ELECTRONICS BOOK SERIES

Copyright © 1975 by McGraw-Hill, Inc. All rights reserved. Printed in the United States of America. No part of this publication may be reproduced, stored in a retrieval system, or transmitted, in any form or by any means, electronic, mechanical, photocopying, recording, or otherwise, without the prior written permission of the publisher.

 McGraw-Hill Publications Co.
1221 Avenue of the Americas
New York, New York 10020

Microprocessors

Edited by Laurence Altman
Senior Editor, *Electronics*

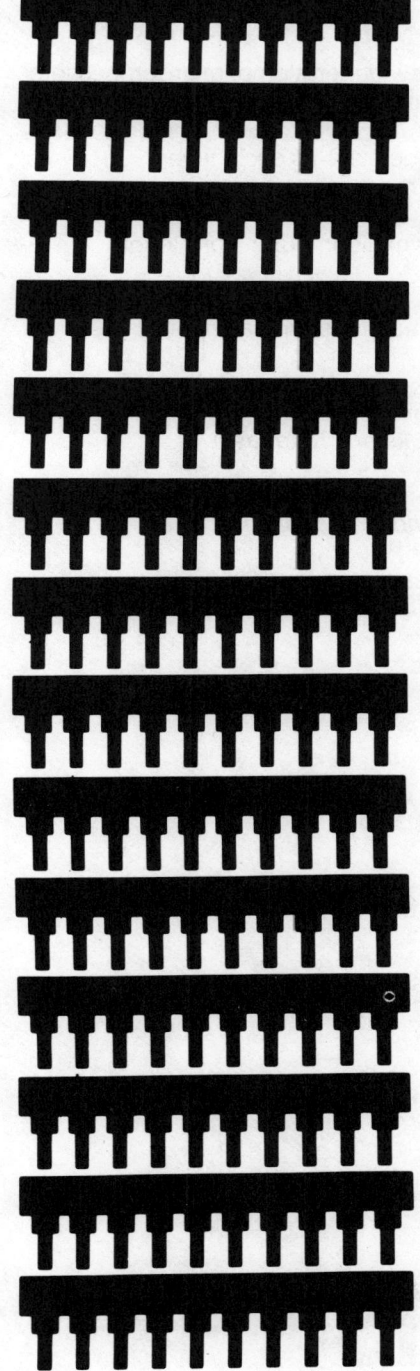

Electronics®
Book Series

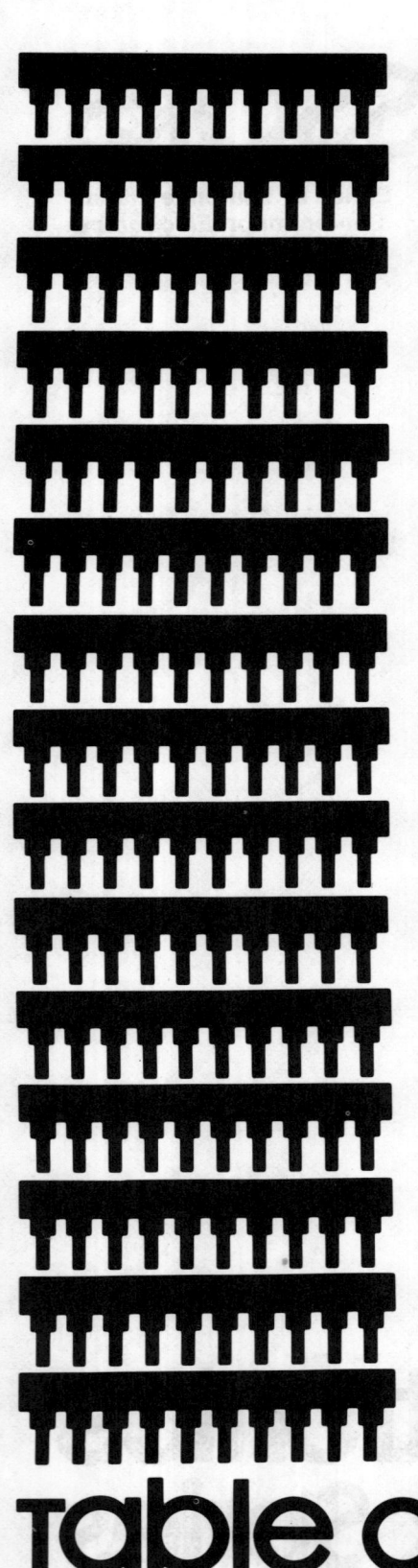

table of contents

vi Introduction

1 Part I—Device Technology

2 Standard parts and custom design merge into four-chip processor kit
F. Faggin and E. Hoff

7 Fast 8-bit microprocessor is versatile
Laurence Altman

9 N-channel MOS technology yields new generation of microprocessors
Link Young, Tom Bennett and Jeff Lavell

16 In switch to n-MOS, microprocessor gets a 2-μs cycle time
Masatoshi Shima and Federico Faggin

22 Single-chip microprocessor employs minicomputer word length
George F. Reyling Jr.

29 Four-chip microprocessor family reduces system parts count
David Chung

35 Twelve-bit microprocessor nears minicomputer performance level
Tadaaki Tarui, Keiji Namimoto and Yukihara Takahashi

41 Bipolar LSI computing elements usher in new era of digital design
Justin Rattner, Jean-Cloud Cornet, and M. E. Hoff, Jr.

49 I²L takes bipolar integration a significant step forward
Richard Horton, Jesse Englade and Gerald McGee

57 Schottky-TTL controller put on a chip
Laurence Altman

59   Part II—Designing With Microprocessors

60   Designing with microprocessors instead of wired logic asks more of designers
Bruce Gladstone

74   Preparation: The key to success with microprocessors
Robert Lewandowski

80   High-level language simplifies microcomputer programing
Gary A. Kildall

87   PLAs enhance digital processor speed and cut component count
George Reyling Jr.

93   Designing microprocessors with standard-logic devices: Part 1
Robert Jaeger

99   Designing microprocessors with standard-logic devices: Part 2
Robert Jaeger

105   ROMs in microprocessors can test themselves
John B. Peatman, David G. Dack, and David A. Warren

106   Counter keeps track of microprocessor interrupts
Douglas M. Risch

107   Part III—Applications

108   Single-chip microprocessors open up a new world of applications
Laurence Altman

115   Diverse industry users clamber aboard the microprocessor bandwagon
Electronics Staff Editors

117   Industrial—*Alfred I. Rosenblatt*
122   Communications—*Stephen E. Scrupski*
126   Consumer/Commercial—*Gerald M. Walker*
130   Computers—*Wallace B. Riley*
133   Instruments—*Michael J. Riezenman*
137   Design—*Wallace B. Riley*
139   Processors and product costs
William Davidow

143   Part IV—Microprocessor Round-up
From the pages of *Electronics*

154   Index

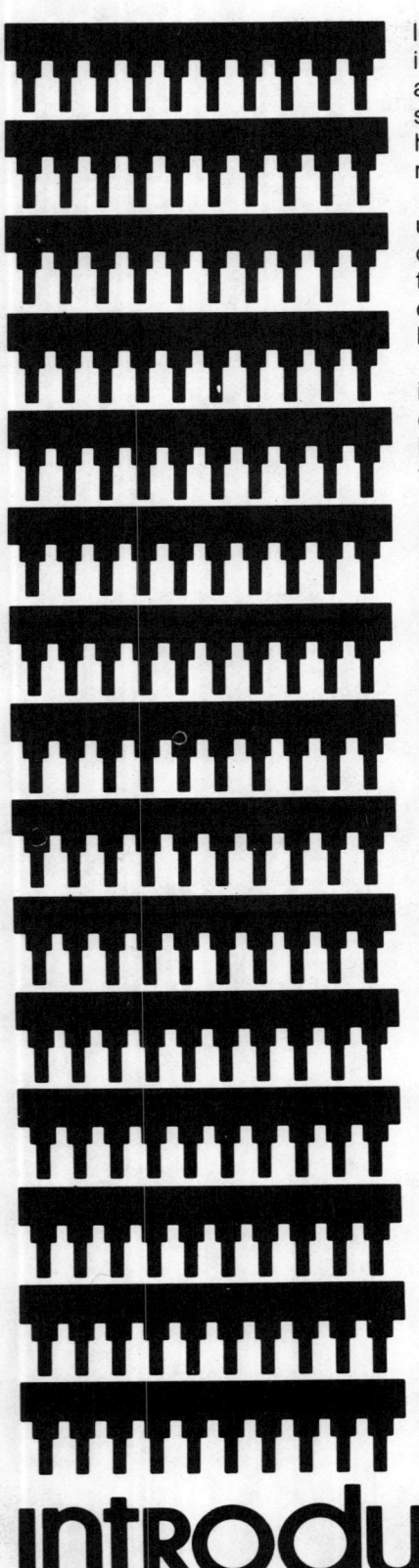

introduction

Inexpensive digital control: that's what makes the microprocessor the most important semiconductor development in over a decade. A designer adds a handful of standard circuits to the chip (or chips), then programs the assemblage to match his special system needs. Equipment capability is enhanced, there is enormous design flexibility, and the design job goes much faster and costs much less than ever before.

Many microprocessors are so new, however, that no textbook on their use exists. In an attempt to fill the gap, the most recent articles published on this topic in *Electronics* magazine have been collected into this book, the aim of which is to put the implications of microprocessors for system design into perspective and to provide practical information on how to utilize the devices.

Part 1 contains descriptions of 10 different available divide types, starting with Intel's original 4-bit four-chip MCS-4, going on to the second-generation 8-bit n-channel microprocessors, and ending with the very latest bipolar LSI processor designs built with integrated injection logic and new forms of Schottky TTL technology.

Part 2 answers design questions that bother users of microprocessors: how the technique differs from the familiar hard-wired logic approach; what knowledge is a prerequisite for utilizing a microprocessor in a system; what software language to choose and how to use it, and even such nuts-and-bolts topics as how to breadboard microprocessing systems.

Part 3 deals with the scores of applications now profiting from microprocessing techniques. All sectors of the equipment industries are covered—industrial, communications, consumer, commercial, computers, and instruments.

Finally, Part 4 chronicles the growth of the microprocessor throughout the last few years. These news items from *Electronics* show how the momentum has built up from the first signs of a powerful new technique to the landslide that is rapidly transforming digital-system design.

Readers unfamiliar with the conventions used in *Electronics* may be puzzled by the sets of initials, like TTL, that appear throughout the articles without apparent explanation. In most cases, however, these initials closely follow (or are closely followed by) the phrases they stand for, e.g. TTL usually occurs only after transistor-transistor logic has been spelled out in full.
—Laurence Altman

Part 1

Device Technology

Standard parts and custom design merge in four-chip processor kit

Processors of various degrees of complexity can be designed from three standardized chip elements and a fourth, a read-only memory, customized 5 to each user's specific purpose by his own microprogram

by F. Faggin and M. E. Hoff, *Intel Corp., Santa Clara, Calif.*

☐ A vast new array of applications has opened up with the advent of low-cost minicomputers that the user can microprogram himself for any number of repetitive functions. These applications range from control of computer peripheral devices to hospital patient monitors to gaming machines.

Such widespread use of microprogramed minicomputers is made possible by large-scale integration that brings the cost about two orders of magnitude below the cost of the most inexpensive conventional minicomputer. One such computer, the Intel MCS-4, is composed of only four kinds of LSI chips. Three of these chip modules—a read/write memory, a processor, and a shift register—are standardized designs. The fourth module, a read-only memory, is programed to the user's specifications.

Among the potential applications for these microprogramed machines are, generically speaking, office equipment, process control, and instrumentation. More specific examples abound in these and other categories: billing machines and point-of-sale terminals; numerically controlled machines and traffic control, spectrum analyzers, navigational receivers, hospital patient monitors, intelligent terminals, and others.

The MCS-4 consists of the 4001 read-only memory (ROM), which also contains a four-bit input/output section, or port; the 4002 read/write memory (RWM), which includes both main storage and status memory, and a four-bit output port; the 4004 four-bit central processing unit (CPU); and the 4003 shift register (SR) for extending output functions—actually a medium-scale circuit because it holds only 10 bits and is on a relatively small chip. Input lines can be expanded with standard MSI multiplexers.

Unexceptional chip size

All employ p-channel silicon-gate MOS circuitry and have conventional measurements typical of today's smaller LSI circuits—53 by 85 mils for the shift register and roughly 110 by 150 mils for the other three. Circuit density is quite high; each chip holds more than these measurements imply. The standard LSI circuits—the RWM, the SR, and the CPU—are produced in high volume, and the only specialized part of the design—the ROM—uses the already proven economy of mask programing. Because the customer can maintain the mask patterns for his ROMs as proprietary, he still has the advantages of a custom design, without the high cost that usually accompanies custom designs.

The I/O port of the ROM contains latches that store data being transferred from the computer's data bus to the outside world—that is, the remainder of the system in which the computer is used. Should such external equipment require more than the number of output

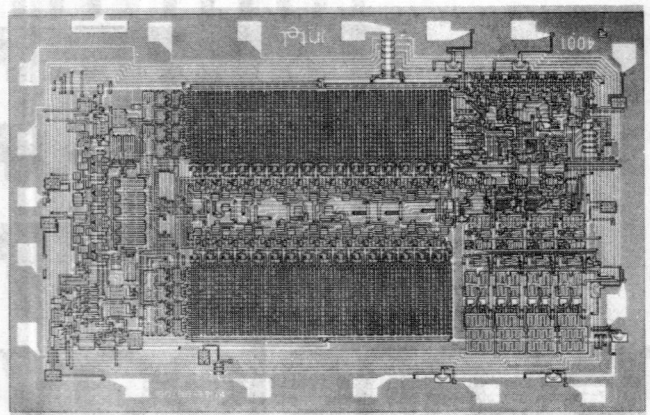
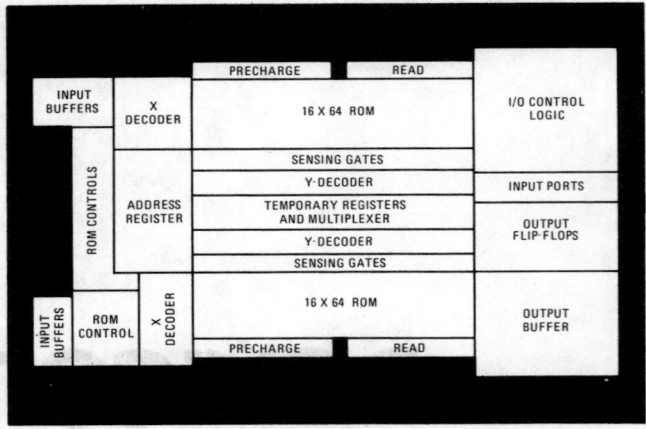

1. Read-only memory. This array of 256 eight-bit words can be used from one to 16 times in a computer made from the 4-chip microcomputer set MCS-4. Chip also contains multiplexing and demultiplexing circuits to permit it to transmit and receive words through the processor's data bus, four bits at a time, and buffers for transferring data from the bus to the outside world.

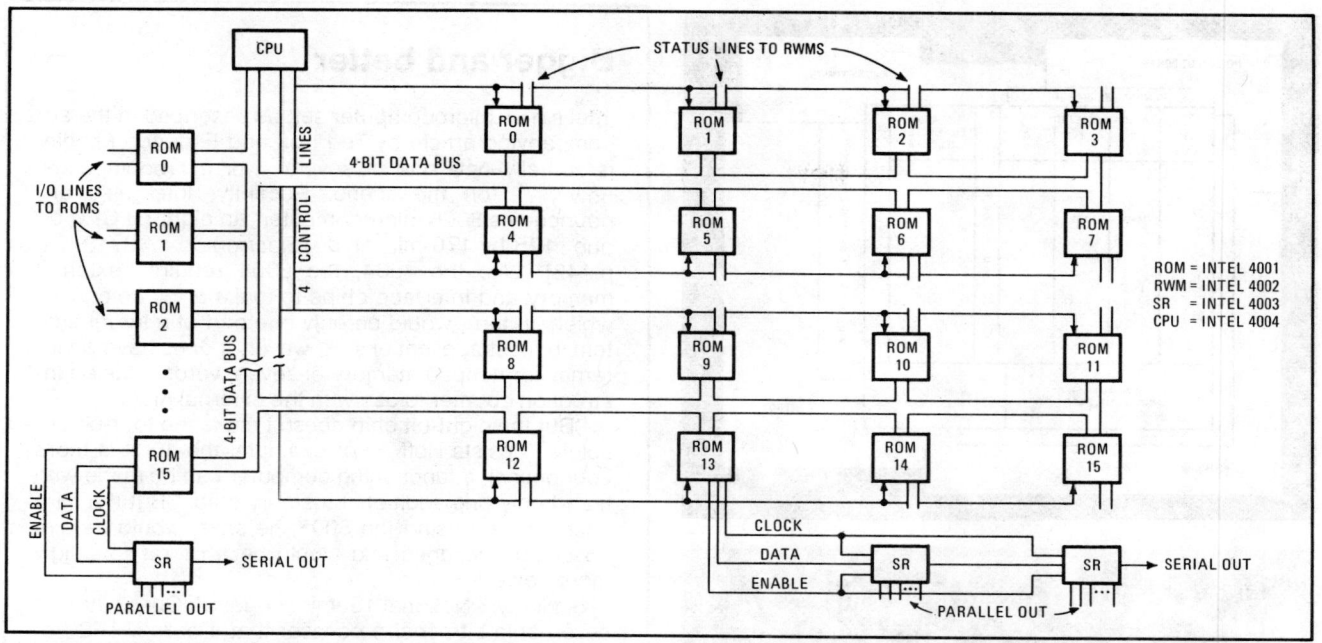

2. Maximal. Up to 16 ROMs and 16 RWMs can be attached to one processor in the new chip set. Input and output are also handled through these chips; output can be expanded beyond four bits in parallel through shift registers.

lines provided by the ROMs and RWMs, the SR makes more lines available, as described below.

The status memory portion of the 4002 RWM is really only an extension of the main memory, differing from the latter primarily in its means of access. It is useful for storing labels, exponents, signs, and other control information associated with the data stored in the main memory.

A typical computer configuration uses one CPU, together with several RWMs and ROMs, and perhaps a few SRs. These configurations are flexible, economical, and easy to design.

Flexibility comes from easy program changes, ease of changing capacity, small size, and low power dissipation. A short design cycle is possible because the system is controlled by a microprogram, which is inherently easier to design and implement than either random logic or custom LSI circuits.

The system is economical to manufacture because all the chips come in standard 16-pin dual in-line packages that lend themselves to automatic insertion and enable the customer to implement rather complex functions with relatively few chips. Furthermore, because three of the four chips are standardized, the customer is not faced with a development charge for them, while mask charges for a new ROM are far less than development charges for custom LSI chips. Furthermore, even these mask changes can be saved, particularly during prototype development, by using electrically alterable ROMs.

Minimum system

The smallest possible system would require one CPU and one ROM. The latter, which contains 256 words of eight bits each, as shown in Fig. 1, would hold programs and subroutines for the CPU, and perhaps some fixed data. The maximum amount of ROM that can be directly addressed is 16 chips or 4,096 bytes (see Fig. 2). While these 4,096 bytes require a 12-bit binary address, the ROM communicates with the CPU over a four-bit-wide data path. Therefore the ROM contains, in addition to the usual decoding circuits, a demultiplexer to permit the address to come in three four-bit chunks and a multiplexer to divide the output word into two more four-bit chunks.

The CPU delivers the three address chunks in three cycles. The first two of these select one byte in each ROM chip, while the third selects one chip out of all the ROMs, which delivers its byte to the data bus. Following these three address cycles are two more cycles during which the CPU accepts the eight bits from the ROM--four during each cycle.

The ROM chip itself contains the logic circuitry required to keep track of which data transfer is in process at any time, so that it can react to each one in the proper way.

Read/write memory

Each RWM (Fig. 3) contains 80 characters of four bits each, organized as four 20-character registers. In each register, 16 characters are part of the main storage, and the other four characters belong to the status memory previously mentioned. Therefore, the 16 chips in the largest memory configuration contain 64 registers, or 1,024 characters of main storage and 256 characters of status memory.

The CPU controls both the RWM and the ROM chips through six control lines. One of the six synchronizes the clocks of all chips to that of the CPU. The other five, called command lines, control the chip addressing and the input/output function. These six control lines permit the single family of chips to be used in a wide variety of system configurations, suitable for many applications.

If more than the 16 ROMs and 16 RWMs are needed for a particular application, external interface circuits and bank switching techniques similar to those used in

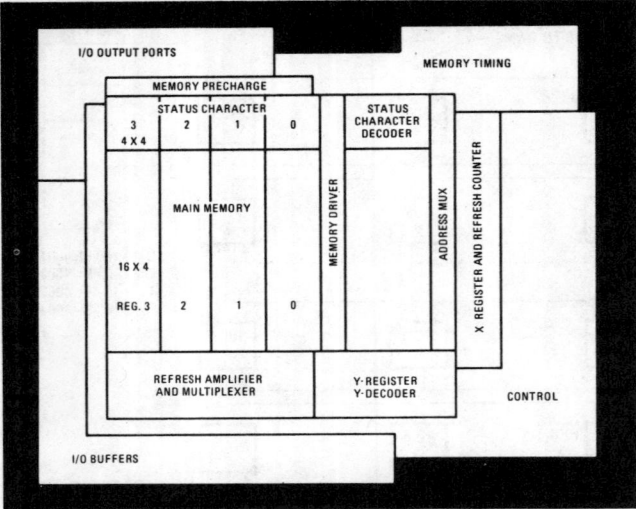

3. Read-write memory. Four 16-character data registers and four 4-character status registers appear in the rectangular array at left center in this photo. Remainder of chip holds control and timing circuits, and output buffers similar to those in the ROM.

Bigger and better

Intel's new microcomputer set, as described in the accompanying article by Ted Hoff and Federico Faggin, is actually only one of several 4-bit microcomputers now on the scene. Recently, Intel also announced its 8008 microcomputer, an eight-bit CPU on one 125-by-170-mil chip [*Electronics*, 3/13/73 p.143]. Like the 4004, the 8008 requires external memory and interface chips to make a full computer, which, in turn, would be only one part of a larger system in most applications. However, it does have an internal scratchpad memory of seven words, plus an instruction counter to use with the external memory.

"But the eight-bit chip doesn't make the four-bit obsolete," insists Hoff. "For example, the 4004 is more economical; a functioning computer can be made with it and only one additional memory chip." But the minimum system using the 8008, he says, would require 15 or 20 packages and would be a correspondingly more powerful system.

Similarly, National Semiconductor Corp. has a seven-chip bit-serial processor that it calls MAPS, for microprogramable arithmetic processor system [*Electronics*, 4/10/73 p.121]. The chip set comprises an arithmetic unit, a set of registers, a timing circuit, two ROMs, a keyboard interface, and a static data monitor; the last is used with the interface for large keyboards, in somewhat the same way as Intel's second application example [p. 5]. —Editor

some minicomputers permit the necessary number of additional memory chips of either type to be connected.

The SR, a 10-bit static shift register into which data is loaded serially, has output lines that are accessible in parallel. Logic included on the chip disables the output lines until all desired data has been shifted into it from a ROM or RWM.

The CPU is a small but complete processor (Fig. 4) capable of executing 45 different instructions in a basic instruction cycle of 10.67 microseconds. It is built around a four-bit adder, and has a set of 16 four-bit scratchpad registers. Internally, the CPU is strictly binary; but for applications using decimal arithmetic, the binary result of adding two binary-coded decimal digits can be returned to BCD by a special instruction.

Of particular interest is the set of four 12-bit address registers that permit as many as three levels of subroutine nesting. During the execution of a program, when a jump to a subroutine is encountered, the instruction address register contains the address of the next instruction to be performed after the subroutine is executed. Its contents must be temporarily stored to permit the main program to resume following the subroutine. In the 4004 CPU, the subroutine may itself branch to a second subroutine, and that one to a third; three of the four address registers store three address words for this nesting process, while the fourth holds the address of the current instruction.

Extended capability

For a complex system, requiring more extensive processing capability, multiple processors can be used. In such a system with two central processing units, one CPU could be dedicated to control functions and the other to arithmetic functions. They could communicate with each other through the I/O ports, or they could share a common memory through a minimum of external circuitry.

Each 10.67-μs instruction cycle is divided into eight machine cycles of 1.33 μs each, as shown in Fig. 5. During the first three of these, an address is sent out to the ROM. Data from the ROM is returned to the CPU during the next two cycles and is processed during the last three. Some instructions require an additional 10.67-μs cycle to fetch eight more bits from the ROM.

The individual machine cycles are driven by a two-phase clock running at 750 kHz.

Steps in design

All four LSI chips may operate with a single –15 volt supply voltage with respect to ground; or they may be made compatible with transistor-transistor logic by operating them between –10 volts and +5 volts.

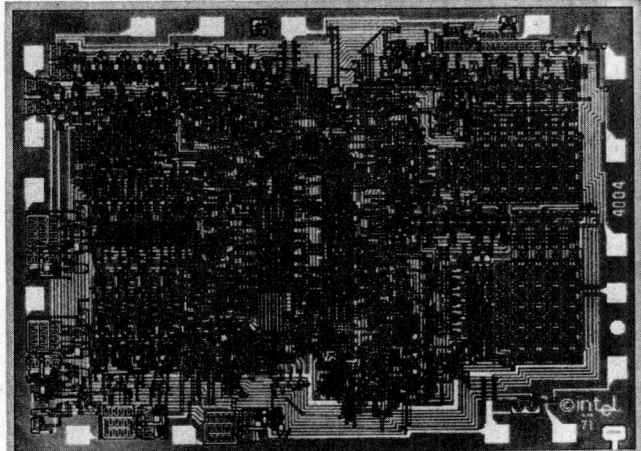 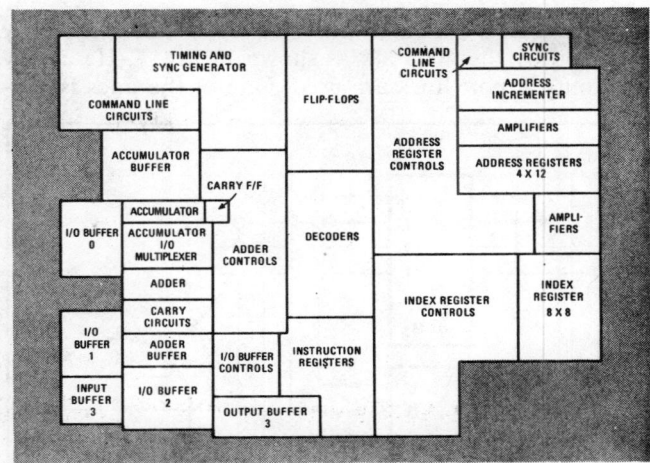

4. Processor. Heart of the four-chip set, this central processing unit is a small but complete general-purpose computer that can execute 45 instructions. The four-bit adder, its central component, is at left center, as key diagram shows. Address registers at right are important features. Processor works exclusively in binary, but has a special instruction that translates a pure binary sum to decimal form. Four white lines around left, bottom, and right are bus interconnecting major sections on chip.

For a particular application, designing a system around the MCS-4 is quite simple. There are essentially seven steps:
- Define the input/output requirements in terms of the peripheral equipment that will be needed.
- Define the amount of storage needed, and from that determine the number of RWM chips.
- Define the amount of control and/or program, and thus the amount of read-only storage needed; this determines the number of ROM chips. (This step may involve an iterative procedure.)
- Specify shift registers as needed to increase the capacity of output lines.
- Write the program.
- Build a prototype system, implement the program and controls in electrically programable ROMs, and get the bugs out.
- Submit the program for manufacturing mask-programed ROMs for volume production.

In defining the input/output requirements, the first step in the design sequence, a number of software/hardware alternatives are available. For example, if the system includes a keyboard, it will interface with the computer's data bus through either a ROM or a RWM. This interface may be capable of eliminating bounce from the key depressions, encoding the data, and rejecting the results of a multiple key depression; or all these functions may be implemented in software and executed in the CPU.

Keyboard design

An approach that uses little hardware and a moderate amount of software, shown in Fig. 6, places each key at the intersection of one input line of a ROM port and one output line of another ROM or RWM port. The program continually scans the keyboard by sequentially placing a single binary 1 on each output line; if any key has been depressed, that 1 reappears on the corresponding input line. The particular combination of output and input lines establishes the key's identity, and may be translated by a code conversion routine in the CPU into a command or character in conventional ASCII or other code. By requiring an encoded character to appear on several successive scan cycles, the CPU obtains key debouncing. With other suitable programs the CPU can detect multiple keying or key rollover.

5. Eight-in-one. Instruction cycle of 10.67 microseconds comprises eight 1.33-μs machine cycles in 4004 CPU. First two cycles transmit address of desired word in ROM, third selects one of up to 16 ROMs. Then the addressed word returns to the CPU in two cycles; instruction is executed in remaining three cycles, plus another full eight if needed. Clock frequency is 750 kHz.

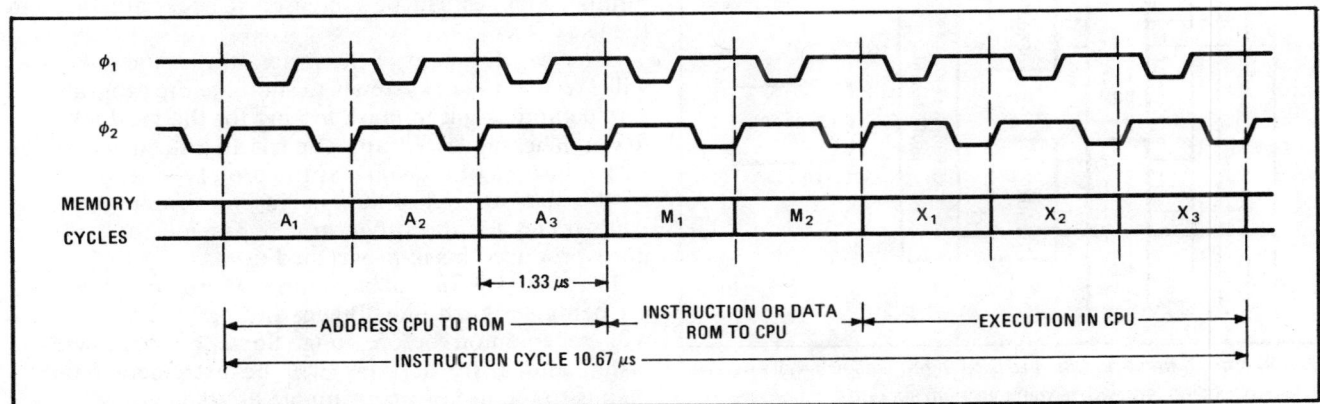

A larger keyboard may be more conveniently scanned by the 4003 SR, as shown in Fig. 7. Here only two output port lines are used. One of the lines is programed to provide a clock pulse for the shift register, and the other supplies data. A single binary 1 is loaded into one end of the register and shifted along it; the parallel outputs effectively scan the large keyboard, and appear at the input port just as with the previous example.

A third design that uses the most hardware and very little software, shown in Fig. 8, requires an external diode encoder and debouncing circuits. In this arrangement the key depressions are read directly into the computer without any scanning.

The amount of read-write storage depends on the number of characters to be stored at one time and the number of bits that are to be stored in read/write storage as opposed to ROM.

For example, if a particular computer is to work with 16-digit numbers and may have to store 10 such numbers at any one time, these numbers will occupy the main-storage registers in three RWM packages, leaving two spare registers in one of the packages. These three packages also contain status memory with a capacity of 48 characters or 144 bits.

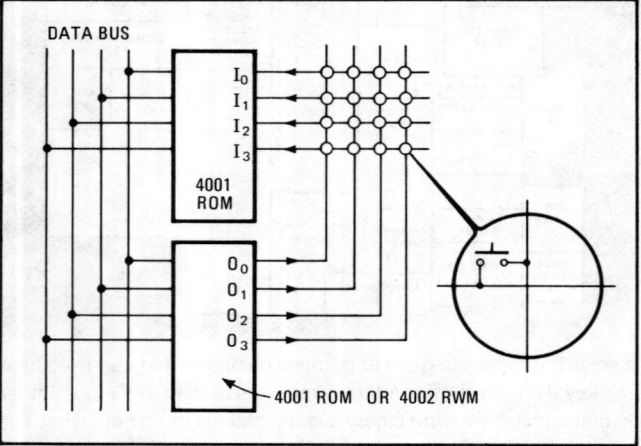

6. Keyboard interface. For data entry to system, the MCS-4 scans all columns on keyboard; signal reappearing on a row input shows that a key has been depressed, and timing of signal relative to scan identifies the key. Program then encodes the signal, and also eliminates bounce and multiple keying.

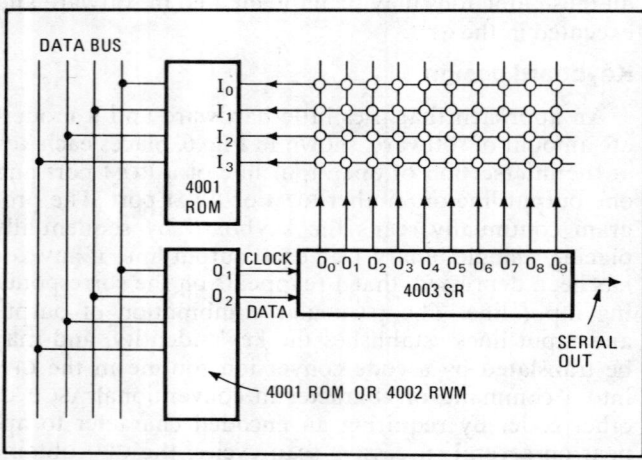

7. More hardware, less software. For larger keyboards, the 4003 shift register extends the scan while simplifying its operation.

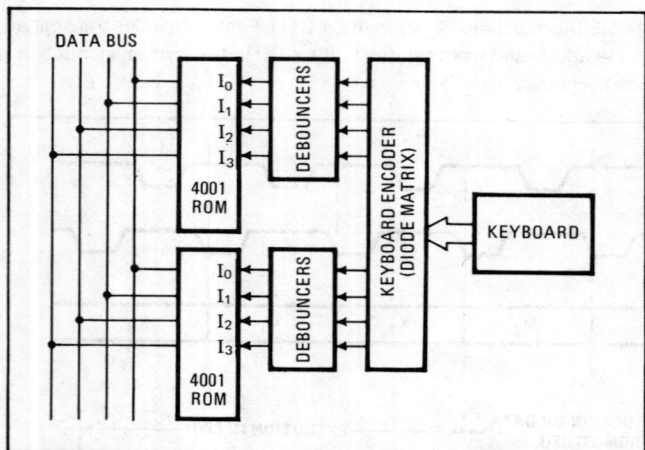

8. Still more hardware. Direct approach requires external encoding and debouncing, and works with minimum support from program.

Calculating ROM needs

In most applications using the MCS-4 chip family, normal programs are stored in the ROM. However, when the user desires to load programs at execution time, it is open to him to program the MCS-4 to operate in interpretive mode.

In this mode, the program in the ROM fetches "data" from RWM and interprets it as new instructions for the CPU, jumping as required to subroutines kept in the ROM. Interpretive mode programs may also run with pseudo-instructions kept in ROM; such programs often use ROM more efficiently than conventionally written programs. In either case, the designer planning to use interpretive mode must allow space for the programs when defining his memory requirements.

Determining the amount of read-only storage is a good deal more difficult. It depends on the system complexity and sophistication. The ability to make an educated guess early in the design process largely depends on experience.

With the number of ROM and RWM chips established, another look at I/O requirements may be in order if the number of I/O lines provided by these packages is substantially different from that assumed in the first step of the design process. But if the I/O layout is firm, the number of lines can be increased if necessary through the use of SRs.

After development of the program that the computer will execute, the next step is to simulate the program before committing it to mask tooling for the production of ROMs. The suggested approach is to use programable ROMs, instead of the 4001, at the prototype stage. When all the bugs are out of the system in the simulation, the truth tables for the program can provide the data for mass-produced mask-programed ROMs.

The MCS-4 is just a beginning. More complex CPUs are being designed [see "Bigger and better," p. 4], and will be common before long. Some of them will be faster, and some of them will be extremely flexible, thanks to the use of programable ROMs. □

Fast 8-bit microprocessor is versatile

Rockwell's p-channel system comes with CPU chip, 256-by-8 RAM, direct-memory-access controller, and enlarged input/output chip

by Laurence Altman, Solid State Editor, *Electronics*

The first microprocessor available as a standard product is less than four years old. But already, semiconductor manufacturers are introducing second-generation models with enlarged instruction capacities, higher speeds, and greater flexibility for an ever-expanding range of applications.

Intel and Motorola have already announced n-channel 8-bit additions to their microprocessor family [*Electronics*, 4/18/74, p. 81]. Now, Rockwell International's Microelectronic Device division, Anaheim, Calif., joins the club by adding an 8-bit system to its 4-bit version, already on the market. Built with p-channel technology, the PPS-8 offers more than 90 instructions, can directly address more than 16,384 bytes of read-only memory, plus a like amount of random-access memory. Complete instruction time is 4 microseconds.

The peripheral devices available are the RAM (a full 256 by 8 bits), the direct-memory-access controller (DMAC), and an expanded input/output chip, called the GPIO #2.

The microprocessor chip has somewhat the same organization as the 4-bit CPU in Rockwell's PPS-4, except that, instead of having save registers, the addresses were put directly into the first 32 addresses of RAM. This implements a 32-deep first-in, last-out stack.

Michel Ebertin, director of new-product development at the division, points out that the PPS-8 follow-on system is constructed exactly like the PPS-4 system so the same memories and simulators can be used with both systems to give the user "instant system-upgrading." Says Ebertin, "We've kept the same bus system and the same timing, so that the same ROMs can be used with both systems; the same system simulators or assembler boxes can be used." In addition, all the input/outputs that were developed for the 4-bit system can be used in the 8-bit system because of a special instruction, called the IO4, which allows the 8-bit system to read in or out with only 4 bits.

Flexibility. Ebertin also points out

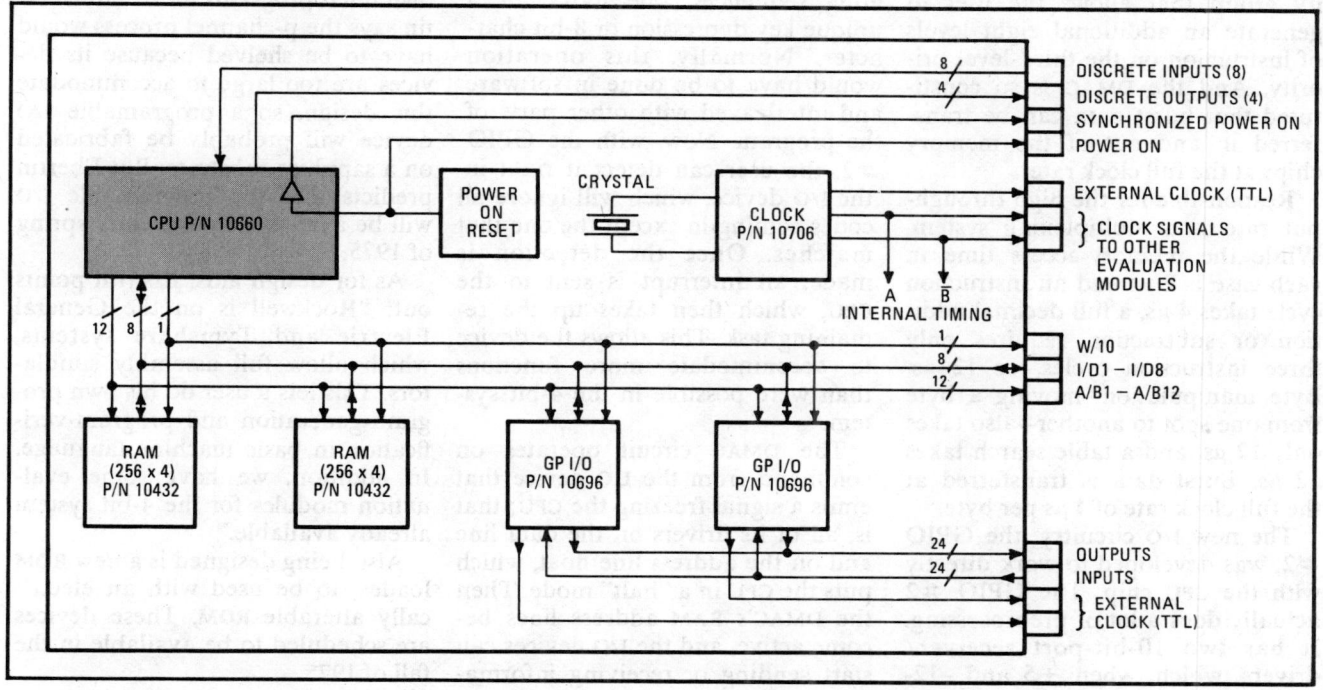

One version. Typical 8-bit parallel processing system includes microprocessor (in color), RAMs, and input/output and clock circuits.

that the 8-bit system is designed so that most of its 90 basic instructions are modifiable for maximum flexibility. Says Ebertin, "We've included the capability for packed binary [-coded] decimal logic, so that in a sophisticated high-speed decimal machine, the speed of calculations can be doubled because now, one add-time calculates two digits, rather than one." What's more, the system has three levels of priority built in, as well as, via the new I/O devices, a daisy-chain priority group that allows the user to generate an additional eight levels of instruction on the third-level priority. And the DMAC is so constituted that burst data can be transferred in and out of the memory chips at the full clock rate.

Responsible for the high throughput rate is a multiplexing system. While the memory-access time in each case is 2 µs and an instruction cycle takes 4 µs, a full decimal addition or subtraction requires only three instruction cycles, or 12 µs. Byte manipulation—moving a byte from one spot to another—also takes only 12 µs, and a table search takes 12 µs. Burst data is transferred at the full clock rate of 4 µs per byte.

The new I/O circuitry the GPIO #2, was developed to work directly with the CPU chip. The GPIO #2 actually does a lot of preprocessing. It has two 10-bit-port receiver/drivers, which, when +5 and −12-volt supplies are used, become fully TTL-compatible. The GPIO #2 receives commands from the CPU, which are stored in two function registers. These command the input/output ports, telling the device whether to copy and send the commands to the CPU, send them out either in parallel form or in serial form, or store the data in the CPU registers.

This flexibility is advantageous, for instance, in a point-of-sale terminal, where, as part of the operating sequences, one looks for a unique key depression or 8-bit character. Normally, this operation would have to be done in software and interleaved with other parts of the program. Now, with the GPIO #2, the user can detect it right in the I/O device, which will ignore all codes coming in except the one that matches. Once the detection is made, an interrupt is sent to the CPU, which then takes up the remaining task. This allows the device to accommodate more functions than were possible in the 4-bit system.

The DMAC circuit operates on command from the I/O device that emits a signal freezing the CPU; that is, all of its drivers on the data line and on the address line float, which puts the CPU in a "halt" mode. Then the DMAC's RAM address lines become active, and the I/O devices can start sending or receiving information at full clock rate into and out of the memory.

Coming. Other peripheral devices at the conceptual stage for the PPS-8 system are a floppy-disk controller, a CRT controller, and a programable I/O device. The programable I/O points to a complete processing system—RAM, ROM, CPU, clock, and I/O—on one chip. By allowing the I/O device to be microprogramed, the I/O function can be reduced to a one-chip device, and each customer could generate his own microprograms for it. But Ebertin says the p-channel process would have to be shelved because its devices are too large to accommodate this design, so a programable I/O device will probably be fabricated on a sapphire substrate. But Ebertin predicts that the programable I/O will be available by the early spring of 1975.

As for design aids, Ebertin points out: "Rockwell is on the General Electric and Tymshare systems, which allow full assembly simulators. This lets a user do his own program-generation and program-verification in basic machine language. In addition, we have some evaluation modules for the 4-bit system already available."

Also being designed is a new ROM loader, to be used with an electrically alterable ROM. These devices are scheduled to be available in the fall of 1975.

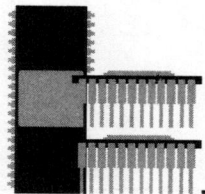

N-channel MOS technology yields new generation of microprocessors

The latest microprocessor chips are faster than p-MOS devices and handle many more peripherals; often, too, as in Motorola's M6800 family, a CPU chip will come in a matched set of memory and input and output chips, simplifying system production

by Link Young, Tom Bennett, and Jeff Lavell,
Motorola Semiconductor Products Inc., Phoenix, Ariz.

□ The great promise that programable LSI circuits have for all kinds of control applications is fulfilled in the second generation of microprocessors, such as Motorola's and Intel's 8-bit devices. These new n-channel MOS chips have many more instructions and need much less in the way of costly systems circuit support than did the first wave of 4- and 8-bit p-channel systems. Their level of computing power is also high, and they are versatile and easy to use.

The n-channel metal-oxide-semiconductor microprocessors are completely self-contained. They are designed to work directly with a minimum number of memory and peripheral support chips, all of which are supplied in coordinated families to allow them to operate off the same voltage and power-supply conditions as the central processor chip.

A typical set contains the CPU chip, a random-access memory for fast scratch-pad logic control, a read-only memory for storing the system's program parameters, and a set of input and output chips. These input/output chips enable the CPU to control a large variety of industrial and communications equipment: process and manufacturing control systems, peripheral and terminal hardware, parameter-control systems of all types—from microcomputers in the automobile to control systems

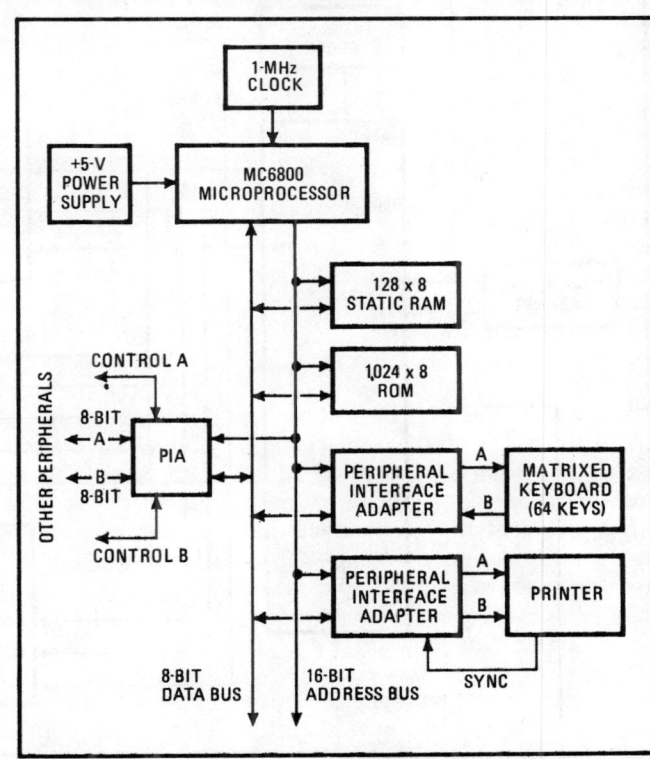

1. Eight-bit family. Motorola's M6800 family of components is organized around the concept of the parallel data bus. Consequently, all memory and peripheral interface adapter (PIA) chips are simply designed to hang on its CPU's eight bidirectional data lines.

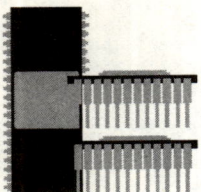

matrix. All instructions operated on complex 4-bit data signals, as did even simple word fetches for each instruction. Still more restrictive was the fact that input and output access was serial, not parallel, limiting the number of peripherals that could work with the CPU. Instruction speeds were also slow—it could take 80 microseconds to execute one—and power-supply requirements were complex and costly.

For larger systems, the 8-bit MSC-8 microprocessor chip set (Fig. 3) could be used, but it was not a self-contained system, requiring external TTL for any application. It was, however, quite powerful: the 8008 CPU of that system can interface with 16,384 8-bit words of read-only, random-access, or shift-register memory. It was also quite economical to build: all communication between functional units and the CPU is carried out over the single 8-bit data bus, a sync line, a ready line, an interrupt line, and just three status lines. Its low cost, together with its respectably fast instruction execution time of 12.5 microseconds, makes the 8008 microprocessor still very useful for moderate-performance systems in point-of-sale terminals, credit-card verifiers, calculators, and other keyboard-addressed applications.

It does, however, fall short of being a useful general-purpose microprocessor chip set, primarily because, unlike its 4-bit predecessor, the MCS-4, it is not a system of compatible parts. Indeed, it requires many small-scale packages to build even a moderately powerful system—a simple modem hook-up would need about 50 TTL packages, increasing circuit board area and systems costs.

Another problem is addressing it. True, its 18-pin package saves board space, but it must be multiplexed both for address and data on common input/output pins, which in the end lengthens excessively the time it takes to execute an instruction. Not only that, the need for seven control registers on the CPU chip makes it difficult to manage the logic cycles, limiting subroutines and creating problems in programing and interrupt handling. Finally, its outputs are compatible, not with standard TTL, but with rarely used low-power TTL, so that circuits are needed to boost voltage level in most applications.

Most of these problems were overcome with National Semiconductor's IMP-16 (Fig. 4), a 16-bit microprocessor set that for the first time provided full mini-

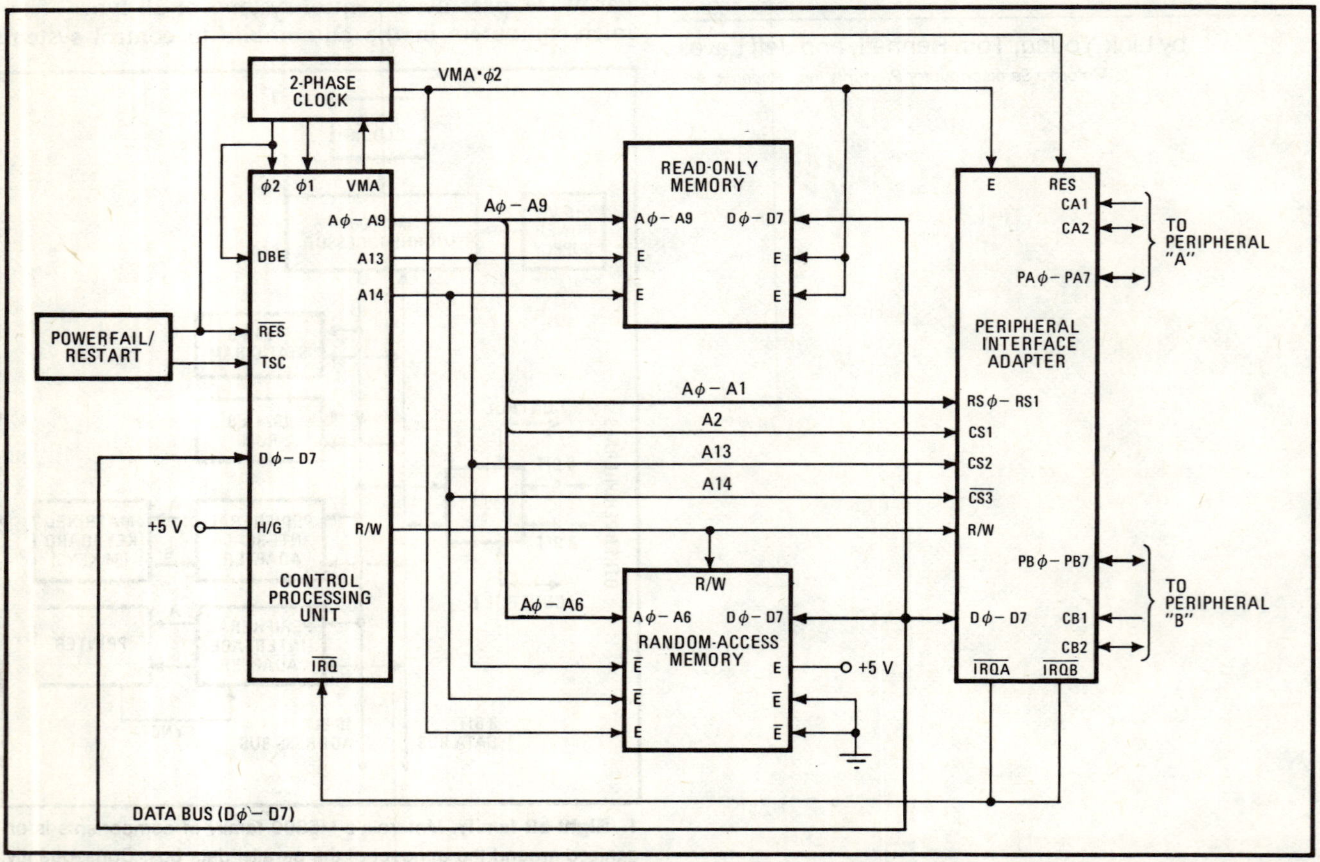

7. At a minimum. The minimum M6800 system configuration contains four functional blocks but can be expanded to 10 modules of memories, I/O adapters, and even additional CPUs on the same data bus with no external interface packages.

computer CPU capability on a single board. Designed to operate on both ends of the MCS-8 performance curve, this p-channel microprocessor unit is central to a family of systems with typical execution times of 4.5 to 10 μs for a system and 9 to 18 μs for a 8-bit system. Although it gained wide strong acceptance for many 16-bit minicomputer applications, it has been less used for 8-bit systems because the designer is forced to use microprograming—a far more complicated task than the programing techniques required for any of today's 8-bit microprocessors. (Because of this, National has now designed 4-bit and 8-bit versions of the basic IMP system.)

The problem then from a design point of view is how to incorporate the maximum system flexibility into an 8-bit unit, make it self-contained, have it offer a large variety of instructions, but nevertheless require the fewest possible external parts. Motorola's newly announced MC6800 microprocessor set and Intel's 8080 are examples of just such a system (Fig. 5). Using implanted n-MOS silicon-gate technology instead of slower p-MOS and operating from a single clock, each is based on a single 40-pin package containing a CPU chip that's far more versatile than previous microprocessor products. (For details of the 8080, see pp. 16-21 .)

The M6800 family

The M6800 microprocessor set incorporates many of the qualities of the 8080, but exhibits additional flexibility because it requires fewer external circuits to implement most control and communication systems. The fact that the family can operate from a single +5-V power supply immediately reduces system cost by about $20 over a typical 8080 system, which needs three power supplies. What is more, the peripheral memory and input/output logic adapters, instead of needing external logic packages, have been designed so that they

---

The M6800 microprocessing family

The family comprises five chips: a single-chip central processor unit, a 128-by-8-bit static random-access memory, a 1,024-by-8-bit read-only memory, and one from each of two groups of input/output interface circuits—a peripheral interface chip designed to provide a buffer to terminal and peripheral systems, and a communications interface adapter circuit for interfacing communications hardware. They all operate from one 5-V power supply, and for many applications require far fewer interface packages than other microprocessor sets.

Basis of the M6800 family is the CPU chip (MC6800) packaged in a 40-pin DIP (see figure). Built with ion-implanted, n-channel silicon-gate technology, this chip contains all the functions required for multi-instruction processing: an arithmetic and logic unit, instruction decode and address registers, an instruction register, all of the clock and logic circuits required for timing, and a full complement of data-bus input and output matrices and address bus drivers.

The equivalent of about 120 MSI TTL packages, the chip provides 72 self-contained basic instructions that have decimal and binary arithmetic capability. The variable-length instructions include double-byte operations (such as increment or decrement, load, store and/or compare) and have tri-state outputs, two-accumulator capacity, and enough registers to provide seven addressing modes. A typical instruction time is under 5 microseconds, and there is direct memory access on the chip. Up to 64 bytes of memory can be addressed in any combination of RAM, ROM, or peripheral registers.

All other members of the set (see table) have been designed specifically to work directly with the CPU chip from the same 5-V power supply. The peripheral adapter (MC6820) is a bidirectional unit with two parallel 8-bit outputs that can either drive two peripherals or, if tied together, provide a higher throughput. The adapter can interface with Teletype and display terminals, with cassettes and test equipment, with keyboards and control panels, and even with large computers for time-shared expansion of computer capability.

The communications interface adapter (MC6850), on the other hand, couples the processor to most standard modems for communications with other computer systems via telephone lines. For still more system flexibility, it's possible to use without adapters not only the static RAM and ROM in the table but other memories, too.

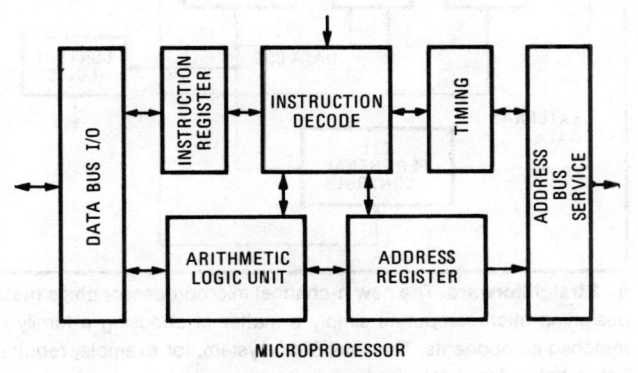

MICROCOMPUTER FAMILY OF CIRCUITS
8-bit microprocessing unit
128-by-8 static random-access memory
1,024-by-8 read-only memory
Peripheral interface adapter
Asynchronous communications interface adapter
0–600-b/s low-speed modem (compatible with Bell 100 series)
Quad, bidirectional data/address bus extender

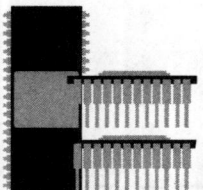

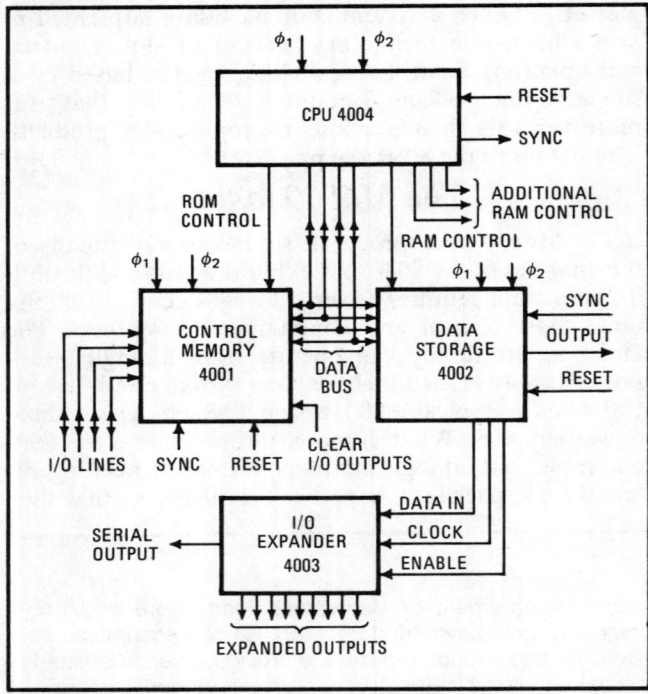

2. Basic computer. One of the first microcomputer chip sets to have been fabricated comes from Intel. Called the MSC-4, it consists of four simple LSI blocks and provides 45 instructions with an instruction cycle time of 10.8 microseconds.

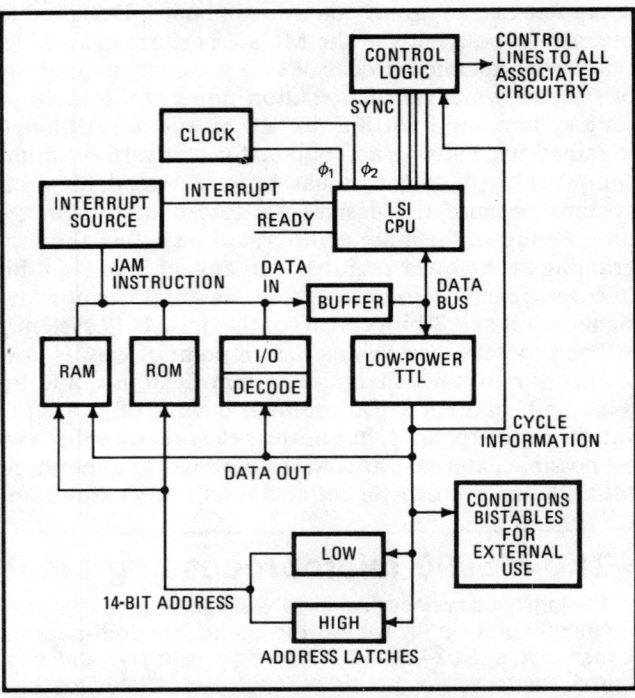

3. Heavy duty. The first 8-bit microcomputer system, Intel's MSC-8, can interface with over 16,000 8-bit words of read-only, random-access, or shift-register memory. Its drawback: substantial external circuitry is needed for most applications.

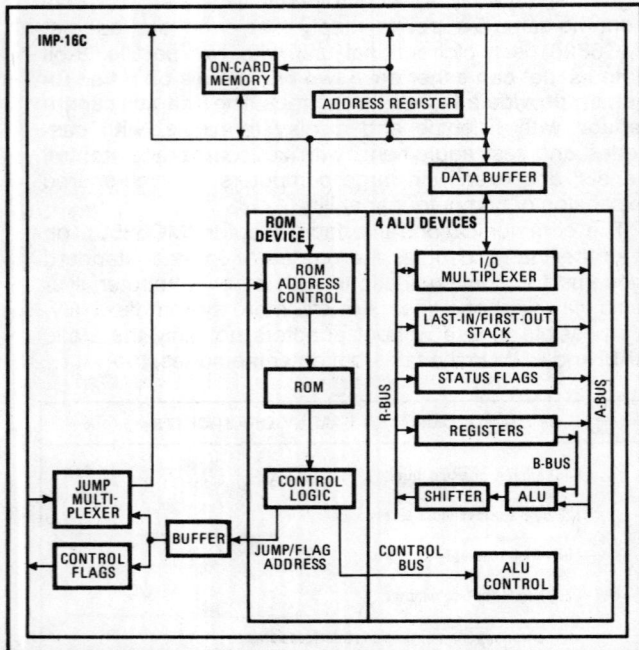

4. Sixteen bits on a board. National's IMP-16 architecture supplies a full 16-bit minicomputer capability on a single pc board. Microprogramable ROMs control the four 4-bit arithmetic logic units that do the processing. Four- and 8-bit versions are also available.

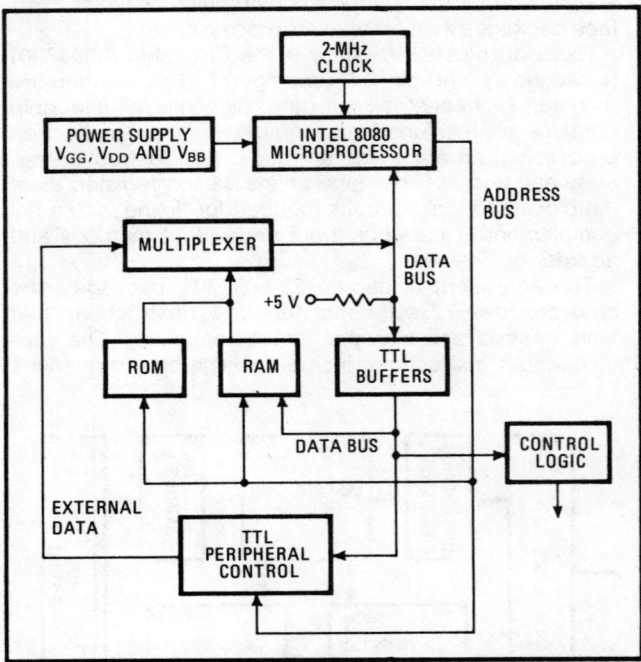

5. Straightforward. The new n-channel microprocessor chips make designing microcomputers simply a matter of choosing a family of matched components. This Intel 8080 system, for example, requires only a half a dozen standard products.

for traffic lights—and anywhere else that random-logic computer control needs optimizing.

These second-generation n-channel units expand considerably on the system benefits offered by the first microprocessors. Over 70 instructions may be available, as against about 40 for the largest p-channel unit. As few as four packages are required to build a complete 8-bit microcomputer. Moreover, in the Motorola family, the M6800, TTL compatibility is achieved with only a single +5-volt power supply, instead of the usual three supplies. Therefore, board space, package count, and component costs are reduced, even while system capacity is increased.

Other benefits to the system

Consequently, as with all microprocessor system designs, board layouts are simplified. The complex interconnections required for large numbers of conventional ICs are replaced by ROMs. The only interconnect wiring on printed-circuit cards runs between the various address and data buses and input/output devices.

The cost savings are not limited to direct circuit component costs but they extend to other, related, system hardware costs. Connectors can be decreased in number, cabling can be simplified, the card cage can be reduced in size, and so on. Associated indirect costs also fall, of course, since assembly takes less time, documentation is simpler, and maintenance is easier.

Equally important to cost savings in hardware systems is the ability of system engineers to build a proposed design quickly. No hardwire logic need be simulated, optimized, or breadboarded. The logic design portion of the cycle now becomes the manipulation of functional building blocks, where the control sequence takes the form of writing a software program into an external ROM. Breadboarding consists of interconnecting a few LSI packages.

Design changes, too, are simply a case of modifying the control program, in contrast to designing and laying out the logic afresh. The various microprocessor manufacturers offer the use of simulators, so that most of the design can be verified even before it is committed to hardware. This all cuts at least 90% from the design time.

The numerous instructions and system versatility despite the very few packages stems directly from the organization of the new CPU chips. For example, the MC6800 chip is organized around the popular parallel data bus concept (Fig. 1), so that all the memory and peripheral interface chips simply hang on the MC6800's eight bidirectional data lines (16 address lines are provided). Up to 10 LSI chips can be directly attached to the bus for operation up to 1 megahertz. To drive still more peripherals, a bipolar extender can be added.

This direct access to a variety of interface and peripheral equipment, obtained with a minimum of packages (see "The M6800 microprocessing family," p. 11) is a tremendous advance on many of the early microprocessor chip families—even though the first single-chip microprocessor was introduced just two years ago.

Intel's MCS-4 and MCS-8 and Rockwell's PPS-4, which all used p-MOS silicon-gate technology, were excellent starting points, in that they were self-contained sets of circuits requiring no external logic. In the 4-bit MCS-4, for example, the CPU, random-access memory, and read-only memory interfaced optimally as a set (Fig. 2). However, these first microprocessors had major limitations. Selecting correct memory locations required complex address logic: 12-bit addresses needing three 4-bit words had to be multiplexed onto the CPU's input

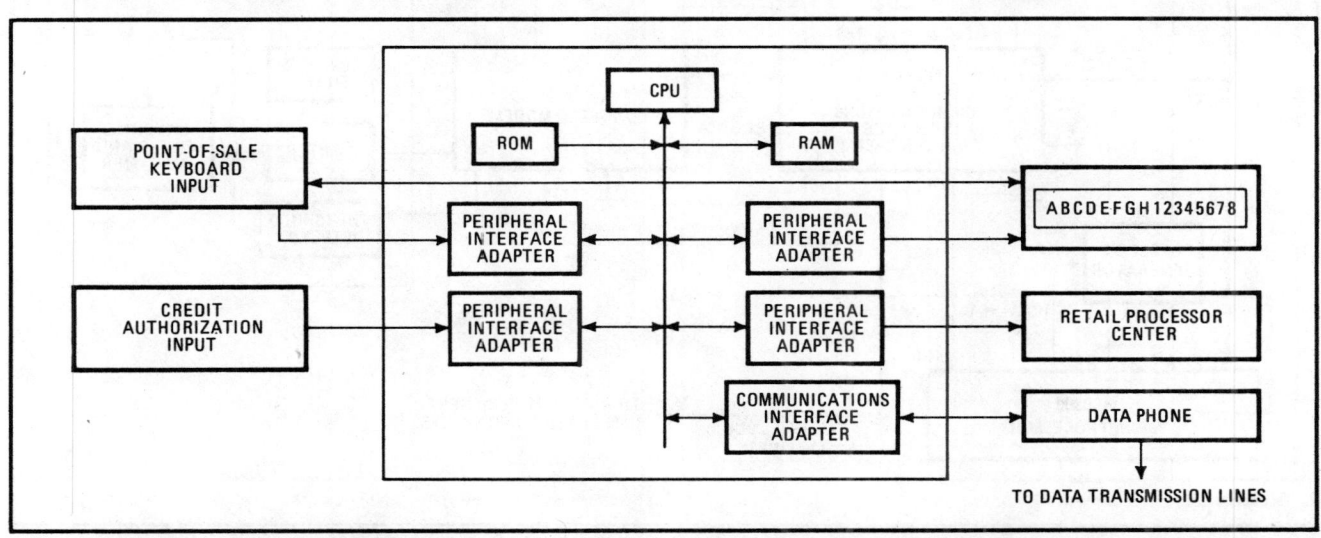

6. Selling well. With microprocessor design techniques, systems such as this point-of-sale installation are capable of being implemented with only five or six circuit blocks, which are designed to work directly with the basic CPU family.

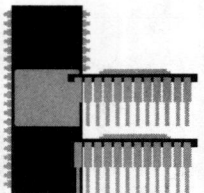

can work directly with the chip containing the CPU.

The smallness of the package count is dramatically illustrated by the comparison of the breadboard, engineering model, and final chip design of an MC6800-type CPU (see photograph on p. 82). The breadboard, a gate-to-gate implementation of the CPU employing basic gates and flip-flops, needs five 10-by-10-inch boards containing 451 packages. The engineering model is a functional implementation of the design and made extensive use of MSI logic packages and programable ROMs to reduce package count to a mere 114, packed into a single 10-by-10-in. board by means of today's most effective hardwire logic techniques. Yet all this is replaced by the single 40-pin package containing the CPU chip. The example epitomizes the impact LSI chip design is having on the implementation of complex computer functions.

The new n-channel microprocessors go still further, by addressing themselves to other parts of the system as well. For the families of circuits are designed to minimize assembly costs by reducing the number of ancillary parts necessary to realize a design.

Consider the block diagram of a typical small terminal, a generalized point-of-sale terminal (Fig. 6). Since every CPU needs several peripheral interfaces, one key to cost-effective designs with a microcomputer lies in the input/output interface.

Indeed, anything that has to interface with a microcomputer ought to be compatible with the data-bus arrangement and with the particular addressing scheme. Moreover, this bus-compatibility requirement holds good for not only in the input/output area but in the memory area as well. Consequently, since a microprocessor is a word-oriented system, more and more word-oriented memories are beginning to appear.

The M6800 family is directed at just these system needs. It includes flexible input/output adapters and word-oriented memories, in addition to the basic microprocessing unit, as indicated in the minimum system configuration of Fig. 7. This system can maintain its 1-MHz level of operation even when expanded to 10 modules (memories, input/output adapters and additional CPUs) on the principal data bus, with no external interface package.

In order to handle applications that require 1-MHz operation with more than 10 modules on the data bus, bus extenders are provided. For systems that do not require 1-MHz operation, up to 30 modules can be added to the data bus without requiring bus extenders—for example, more than 20 modules can be added to the data

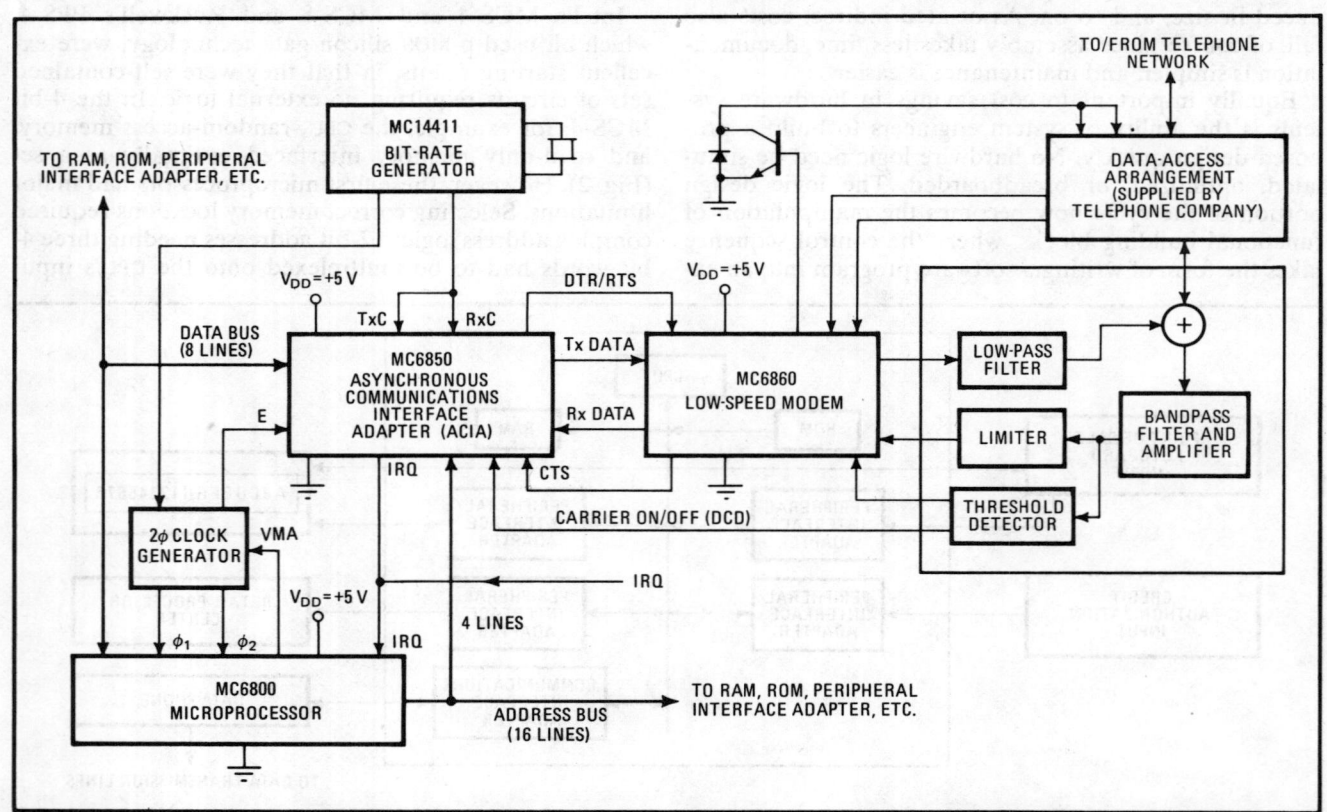

8. Communicating. A boon for communications systems, this microprocessor setup can be implemented using standard communication interface adapters (CIAs). These adapters' function is to give the CPU system access to any standard modem.

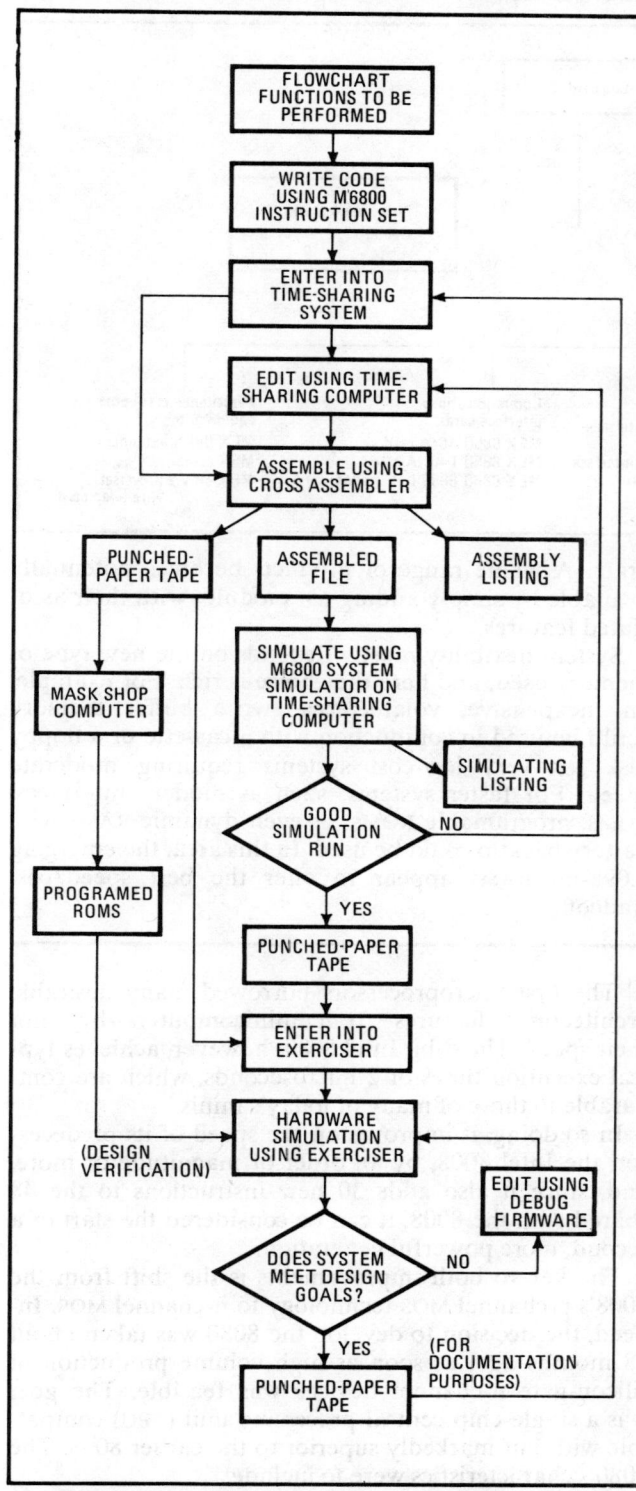

9. Working up the software. This design sequence, which is organized for ease of use with the GE time-sharing network, allows the designer to enter his specific program, which is then simulated on a cross assembler resident in the GE computer.

bus in a design for a typical 500-KHz control system.

Another example of how few packages are necessary with microprocessors is given by a typical modem communications system (Fig. 8). Here the asynchronous communication interface adapter performs the basic serializing/deserializing function required to interface the modems with the CPU. It also provides such additional logic capability as start, stop, and parity compensation. It can be used with a line driver/receiver for high-speed data transmission up to 5,000 bits per second, or with standard modems like the single-chip Bell 100 Series low-speed modem. Significantly, the 116 TTL and modem packages formerly required by this system are here replaced by only seven packages. The assembly costs alone are reduced by as much as two thirds.

Using the microprocessor

Most microprocessor manufacturers supply the software required to program their devices in a form usable with readily available computer systems. The software programs for the MC6800, for instance, are currently available on the ubiquitous GE time-sharing network. A designer might use them in the sequence shown in Fig. 9. Working with the GE edit program, the designer enters his specific applications program, which is simulated on a cross assembler resident in the same host computer. The cross assembler checks for obvious errors and violations and indicates them to the designer.

After the program has been assembled, the designer has two choices—to go to hardware directly, or to simulate his system by making use of the large GE host computer containing all the parameters of the particular system. If he chooses to simulate and his program works, he can then go to the hardware stage. If his program does not run, the simulator will pinpoint his problem areas, and he can modify his program and go through the loop again. This process can be continued until the designer is completely satisfied with his program.

In addition, exercisers, hardware, and programs are provided by many manufacturers to verify breadboard operation. In the system that is described in Table 1, the designer chooses the cards required to breadboard his system, plugs them into the machine, cables the input/output cards to his various peripherals, reads his program in through the TTY, or equivalent, network that interfaces to the debugging card. His program is contained in the read/write memory until it is debugged.

Then, in the debugging stage, a panel switch enables the flexible RAM to look like the appropriate ROM. If his program does not run, the exerciser will help him find out why and enable him to modify the program.

It's estimated that exercising aids like the off-the-shelf software and the Motorola Exorciser can save the designer from six to 12 man-months by providing him

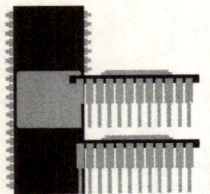

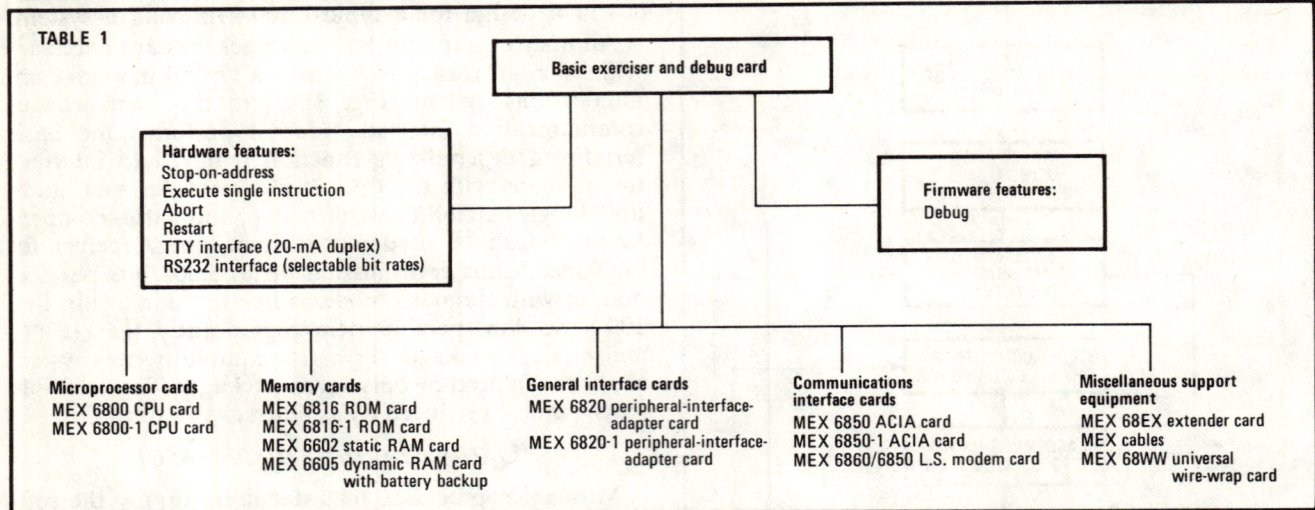

TABLE 1

Basic exerciser and debug card

Hardware features:
Stop-on-address
Execute single instruction
Abort
Restart
TTY interface (20-mA duplex)
RS232 interface (selectable bit rates)

Firmware features:
Debug

Microprocessor cards
MEX 6800 CPU card
MEX 6800-1 CPU card

Memory cards
MEX 6816 ROM card
MEX 6816-1 ROM card
MEX 6602 static RAM card
MEX 6605 dynamic RAM card
with battery backup

General interface cards
MEX 6820 peripheral-interface-adapter card
MEX 6820-1 peripheral-interface-adapter card

Communications interface cards
MEX 6850 ACIA card
MEX 6850-1 ACIA card
MEX 6860/6850 L.S. modem card

Miscellaneous support equipment
MEX 68EX extender card
MEX cables
MEX 68WW universal wire-wrap card

with a convenient method of communicating with the microcomputer.

Systems that are based on microprocessors are cheaper to manufacture, require shorter design cycles—and are also easier to modify or upgrade. The personality or function of the system, being determined by a master control program stored in a memory, is changed simply by modifying that program.

In the case of market testing, systems can be adapted in the customer's own environment to meet his needs better. For the first time a manufacturer has the capacity to make his product smarter and add features at any instant simply by expanding his master control program. A whole range of products becomes potentially available by simply adding LSI modules with their associated features.

System flexibility mostly depends on the new type of memory used, and here the choice is rich. For example, an inexpensive, volatile read/write buffer memory could be used in conjunction with a cassette or a floppy disk for very low-cost systems requiring moderate speed. For faster systems, such as modem interfaces, ROMs, programable ROMs, or even dynamic RAMs with battery backup could be used. In this area, the emerging 4,096-bit RAMs appear to offer the best speed/cost tradeoff. □

In switch to n-MOS microprocessor gets a 2-μs cycle time

Intel's 8-bit successor to its 4-bit p-MOS CPU chip has 30 extra instructions, is 10 times faster

by Masatoshi Shima and Federico Faggin,
Intel Corp., Santa Clara, Calif.

□ The first microprocessors borrowed many desirable architectural features from minicomputers—but not their speed. The 8-bit Intel 8080, however, achieves typical execution times of 2 microseconds, which are comparable to those of many of today's minis.

In so doing, it improves on the speed of its predecessor, the Intel 8008, by an order of magnitude or more, and, since it also adds 30 new instructions to the 48 shared with the 8008, it can be considered the start of a second, more powerful generation.

The key to both improvements is the shift from the 8008's p-channel MOS technology to n-channel MOS. Indeed, the decision to develop the 8080 was taken about 18 months ago, as soon as high-volume production of silicon-gate n-channel devices was feasible. The goal was a single-chip central processing unit (CPU) compatible with but markedly superior to the earlier 8008. The 8080's characteristics were to include:

■ A 10:1 speed improvement over the 8008.
■ None of the known limitations of the 8008 (such as interfacing problems and lack of multiple interrupts).
■ Improved functional capability plus retention of all

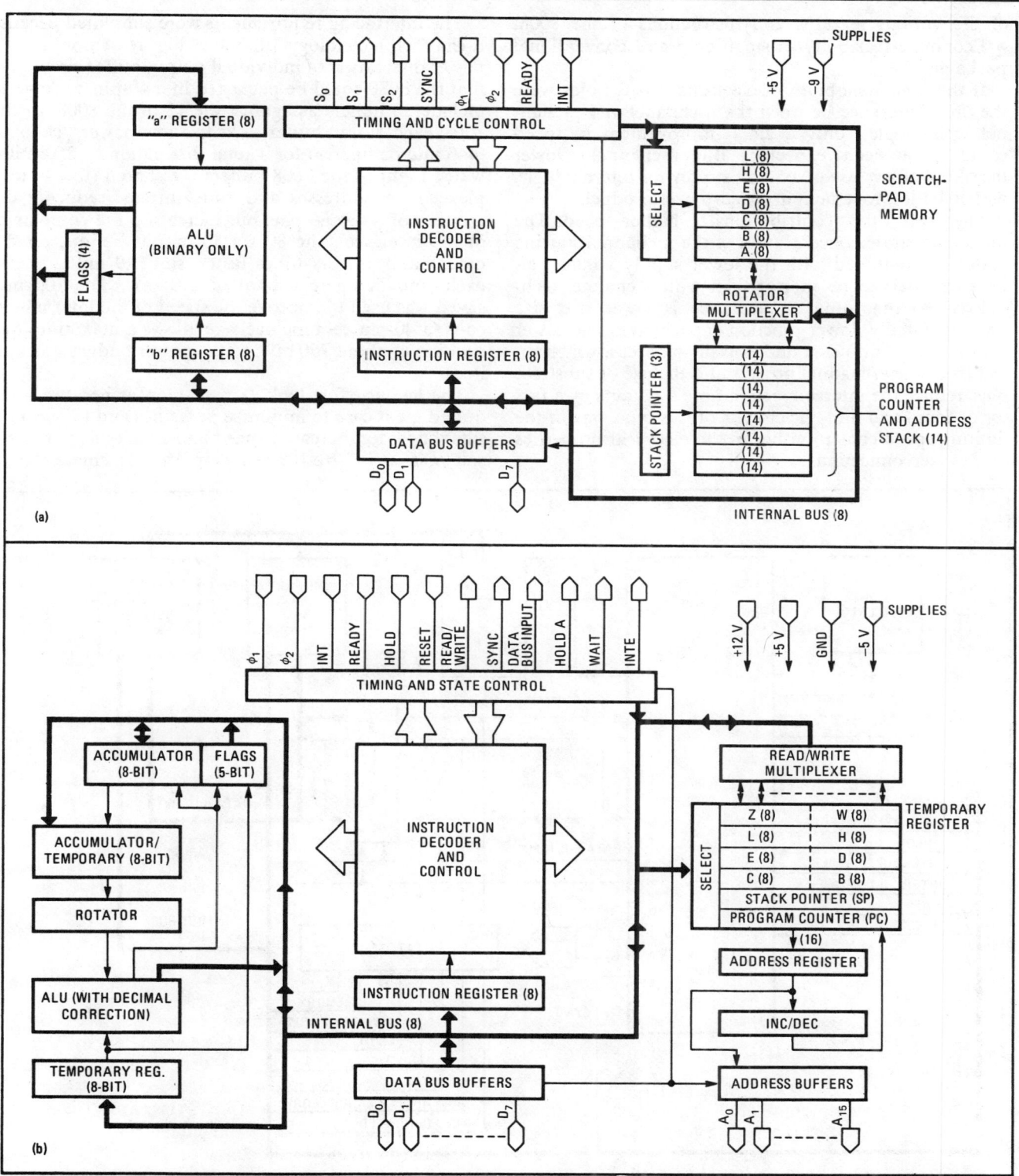

1. Comparison. Intel's earlier single-chip microprocessor, the 8008, has a separate scratch-pad memory and address stack (a). In the 8080, these have been combined into the six 16-bit registers (b). The accumulator has been moved into the arithmetic and logic unit, avoiding the use of the internal bus for data transfers between the scratch pad and the ALU during arithmetic and logic operations.

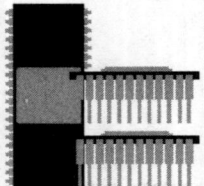

of the various features and instructions of the 8008.
- Economic feasibility—a small chip and conventional packaging.

If the higher mobility of electrons versus holes were the only difference between the n-channel and p-channel technologies, only a 2.4:1 improvement in speed could have been expected. But n-channel's lower threshold allows use of a 5-volt supply for internal logic, with a 4:1 improvement in speed-power product.

There are other contributions to higher speed. The higher substrate concentration of the n-channel starting material, combined with the lower supply voltage, allows channels to be shorter than with p-channel technology, so that input capacitance is lower and size smaller. Finally, lower junction capacitances and lower resistivities of diffusion and polysilicon areas, which result from the n-channel process and the use of substrate bias, reduce the interconnection time constants by a factor of four—and, in logic circuits of this type, one of the limiting speed constraint lies in the electrical properties of the interconnections.

The interfacing requirements were simplified because n-channel technology allows a big reduction of the power dissipation of individual output buffer circuits, so that the 8080 could be packaged in a 40-pin package to include 30 buffers as against the 12 of the 8008. In the 8008, each output buffer sinks two low-power TTL loads (440 microamperes) for a total dissipation of 250 milliwatts. Eight of the 8008 buffers are shared (time-multiplexed) for addresses and data outputs, reducing the number of package pins but increasing the complexity of the interface. The 8080's 30 output buffers, on the other hand, are six times faster, sink 1.9 milliamperes each, and dissipate a total of 150 mw. The 100 mw saved was used to improve the speed of the internal circuits (a 40-pin ceramic package allows a maximum dissipation of about 750 mw, so the power budget was limited).

The layout effort took 18 man-months because it required great care to minimize parasitics and to optimize signal flow for increased speed and smaller size. The result was a 165-by-191-mil chip that is smaller than

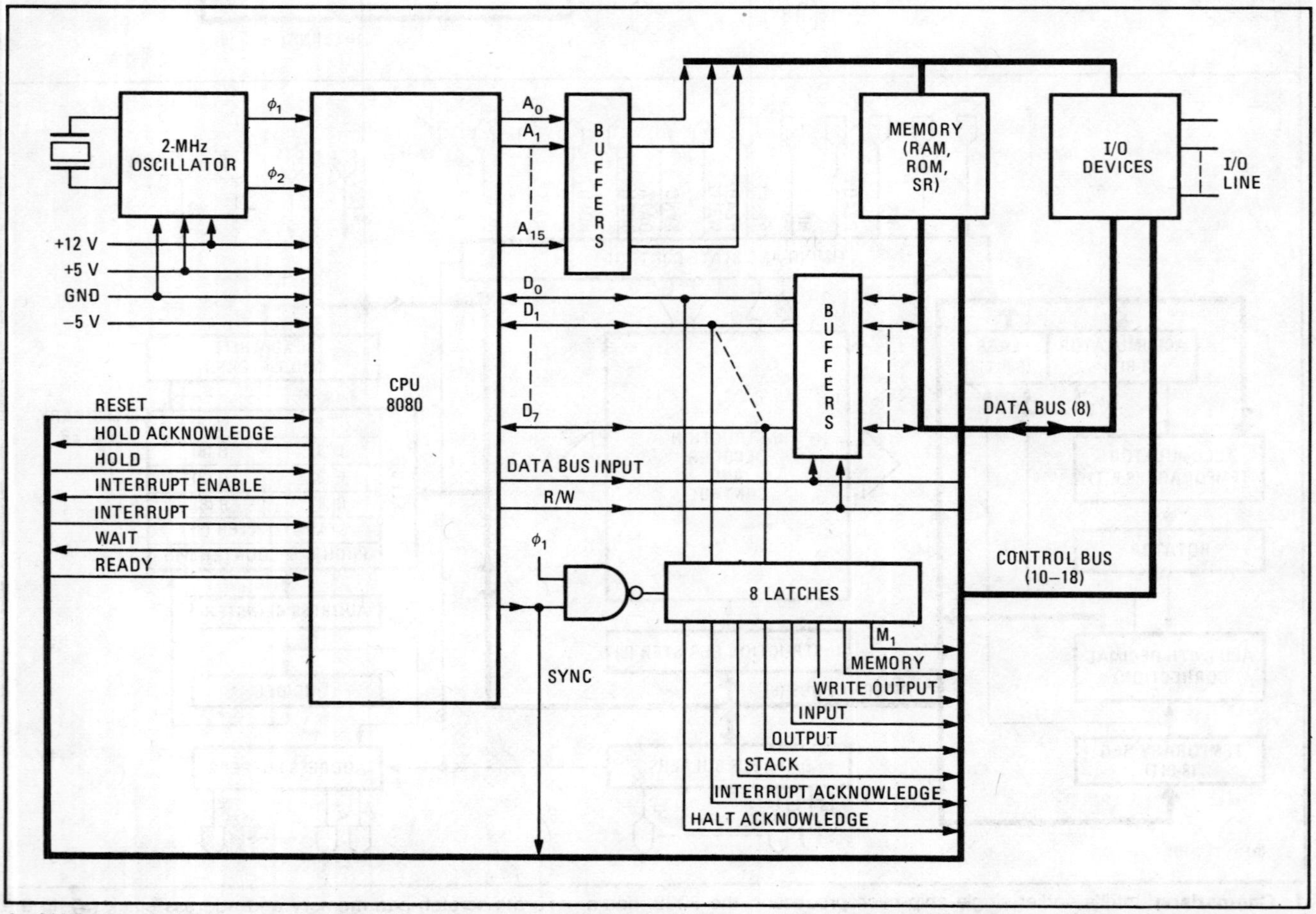

2. 8080 at work. When connected in a microprocessor system, the 8080 requires only six external TTL packages, as against the 20 needed by the 8008. The address bus can access up to 64 kilobytes of memory and up to 256 input and 256 output ports.

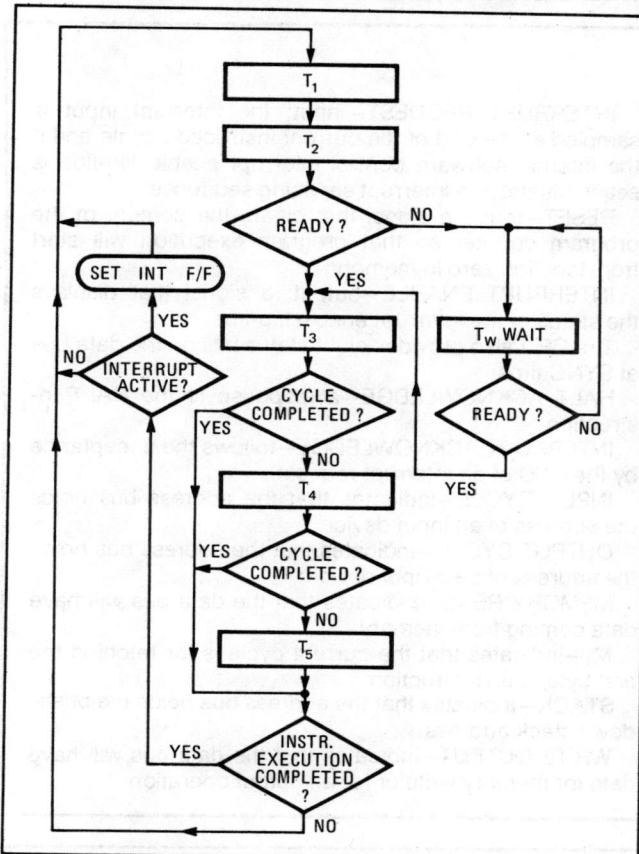

3. State diagram. A typical machine cycle requires three to five states. The operation is basically as follows: during T_1, the content of the internal address register is sent to the address bus; during T_2, READY is tested; during T_3, data is transferred between the CPU and memory or I/O devices; T_4 and T_5 are used when necessary to complete the instruction execution; and finally, the circuit goes back to T_1 for the next machine cycle. Only after the last state of the last machine cycle is the interrupt request line tested.

many of today's single-chip calculators. Great effort went into both logic and circuit design minimization, as a result of which the complex functions of the 8080 were implemented in only about 5,000 transistors.

The effectiveness of a CPU can be measured by its execution speed and memory storage requirements for a representative class of practical benchmark programs. The real improvement in performance is highly dependent on specific applications. If the 8080 had only the same 48 instructions as the 8008, it would handle the same problems about eight times faster (and five times faster than the 8008-1, a high-speed version of the 8008). However, with the 30 new instructions, the 8080 offers speed improvements on the order of 10:1 to 20:1 with smaller storage requirements—from 95% to 70% for an equivalent program written for the 8080.

The internal organization of the 8080 is shown in Fig. 1b, while Fig. 1a shows the same detail for the 8080.

The most important change concerns the internal memory organization. The 8008 has separate memories: an address stack—eight 14-bit registers which comprise one program counter storing the current effective address and seven others that store the addresses of nested subroutines—and a scratch pad, which contains the 8-bit accumulator and six additional 8-bit registers used for memory addressing and temporary storage of operands. In the 8080, these memories have been combined into a single internal 16-bit-wide memory with paired 8-bit register organization. The 8080's program counter and stack pointer, also each 16 bits wide, replace the 8008's internal address stack.

The 8008 has an internal 3-bit stack pointer, which gives the user up to seven levels of nesting of subroutines. The 8080's 16-bit stack pointer can address up to 64 kilobytes of external stack memory, providing essentially as many nesting levels as needed.

The 8080's accumulator and its associated circuitry have been moved into the arithmetic logic unit (ALU) section, to speed up the operation of the processor (data transfers between memory and ALU on the internal data bus are therefore not required for arithmetic and logic operations). Notice that the 8080 memory is double-ended—information can be transferred from the internal bus 8 bits at a time, while 16-bit transfers can take place from the address register.

Extra benefits

This organization yields a number of other new features for the 8080. The most important are:

- New instructions allow the contents of any register pair (B-C, D-E, H-L, or ACCUMULATOR-FLAGS) to be quickly stored and retrieved by being "pushed into" or "popped from" the top of the external memory stack. This is a fast way to save the machine status (the contents of the registers) when an interrupt occurs and then restore the status after the interrupt has been serviced. The stack can also be used as an extension of the internal registers.
- Other new instructions allow easy manipulation of addresses and the memory stack, since the registers B-C, D-E and H-L, and STACK POINTER can be incremented and decremented with 16 bits in parallel.
- The temporary register pair W-Z can be used as a program counter to hold a direct address to quickly load or store H-L or ACCUMULATOR. Also possible are double precision additions between any register pair and H-L.
- Fast, parallel transfers of H-L to PROGRAM COUNTER or STACK POINTER are now possible with a minimum amount of internal control logic.
- The addition of decimal correction to the ALU section enables binary and BCD arithmetic to be performed at about equal speeds.
- The addition of many new, easy-to-use control and

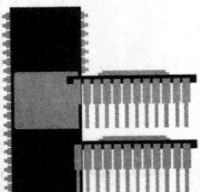

The 8080's inputs and outputs

The Intel 8080 takes four control inputs and generates six control outputs:

SYNC—output; a synchronizing signal that indicates the beginning of each memory cycle.

DATA BUS INPUT—output; a signal that indicates when the data bus is in the receiving mode, i.e. when data is expected by the CPU.

READY—input; a signal to the CPU that valid data is available. If not activated, the CPU enters a WAIT state.

WAIT—output; a signal that acknowledges that the CPU is in the WAIT state.

WRITE—output; a signal that tells the memory and output devices that valid data from the CPU is available on the data bus.

HOLD—input; a signal used by an external device to request access to the CPU address and data bus. Request is granted upon completion of memory access and it is acknowledged on the HOLD ACKNOWLEDGE output pin. The CPU address and data buses become floating (in a high-impedance state), but internally, the CPU completes the execution of the current memory cycle. After that, the CPU idles for as long as HOLD is active. HOLD and HOLD ACKNOWLEDGE can be used for DMA (direct memory access) control and in multiprocessor applications.

HOLD ACKNOWLEDGE—output; signals acknowledgment of the HOLD state.

INTERRUPT REQUEST—input; the interrupt input is sampled at the end of the current instruction cycle and if the internal software control interrupt enable flip-flop is set, it initiates the interrupt servicing sequence.

RESET—input; a signal that clears the content of the program counter so that program execution will start from location zero in memory.

INTERRUPT ENABLE—output; a signal that displays the status of the interrupt enable flip-flop.

The CPU also provides eight status bits on the data bus at SYNC time:

HALT ACKNOWLEDGE—a response to the HALT instruction.

INTERRUPT ACKNOWLEDGE—follows the acceptance by the CPU of an interrupt request.

INPUT CYCLE—indicates that the address bus holds the address of an input device.

OUTPUT CYCLE—indicates that the address bus holds the address of an output device.

MEMORY READ—indicates that the data bus will have data coming from memory.

M_1—indicates that the current cycle is for fetching the first byte of an instruction.

STACK—indicates that the address bus holds the pushdown stack address.

WRITE OUTPUT—indicates that the data bus will have data for memory write or for an output operation.

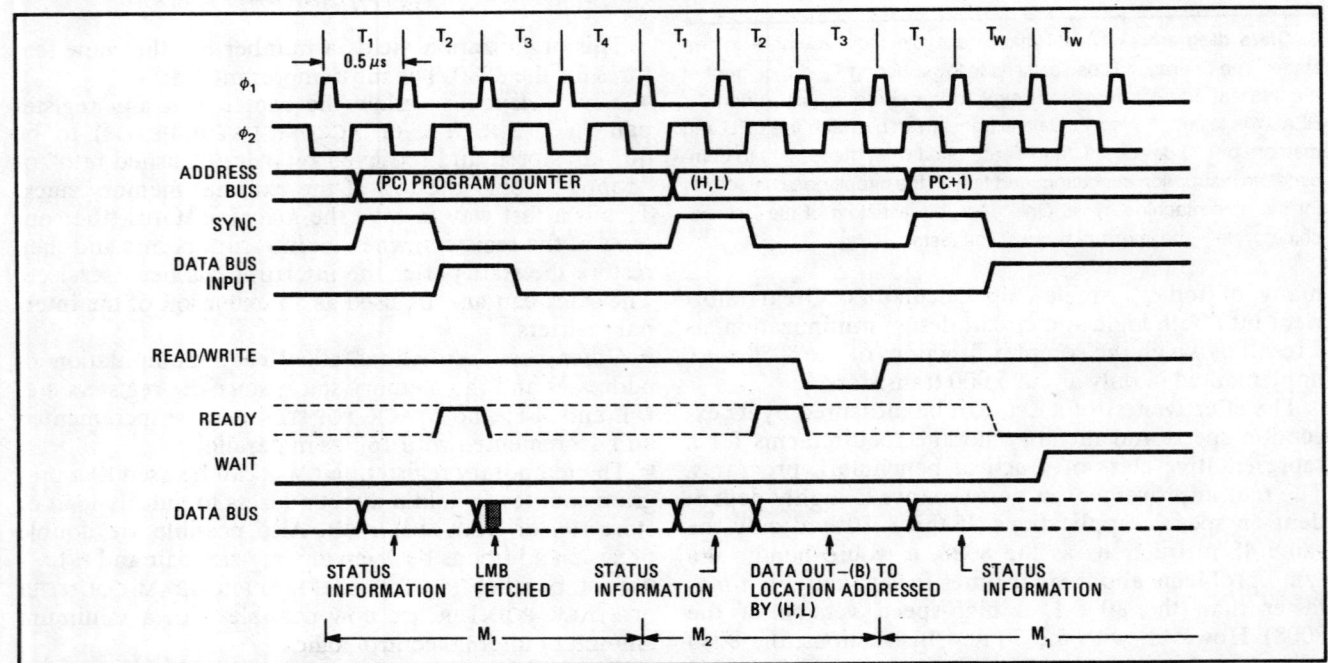

4. Timing. The instruction LMB (load the content of register B into the location addressed by the contents of registers H and L) requires two machine cycles (M_1 and M_2). During M_1, the address bus holds the program counter contents, and during M_2 it holds the contents of the H-L register pair. DATA BUS INPUT shows when the CPU expects data from the data bus. WRITE shows when data from the CPU is available on the data bus. READY shows that valid data is available to the CPU. The bottom waveform shows the corresponding data-bus actions.

status signals simplifies interfacing, allows direct memory access, and helps in program debugging.

Figure 2 shows how the 8080 interfaces with outside chips to make a microprocessor system. An external crystal-controlled oscillator supplies two non-overlapping clocks, ϕ_1, and ϕ_2. Buffers interface to external address and data buses, and a gate and eight latches set up status bits during sync time. All inputs and outputs are TTL-compatible, with the exception of the two clocks, which require +12 V. A memory and the input-output devices complete the system.

The amount of external interface logic necessary to implement any system depends on that system's complexity. The minimum requirement is six packages of conventional TTL (the 8008 needs at least 20).

External signals are organized on three buses. An address bus with 16 lines addresses up to 65 kilobytes of memory and up to 256 input and 256 output ports. A bidirectional eight-line data bus carries data to and from memory and I/O ports. A control bus synchronizes the CPU, external memory, and I/O devices, and also has the job of handling interrupts, direct-memory-access (DMA) controls, and CPU status information.

Instructions in the 8080, as in the 8008, use one, two, or three bytes of storage. Each instruction requires from one to five machine (or memory) cycles for fetching and execution. Machine cycles are called $M_1, M_2, \ldots, M_5$. Each machine cycle requires from three to five states—$T_1, T_2, \ldots, T_5$—for its completion. Each state has the duration of one clock period (0.5 microsecond). There are three other states (WAIT, HOLD, and HALT) which last one to an indefinite number of clock periods, as controlled by external signals. Machine cycle M_1 is always the operation-code fetch cycle and lasts four or five clock periods. Machine cycles M_2, M_3, M_4, and M_5 normally last three clock periods each.

To understand the basic operation of the 8080, let's refer to the simplified state diagram shown in Fig. 3, starting at cycle M_1 and state T_1.

During T_1 the content of the program counter is sent to the address bus, SYNC is true, and the data bus has status information pertaining to the cycle that is currently being initiated. T_1 is always followed by another state, T_2, during which the condition of the READY input is tested. If READY is true, T_3 is entered; otherwise, the CPU will go into the wait state (T_w) and stay there for as long as READY is false. READY thus allows the CPU be synchronized to a memory with any access time and to any I/O device. Also, by controlling the READY line, the user can single-step through his program.

During T_3, the data coming from memory is available on the data bus and is transferred into the instruction register (during M_1 only). The instruction decoder and control sections then generate the basic signals to control the internal data transfers, the timing, and the machine-cycle requirements of the new instructions.

At the end of T_4, if the cycle is complete, or else at the end of T_5, the 8080 goes back to T_1 and enters machine cycle M_2, unless the instruction required only one machine cycle for its execution. In such cases, a new M_1 cycle is entered. The loop is repeated for as many cycles and states as required by the instruction.

It is only during the last state of the last machine cycle that the interrupt request line is tested and a special M_1 cycle is entered, during which no program-counter incrementing takes place and INTERRUPT ACKNOWLEDGE status is sent out. During this cycle, one of eight possible single-byte calls will be sent to the CPU by the interrupting device.

Execution times

Instruction state requirements range from a minimum of four states for non-memory referencing instructions, like register and accumulator arithmetic instructions, up to a maximum of 18 states for the most complex instructions—such as XTHL (exchange the contents of registers H and L with the content of the top two locations of the stack). At the maximum clock frequency of 2 megahertz, this means that assembly-language instructions can be executed in 2 to 9 μs.

As an example of 8080 timing, Fig. 4 shows the timing diagram for the one-byte, two-cycle instruction LMB (load the content of register B into the memory location addressed by the contents of registers H and L). This example also illustrates the timing when a WAIT state is entered after the execution of LMB. Notice that seven states (a total of 3.5 μs) are required to fetch and execute the LMB instruction. The same instruction would require 28 μs by the 8008, 17.5 μs by the faster 8008-1.

Though this example demonstrates an 8:1 improvement in speed over the 8008, the real impact of the new 8080 will not be as a replacement for the 8008. The 8008 has, after all, adequate speed for a large number of applications. The 8080 will be used in new systems that were not feasible before because the first-generation microcomputers were not powerful enough. □

COMPARING THE GENERATIONS		
	INTEL 8008	INTEL 8080
Technology/threshold voltage	p/1.5–2.5 V	n/0.8–1.4 V
Supply voltage	+5, −9 V	+12, +5, 0, −5 V
Number of pins on package	18	40
Number of interface chips	20	6
Number of instructions	48	78 (48 + 30)
Instruction execution speed	12–22 μs	2–9 μs
Internal memory type/number of bits	dynamic/168 bits	static/104 bits
Chip size (mils)	124 × 173	164 × 191
RAM size/speed (typical systems)	256/1 μs	1,024/500 ns
ROM size/speed (typical systems)	2,048/1 μs	4,096/600 ns

Single-chip microprocessor employs minicomputer word length

By providing 16-bit instructions and addresses and a choice of 8- or 16-bit words for data processing, a new microprocessor speeds up operation and simplifies programing for many applications

by George F. Reyling Jr., *National Semiconductor Corp., Santa Clara, Calif.*

☐ Because the development cost of custom large-scale integrated circuits can only be justified by high product volumes, LSI-chip designers have turned to developing standard circuits that can be customized by programing: the read-only memory, the programable logic array, and now the programable microprocessor.

The 8-bit word length of the first single-chip microprocessors does, however, handicap them for the many applications that require 16-bit words for instructions and memory addresses. For these jobs, a new single-chip device, the processing and control element (PACE), has been developed that provides 16-bit instruction and address-processing plus a choice of either 8-bit or 16-bit data processing. It not only is faster, but it also needs shorter programs, and hence less memory.

In complex microprocessor applications, the chip with the 8-bit word length may have to use double-precision arithmetic to attain the necessary data accuracy. Worse still, multiple registers are needed to form 16-bit memory addresses, and multiple accesses to memory must be made to fetch multibyte instructions—yet fetching instructions and forming addresses are the operations most frequently performed by processors.

This adds up to a strong case for optimizing the word length for a processor's instruction set and addressing capabilities rather than the data it is handling. Indeed,

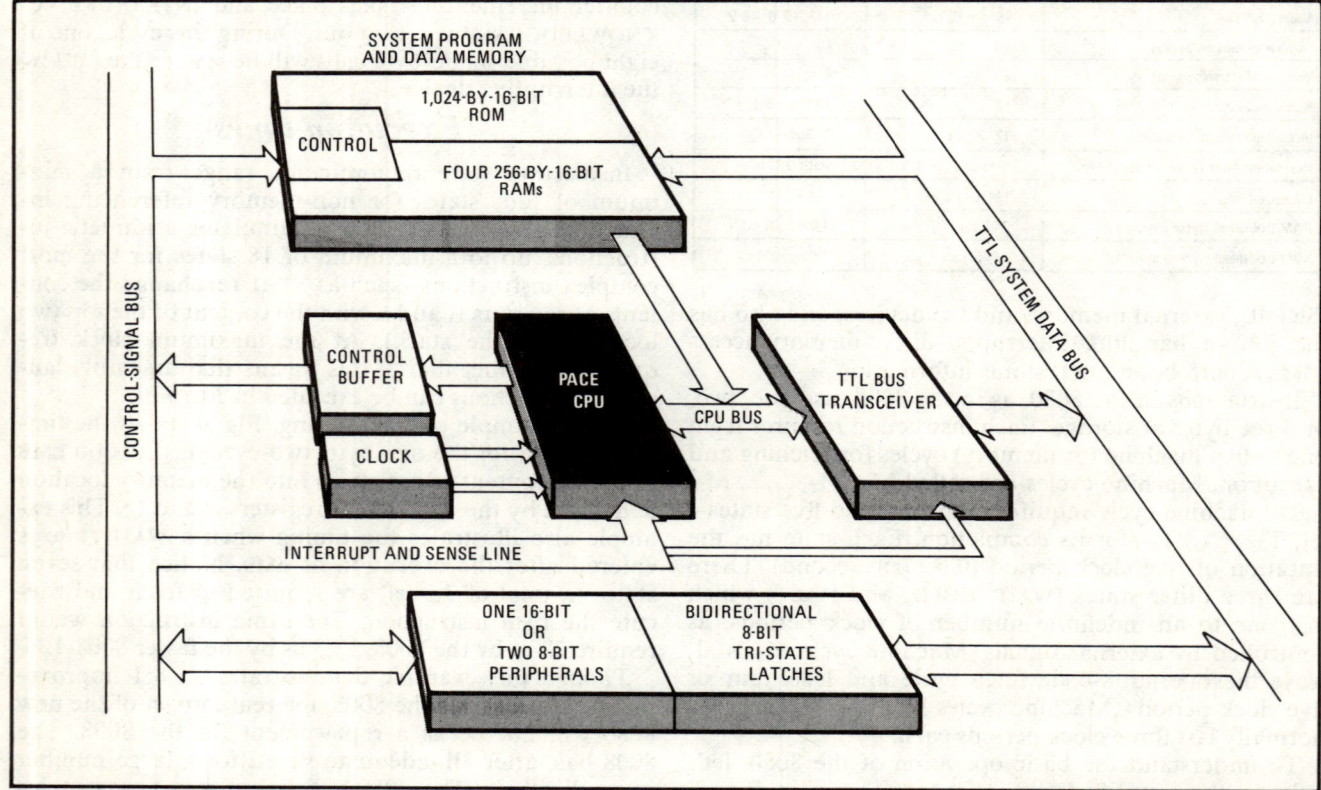

Few parts. The PACE chip allows a complete microcomputer system to be built with a minimal parts count. This system requires five integrated circuits for the 16-bit central processing unit, clock, and buffering circuits, six ICs for the memories, and two ICs for interfacing.

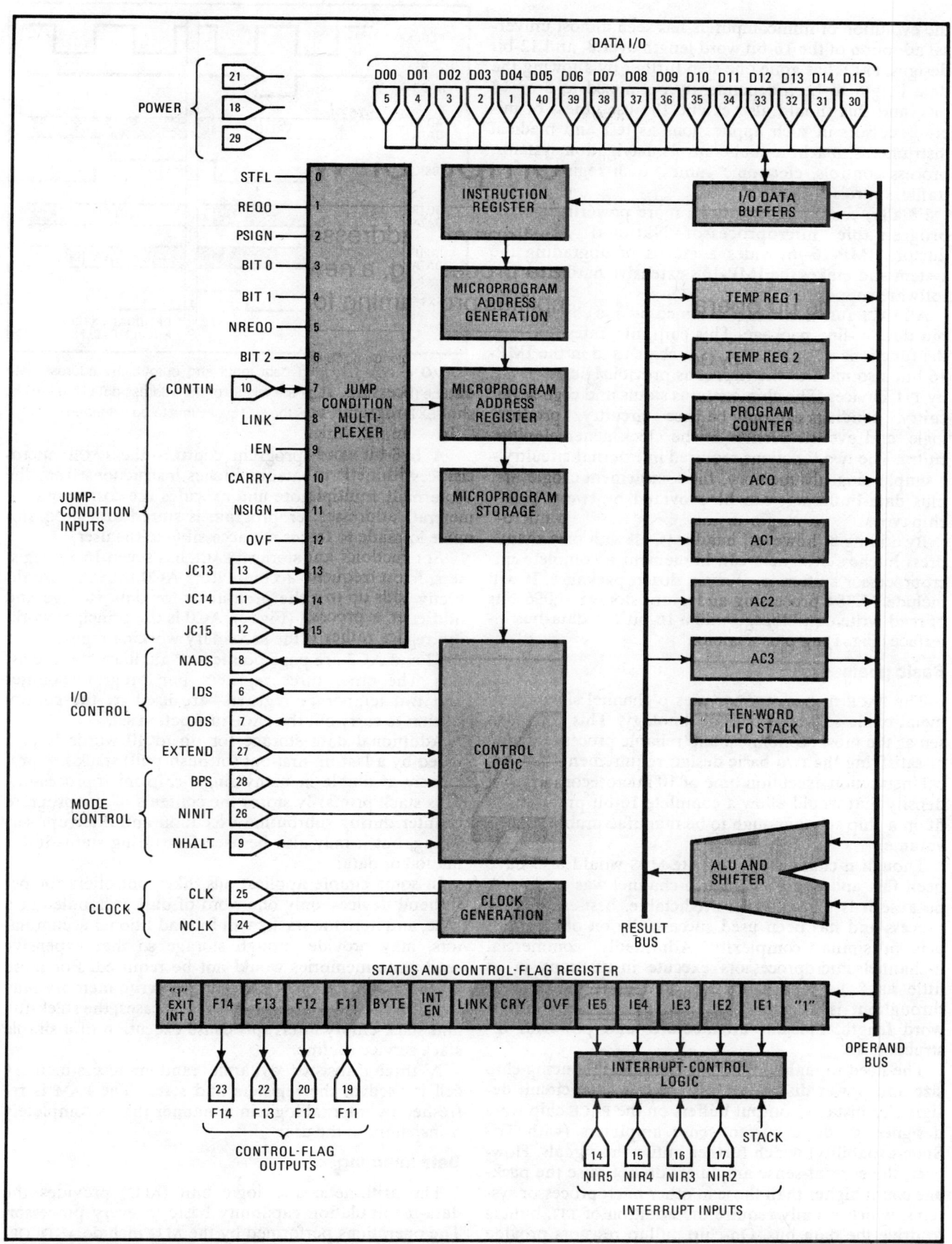

2. On the inside. Seven 16-bit registers are included in PACE, along with a last-in, first-out stack for additional storage of up to 10 words. The status-flag register can be loaded from any accumulator. The byte flag is used to specify 8-bit or 16-bit data lengths.

the evolution of minicomputers has seen almost universal adoption of the 16-bit word length over 8- and 12-bit designs. PACE has gone one step further by allowing the data length to be independently optimized to 8 or 16 bits, and this should also extend the usefulness of microprocessors in such applications as test and medical instruments, machine-tool controls, navigation systems, process controls, electronic games, cash registers, and traffic controls.

Finally, compatibility with a more powerful, microprogramable microprocessor—National Semiconductor's IMP-16—provides a means of upgrading the system and makes the IMP-16's extensive hardware and software support available to PACE.

All PACE functions are performed by one chip in a 40-pin dual in-line package. This chip integrates not only the functions of the five MOS LSI chips used in the IMP-16 but also most of the functions previously carried out by TTL devices. The chip contains status and control circuitry, conditional-branch sense circuitry, interrupt logic, and even a portion of the clock generation circuitry. The two functions required in external circuitry—a simple, single-phase, true and complement clock input plus data-buffering—can be provided by two separate chip types.

By adding a ROM and four RAMs, all with on-chip address latches, designers can implement a complete microprocessor system in about a dozen packages. It will include 16,384 bits of ROM program storage, 4,096 bits of read-write data storage, and a 16-bit TTL data-bus interface (Fig. 1).

Basic goals

The PACE microprocessor uses p-channel silicon-gate metal-oxide-semiconductor technology. This was chosen as the most economical and reliable process capable of satisfying the two basic design requirements: a typical instruction execution time of 10 microseconds, and a density that would allow a complete 16-bit processor to fit on a chip small enough to be manufacturable in high volume.

Though n-channel silicon-gate MOS would also have been fast and dense enough, p-channel was preferred, because it is today's most predictable, best-established process and has been used successfully on other products of similar complexity. Admittedly, commercial n-channel microprocessors execute instructions in as little as 2 µs, but its designers believe that PACE's throughput is as good or better, thanks to its 16-bit word length, efficient architecture, and powerful instruction set.

The need to maintain high speed while reducing chip size and power dissipation also affected the circuit design. For instance, output buffers on the PACE chip were designed to drive current-sense amplifiers (with Tri-State capability) which further buffer the signals. However, the current-sense amplifiers do not raise the package count higher than those in other microprocessor systems, which usually require the addition of TTL buffers to drive the data bus. On-chip pullup resistors provide TTL-compatible inputs, and the use of dynamic logic also keeps power dissipation down.

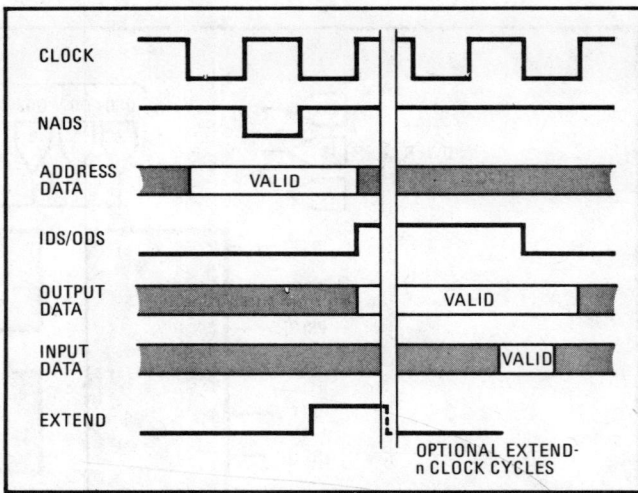

3. I/O controls. During data input and output, the address data strobe (NADS) occurs in the middle of the address-data time period. The EXTEND input allows the I/O cycle time to be extended.

A built-in microprogram controls the PACE microprocessor as it repeatedly fetches instructions from the external program store and executes the corresponding operations. The microprogram is stored in a programable logic array that is not accessible to the user.

For internal data storage, PACE has seven 16-bit registers, four of which—accumulators AC0 to AC3—are directly available to the programer for data storage and address formulation (Fig. 2). AC0 is the principal working register, AC1 is the secondary working register, and AC2 and AC3 are page pointers or auxiliary data registers. The other three registers—one program counter and two temporary registers—are used by the control section to carry out the PACE instruction set.

Additional data storage for up to 10 words is provided by a last-in, first-out (or push-pull) stack not previously available in many single-chip microprocessors. This stack primarily stores the contents of the program counter during subroutine execution and interrupt servicing, but it may also be used for storing status information or data.

In some simple applications, like controllers for peripheral devices, only one word of data is handled at a time, and here the stack, with four additional accumulators, may provide enough storage so that expensive read-write memories would not be required. For more complex applications, external read-write memory may be used as a stack extension. In such cases, the stack-full and stack-empty interrupts cause execution of a simple stack service routine.

A three-transistor dynamic random-access-memory cell is used in the registers and stack. The RAM is refreshed by internal logic in a manner that is completely transparent to the user.

Data handling

The arithmetic and logic unit (ALU) provides the data-manipulation capability basic to every processor. The operations performed by the ALU include AND, OR, XOR, complement, shift left, shift right, mask byte and sign extend. PACE can add four-digit-per-word binary-

PACE INSTRUCTION LIST

BRANCH INSTRUCTIONS

BOC	Branch on condition
JMP	Jump
JMP@	Jump indirect
JSR	Jump to subroutine
JSR@	Jump to subroutine indirect
RTS	Return from subroutine
RTI	Return from interrupt

SKIP INSTRUCTIONS

SKNE	Skip if not equal
SKG	Skip if greater
SKAZ	Skip if and is zero
ISZ	Increment and skip if zero
DSZ	Decrement and skip if zero
AISZ	Add immediate, skip if zero

MEMORY DATA TRANSFER INSTRUCTIONS

LD	Load
LD@	Load indirect
ST	Store
ST@	Store indirect
LSEX	Load with sign extended

MEMORY DATA OPERATE INSTRUCTIONS

AND	And
OR	Or
ADD	Add
SUBB	Subtract with borrow
DECA	Decimal add

REGISTER DATA TRANSFER INSTRUCTIONS

LI	Load immediate
RCPY	Register copy
RXCH	Register exchange
XCHRS	Exchange register and stack
CFR	Copy flags into register
CRF	Copy register into flags
PUSH	Push register onto stack
PULL	Pull stack into register
PUSHF	Push flags onto stack
PULLF	Pull stack into flags

REGISTER DATA OPERATE INSTRUCTIONS

RADD	Register add
RADC	Register add with carry
RAND	Register and
RXOR	Register exclusive-OR
CAI	Complement and add immediate

SHIFT AND ROTATE INSTRUCTIONS

SHL	Shift left
SHR	Shift right
ROL	Rotate left
ROR	Rotate right

MISCELLANEOUS INSTRUCTIONS

HALT	Halt
SFLG	Set flag
PFLG	Pulse flag

---

coded-decimal (BCD) data, as well as straight binary data, thus eliminating the program-storage and execution time usually required for BCD-to-binary conversions. This is useful in such BCD-oriented applications as display controllers, electronic cash registers, billing systems, accounting machines, navigation aids, and industrial controllers and test systems.

The programer, using a status flag, sets the ALU to operate on either 8- or 16-bit data. This option allows character-oriented and other 8-bit applications to be executed using an 8-bit peripheral data bus and read-write memory, while address formation and instruction storage can be implemented in 16 bits.

Data transfers

All input/output transactions consist of an address-output interval (in which the address specifies an external memory location or peripheral device) followed by a data-transfer interval. If 8-bit data is being transferred, the unused bits can be treated as "don't care" bits by the hardware.

Address and data transfers between PACE and external memories or peripheral devices take place over 16 data lines (Fig. 2) and are synchronized by four I/O control signals: NADS (address data strobe), IDS (input data strobe), ODS (output data strobe), and EXTEND (Fig. 3).

The NADS pulse occurs in the center of the address-data time period and may be used to strobe the address into an address latch on the external ROM or RAM. (Such memories are commercially available with address latches on the chip.) The IDS and ODS indicate the type of data transfer and may be used to enable Tri-State I/O buffers and to gate data into registers or memories. The EXTEND input allows the I/O cycle time to be extended by multiples of the clock cycle and thus adapted to various memory and peripheral devices or to direct-memory-access/bus operation.

The EXTEND input and all other signal inputs to PACE are designed to accept signals that are asynchronous with respect to the clock signal. Clocks for the dynamic logic are derived internally from single-phase true and complement clock inputs. These inputs are divided by the internal circuitry into the eight clock phases that constitute a microinstruction cycle.

Data transfers occur at two times: during each access to an instruction (usually contained in a ROM) and during the access to data (usually contained in a RAM) called for by a memory-reference instruction. (Memory-reference instructions in PACE could perhaps more properly be called I/O-reference instructions, since the same instructions control all data transfers, whether with memory, peripheral devices, or a central processor's data bus.)

The same buses are used for memory and peripherals, saving system hardware. This unified-bus architecture contrasts with that of many other microprocessors and minicomputers, in which one instruction type (I/O class) communicates with peripheral devices and an-

Memory addressing in PACE

Part of the PACE microprocessor's powerful instruction set is a flexible method of addressing the memory. This method makes it possible to reference three sequences of 256 words located anywhere in the 65,536-word memory, as well as another 256 words in fixed positions.

The fixed words from what is called a "base" page, and the others form three "floating" pages. The mode of addressing is specified by the 2-bit XR field (bits 8 and 9) of the 16-bit instruction, as shown in the figure.

When the XR field is 00, it specifies base-page addressing. The base page may consist of either the first 256 words in the memory, or the first 128 plus last 128 words. The base-page-select (BPS) signal input decides which option will be used.

To address the first 256 words of memory (locations 0–255), BPS is set to 0, and the 16-bit memory address is formed by setting bits 8 through 15 to zero and by using bits 0 through 7 to specify one of 256 locations.

If BPS is 1, the 16-bit memory address is formed by setting bits 8 through 15 equal to bit 7 and by using 0 through 6 to locate the first 128 words of the memory (when bit 7 is 0) and the last 128 words (when bit 7 is 1). This technique is useful for splitting the base page between read-write and read-only memories or between memory and peripheral devices, so convenient base-page addressing can access data or peripherals.

When the XR field is 01, it specifies that addressing be relative to the program counter (PC). In this mode, the memory address is formed by adding the contents of the program counter to the value of bits 0 through 7, treated as a two's complement number with sign. That is, the bits 0 to 7 are interpreted as a 16-bit value with bits 8 through 15 set equal to bit 7. This allows numbers from −128 through +127 to be represented. Bits 0 to 7 are called displacement bits, since they can represent a range of words around a center position.

When the XR field is 10 or 11, addressing is relative to an index register, and any memory location within the external 65,536-word address space may be referenced. As before, the displacement field is interpreted as a signed value ranging from −128 through +127. The memory address is then formed by adding the displacement bits to the contents of either accumulator AC 2 (when XR = 10) or accumulator AC3 (when XR = 11). This type of addressing is desirable for those applications that require addresses to be computed at execution time, since addresses can not be modified when a ROM is serving for program storage (as is usually the case with microprocessors as opposed to minicomputers).

OPERATION CODE	INDEX (XR)	DISPLACEMENT (disp)
15 10	9 8	7 0

16 BITS

XR FIELD	ADDRESSING MODE	EFFECTIVE ADDRESS
00	Base page	EA = disp
01	Program-counter relative	EA = disp + (PC)
10	AC2 relative (indexed)	EA = disp + (AC2)
11	AC3 relative (indexed)	EA = disp + (AC3)

---

other instruction type (memory-reference class) communicates with memories. The advantage of the PACE approach is that a wider variety of instructions—in fact, the entire memory-reference class—is available for communicating with peripherals. For example, the DSZ (decrement and skip if zero) instruction can be used to decrement a peripheral-device register, or the SKAZ (skip if AND is zero) instruction can be used to test the register's contents. The LD (load) and ST (store) instruction handle simple data transfers.

Flags and jumps

The PACE flag outputs and jump commands give it flexibility in controlling peripherals. They can be used for many simple control functions, such as start reader and rewind in a tape controller.

The flag and jump conditions also can be used together as a serial I/O port, eliminating the hardware that would otherwise be required to interface to the data bus and to decode the device address. The jump condition inputs serve as data-sense inputs, for one bit of data, since their state can be determined by instructions in the program. A flag, on the other hand, can be set and cleared and serve as an output for one bit. For example, for a teletypewriter, a flag output becomes a serial bit-stream output, and the jump a serial bit-stream input.

All status and control bits for PACE are contained in a single status-flag register (Fig. 2), the contents of which may be loaded from or into any accumulator on the stack. This makes it convenient to test, store, and even—where a specific group of bits are of interest—to mask status. In addition, a number of status bits may be tested directly by the conditional-branch instruction, and any bit may be individually set or reset.

The bits in the 16-bit status-flag register serve various functions:
- The carry flag is set to the state of the carry output that results from binary and BCD arithmetic instructions and can serve as a carry input for some of these instructions.
- The overflow flag is set if an arithmetic overflow results from a binary-arithmetic instruction.
- The link flag serves as a 1-bit extension for certain shift and rotate instructions.
- The byte flag is uniquely important, since it is used to specify an 8-bit data length for data-processing instruction while arithmetic operations for address formation remain at the 16-bit data length. (In the 8-bit data mode, modifications of the carry, overflow, and link flags are based on the 8 least-significant data bits only).
- Six status flags enable the interrupt request lines.
- Four flags (bits 11–14) can be assigned functions by the programer. These flags drive output pins and may be used as direct controls for external system functions or as software-status flags.
- Bits 0 and 15 of the status register are not intended for use and always appear as a logic 1.

In the past, microprocessors' interrupt features have

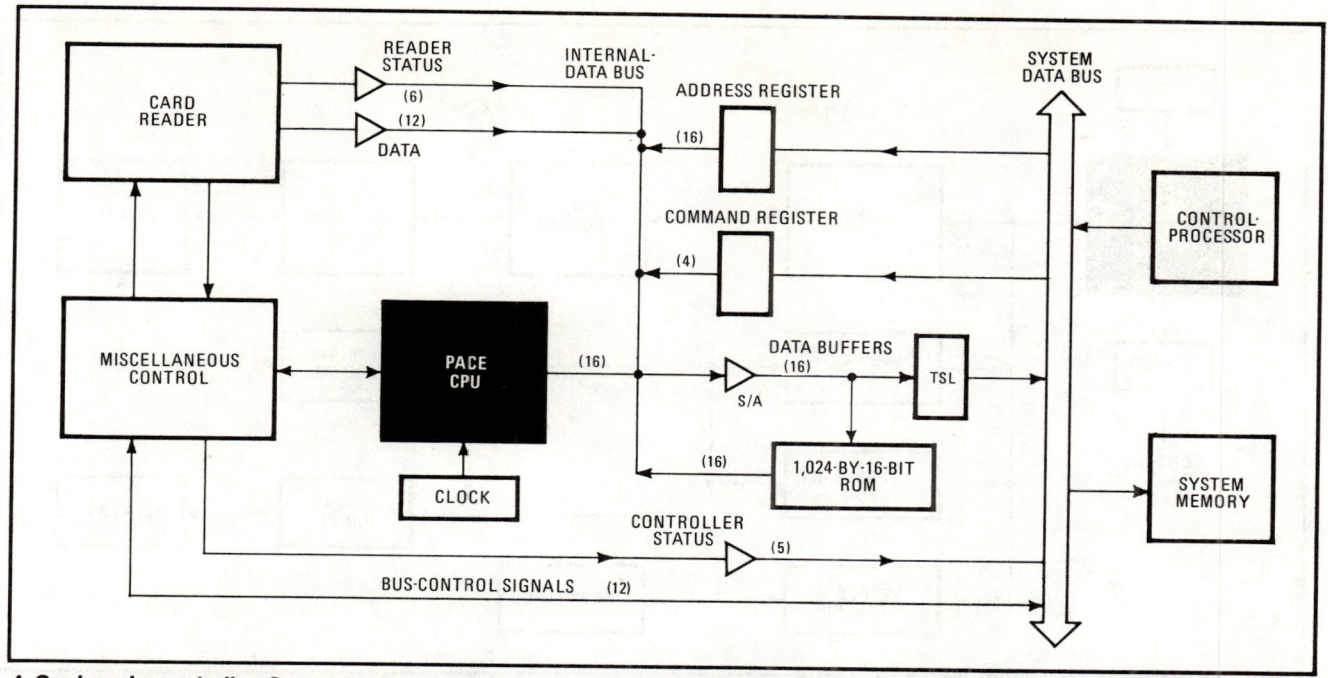

4. Card-reader controller. One application of PACE is in a card-reader controller, which requires about 20 IC packages. A central processor commands the controller to complete various operations, and the controller generates timing and control signals for the card reader.

been inadequate for many applications and have also required excessive hardware and software. Yet interrupts are essential in those applications where alarm conditions or transient conditions must be serviced immediately, as in controls for automobiles, chemical processes, or machine tools. They are also useful in many other systems to eliminate the program overhead required to scan asynchronous system inputs, as in a controller for multiple terminals or for an intersection traffic light.

Six interrupt levels

The PACE microprocessor, however, provides a six-level, priority-interrupt structure. As a result, the interrupting device's level is automatically identified, and all devices on an interrupt level can be enabled or disabled as a group, independently of other interrupt levels. An individual interrupt-enable is provided in the status register for each level, and a master interrupt-enable (IEN) is provided for all five lower-priority levels as a group. Negative-true interrupt request inputs allow several interrupts to be "wire-ORed" on each input.

The PACE interrupt system can save considerable hardware and software in applications that tend to need several interrupts. The on-chip priority logic and subsequent "vectored" (or immediate) branch to the interrupt routine can eliminate many of the logic circuits that are often required with other microprocessors. For example, PACE can internally resolve priority questions and immediately put an address vector onto the data bus. The interrupt-servicing capability in addition saves the program-storage-and-execution time that would otherwise be required to access the appropriate interrupt-service routine.

The PACE microprocessor's 337 individual instructions are a general-purpose mix of 45 types of instructions. The mix is powerful enough to allow program-coding to be considerably more efficient than with most microprocessors, and it also compares favorably with many minicomputers.

The memory-reference instructions, for example, use a flexible memory-address scheme to provide one fixed, or "base," page of 256 words in the external memory, and three "floating" pages, which allow the user to pick out 256 words anywhere in the memory. The floating pages can be selected according to the contents of the program counter or either of the two accumulators (see "Memory addressing in PACE").

Instruction types

Among the types of instruction used in PACE are:
- Branch instructions, which allow transfer of control to anywhere in the 16-bit addressing space.
- Conditional branches, which allow testing of any one of 16 conditions, including status flags, the contents of the principal working register (AC0), and user inputs to the chip.
- Skip instructions, which provide additional testing capability and comparisons of memory without altering data.
- Memory-data-transfer instructions, for transferring data between the accumulators and either memory or peripheral devices.
- Load-with-sign-extended instructions, which convert 8-bit, two's-complement data to 16-bit data, allowing 16-bit address modification when the 8-bit data length has been selected.
- Memory-data-operate instructions, for operations between the principal working register (AC0) and memory or peripheral data. They include both binary and BCD arithmetic instructions (no correction required).
- Register-data-transfer instructions, which provide a

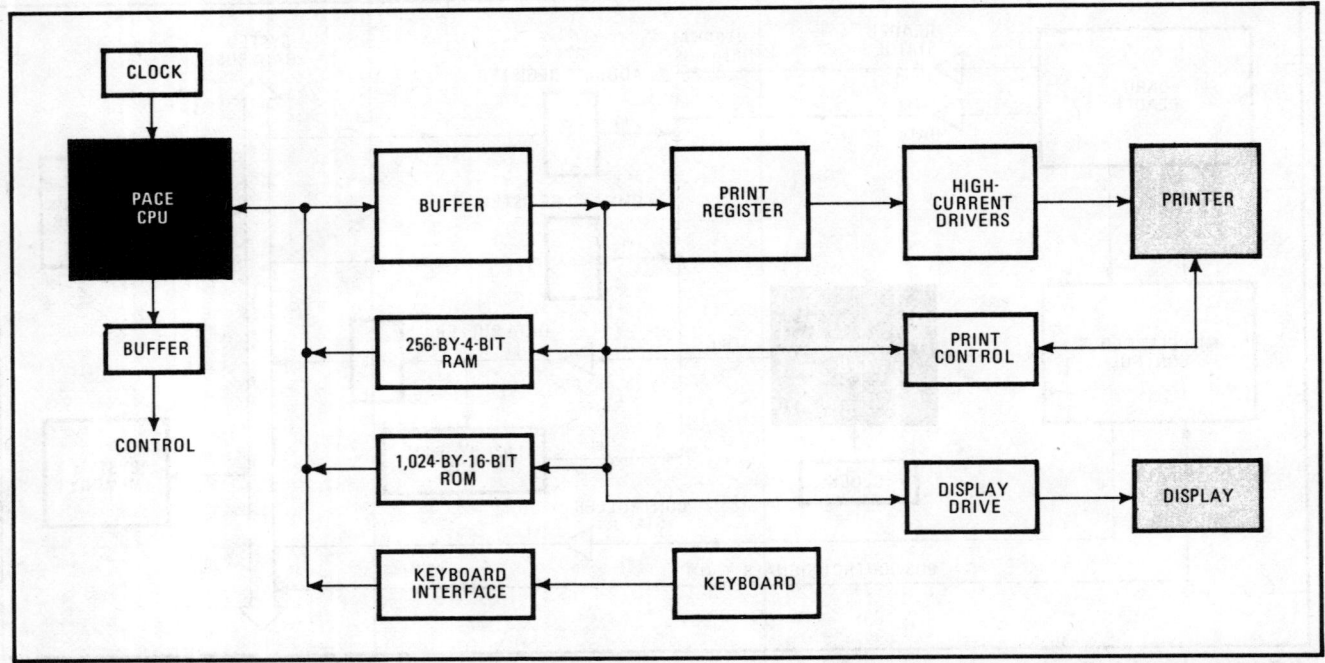

5. Cash register. An electronic cash register using PACE can perform such functions as tax computations and multiple-item pricing. The entire system has been built with 35 IC packages, eight of which comprise the CPU and the memory.

complete set of transfer possibilities between the accumulators, flag register, and stack, and which include the capability to load immediate data.
- Register-data-operate instructions, for logical and arithmetic operations between any two accumulators. They may be used to modify addresses and data and to reduce the number of time-consuming memory references in a program.
- Shift-and-rotate instructions, which allow eight different operations that are useful for multiply, divide, bit-scanning, and serial input-output operations.
- Miscellaneous instructions, including the capability to set or reset any of the 16 bits of the status-flag register individually

Two applications

A card-reader controller and an electronic cash register illustrate the use of the PACE microprocessor.

The card-reader controller (CRC) is designed to interface with a system that is under the control of a central processor and has a direct memory-access channel (Fig. 4). The central processor issues commands to the CRC over a 16-bit multiplexed data bus. The CRC then responds to these commands by generating appropriate timing and control signals to the card reader and by monitoring the card reader's data and status outputs. Data read from the card is then transferred directly to the system memory over the data bus, and the CRC generates an interrupt to the central processor to signal completion of the order or the occurrence of an error condition.

The CRC has two modes of operation. In the bootstrap mode, a control-panel switch causes one card to be read and its data deposited in packed form in the first 40 locations of system memory. In the normal mode, the CRC also transfers data directly to memory, but does so under control of the central processor.

Data output from the PACE chip is buffered with sense amplifiers, which drive the 1,024-by-16-bit ROM chip (with internal address latch) and the Tri-State system data-bus buffers for time-multiplexed address and data output. Input commands to the CRC are received in the 4-bit command register, while the address register stores those system-memory starting addresses specified by the read commands.

The PACE priority-interrupt inputs are very useful in this application. They monitor the index pulses and signals for motion check, hopper check, and read error. The jump-condition inputs monitor less critical signals, such as reader-ready. Control-flag outputs drive the reader's card-pick input and gate data from the register onto the internal data bus.

The total controller function, including memory and I/O, requires about 20 packages. This is a quarter the number required for a TTL MSI version (which also does not include character conversion). The PACE design, with its programable feature, also allows easy modifications for changes in command requirements or for a variety of card readers.

The electronic cash register (Fig. 5) consists of the CPU, memory, a 6-digit display, and 18-column printer, and a keyboard. In addition to providing all the functions of a mechanical cash-register, the system performs automatic tax computations and multiple-item pricing. The 256-by-4-bit RAM with on-chip address latches provides the programer with 32 8-digit registers to store totals, calculate taxes, and so on.

The CPU and memory section is implemented with only eight packages, while the entire system requires approximately 35 packages. Again, effective use is made of the interrupts, jump conditions, and flags to reduce hardware and software requirements. □

Four-chip microprocessor family reduces system parts counts

Basic two-chip system, consisting of microprocessor and read-only memory, handles simple applications by itself but can also be built into complex multiprocessing systems with the aid of memory access and interface chips

by David Chung, *Fairchild Semiconductor Corp., Mountain View, Calif.*

☐ A system designer's enthusiasm for the one-chip microprocessor often fades once he starts developing an actual system. True, the chip replaces dozens of MSI logic chips or hundreds of small-scale ICs. But it may require the addition of several logic and memory circuits and a couple of clocks before becoming even a minimally self-contained system. Probably the microprocessor will also need address and data buffering if it is to be used with peripherals, and then there are clock-generation and timing circuits, memories and input/output control, multiplexing, and interrupt capability to be considered.

What the system designer needs is a group of just a few compatible chips capable of handling all these functions. What the chip manufacturer needs is processing technology and a system architecture that will pack these functions on small chips, since only small chips will assure the high production yields that keep costs low. The F8 family of four n-channel chips provides the necessary circuit density by combining the MOS version of Fairchild's Isoplanar process with a novel architecture on which designers in the areas of systems, logic, circuits and software all cooperated.

The F8 chips consist of an 8-bit microprocessor or central processing unit (CPU) with a 2-microsecond processing speed, an 8,192-bit read-only memory organized as 1,024 8-bit words, a memory-interface chips, and a direct-memory-access chip. The CPU communicates with other F8 circuits over an 8-bit bidirectional data bus and five control lines.

The distribution of F8 system functions is unique among microprocessor chip sets. For example, the CPU chip contains much more logic than usual yet does not have a program counter for addressing memory. Instead, each ROM and memory interface chip has its own program counter, as well as a stack register and data counter. An incrementer/adder is also located on each of these chips so that addresses may be modified locally. Thus the need for a 16-bit address bus between chips is eliminated, and the CPU and ROM are left with 16 pins free for use with input/output devices.

Five system-design advantages

The chip set helps its users meet five system-design objectives: cost-effectiveness, minimum parts count, simple peripheral interfaces, easy expansion through modular architecture, and simplified programing.

Yields on the CPU chip are high and manufacturing costs low because the device is the smallest now being produced—it measures only 181 and 155 mils, despite its unusual number of functions. Also eliminated is the need for external chips and other components, and, with few exceptions, the F8 chips are electrically compatible with many devices, whether a TTL gate or a switch.

For many applications, such as calculators and appliance controllers, a two-chip "minimum" system—CPU and ROM—will suffice, while the other two chips allow the system to move upward into much more complex applications. This minimum system is defined as one that includes a random-access memory, I/O circuits, computing electronics, clock generators, power-on reset circuits, an interrupt structure, a timer, and of course a ROM. Chip size was reduced some 40% by using, not conventional MOS techniques, but the Isoplanar version of n-channel MOS (which is slightly different from the Isoplanar process devel-

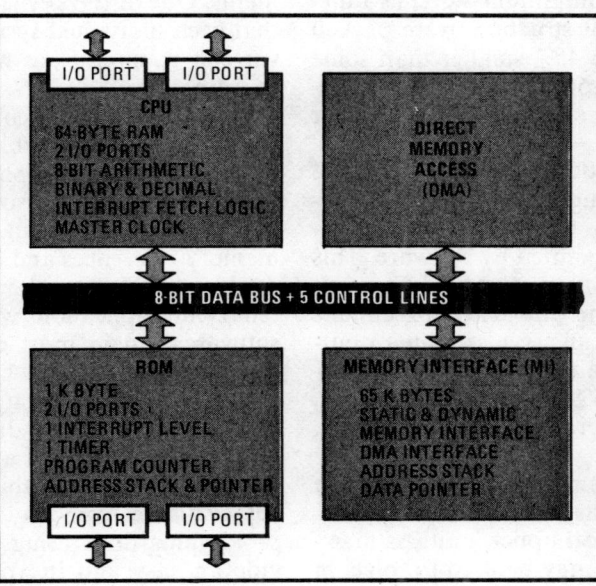

1. The system. The four F8 chips—a central processing unit, read-only memory, memory interface, and direct memory access—communicate over an 8-bit data bus and five control lines.

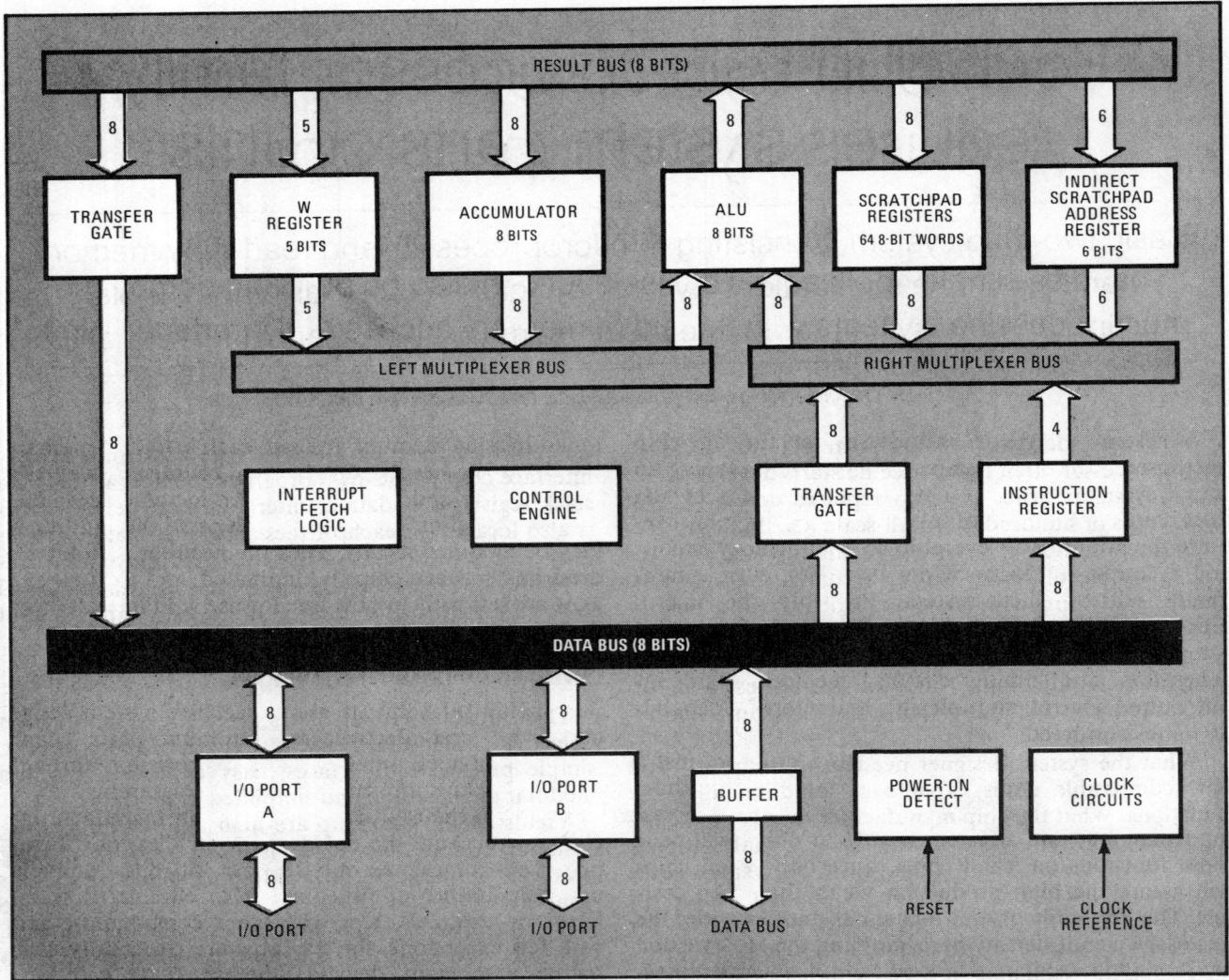

2. Central processor. The F8 CPU chip has two 8-bit input/output ports, which result from placing the 16-bit addressing circuits directly on the mating read-only memory chip. It also has a 64-word-by-8-bit random-access memory for use as a scratchpad.

oped by Fairchild for bipolar integrated circuits). Consequently, the first five of the minimum system's functions, plus part of the interrupt structure, were packed onto a CPU chip that is 10% to 45% smaller than some popular microprocessors that contain only a CPU function. The rest of the interrupt structure and the timer are on the ROM chip.

Direct interfaces can be made with a wide range of peripheral devices because enough hardware is incorporated on the CPU and ROM chips to allow the idiosyncrasies of most I/O devices to be handled by software. This hardware includes the interrupt structure and timer already mentioned, plus encoding and decoding circuits and bidirectional ports, which can serve as input or output lines at different times. As a result, the chips can directly handle approximately 95% of today's I/O devices, including keyboards, printers, readers, displays, modems, and magnetic devices.

The minimum two-chip system is also the basis for a modular architecture that can handle increasingly complex problems with no theoretical upper limit. As many two-chip modules as necessary may be used to solve, in piecemeal fashion, the most complex system requirements. One of the key characteristics of this approach is that each individual system can operate independently, yet can communicate with one system that acts as a coordinator.

There were some architectural tradeoffs. In looking at the frequency with which certain operations are normally performed, emphasis was placed on I/O speed (most F8 microprocessor instructions are I/O-oriented) and lower parts count, although some versatility in memory references and double shift was sacrificed. The double-shift feature, however, is primarily of value for binary multiplication, which also can be done through software, and in most cases, repetitive memory reference can be eliminated by efficient programing.

In fact, carefully thought out software systems should alleviate many of the difficulties facing microprocessor users today. Although a low-cost, nonvolatile RAM (for permanent, but alterable, storage of programs) is not yet available from any supplier, there is a variety of prototyping units using programable ROMs which provide an easy and inexpensive way of developing and

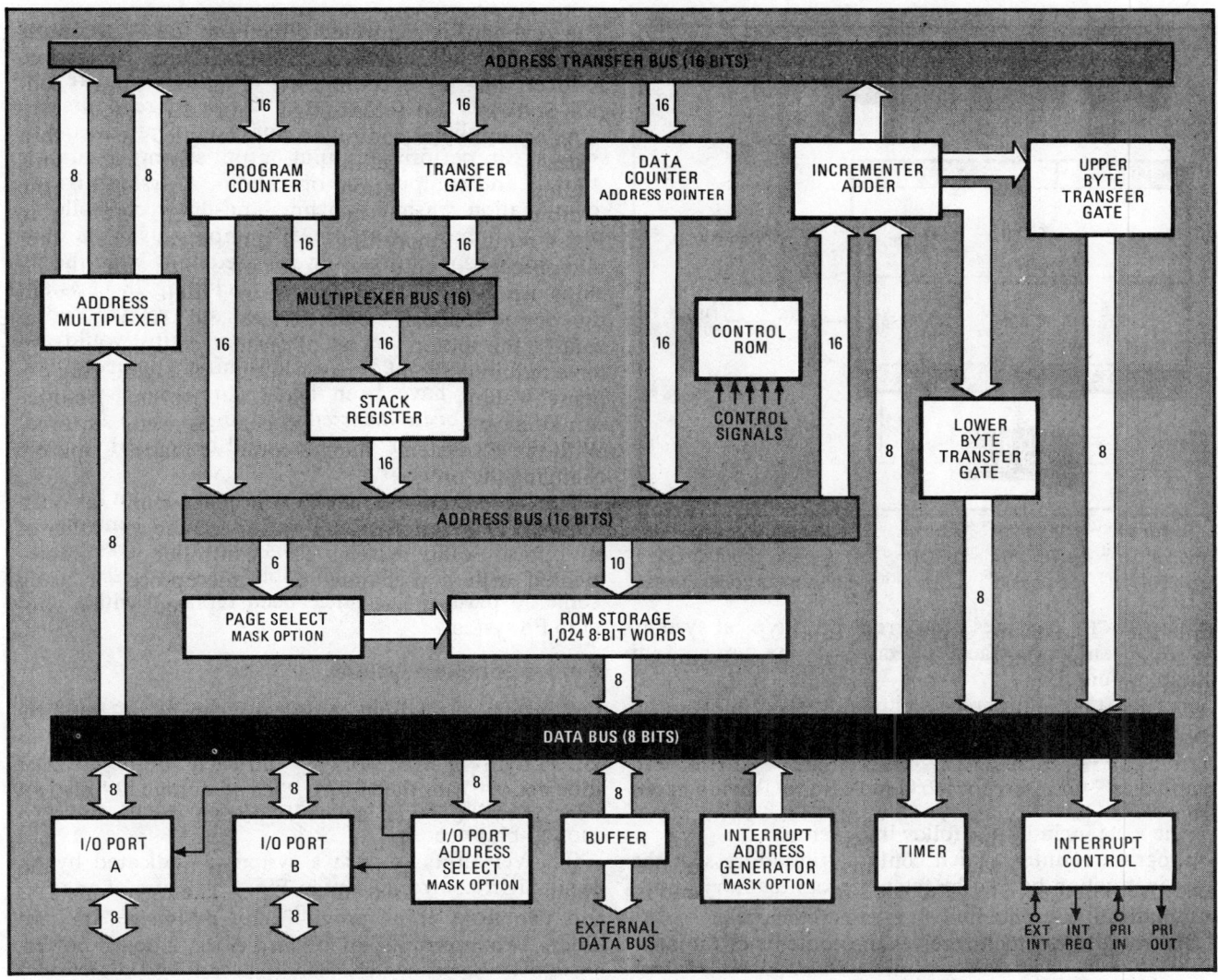

3. Read-only memory. In addition to the 8,192 storage cells, the F8 ROM chip has its own 16-bit program counter and address bus. This frees 16 package pins for use as two 8-bit input/output ports. The ROM also has an interrupt input and a timer.

verifying microprocessor software, even for small-quantity users. Three software packages—an assembler, simulator, and a stand-alone conversational operating system—have been developed, as well as a terminal specially designed for the F8 microprocessor chip set.

The CPU chip

Despite being the smallest 8-bit, n-channel microprocessor chip available, the F8 CPU contains the most logic. It includes the following circuits:
- Arithmetic logic unit, an 8-bit parallel logic network that can be used in binary or decimal functions.
- Accumulator, an 8-bit storage register that stores the results of arithmetic operations and transfers information into or out of the scratchpad memory.
- Scratchpad memory, a group of 64 8-bit registers that serve as read-write memories and may be used as a workspace by a programer.
- W register, which stores the status indications from an arithmetic or logical operation.
- Two bidirectional 8-bit I/O ports, which can be used either for gathering data from external circuits or for outputting data to other circuitry.
- Clock circuits, which generate the necessary two-phase clock signals used by all other parts of the system. Operating frequency is set externally by either an RC network or a separate clock or, if a precise operating frequency is required, a crystal.
- Interrupt fetch logic, which allows CPU operation to be interrupted by a timer on the ROM chip or by an external source. A unique feature of the F8, it permits the microprocessor to operate on a real-time basis and also generates control signals. The combination of timers, priority interrupts, and buffered outputs and inputs allows the F8 to serve as a peripheral controller.
- Power-on detect, another vital circuit, which causes the CPU to disable the interrupt system and also insures that processing starts out from a unique address when power is first applied.

The ROM's role

The ROM, with 1,024 8-bit bytes of storage, is used principally to store programed instructions and nonvolatile data constants that will be fetched as operands

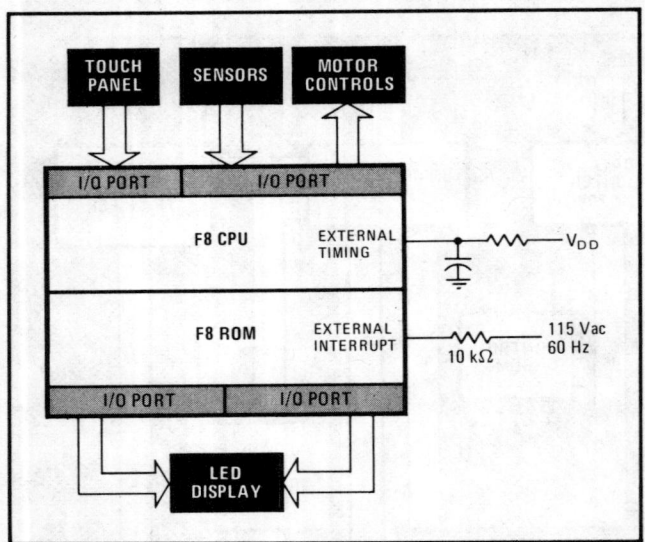

4. Fewer pieces. When an electrical appliance controller was redesigned around the F8 CPU and ROM chips, its parts count dropped from 250-plus to 55, including LEDs and motor-control components.

while the CPU executes a program. In a typical system, the ROM can be interfaced directly with the CPU without buffer circuits.

The ROM has a different architecture from the kind of ROM commonly used with microprocessors. In addition to storage cells, each ROM contains circuits that enable it to add a second interrupt level and also to provide extra processing capability independent of the CPU.

The ROM includes the following circuits:
- Program counter, which contains the address of the next instruction byte to be fetched from memory and is automatically incremented after each fetch cycle.
- Stack register, which receives the contents of the program counter whenever an interrupt is generated and also aids in developing a multilevel program function.
- Data counter, which acts as a self-incrementing pointer for conveniently referencing data addresses in memory; because it is 16 bits long, it can address up to 65-k bytes of memory.
- I/O ports, which are fully bidirectional and contain storage latches and Schmitt triggers at the input for noise rejection, thus eliminating the need for external latches and external noise-rejection circuits.
- Interrupt address generator, which provides the next instruction address when an interrupt occurs.
- Timer, which greatly increases the versatility of the system, since it can interrupt the CPU's performance of routine tasks and switch it to servicing real-time equipment after a preset time interval. For example, as data is transmitted to a printer, the timer keeps track of the elapsed time and at the end of the transmission starts the next operation automatically, without the usual loop delay for interrogations from the CPU. The timer also is useful for generating waveforms (which can be changed by software) for control functions.

A two-chip system

The two-chip F8 microcomputer is suitable for small data terminals, controllers, and specialty calculators. The keyboard is connected directly to the F8 I/O ports without special interfaces. Switch-bounce protection, rollover, and key encoding are all under software control. Software also decodes signals for LED readouts.

As an appliance controller, for example, the two-chip system can perform all input-output sensing, actuating, timing, and computation operations. A system like the combination washing-machine-and-dryer controller in Fig. 4 required more than 250 components when other microprocessor chip sets were used, but with the F8 chips uses only 55 components, including 28 LEDs and the power semiconductor devices and relays used to control the motors. A set of custom chips would also have required about 50 parts, but initial engineering expense would have been heavy and severe penalties would have been incurred if changes were required. With the F8 system, changes could be made by merely changing the program.

The same dramatic reduction in parts count has been achieved in yet another application—as the controller of an optical wand system. This controller was implemented with a p-channel 8-bit microprocessor using some 50 parts. It has since been replaced with a two-chip F8 system.

A more complex system

A system of medium complexity can be designed by adding more ROMs. The 16-bit addressing permits up to 65,536 bytes of ROM storage—and each additional ROM adds not only another 1,024 bytes of storage but also an extra interrupt level, an extra system timer, and two more 8-bit I/O ports.

The versatility of such a system is indicated by the traffic-light-control system in Fig. 5. The use of one CPU and two ROM chips provides the designer with two timers, two interrupts, an inboard clock, inboard power-on reset, inboard switch decoding, and 48 bidirectional I/O bits. This system could be tied to vehicle detectors in the road, to monitor traffic for left-turn lanes as well as through-traffic flow in four directions. It would also react to interrupts from the pedestrian control buttons at each corner. There also is sufficient I/O capability to permit communication with and control of neighboring intersections and to allow the system to be operated manually or tested for proper operation.

Five F8 features are of particular interest for this type of application. One of the interrupts can eliminate the need for such external circuits as a comparator to compare a count of the cars with a predetermined value to cause the light to change. (The CPU can handle the simple arithmetic of counting cars.) This interrupt also eliminates the need for continuous polling of traffic count by the microcomputer. The second interrupt would be ideal for permitting pedestrian control to override the automatic system. The internal clock, with an external crystal, can also control light routines.

The two timers permit simultaneous counting of delay for vehicle signals and flashing warning lights for pedestrians. The inboard power-on reset acts in case of power failure to start the system automatically when power is renewed. The bidirectional I/Os have built-in latches that eliminate the need for external latches for the job of "holding" commands for lights as well as the momentary commands provided by timers and sensors.

More complex requirements still can be broken down so that they can be handled by more than one microcomputer. For this purpose, the two additional F8 chips may be used.

A memory-intensive system

The memory interface chip allows standard memory chips, such as the 1103, the 2102, or 4,096-bit memories, to be incorporated into the F8 system. One version of the memory-interface chip handles static memory elements such as the 1,024-bit 2102 RAM, and another version interfaces with dynamic memories, such as the 1,024-bit 1103 RAM and the 4,096-bit RAM, with on-board refresh logic for 4-k memories. The second version also provides interface signals required by the direct-memory-access chip.

This memory-access chip, which cannot be used without the second version of the interface chip, is used to set up a high-speed data path between the F8 memory and a high-speed peripheral (such as a magnetic-tape unit), a first-in, first-out memory, or another two-chip F8 microcomputer.

A typical application is a printing credit-verification terminal (Fig. 6). Such a system requires high performance and yet must be low in cost if it is to reach a large market. Only four different F8 chips are required to handle a keyboard input, visual display, card reader, and printer as well as provide a modem interface and memory interface for external RAM storage. Such a system might be compared to a "bare mini" in terms of utility, but it costs less and has fewer parts and a more flexible I/O structure.

Using additional chips, independent F8 microcomputers can be connected into a synergistic multiprocessing complex in which each system can operate independently yet can be controlled by one CPU that is established as the coordinator. Three microcomputers, each having a CPU and two ROMs, use the memory interface and direct-memory-access chips to share RAM storage, which serves as an efficient three-way exchange.

In this system, all three microcomputers can operate

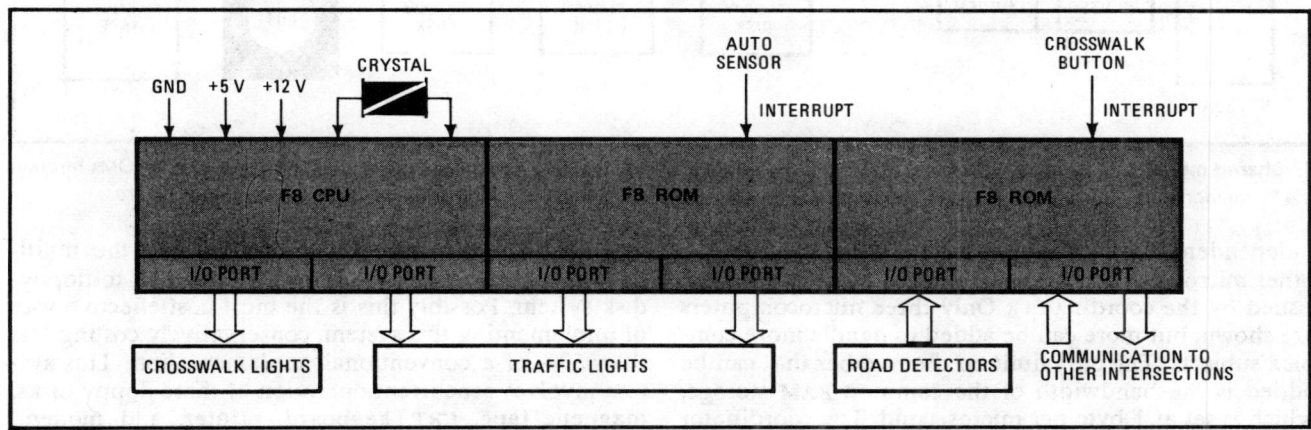

5. Versatile. As a traffic-light controller, one F8 CPU and two F8 ROMs can count passing autos, provide a pedestrian crosswalk interrupt input, and also time the traffic-light changes. An external crystal precisely sets the clock frequency.

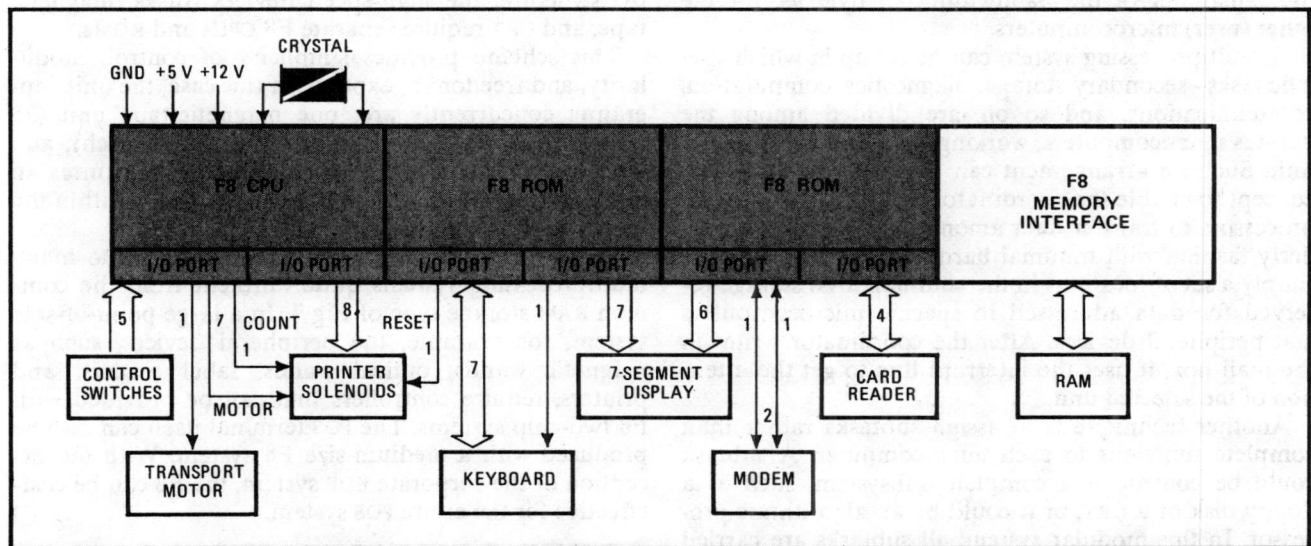

6. In charge. In a credit verification terminal, one F8 CPU, two F8 ROMs, and an F8 memory interface circuit can handle all the inputs and outputs. Each I/O port handles eight bits, which can be allocated among the various I/O devices.

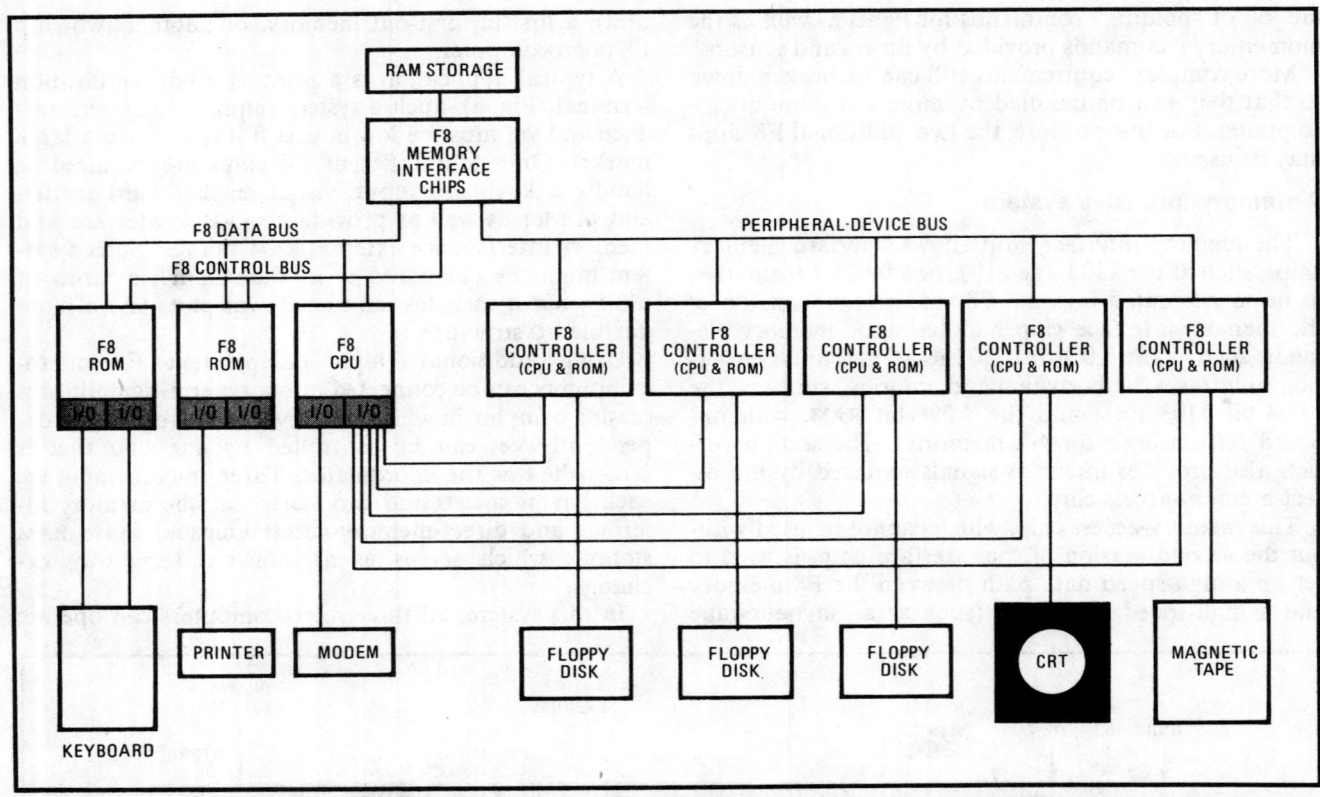

7. Shared memory. In a key-to-floppy-disk system, a single random-access memory can be used by several F8 CPUs and ROMs through the F8 memory-interface chips. Information bandwidth is wide enough to handle more than the three floppy-disk units shown here.

independently, with no waiting for the operation of another microcomputer (although general instructions are issued by the coordinator). Only three microcomputers are shown, but more can be added to handle more complex subjects. The only limit on the number that can be added is the bandwidth of the common RAM storage, which is set at 1 byte per microsecond. The coordinator microcomputer has priority access to the common RAM storage. Its maximum access time is 0.5 byte/μs, leaving the remainder of the bandwidth, 0.5 byte/μs, for the other (user) microcomputers.

A multiprocessing system can be set up in which specific tasks—secondary storage, diagnostics, computation, communications, and so on—are divided among the various microcomputers, working from one RAM storage unit. Such an arrangement can exploit the "mail-box" concept to enable the coordinator CPU and other microprocessors to transfer data among themselves in an orderly fashion with minimal hardware. The mail box is simply a set of locations in the common RAM storage reserved for data addressed to specific microcomputers and peripheral devices. After the coordinator writes in the mail box, it uses the interrupt line to get the attention of the selected unit.

Another technique is to assign subtasks rather than complete functions to each microcomputer. A subtask could be control of a complete subsystem, such as a floppy disk or a CRT, or it could be an algorithmic processor. In this modular system, all subtasks are carried out as part of a total program which is controlled by the coordinator.

Figure 7 shows a specific application of the multiprocessing concept as applied to a keyboard-to-floppy-disk system. Possibly this is the most cost-effective way of implementing this system, conservatively costing less than 50% of a conventional implementation. This system involves concurrent operation of three floppy disks, magnetic tape, CRT, keyboard, printer, and modem. While the low-speed devices (the keyboard, printer, and modem) can be adequately handled by the programed I/O structure, the high-speed devices (disks, magnetic tape, and CRT require separate F8 CPUs and ROMs.

This scheme provides simplicity of control, modularity, and freedom to expand. In this case, the units operating concurrently are: one magnetic-tape unit (25 μs/byte; three floppy-disk units (32 μs/byte each); and a CRT unit (71 μs/byte). This combination requires an aggregate bandwidth of 0.1478 byte/μs—well within the F8's 0.5-byte/μs bandwidth.

However, the F8 chips can be structured into many multiprocessing systems quite different from the common RAM storage type of Fig 7. In a large point-of-sale system, for example, the peripheral devices, such as magnetic wands, optical wands, label readers, and printers, require controllers that can be provided with F8 two-chip systems. The POS terminal itself can also be produced with a medium-size F8 system. With the exception of the corporate EDP system, the F8 can be cost-effective for the entire POS system. □

Acknowledgement
The author is grateful to Thomas Longo for his leadership in developing the Isoplanar n-channel MOS process and the system partitioning used in the F8.

Twelve-bit microprocessor nears minicomputer's performance level

Microprogramed central processing unit on a single chip can handle 12 bits in parallel, respond to eight levels of interrupt, and use an asynchronous bus for both internal and external communications

by Tadaaki Tarui, Keiji Namimoto, and Yukiharu Takahashi, *Tokyo Shibaura Electric Co., Tokyo, Japan*

□ A recently developed microprocessor offers a level of performance generally considered beyond the capabilities of even these versatile devices. Among its many powerful functions are a maskable eight-level interrupt and direct memory-access capability.

Like other microprocessors introduced during the past two years, the Toshiba TLCS-12 is fabricated in the form of an MOS large-scale integrated circuit. One of its unusual features is its 12-bit word length, whereas words in other common microprocessors are limited to 4 or 8 bits. Furthermore, the TLCS-12 is organized around a common asynchronous bus, through which the functional units on the chip communicate with each other and also with external memory, input/output registers, and other system elements.

Other significant features include a microprogram in a read-only memory within the microprocessor chip itself, an internal clock generator, and bit-handling instructions capable of modification for indexing and indirect addressing, an automatic start capability, and eight general registers.

The TLCS-12 can not only handle interrupts, but after an interrupt has been processed, the microprocessor can restore to a general register the previous program-status word from temporary storage in the main memory to resume the interrupted program. Although this concept was first used in large computers about 10 years ago, this is the first time it has been used in a microprocessor.

The 12-bit bidirectional bus contained in the microprocessor itself is also the backbone of the system built around the microprocessor. Data and addresses are both transferred along this bus, but not at the same time. The microprocessor, all memory chips, and input/output registers are connected to the common bus and communicate with one another along it asynchronously, so that devices of any speed can be used.

As shown in Fig. 1, a useful microcomputer system requires several ICs in addition to the TLCS-12 microprocessor. A minimum system configuration consists of one microprocessor, three memories, and one memory control unit. The memories may be either read-write, read-only, or a combination. For efficiency and convenience, input/output controllers, an interrupt register, and a control console can be added. The system operates through a range of -40°C to +125°C.

All these devices are mounted in dual in-line packages, and all except the interrupt latches are made with p-channel silicon-gate enhancement/depletion technology. On each chip, those circuits that drive the bus have three-level outputs so that they can be disconnected when not in use.

Central processor has ROM control

The microprocessor itself is a fully parallel 12-bit processor on a chip. It contains a 12-bit parallel arithmetic and logic unit with fast-carry logic and five working reg-

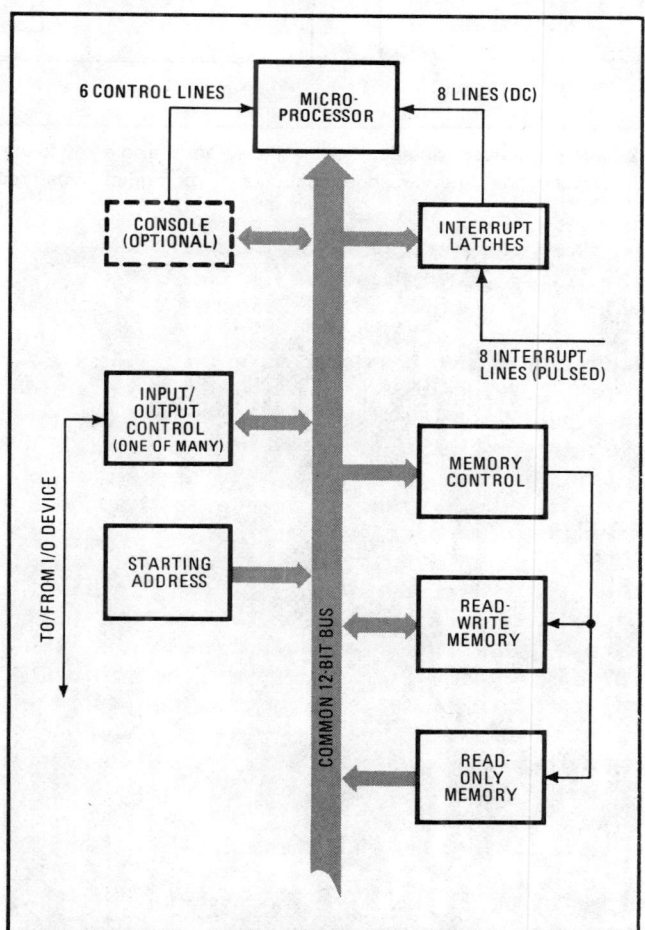

1. Spine. The 12-bit bidirectional bus (color) communicates with external devices and also interconnects functional units within the microprocessor itself, transferring both data and addresses.

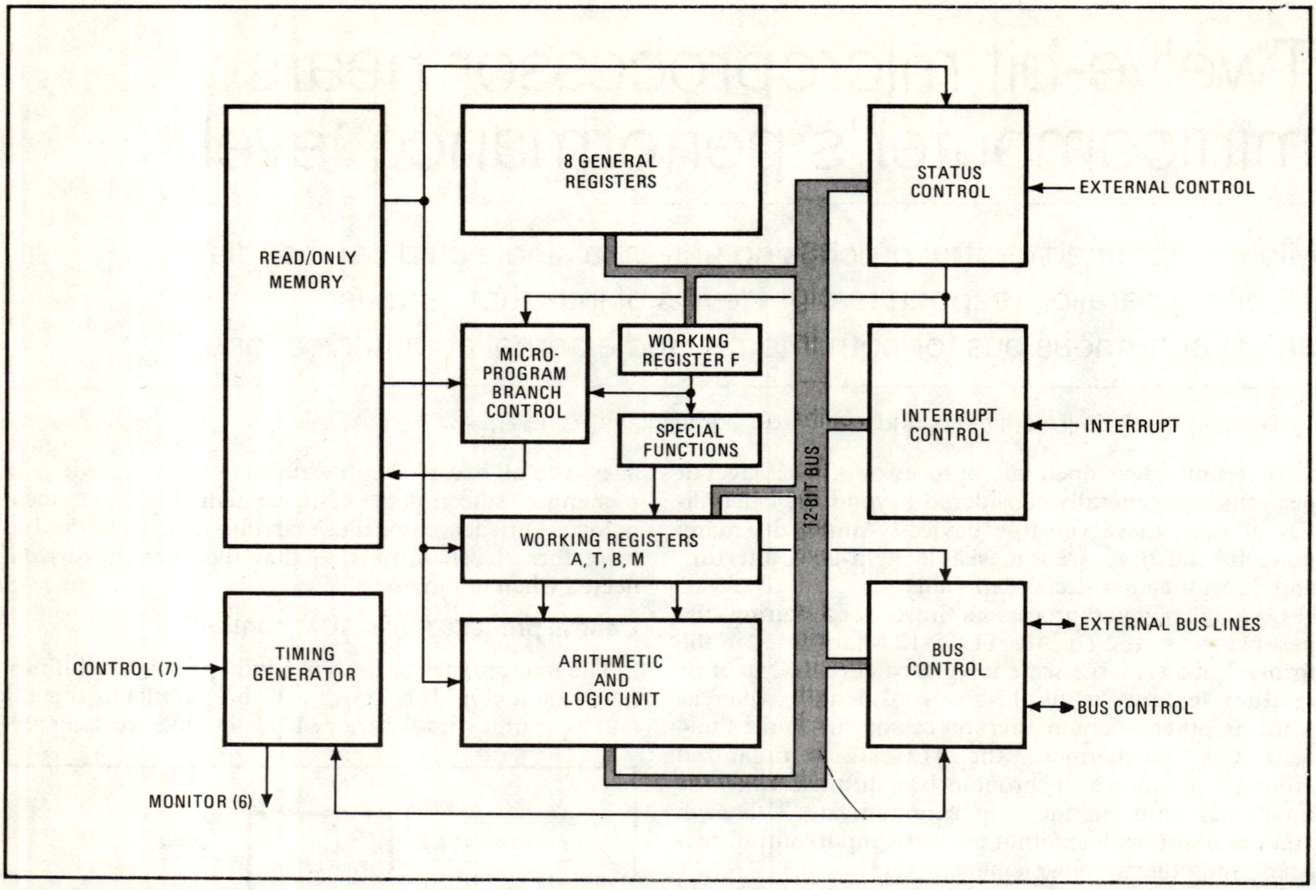

2. Microprocessor details. This block diagram is also a key to the photo (Fig. 3). Arithmetic and logic unit (bottom center) performs most major functions of device, under control of microprogram in read-only memory (top left).

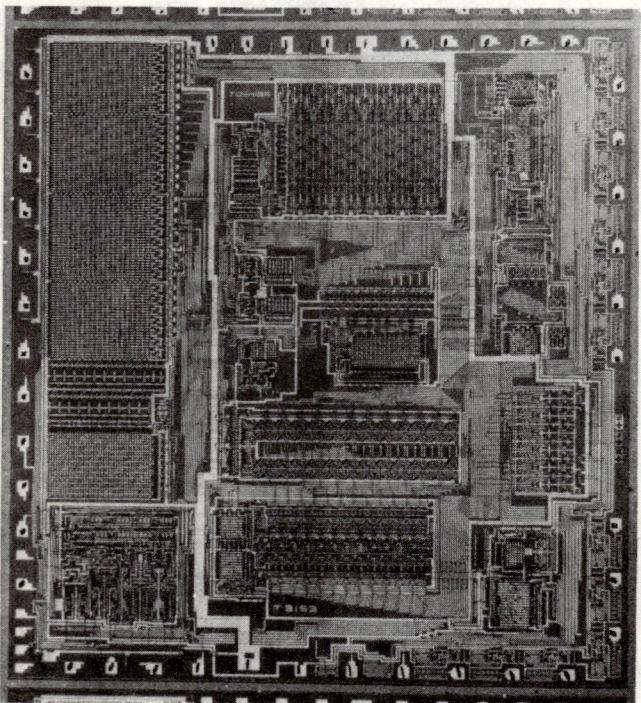

3. Microprocessor chip. The 12-bit bus, which interconnects the section of the chip and external devices as well, is visible as a set of more or less vertical zigzag lines, just right of center.

isters, a 4,000-bit microprogram in a read-only memory, eight 12-bit general-purpose registers, a timing generator, and an external bus controller. The functional blocks shown in the block diagram (Fig. 2) and also visible in the photograph (Fig. 3) are interconnected via the 12-bit bus, which zigzags up and down slightly to the right of the center of the photograph.

Fast-carry logic divides the bits of a computer word into groups and generates the carry from group to group. In the TLCS-12, the groups contain 1 bit, 3 bits, 4 bits, 3 bits, and 1 bit, respectively (Fig. 4), generating a carry substantially more quickly than would a simple bit-to-bit carry, which, however, is used within the groups. The bit-to-bit carry out of any bit position depends, in part, on the carry into that position; thus, under certain circumstances, a single carry can ripple from the least-significant-bit position along the full length of the word. Enough time must be allowed for an add operation to permit this ripple carry. But with carry lookahead, the ripple occurs in parallel in separate groups, which speeds up the add operation accordingly.

Had the groups all been the same length in the TLCS-12, as they have been in many other processors over the past 15 years or so, circuit fan-in and fan-out would have been so large that circuit propagation delays, which depend on fan-in and fan-out, would have canceled the reduction in carry-propagation time.

The five working registers are designated A, T, B, M,

and F. The F register usually contains the instruction to be executed; the A and T registers drive one input of the arithmetic unit, and the B and M registers drive the other input. All five of these registers are loaded from the internal bus, and the arithmetic unit's output is returned to the bus.

Of the eight general-purpose registers, seven are available to the user, and the eighth is reserved for the program-status word, which stores information about the current state of the microprocessor and the program being executed—for example, the address of the next instruction, the status of various indicators in the microprocessor, and so on.

As a rule, whenever an interrupt occurs, the program-status word is replaced by another word that defines the state of the microprocessor for the servicing of that interrupt. When the interrupt is out of the way and the microprocessor can return to its main program, the original status word is brought back from the main memory, where it had been temporarily stored, and replaced in the register.

A special-function unit generates address components, shifts data to the left or right, or identifies bit positions to be processed by subsequent microinstructions. An external bus-control unit links the microprocessor to other ICs in the system by transmitting and receiving timing signals that coordinate unrelated clock frequencies and phases in separate chips.

The microprogram, which defines the microprocessor's basic characteristics, is stored in a read-only memory from which it controls the data paths everywhere in the microprocessor during every machine cycle—as in most microprogram-controlled computers. Each microinstruction is 29 bits wide and is divided into several fields or micro-orders. Up to 128 microinstructions can be installed.

The entire microprocessor contains approximately 11,000 p-channel MOS transistors on a chip measuring 5.5 by 5.9 millimeters, in a 42-pin DIP. Logic transistors operate in enhancement mode, and load transistors in depletion mode; a single 5-volt power supply drives both. For the output-driver circuits, which have three-state outputs for connection to the bus, both +5 and −5 V are necessary. All circuits are made with silicon-gate transistors with a channel length of 6 micrometers— compared to 8 or 10 μm in most p-MOS transistors.

This small size is made possible, in part, by the use of silicon instead of metal for the gate and in part by the use of a new process for growing the doped polysilicon layer. In fabrication, boron-doped polysilicon is used for low sheet resistance and high growth rate. The necessary impurities are added to both the enhancement-mode and depletion-mode transistors by an ion-implantation process.

External circuits are conventional

None of the other circuits that go with the TLCS-12 microprocessor are particularly unusual. The read-write memory, for example, is a static 512-bit device, organized as 128 words of 4 bits each; its access time is 300

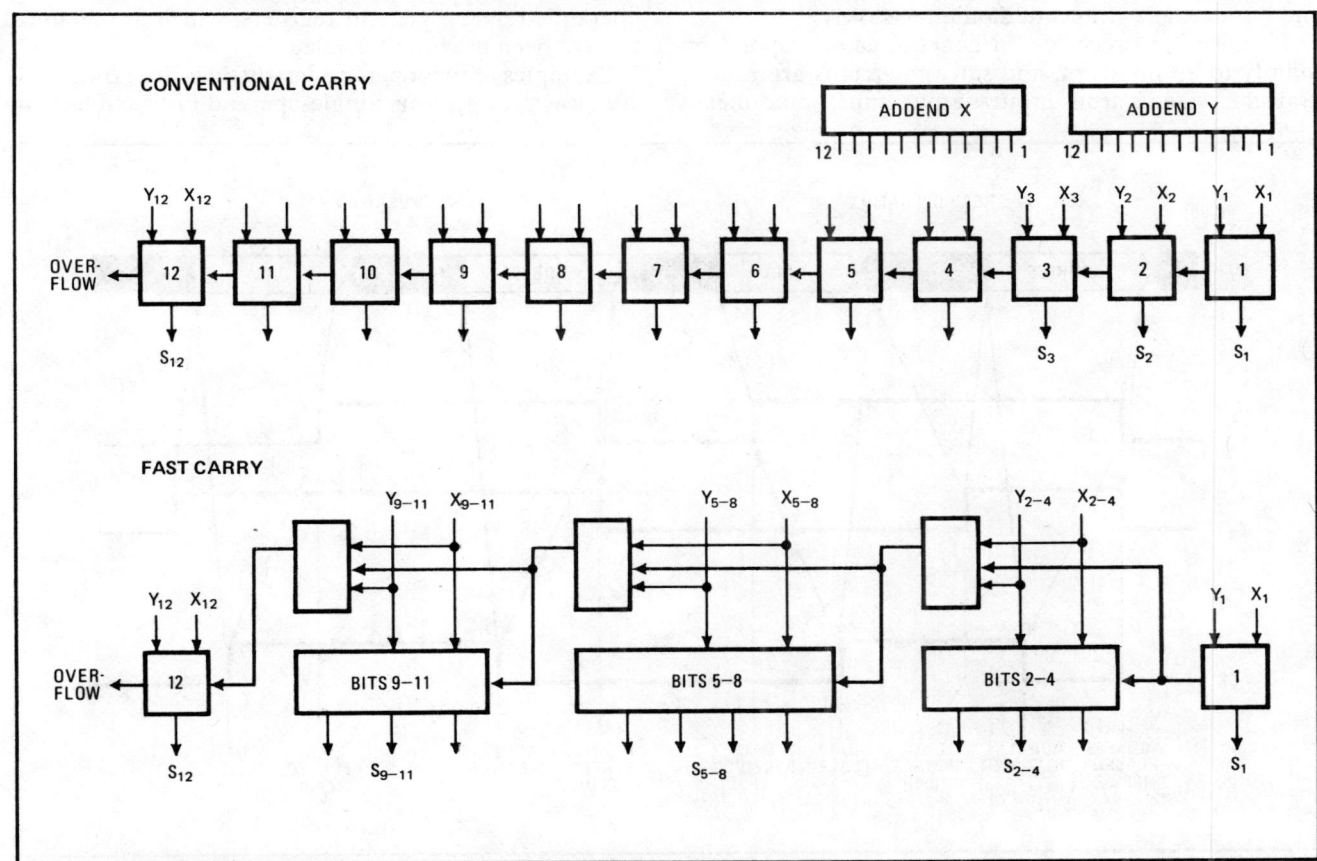

4. Fast-carry logic. By generating a carry signal from groups of bit positions instead of singly, the carry can be propagated along the full word length more quickly, sharply decreasing the time required for arithmetic operations.

nanoseconds, and it dissipates 400 milliwatts.

The external read-only memory, while unusual, is not original with this system. It is a reprogramable stacked-gate MOS device, based on the floating-gate avalanche-injection principle, but provided with an overlying control gate. In this technology, the gates of the MOS transistors are buried in a layer of oxide and remain unconnected to any external signal, but a control gate is further provided on the top. When a large negative signal is applied to the source and drain of the transistor, and a large positive signal is applied to the control gate, negative carriers are injected into the buried gate by an avalanche effect.

When the signal is removed, an excess of negative carriers remains in the gate, opening a conducting channel in the n-type substrate. The excess remains until the gate is irradiated with ultraviolet light, which discharges the gate and permits the memory to be reprogramed. The chip used in the Toshiba system can be programed in 5 seconds; after programing, its access time is 600 ns and its dissipation 400 mw.

Data is transferred between the microprocessor and either a read-write or a read-only external memory by the memory-control unit, which responds to the control signals on the bus that originate in the microprocessor's bus-control unit. The memory-control unit generates address, read/write, and chip-select signals for the memories themselves. A similar unit performs similar functions with respect to input/output units. The two controls differ primarily in their address range and the timing, since many units— particularly those used with microprocessors—transmit data quite slowly.

Because the processor, in general, can't respond instantly to an interrupt, and since interrupts are usually transient signals from input/output units, some means is required to catch and hold interrupts until the microprocessor can respond to them. This function is performed by the interrupt-latch unit, which is simply an array of eight latches that can be set by the external interrupt and reset by the microprocessor. Masking, if and when appropriate, is performed inside the microprocessor, and is therefore not part of the latch unit's function.

Input and output buffering is handled in the input/output register, which is actually a pair of registers—one for 4 bits and one for 8 bits. These have independent control signals and can therefore be used separately for different devices, or they can be connected to parallel for use with a single unit that transmits 12-bit words.

Instruction set is microprogramed

As in all microprogramed computers, the instruction set can be changed by altering the microprogram. However, as with all microprograms stored in ROMs, such alterations are uneconomical because of the cost of changing masks, except when large quantities of microprocessors are built with the new instruction set. (The ROM in the microprocessor is not to be confused with the PROM in a separate IC.)

The standard instructions used in the TLCS-12 are of four types: two-operand instructions, one-operand instructions, branch instructions, and complex types. Two-operand instructions include address modification through either indirect addressing or indexing. Address modification applies only to the second operand; both operands refer to general registers, which are assumed to have been previously loaded.

Examples of two-operand instructions are LOAD, ADD, SUBTRACT, and SWAP. Single-operand instructions work

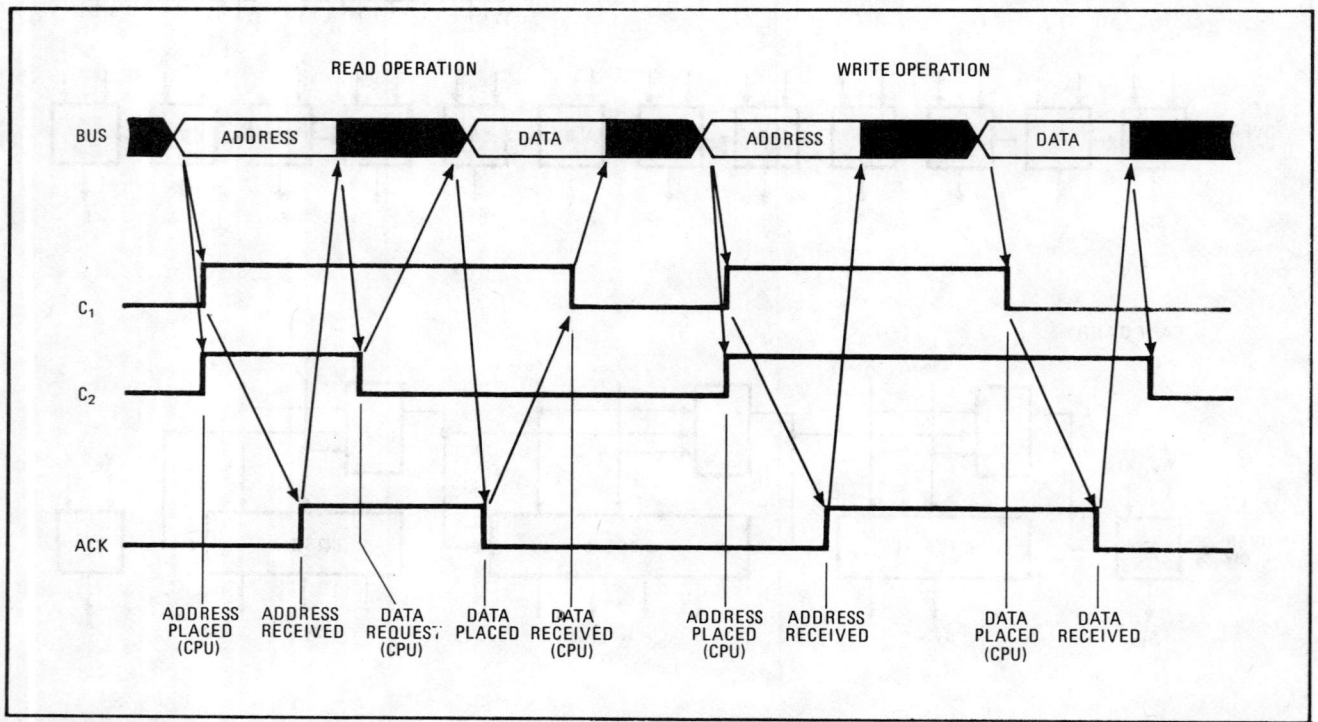

5. Handshaking. Every event involving the bus must await an overt response from a device connected to the bus, in a sequence sometimes called "handshaking." Thus, its operation is kept independent of all internal device timings.

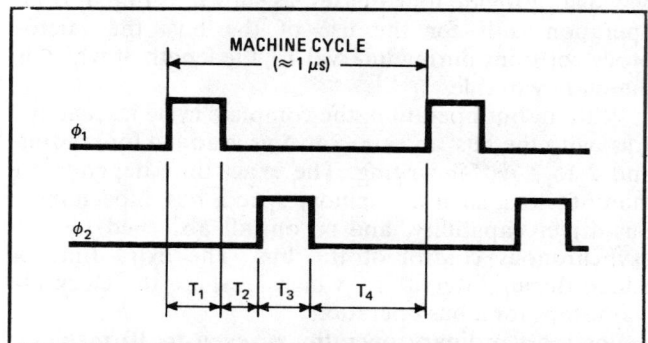

6. Internal timing. Microprocessor generates its own clock signals, skewed into four phases. During T_1, the results of the preceding cycle are placed into internal registers. Microprogram branch control is set up during T_2, and following that, the proper microinstruction is placed in the ROM output register during T_3. The microinstruction is executed during T_4; if the instruction calls for the use of the external bus, the clock is stopped in this phase.

with either the contents of a general register or a single bit in that register. They include such operations as SHIFT, INCREMENT or DECREMENT, and, among bit-oriented instructions, SET, CLEAR, INVERT, and TEST.

Branch instructions include, of course, the unconditional branch and conditional branches that rely on the results of prior instructions, such as BRANCH ON PLUS, BRANCH ON ZERO, and so on. Finally, most of the complex instructions include two or more simple steps in one instruction. Examples are CLEAR AND INCREMENT, CLEAR AND COMPLEMENT, and COMPLEMENT AND INCREMENT.

The total instruction set of the TLCS-12 contains about 108 instructions, some of which are very powerful. As in many other processors, the exact number of instructions depends on whether certain variations are counted separately. Thus the performance of the microprocessor approaches that of standard minicomputers, and the unit can do many kinds of jobs with fewer steps than can most other microprocessors.

Implementing the eight-level interrupt

Because the eight interrupt lines into the microprocessor have independent priorities, an interrupt on any one of them is accepted when the corresponding mask bit is 1 and no higher-priority interrupt is being requested. The mask bits are part of the program-status word previously mentioned.

An extra mask bit can mask all the interrupt lines at once, as when the microprocessor is itself busy with a critical and perhaps time-dependent task. Recognizing the interrupt (when not masked), choosing the highest-priority request, and linking the interrupt service routine to and from the main program are controlled by the hardware, not by the microprogram.

Interrupt capability in the microprocessor places certain restrictions on the use of external memory to guarantee that a place is always available to store a program-status word without wiping out something else that might still be needed. In the TLCS-12, the highest priority interrupt always causes the current program-status word to be exchanged with a new program-status word that is kept in location 8.

Adjacent locations are reserved for lower interrupt levels; in an application requiring all eight interrupts, locations 8 through 15 must be reserved. Where fewer interrupt levels are used, less space in memory is needed, but the reserved space always begins at memory location 8.

The asynchronous bus, both inside and outside the microprocessor, is completely under microprocessor control. A request for bus operation, issued by the microprogram, starts the bus controller on the chip. First, the controller stops the microprocessor's internal clock, and then runs the bus asynchronously with two output signals and one input signal. The two output signals, called C_1 and C_2, rise at the same time, indicating that an address to an external device (memory or input/output) is on the bus. As shown in Fig. 5, the receipt of this address by the appropriate device is acknowledged by the rise of the incoming ACK line to the bus controller. At this time, the microprocessor can remove the address from the bus; if C_2 falls while C_1 stays up, the device is requested to place data on the bus for the microprocessor to read. When the device responds to the request, it drops ACK. Then, when the microprocessor has the data, the controller drops C_1, and the device is free to release the bus.

On the other hand, when the microprocessor removes the address from the bus and leaves both C_1 and C_2 up, it is preparing to send data to the device in a write operation. After the address has been replaced by the data, C_1 falls while C_2 stays up, requesting the previously addressed device to pick up the data. The device acknowledges receipt by dropping ACK, after which the bus controller can release the bus, drop C_2, and generate a restart pulse for the microprocessor clock. Normal operation is resumed.

External control

Although the microprocessor ordinarily runs under internal control, it can also be controlled from a manual console for diagnostic purposes, program debugging, and the like. Seven control schemes cause, respectively, a single instruction to be executed, the program counter (part of the program-status word) to be set to a number previously placed on the bus, the contents of the pro-

---

Defining the terms

In this article, the word "microprocessor" refers to a complete processing unit on one large-scale integrated circuit. In some circles, the word refers to that particular collection of logic, in IC form or otherwise, that is controlled by a microprogram.

At one point, a reference is made to a condition code, a particular bit in a program status word, as the basis for a conditional branch. Unfortunately, these two similar terms can be easily confused, although they have only a tenuous relationship to one another.

Conditional branch instructions can be defined for any of a large number of conditions, such as positive, zero, or negative results of a preceding operation, the zero or nonzero state of a register, and many more. The condition code is only one such condition.

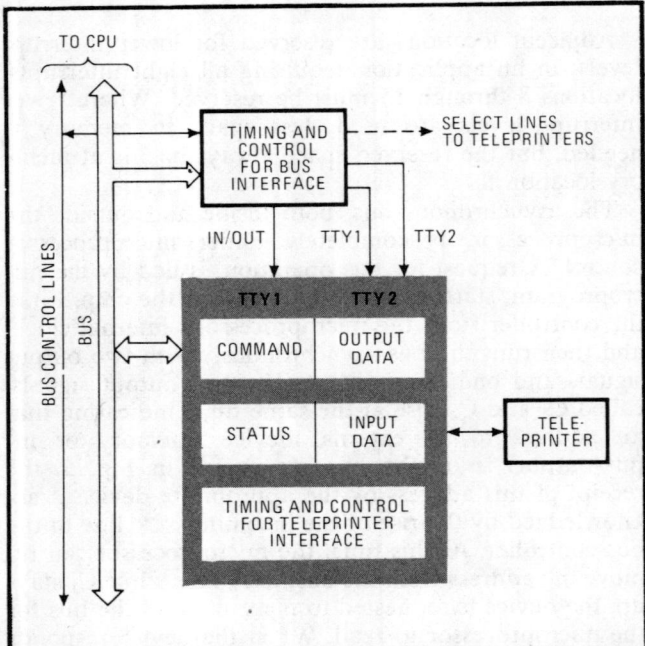

7. Input/output control. For a teleprinter, controller includes two registers for inbound and outbound data. Portions of the same physical registers, which nevertheless have different addresses, hold control and status information. Timing and control section responds to bus-control signals, guides data to and from the teleprinter itself, and generates interrupts for the microprocessor.

gram counter to be placed on the bus (thus permitting the operator to designate what instruction is to be executed next in the program), the contents of a specified memory location to be read or written, or a single microinstruction to be executed during a test. Last but not least, of course, is the NORMAL RUN signal.

This NORMAL RUN command assumes that the microprocessor has been previously initialized—that the various control flip-flops specify a normal state for the processor, that the address of an executable instruction is in the program counter, and that all necessary data and instructions are available for the microprocessor's use. This initialization process, necessary every time the microprocessor is started, is executed by an automatic-start sequence that is built into the microprocessor. The automatic-start sequence is designed for use in a system that does not include a manual console—that is, in fixed-program applications.

Initializing the system

A short-duration pulse applied to the microprocessor's initialization terminal resets all the flip-flops, loads the program counter with the contents of memory location 4095, and clears the remainder of the program-status word. To utilize this sequence, the address of the first instruction in the program must previously have been stored in location 4095, a step easily taken by any program-preparing software. The address 4095, in binary, is a string of 12 1s, or every bit in a word turned on; this location, like those reserved for interrupt processing, is not available to the user.

An internal clock generator in the microprocessor produces a two-phase timing signal skewed in such a way as to provide four phases, as shown in Fig. 6. If an operation calls for the use of the bus, the microprocessor stops during interval T_4, the length of which is therefore variable.

Without bus operation, the complete cycle lasts about 1 μs; with the bus, an extra 3 to 5 μs is added for reading and 2 to 3 ns for writing. The exact time depends on many factors, such as memory speed, bus capacitance, bus-driver capability, and so on—all absorbed by the asynchronous control of the bus. The extra time is added during interval T_4, which is where the clock always stops for a bus operation.

For most ordinary operations, seven to 10 machine cycles are necessary when only the general registers are used; one extra cycle is needed for a read operation (plus the delay of the asynchronous bus). If the addresses are indexed, two or three extra cycles within the microprocessor are needed, and the read operation takes three extra cycles instead of one. For more complex tasks, such as MULTIPLY, as many as 40 machine cycles are required, or 43 with indexing.

An additional advantage of the internal clock generator in the TLCS-12 is its automatic frequency compensation with temperature. As the ambient temperature increases, the logic circuits in the microprocessor slow down, and delays within the circuits are increased. But the clock slows down to the same degree, tracking the changes in circuit delay. However, this advantage has a tradeoff. It is impossible to measure time precisely by counting machine cycles, instruction executions, or the like, because the execution time varies with the temperature.

Interfacing input/output

All input/output devices communicate with the microprocessor through the common bus. Between the actual device and the bus, however, a device-control unit is necessary. In general, the control unit consists of one or more buffer registers that can be the same kind for all controllers—the kind shown in Fig. 7, for example—plus timing and control circuits that are tailored to the particular kind of device. These control circuits could, for instance, respond to the C_1 and C_2 bus-control signals and generate the ACK signal to the bus controller; they would also select, time, and otherwise control the device itself.

A typical device-control unit (Fig. 7) would control a teleprinter—a Teletype model ASR-33 is commonly used. This controller uses two 12-bit buffers— one for input and one for output. Since the data to and from teleprinter requires only 8 bits, the buffers have 4 bits in each direction to spare, which in this design are utilized for command and status information.

The 8-bit part and the 4-bit part have different addresses to distinguish them for the bus controller in the microprocessor. One or the other 12-bit register is specified by an additional IN/OUT signal generated by the control circuitry in response to the fall of C_1 and C_2, whichever is first. The control circuitry could also generate an interrupt signal when data arrives from the teleprinter in the data-input register. The interrupt routine, in this case, would include a READ instruction to transfer the data from the register to the microprocessor. □

Bipolar LSI computing elements usher in new era of digital design

Schottky bipolar chip set that is compatible with standard memories outdoes MOS microprocessors in performance and flexibility—the user microprograms it, and it can be configured to fit many computation and control functions

by Justin Rattner, Jean-Claude Cornet, and M.E. Hoff, Jr., *Intel Corp., Santa Clara, Calif.*

☐ Microprocessors have popularized programable LSI technology as a replacement for discrete logic and custom ICs[1]—at least, in the lower-speed applications for which the performance of metal-oxide-semiconductor technology is suited.

But high-performance applications are no longer beyond the reach of the microprocessor revolution. A family of computing elements has been developed using Schottky bipolar LSI technology, and it is not only faster but also far more flexible than its MOS predecessors. The new bipolar chips can be arranged in a number of different system organizations, and they are also microprogramed by the system designer to perform a number of different processing functions.[2,3]

Furthermore, systems built with this large-scale integrated circuitry are much smaller and less costly and consume less energy than equivalent designs using lower levels of transistor-transistor-logic integration. Even allowing for ancillary logic circuits, the new bipolar computing elements cut 60% to 80% off the package count in realizing most of today's designs made with small- or medium-scale-integrated TTL.

For example, an entire 16-bit processor (Fig. 1) can be assembled on one six-inch-square printed-circuit board. Such a processor is capable of typical register-to-register add cycle times of less than 125 nanoseconds. In

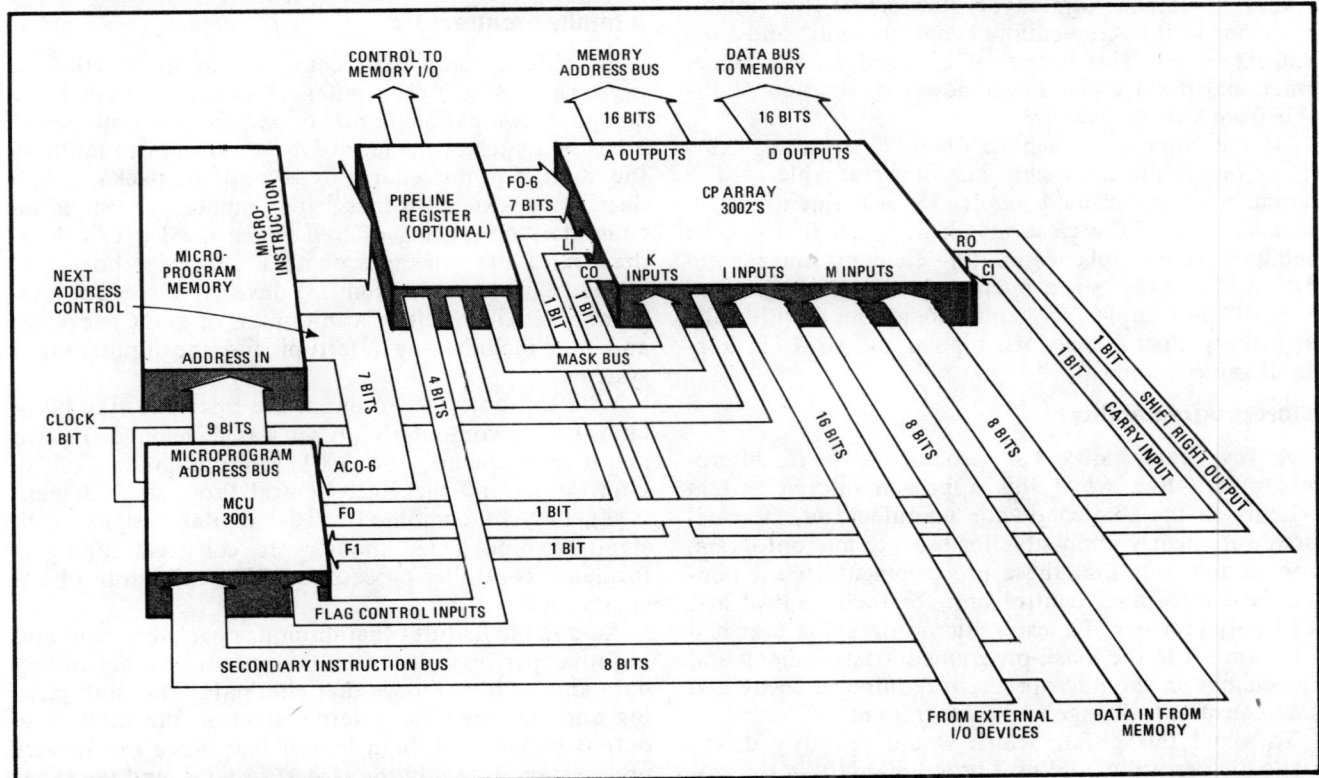

1. Bipolar microcomputer. Block diagram shows how to implement a typical 16-bit controller-processor with new family of bipolar computer elements. An array of eight central processing elements (CPEs) is governed by a microprogram control unit (MCU) through a separate read-only memory that carries the microinstructions for the various processing elements. This ROM may be a fast, off-the-shelf unit.

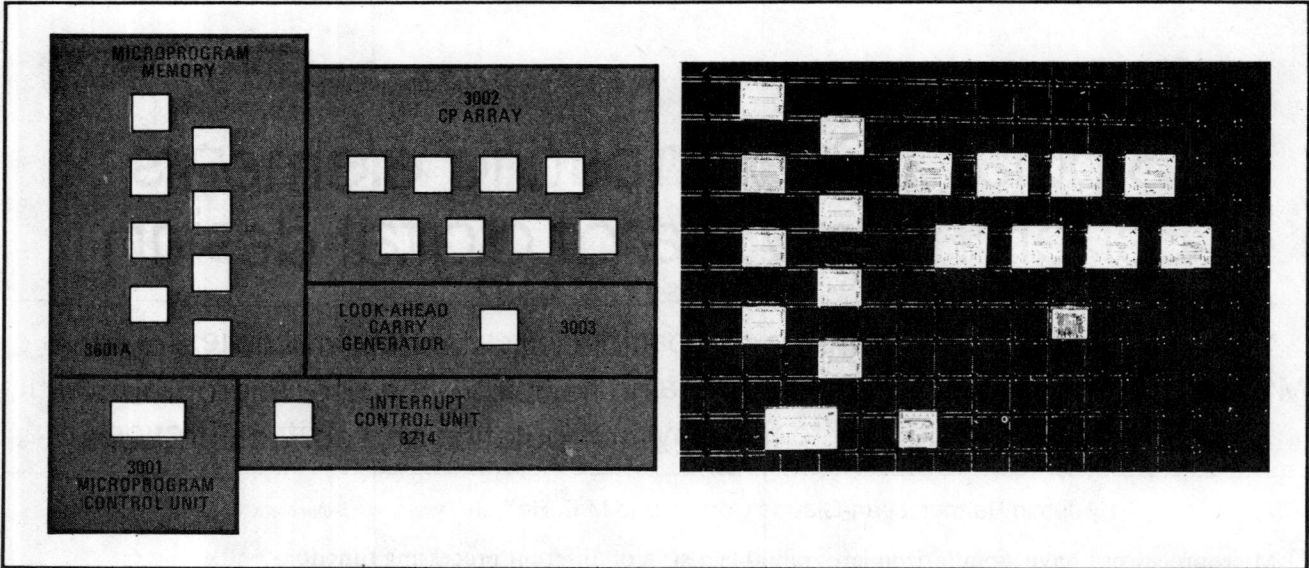

2. Family portrait. Four members of the Intel 3000 Schottky bipolar microcomputer chip set are shown here on an old transistor wafer. Interconnecting them in different combinations results in a wide range of low-cost, high-performance control and computation systems.

terms of raw computing power, that's over 15 times faster than Intel's 8080, the fastest n-channel MOS microprocessor,[4] and at double the word size.

Every LSI circuit technology confronts the chip architect and the device engineer with an assortment of design and manufacturing tradeoffs. Such factors as gate complexity, power dissipation, and propagation delay must all enter into the selection of a suitable component organization.

MOS LSI technology favors the single-chip microprocessor with its conventional control section and fixed instruction set. This judgment is based on the higher functional density and lower power dissipation realizable from MOS technology.

On the other hand, Schottky bipolar technology currently favors the multi-chip microprogramable organization. Microprogramed bipolar LSI is eminently practical because of the close match in speed that can be obtained from bipolar computing elements and memories. Additionally, since microprograming circumvents most of the complex sequential logic found within the single-chip microprocessors, bipolar die sizes are kept small and economical.

Microprogramability

A few early MOS LSI processors were microprogramed. But, while this approach offered certain benefits to the semiconductor manufacturer,[5] the devices were nearly impossible for users to microprogram. The trouble was that these processors utilized a nonstandard integrated control unit for their control and read-only memory. To test a microprogram, a user had to commit it to the mask-programed ROM element, and any change in the microprogram required a costly and time-consuming change to the program mask.

To avoid this pitfall, which would seriously downgrade the versatility and user programability of the new microcomputer set, the decision was made to utilize standard bipolar LSI memories—electrically programable and mask-programable read-only memories, as well as random-access memories, as options for storing the micro-instructions for the LSI computing elements. RAMs can hold the microprograms in developmental systems to simplify debugging. PROMs can be used to build and test prototypes or even in the production of low-volume systems. High-volume applications can commit their microprograms to compatible mask-programed ROMs. In every case the use of standard off-the-shelf components minimizes memory costs.

A family architecture

To reduce component count as far as practical, a multi-chip LSI microcomputer set must be designed as a complete, compatible family of devices. The omission of a bus or a latch or the lack of drive current can multiply the number of miscellaneous SSI and MSI packages to a dismaying extent—witness the reputedly LSI minicomputers now being offered which need over a hundred extra TTL packages on their processor boards to support one or two custom LSI devices. Successful integration should result in a minimum of extra packages, and that includes the interrupt and the input/output systems.

With this objective in mind, the Intel Schottky bipolar LSI microcomputer chip set was developed. Its two major components, the 3001 Microprogram Control Unit (MCU) and the 3002 Central Processing Element (CPE), may be combined by the digital designer with standard bipolar LSI memory to construct high-performance controller-processors with a minimum of ancillary logic.

Among the features that minimize package count and improve performance are: the multiple independent data and address busses that eliminate time multiplexing and the need for external latches; the three-state output buffers with high fanout that make bus drivers unnecessary except in the largest systems, and the separate output-enable logic that permits bidirectional busses to be formed simply by connecting inputs and outputs together.

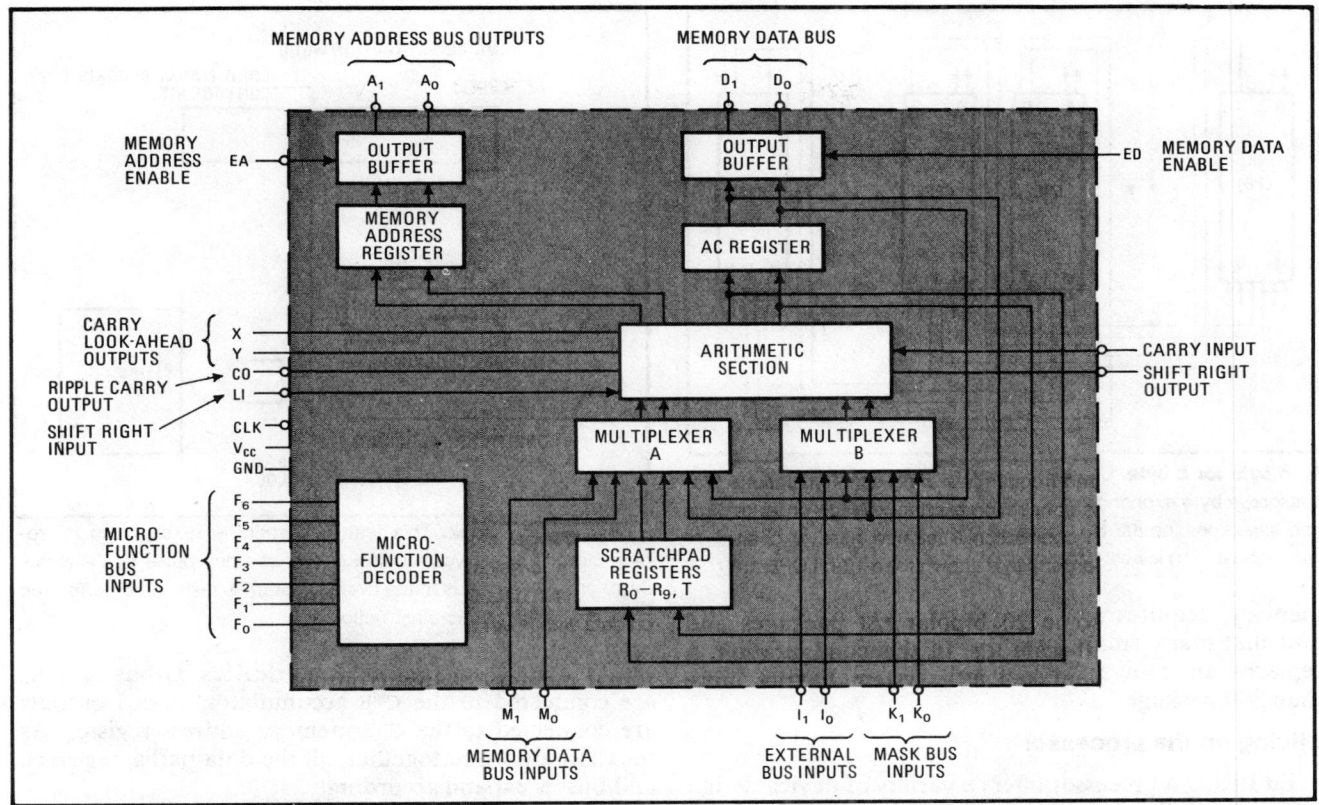

3. Central processing element. This element contains all the circuits representing a two-bit-wide slice through a small computer's central processor. To build a processor of word width N, all that's necessary is to connect an array of N/2 CPEs together.

Each CPE represents a complete two-bit slice through the data-processing section of a computer. Several CPEs may be arrayed in parallel to form a processor of any desired word length. The MCU, which together with the microprogram memory, controls the step-by-step operation of the processor, is itself a powerful microprogramed state sequencer.

Enhancing the performance and capabilities of these two components are a number of compatible computing elements. These include a fast look-ahead carry generator, a priority interrupt unit, and a multimode latch buffer (Fig. 2). A complete summary of the first available members of this family of LSI computing elements and memories is given in the table on this page.

The cost/performance spectrum

The total flexibility of the Intel LSI computing elements is demonstrated by the broad cost/performance spectrum of the controllers and processors that can be constructed with them. These include:
- High-speed controllers, built with a stand-alone ROM-MCU combination that sequences at up to 10 megahertz; it can be used without any CPEs as a system state controller.
- Pipelined look-ahead carry controller-processors, where the overlapped microinstruction fetch/execute cycles and fast-carry logic reduce the 16-bit add time to less than 125 nanoseconds.
- Ripple-carry controller processors (a 16-bit design adds the contents of two registers in 300 nanoseconds).
- Multiprocessors, or networks of any of the above controllers and processors, to provide computation, interrupt supervision, and peripheral control.

These configurations represent a range of microinstruction execution rates of from 3 million to 10 million instructions per second, or up to two orders of magnitude faster, for example, than p-channel microprocessors. Moreover, the increases in processor performance are achieved with relative simplicity. A ripple-carry 16-bit processor uses one MCU, eight CPEs, plus microprogram memory. One extra computing element, the 3003 Look-ahead Carry Generator, enhances the processor with fast carry. Increasing speed further by pipelining, the overlap of microinstruction fetch and execute cycles, requires a few D-type MSI flip-flops.

At the multiprocessor level, the microprogram memory, MCU, or CPE devices can be shared. A 16-bit processor, complete with bus control and microprogram

THE 3000 BIPOLAR LSI FAMILY	
3001	Microprogram control unit
3002	Central processing element
3003	Look-ahead carry generator
3212	Multimode latch buffer
3214	Priority interrupt unit
3216	Noninverting bidirectional bus driver
3226	Inverting bidirectional bus driver
3601	256-by-4-bit programable read-only memory
3604	512-by-8-bit programable read-only memory
3301	256-by-4-bit read-only memory
3304	512-by-8-bit read-only memory

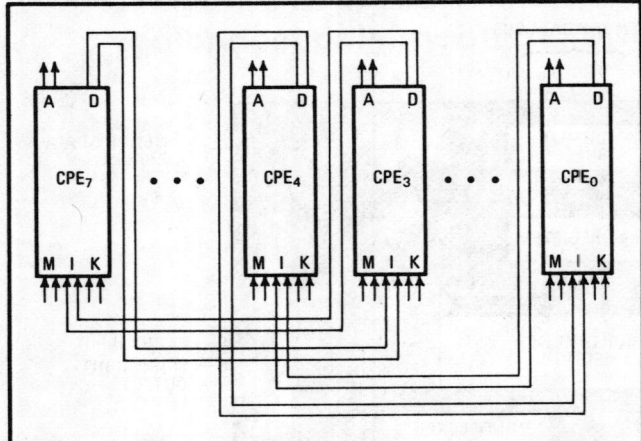

4. A byte for a byte. Used frequently in data-communications processors, a byte exchange connection exchanges high-order outputs and low-order inputs. In connection illustrated here, exchange of two highest- and lowest-order bits is shown for a 16-bit CPE array.

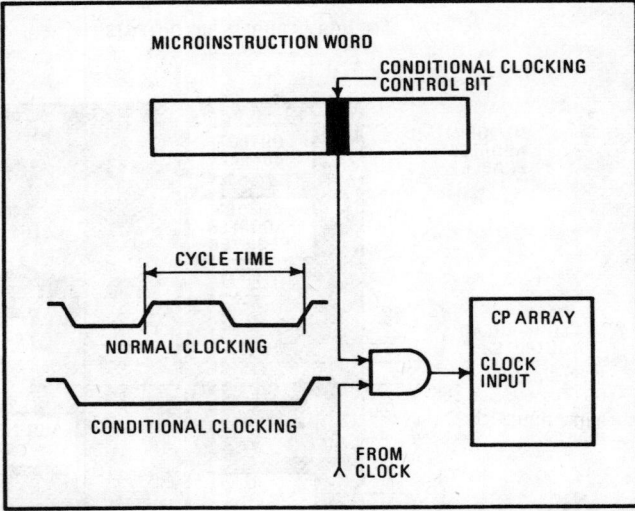

5. Conditional clock. This feature permits an extra bit in microinstruction to selectively control gating of clock pulse to CP array. Carry or shift data thus made available permits tests to be performed on data with fewer microinstructions.

memory, requires some 20 bipolar LSI packages and half that many small-scale ICs. In this configuration, it replaces an equivalent MSI TTL system having more than 200 packages.

Slicing up the processor

Bit slicing a processor offers a variety of device design alternatives. On the one hand, die size restrictions and pin limitations may force a slice to get by with fewer external input and output busses, and as a result, fewer independent data paths than is desirable. This has two unfortunate results.

First, the paucity of data paths causes a proliferation of external latches and multiplexers to create the address, data, and control busses found in a typical processor. Second, the inability of operands, including bit masks, to enter the slice in parallel, severely degrades performance. Multiple microcycles are required to load and operate on data in addition to the overhead cycles needed to multiplex addresses with data on a single output bus.

On the other hand, attempting to put too much logic on a single chip can also seriously degrade performance. For a given amount of power dissipation, which is determined by the selected package and limited by its cost and mechanical intricacy, the functional complexity of a device establishes its power dissipation per function ratio. As a device becomes more complex, the available power per function decreases, and the propagation delay per function increases. Clearly, longer propagation delays mean lower performance.

The organization of the 3002 CPE is a result of balancing the need for a certain number of independent busses and data paths against the current limits on die size and power dissipation.

CPEs form a processor

Each CPE (Fig. 3) carries two bits of five independent busses. The three input busses can be used in several different ways. Typically, the K-bus is used for microprogram mask or literal (constant) value input, while the other two input busses, M and I, carry data from external memory or input/output devices. D-bus outputs are connected to the CPE accumulator; A-bus outputs are connected to the CPE memory address register. As the CPEs are wired together, all the data paths, registers, and busses expand accordingly.

Certain data operations can be performed simply by connecting the busses in a particular fashion. For example, a byte exchange operation, often used in data-communications processors, may be carried out by wiring the D-bus outputs back to the I-bus inputs, exchanging the high-order outputs and low-order inputs as shown in Fig. 4. Several other discretionary shifts and rotates can be accomplished in this manner.

A sixth CPE bus, the seven-line microfunction bus, controls the internal operation of the CPE by selecting the operands and the operation to be performed. The arithmetic function section, under control of the microfunction bus decoder, performs over 40 Boolean and binary functions, including 2's complement arithmetic and logical AND, OR, NOT, and exclusive-NOR. It increments, decrements, shifts left or right, and tests for zero.

Unlike earlier MSI arithmetic-logic units, which contain many functions that are rarely used, the microfunction decoder selects only useful CPE operations. Standard carry look-ahead outputs, X and Y, are generated by the CPE for use with available look-ahead devices or the Intel 3003 Look-ahead Carry Generator. Independent carry input, carry output, shift input, and shift output lines are also available.

What's more, since the K-bus inputs are always ANDed with the B-multiplexer outputs into the arithmetic function section, a number of useful functions that in conventional MSI ALUs would require several cycles are generated in a single CPE microcycle. The type of bit masking frequently done in computer control systems can be performed with the mask supplied to the K-bus directly from the microinstruction.

Placing the K-bus in either the all-one or all-zero state will, in most cases, select or deselect the accumulator in the operation, respectively. This toggling effect of the K-bus on the accumulator nearly doubles the CPE's repertoire of microfunctions. For instance, with the K-bus in the all-zero state, the data on the M-bus may be complemented and loaded into the CPE's accumulator. The same function selected with the K-bus in the all-one state will exclusive-NOR the data on the M-bus with the accumulator contents.

Three innovations

The power and versatility of the CPE are increased by three rather novel techniques. The first of these is the use of the carry lines and logic during non-arithmetic operations for bit testing and zero detection. The carry circuits during these operations perform a word-wide logical OR (ORing adjacent bits) of a selected result from the arithmetic section. The value of the OR, called the carry OR, is passed along the carry lines to be ORed with the result of an identical operation taking place simultaneously in the adjacent higher-order CPE.

Obviously, the presence of at least one bit in the logical 1 state will result in a true carry output from the highest-order CPE. This output, as explained later, can be used by the MCU to determine which microprogram sequence to follow. With the ability to mask any desired bit, or set of bits, via the K-bus inputs included in the carry OR, a powerful bit-testing and zero-detection facility is realized.

The second novel CPE feature is the use of three-state outputs on the shift right output (RO) and carry output (CO) lines. During a right shift operation, the CO line is placed in the high-impedance (Z) state, and the shift data is active on the RO line. In all other CPE operations, the RO line is placed in the Z state, and the carry data is active on the CO line. This permits the CO and RO lines to be tied together and sent as a single rail input to the MCU for testing and branching. Left shift operations utilize the carry lines, rather than the shift lines, to propagate data.

The third novel CPE capability, called conditional clocking, saves microcode and microcycles by reducing the number of microinstructions required to perform a given test. One extra bit is used in the microinstruction to selectively control the gating of the clock pulse to the central processor (CP) array. Momentarily freezing the clock (Fig. 5) permits the CPE microfunction to be performed, but stops the results from being clocked into the specified registers. The carry or shift data that results from the operation is available because the arithmetic section is combinatorial, rather than sequential. The data can be used as a jump condition by the MCU and in this way permits a variety of nondestructive tests to be performed on register data.

A good example of the over-all capability of the CPE is stack pointer or program counter maintenance. Usually this operation requires four microprocessor cycles: fetch the register data, send it to the memory address register, increment the value, and store the result back in the specified register. But the CPE can do it in one microcycle, using any one of its 11 scratchpad registers as the stack pointer or program counter. The desired address is gated through the arithmetic section to the memory address register, and the memory cycle is initiated. Simultaneously, over a separate data path, the address value is incremented by the arithmetic section and sent back to the scratchpad.

By itself the CP array is incomplete as a microprocessor. The arithmetic, logic, and register functions need to be controlled in some orderly fashion, and this is the function of the MCU.

Microprogram control

The classic form of microprogram control incorporates a next-address field in each microinstruction—any other approach would require some type of program counter. To simplify its logic, the MCU (Fig. 6) uses the classic approach and requires address control information from each microinstruction. This information is not, however, simply the next microprogram address. Rather, it is a highly encoded specification of the next address and one of a set of conditional tests on the MCU bus inputs and registers.

The next-address logic and address control functions of the MCU are based on a unique scheme of memory addressing. Microprogram addresses are organized as a two-dimensional array or matrix, as shown in Fig. 7. Unlike in ordinary memory, which has linearly sequenced addresses, each microinstruction is pinpointed by its row and column address in the matrix. The 9-bit microprogram address specifies the row address in the upper 5 bits and the column address in the lower 4 bits. The matrix can therefore contain up to 32 row addresses and 16 column addresses for a total of 512 microinstruction addresses.

The next-address logic of the MCU makes extensive use of this addressing scheme. For example, from a particular row or column address, it is possible to jump either unconditionally to any other location in that row or column or conditionally to other specified locations, all in one operation. For a given location in the matrix there is a fixed subset of microprogram addresses that may be selected as the next address. These are referred to as a jump set, and each type of MCU address control jump function has a jump set associated with it.

Incorporating a jump operation in every microinstruction improves performance by allowing process-

---

Microprograming technology

- **Microprogram:** A type of program that directly controls the operation of each functional element in a microprocessor.
- **Microinstruction:** A bit pattern that is stored in a microprogram memory word and specifies the operation of the individual LSI computing elements and related subunits, such as main memory and input/output interfaces.
- **Microinstruction sequence:** The series of microinstructions that the microprogram control unit (MCU) selects from the microprogram to execute a single macroinstruction or control command. Microinstruction sequences can be shared by several macroinstructions.
- **Macroinstruction:** Either a conventional computer instruction (e.g. ADD MEMORY TO REGISTER, INCREMENT, and SKIP, etc.) or device controller command (e.g., SEEK, READ, etc.).

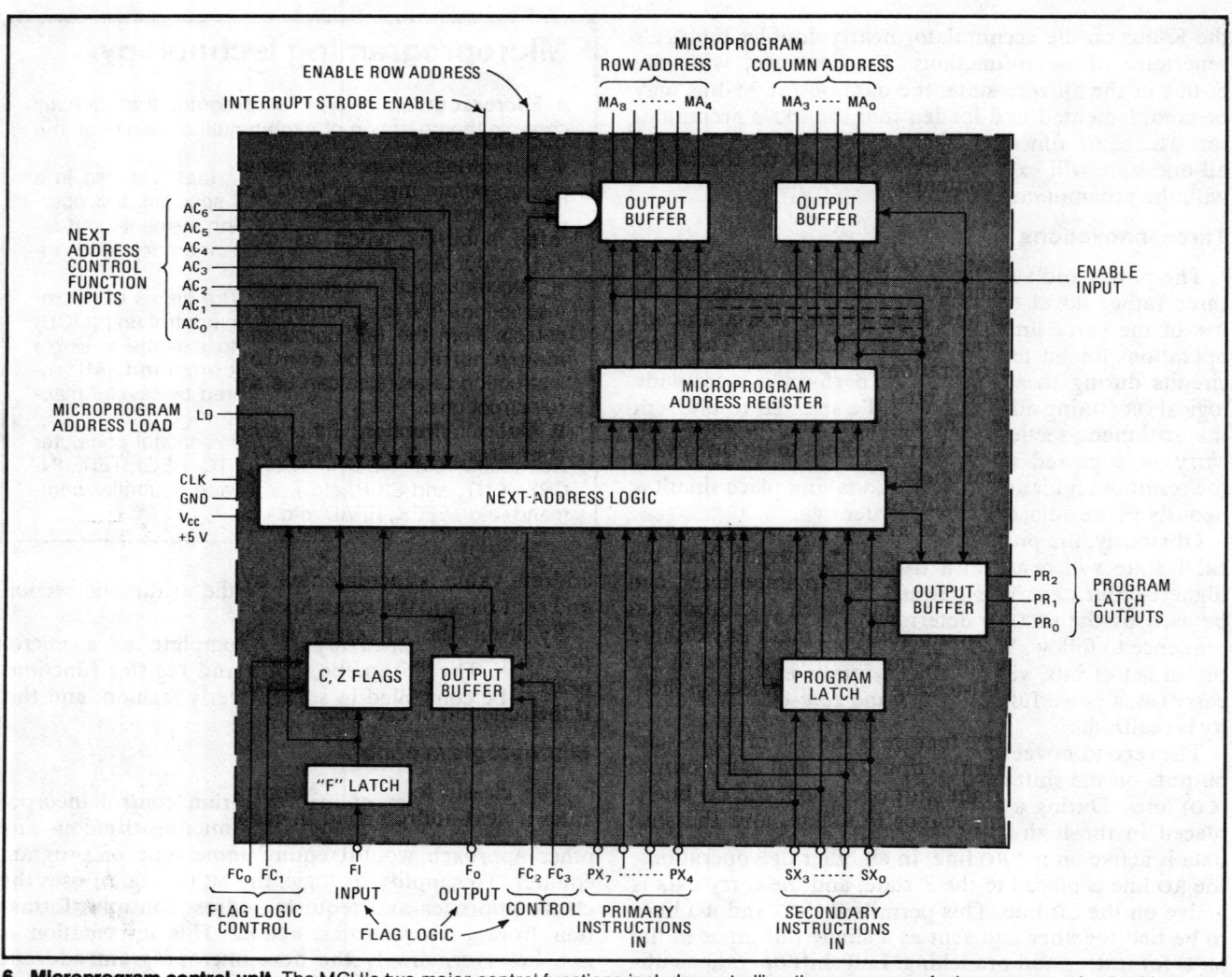

6. Microprogram control unit. The MCU's two major control functions include controlling the sequence of microprograms fetched from the microprogram memory, and keeping track of the carry inputs and outputs of the CP array by means of the flag logic control.

ing functions to be executed in parallel with program branches. Reductions in microcode are also obtained because common microprogram sequences can be shared without the time-space penalty usually incurred by conditional branching.

Independently controlled flag logic in the MCU is available for latching and controlling the value of the carry and shift inputs to the CP array. Two flags, called C and Z, are used to save the state of the flag input line. Under microprogram control, the flag logic simultaneously sets the state of the flag output line, forcing the line to logical 0, logical 1, or the value of the C or Z flag.

The jump decisions are made by the next-address logic on the basis of: the MCU's current microprogram address; the address control function on the accumulator inputs; and the data that's on the macroinstruction (X) bus or in the program latch or in the flags. Jump decisions may also be based on the instantaneous state of the flag input line without loading the value in one of the flags. This feature eliminates many extra microinstructions that would be required if only the flag flip-flop could be tested.

Microinstruction sequences are normally selected by the operation codes (op codes) supplied by the microinstructions, such as control commands or user instructions in main memory. The MCU decodes these commands by using their bit patterns to determine which is to be the next microprogram address. Each decoding results in a 16-way program branch to the desired microinstruction sequence.

Cracking the op codes

For instance, the MCU can be microprogramed to directly decode conventional 8-bit op codes. In these op codes the upper 4 bits specify one of up to 16 instruction classes or address modes, such as register, indirect, or indexed. The remaining bits specify the particular subclass such as ADD, SKIP IF ZERO, and so on. If a set of op codes is required to be in a different format, as may occur in a full emulation, an external pre-decoder, such as ROM, can be used in series with the X-bus to reformat the data for the MCU.

In rigorous decoding situations where speed or space is critical, the full 8-bit macroinstruction bus can be used for a single 256-way branch. Pulling down the load line of the MCU forces the 8 bits of data on the X-bus (typically generated by a predecoder) directly into the microprogram address register.

The data thus directly determines the next microprogram address which should be the start of the desired microprogram sequence. The load line may also be used by external logic to force the MCU, at power-up, into the system re-initialization sequence.

From time to time, a microprocessor must examine the state of its interrupt system to determine whether an interrupt is pending. If one is, the processor must suspend its normal execution sequence and enter an interrupt sequence in the microprogram. This requirement is handled by the MCU in a simple but elegant manner.

When the microprogram flows through address row 0 and column 15, the interrupt strobe enable line of the MCU is raised. The interrupt system, an Intel 3214 Interrupt Control Unit, responds by disabling the row address outputs of the MCU via the enable row address line, and by forcing the row entry address of the microprogram interrupt sequence onto the row address bus. The operation is normally performed just before the macroinstruction fetch cycle, so that a macroprogram is interrupted between, not during, macroinstructions.

The 9-bit microprogram address register and address bus of the MCU directly address 512 microinstructions. This is about twice as many as required by the typical 16-bit disk-controller or central processor.

Moreover, multiple 512 microinstruction memory planes can easily be implemented simply by adding an extra address bit to the microinstruction each time the number of extra planes is doubled. Incidentally, as the number of bits in the microinstruction is increased, speed is not reduced. The additional planes also permit program jumps to take place in three address dimensions (Fig. 8) instead of two.

Because of the tremendous design flexibility offered by the Intel computing elements, it is impossible to describe every microinstruction format exactly. But generally speaking, the formats all derive from the one in Fig. 9. The minimum width is 18 bits: 7 bits for the address control functions, plus 4 bits for the flag logic control; plus 7 bits for the CPE microfunction control.

More bits can be added to the microinstruction format to provide such functions as mask field input to the CP array, external memory control, conditional clocking, and so on. Allocation of these bits is left to the designer who organizes the system. He is free to trade off memory costs, support logic, and microinstruction cycles to meet his cost/performance objectives.

Configuring a processor

The processor organization of Fig. 1 may be varied to enhance speed, reduce component count, or increase data-processing capability. As mentioned earlier, one widely applicable technique for maximizing a processor's performance is called pipelining. To pipeline a microprocessor, a group of D-type flip-flops is hung on the microprogram memory outputs (excluding the address control field) to buffer the current microinstruction and so allow the MCU to overlap the fetch of the next microinstruction with the execution of the current one. If fast carry logic is also used, the microinstruction cycle time is typically less than 125 nanoseconds.

Although almost any number of CPEs may be arrayed (up to 320 bits without buffering, to be exact), a system

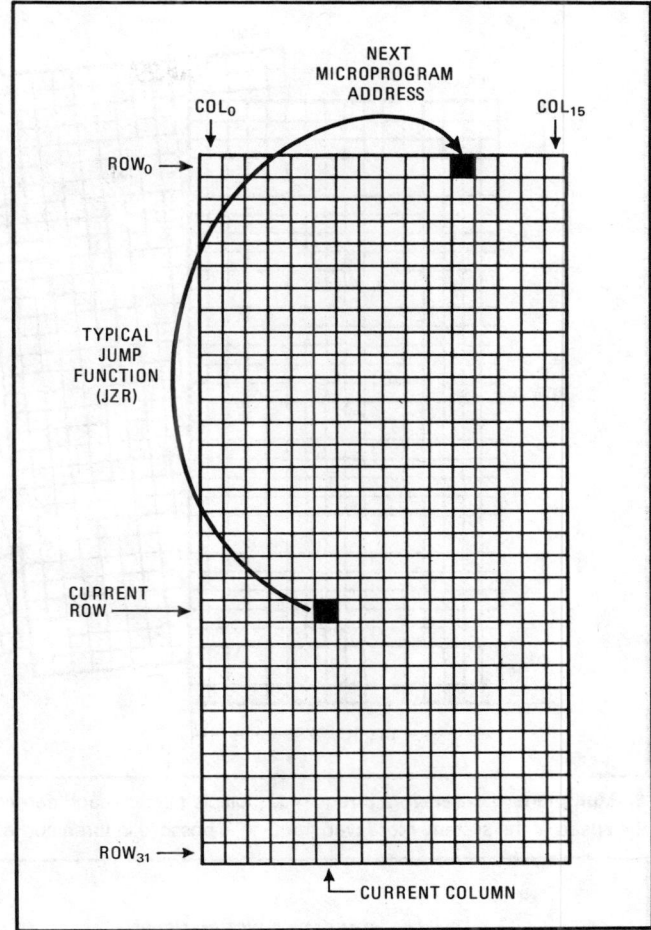

7. Jump function. Microprogram addresses, represented here by boxes, are organized as a two-dimensional array or matrix. Each microinstruction contains a jump operation field that specifies the next microprogram address. Shown here is a typical jump operation from location (row 20-column 5) to (row 0-column 11).

using only a few CPEs may not have a CP array address bus wide enough for the size of main memory required. A good example is the 8-bit processor that needs a 16-bit address bus. Such problems are easily solved. In this case the CP array delivers one byte of the address on its memory address bus outputs and the other byte on its data bus outputs. The tradeoff is that two microcycles are required to send the address to memory.

Another configuration insures rapid servicing of interrupts by combining two CP arrays with one MCU. All of the register contents associated with the interrupted routine are held in one array, while the interrupt service routine is executed on the second CP array. Normal program execution resumes when the MCU regains control of the first CP array.

Multiprocessing is another way to obtaining high performance. Several satellite MCU-CP arrays can share a common main memory—an arrangement that could be used quite effectively in a multi-terminal information system. In a busy system, memory bus conflicts might increase the average processor cycle time, but the speed of the Schottky bipolar computing elements is so great that such delays would be invisible to the users.

As a final example, consider the costly and complex

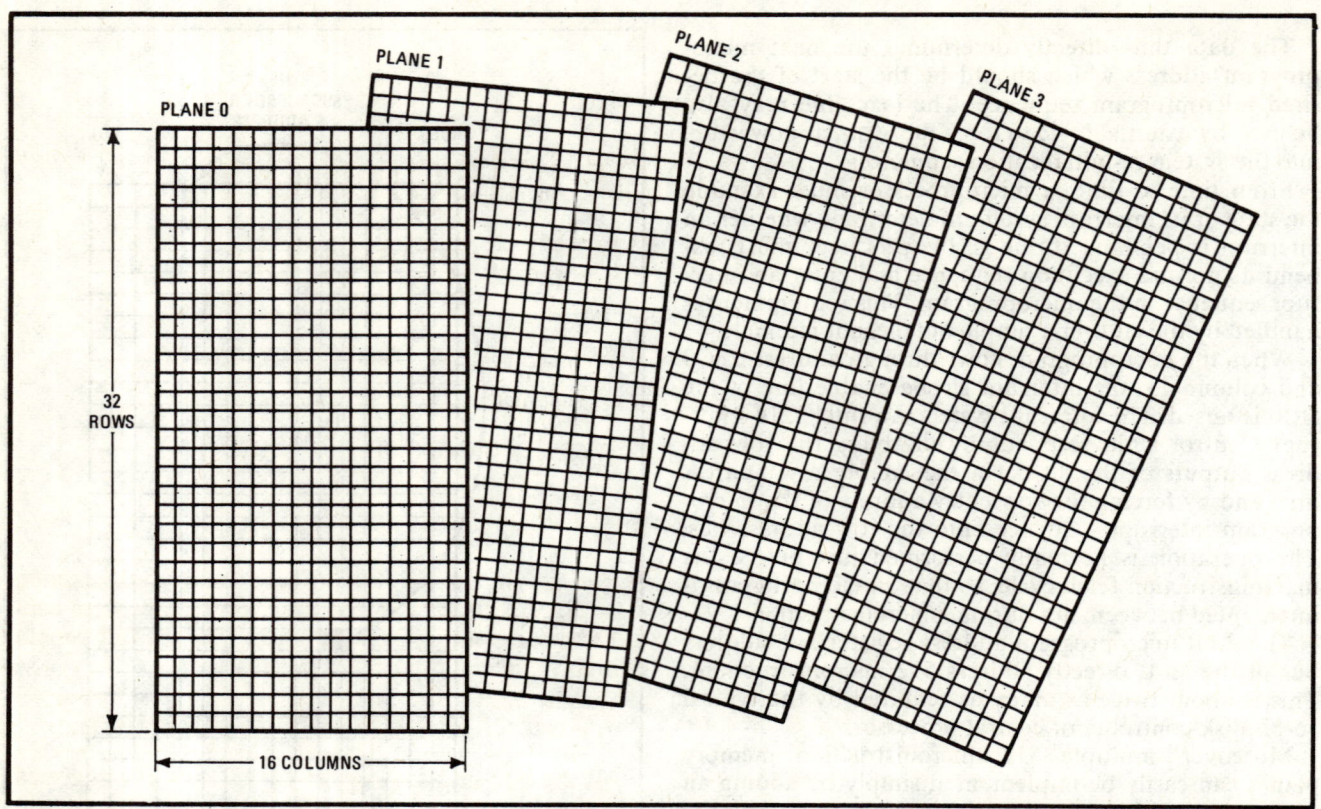

8. Multiplanar addressing. If required, multiple planes, each carrying 512 microinstructions, can be implemented without any sacrifice in the speed of the system. Moreover, jumping is possible in three address dimensions with such a configuration.

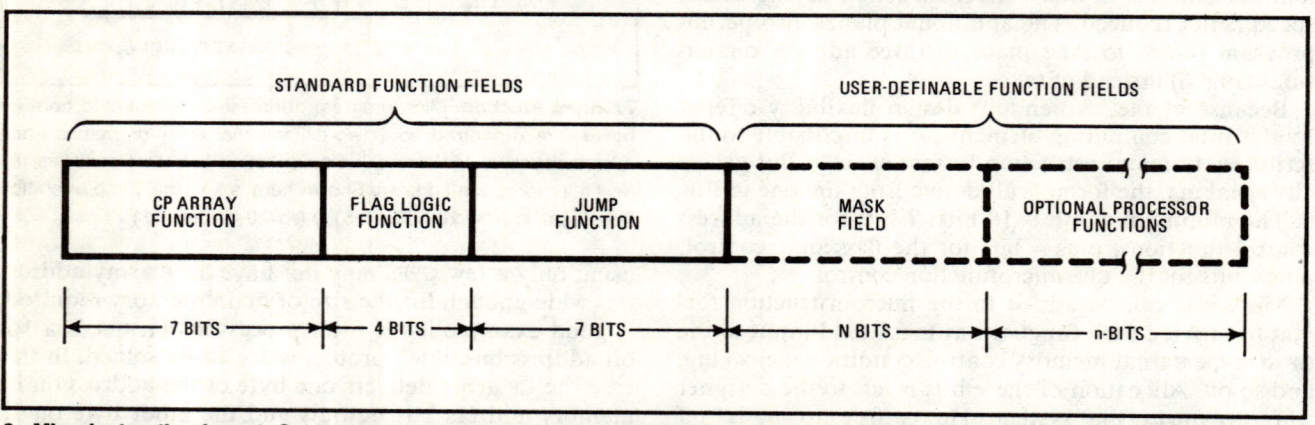

9. Microinstruction format. Only a generalized microinstruction format can be shown since allocation of bits for the mask field and optional processor functions depends on the wishes of the designer and the tradeoffs he decides to make.

controllers available for the inexpensive diskette or floppy disk. The relatively high data-transfer rates and the processing demands of the soft-sectored diskette put this application just beyond the reach of the fastest MOS microprocessors. Existing controllers contain upwards of 250 TTL packages and can only work with one type of media-formatting scheme.

In contrast, a universal diskette controller, adaptable to a variety of formatting schemes through microprograming, requires less than 20 bipolar LSI components, including the MCU, CPEs, and memories. The over-all diskette controller package count is reduced by two thirds.

Intel's Schottky bipolar computing elements are the first LSI technique endowed with the computing and control power of discrete high-speed TTL circuits. In addition, they give the digital designer a degree of flexibility, simplicity, and economy never before available to him. By all indications, bipolar LSI computing elements are destined to become the standard for high-speed design in the next generation of computation and control systems. □

REFERENCES
1. M.E. Hoff, Jr., "New LSI Components," 8th IEEE Computer Society International Conference Digest, 1972, pp. 141–143.
2. S.S. Husson, "Microprogramming: Principles and Practice," Prentice Hall Inc., 1970.
3. P.M. Davies, "Readings in Microprogramming," IBM Systems Journal, Vol. 11, 1972, pp. 16–40.
4. M. Shima and F. Faggin, "In switching to n-MOS microprocessor gets 2-microsecond cycle time," Electronics, April 18, 1974, pp. 95–100.
5. G. Reyling, Jr., "Considerations in Choosing a Microprogrammable Bit-Slice Architecture," Computer, July, 1974, pp. 26–29.

I²L takes bipolar integration a significant step forward

Extraordinary compactness is achieved in new microprocessor while speed is increased up to five-fold over n-channel devices; 4-bit controllers to 16-bit minicomputers can be simulated

by Richard L. Horton, Jesse Englade, and Gerald McGee, *Texas Instruments, Dallas, Texas*

☐ For specialty applications such as watch circuits and linear control elements, integrated injection-logic circuits are already in production. But only with the development of purely digital techniques can system designers realize the full impact of this new bipolar structure. To this end, an extremely compact I²L gate has been devised that does not require isolation between elements within the gate—in contrast to I²L linear types that rely on conventional, space-consuming pn junctions to separate their devices. In the new, non-isolated I²L form, gates shrink to the size of a single transistor, so that, together with their low power capabilities, digital I²L structures may contain thousands of gates on a single high-performing bipolar chip.

With these non-isolated gate structures, a 4-bit bipolar microprocessor chip (Fig. 1) has been built that operates up to five times faster than today's n-channel devices. At the same time, this I²L processor element, which is directly compatible with existing bipolar interface circuits, provides greater instruction capability than n-channel designs. And because the 4-bit device is expandable to larger systems with simple interconnections, this circuit element can handle a wide range of computer functions—from simple 4-bit controller jobs to full 16-bit minicomputer process control functions.

True, the processor speeds achievable with these first-generation I²L gates—propagation delays of 20 to 50 nanoseconds—are not as fast as with today's TTL technologies. But techniques to boost I²L speeds toward the TTL level while still maintaining a compact low-power LSI format are known to be on the way. These integrated-injection logic chips will, for the first time, provide process control and computer system designers with the full benefit of highly efficient bipolar LSI circuits.

Part 1: Fundamental structure.

All the size and low-power advantages of integrated injection logic come directly from shrinking the old direct-coupled transistor logic (DCTL) into a single complementary transistor equivalent. In this scheme (Fig. 2) the resistor in the DCTL gate is replaced by an active current source; the emitter-grounded output transistor pair is replaced by a single multicollector transistor, and a simple pnp transistor is added to serve as the current injector source.

Thus the six transistors of a three-input DCTL gate are reduced to a single I²L transistor pair. The vertical npn transistor Q_1, with the multiple collectors C_1 and C_2, operates as an inverter, and the lateral pnp transistor Q_2 serves as both the current source and active load. No large ohmic resistors are required for either the source or load function. What is perhaps most ingenious, the base of the multi-collector npn transistor is made common with the collector of the lateral pnp current source, while the base of the current source is made common with the emitter of the multi-collector npn. Because of the elements in common (see panel p. 51), the entire I²L gate, when it is configured on silicon, only takes up the room of a single multi-emitter transistor.

Again, the basic I²L

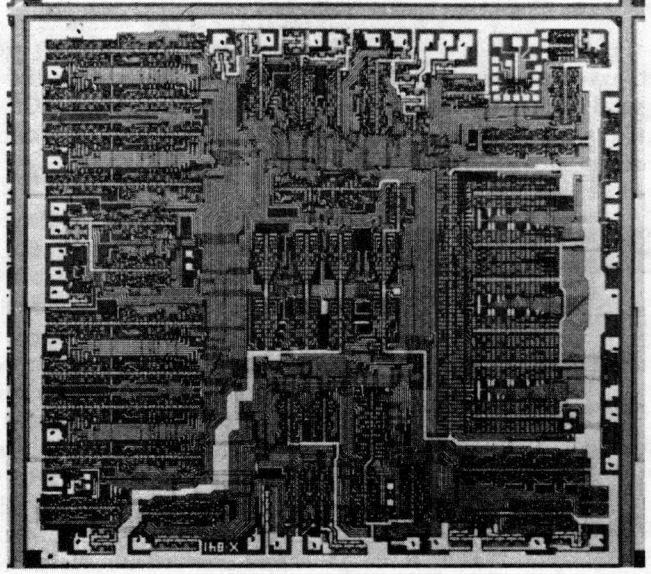

1. The first. Entering the picture is the industries first standard-product microprocessor built with the integrated injection logic bipolar technique. This 4-bit-slice device, SBP0400, bridges performance gap between today's n-channel and Schottky devices.

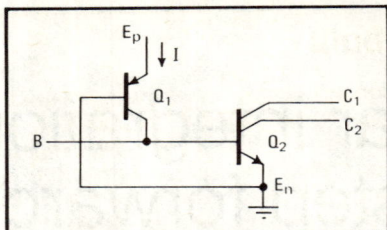

2. Structure. Digital form of I²L has vertical npn transistor Q_1 with multiple collectors C_1 and C_2 operating as inverter; and lateral pnp transistor Q_2 as current-source and load.

structure can take two forms: isolated or non-isolated. The isolated form, which so far has received more public attention [*Electronics*, Oct. 3, 1974, p. 111-118], makes use of a conventional reverse-biased pn junction for component isolation. Since this form of isolation completely separates adjacent devices, it is the isolated I²L structures that are used in circuits containing mixed-component functions.

Fabricated with a 6-mask bipolar process, isolated I²L allows all other standard bipolar and MOS design techniques (Schottky TTL, ECL gates and memories, and n-channel MOS devices, including linear functions) to be combined directly with the I²L gates. This means that along with I²L digital sections, a single low cost monolithic chip can hold such linear and special buffer functions as LED drivers, memory decoders, current regulators, op amps, comparators, oscillators, and very-fast digital TTL or ECL logic.

Indeed, the I²L watch, entertainment and other commercial LSI circuits already in production are made with this technique. This isolated form of I²L can also be combined with Schottky and ECL memory structure to provide fast low-cost bipolar memory designs. Here the I²L-type gates would form the internal array of the memory, while the TTL or ECL transistors would form the peripheral interface elements. RAMs with I²L-type arrays (74S209) have already been built, pointing to a new low-cost bipolar approach to medium-performance (100 ns) memories.

The boss LSI technology

Even as isolated forms of I²L have endless possibilities for combining linear and digital functions into heretofore-unattainable degrees of circuit integration, it is non-isolated I²L that results in the most dense and efficient form of bipolar logic yet devised for the fabrication of very complex digital ICs. Utilizing the single transistor switch with the common ground planes shown in Fig. 2, this logic form capitalizes on the high carrier mobility inherent in bulk silicon structures. It need not be isolated, nor does it require ground metalization, because in this single-transistor gate the output of one gate serves as the input of the next.

Nevertheless, these I²L gates are capable of operating at nanosecond speeds and microwatt power dissipation (Table 1), with a component density 10 times that of conventional bipolar circuits, and twice that of p-MOS. Furthermore, non-isolated I²L circuits can be built with a 4-mask, two-diffusion bipolar process, at high yields—an essential requirement of any LSI process where thousands of gates per circuit must be fabricated on a wafer of complex circuits.

The advantages of the I²L process are shown in Fig. 3, which compares the process complexity and gate-size relationships of the various digital technologies in use today. In process complexity, I²L is simpler than all other techniques except low-performing p-MOS, which requires the same number of mask steps but needs one less diffusion step. And, compared to I²L, the newly-evolved depletion-load MOS technology, being relied on so heavily in today's n-channel memories and microprocessors, requires an additional mask step. It also requires two ion implementation steps as opposed to none for I²L although depletion-load MOS does use one less diffusion. In any case, compared to TTL's 7 masks and 4 diffusions, and C-MOS's 6 masks and 3 diffusions, the I²L process is simplicity itself.

Even so, this process results in the smallest component size of any technology in operation—as Fig. 3 shows, the product is less than one tenth the area of either a conventional TTL or C-MOS gate. Even the newest LSI forms of TTL occupy four times as much space.

Speed-power comparisons (Fig. 4) show still another advantage of I²L gates; they have the lowest speed power product of any technology in use today, approaching a theoretical limit of 0.001 picojoule. Even non-optimized I²L test bars have operated with 100 ns propagation delays while dissipating 100nW of power per gate—surpassing today's best C-MOS circuits.

Constant speed-power

Yet, unlike C-MOS, whose power dissipation rises dramatically at higher speeds, I²L gates can be pushed to speeds of 10 to 20 ns while maintaining a virtually constant speed-power product. Indeed, an I²L gate optimized around a high-speed 50-ns format is the one used in the current 4-bit microprocessor circuit design.

Finally, Fig. 5 shows where I²L processor circuits fit into the spectrum of computer applications. I²L microprocessors can potentially handle all the jobs now being performed by today's MOS systems—from non-real time processing, to calculator jobs requiring millisecond add times, to the 50-ns real-time processing of some mainframe controller systems. Second and third generation I²L designs are expected to significantly extend this capability into higher performance applications (Fig. 6).

Taking the simplest case, one in which a single npn grounded-emitter transistor forms the basic I²L gate,

TABLE 1: COMPARISON OF I²L AND TTL PROPERTIES		
Parameter	I²L	TTL
Packing density (7-μm mask details)	120 – 200 gates/mm²	20 gates/mm²
Speed-power product	4 – 0.2 pJ/gate	100 pJ/gate
Gate delay	25 – 250 ns	10 ns
Power dissipation	6 nW – 70 μW	10 mW
Supply voltage	1 – 15 V	3 – 73 V
Logic voltage swing	0.6 V	5 V
Current range (per gate)	1 nA – 1 mA	2 mA
Interconnect	Single-level	Double-level

How it's built

Designers at Texas Instruments are evaluating a number of I²L fabrication techniques. The one used to build their first microprocessor was chosen for its compatibility with existing TTL production facilities.

An I²L circuit's high packing density is due mainly to the simplicity of designing with a single transistor gate. In the accompanying illustration, for example—working from the bottom up in the cross-section of an I²L gate—the n+ substrate serves not only as the structural base for fabrication, but also as a common ground plane to interconnect all the grounded-emitter transistor gates. This eliminates the need for any surface metallization for ground interconnections. Likewise, the thick n-type epitaxial layer, grown on top of the n+ substrate, serves not only as the grounded-emitter region of the vertical npn switch, but also as the grounded-base region of the lateral pnp injector.

Continuing upward in the cross-section, the first of the two diffusions serves as the p-base region of the vertical npn, and also as the p-collector region of the lateral pnp injector. The second diffusion completes the I²L gate by providing the multiple-collector n+ regions of the vertical npn.

Metallization is then deposited and etched to provide interconnection between various I²L transistor gates. Note that the lateral pnp is integrated into the vertical npn structure and therefore does not exist as a discrete component. Furthermore, a single lateral pnp can be utilized as a current injector for multiple npn gages as long as symmetry in the layout is maintained to avoid current-hogging. Density is enhanced by the simplicity of a single-transistor gate requiring no component isolation.

The similarity existing between I²L and TTL circuits is worth noting. This, essentially, is in the similarity between the basic multi-collector I²L transistor and the common multi-emitter TTL transistor. The I²L multi-collector regions correspond to TTL's multi-emitters, the I²L and TTL bases occupy similar regions, while the I²L emitter and TTL collector reside in the deepest n regions. An I²L multicollector transistor is, in essence, a TTL multi-emitter transistor operated upside down. Transistor logic in I²L structures is implemented by controlling inverse beta, while in TTL structures the forward beta is controlled.

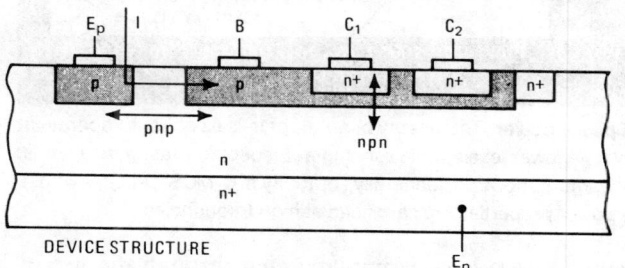

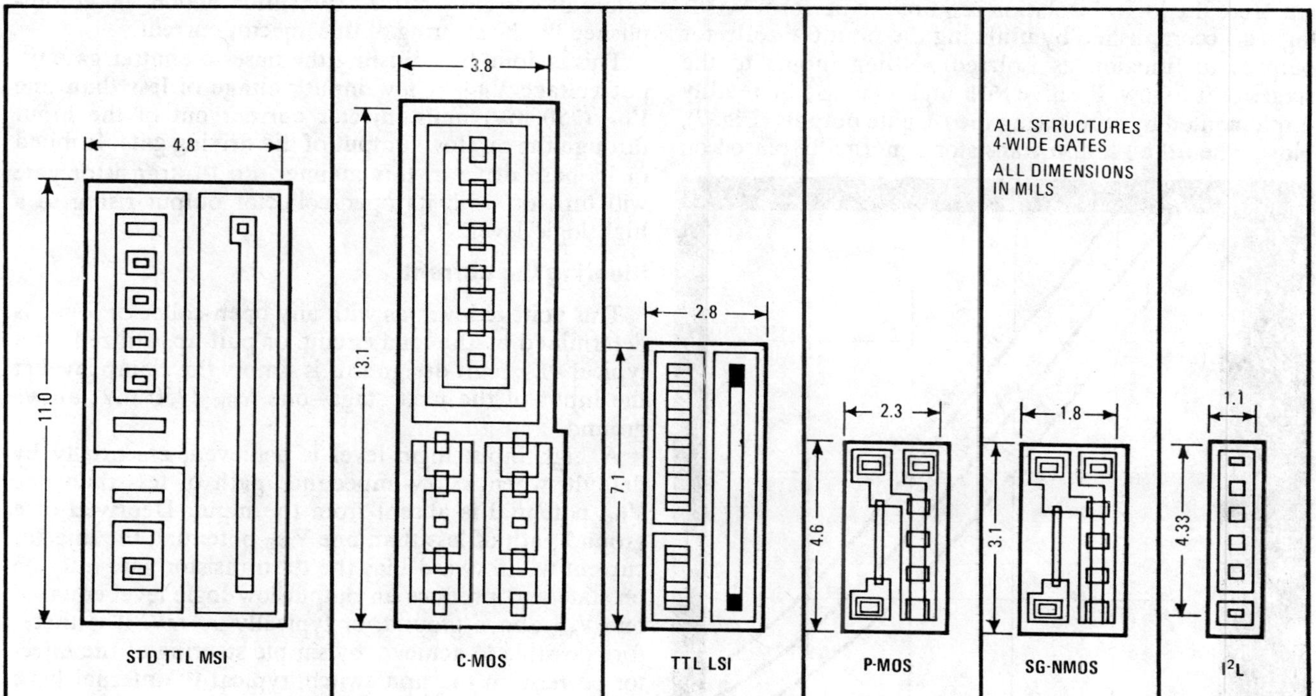

DEVICE STRUCTURE

	STD TTL MSI	C-MOS	TTL LSI	P-MOS	SG-NMOS	I²L
GATE AREA (SQ MILS)	52.8	49.8	19.9	10.6	5.6	4.8
NUMBER OF COMPONENTS	3	3	3	2	2	1
MASK STEPS	7	6	7	4	7	4
NUMBER OF DIFFUSIONS	4	3	4	1	3	2

3. Shaping up. An I²L gate fabricated with non-isolated elements saves space and is simple to build, compared to other techniques. It's simpler than all but p-MOS gates and its 5 square mil area makes it the smallest. All structures shown are 4-wide gates.

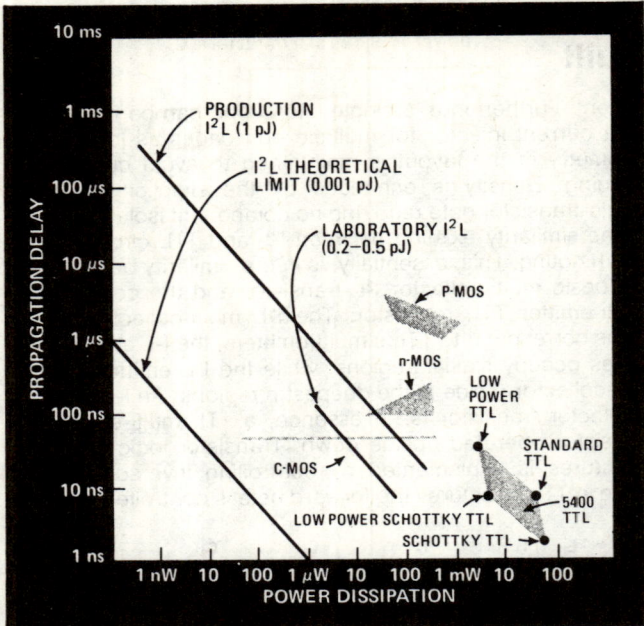

4. Speed/power. The beauty of an I²L gate is its ability to operate at very low power levels while running at respectably fast gate speeds. The same is not true, generally, of today's C-MOS circuits, whose low power properties are sacrificed at high frequencies.

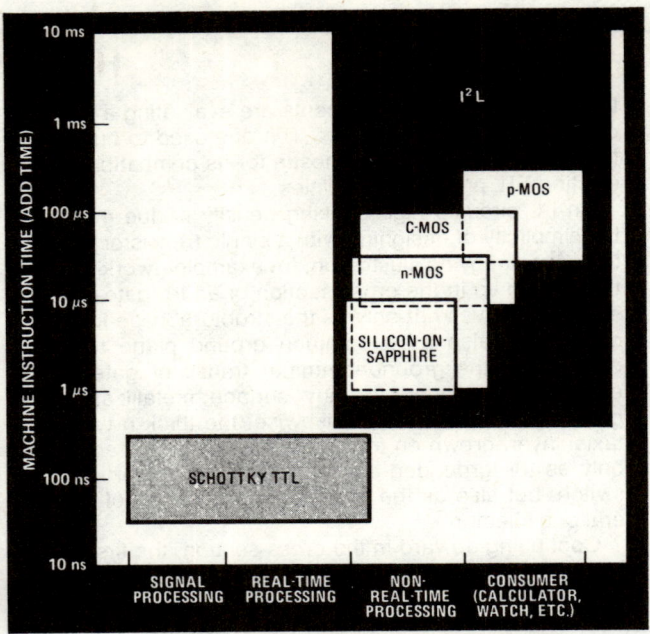

5. Tomorrow. An I²L microprocessor potentially can take over all jobs now being done by MOS units. This includes non-real-time and consumer-type applications. What's more, I²L does overlap into real-time—processing jobs now being handled by TTL products.

positive NAND logic is implemented through the use of a multiple-collector npn switch functioning as an inverter. Here the logical isolation required to perform NAND logic is accomplished by utilizing the multiple-collector outputs to function as isolated ANDing inputs to the stages that follow. Positive NOR logic can also be readily implemented by wire-ORing the I²L gate outputs (Fig. 7). Now, when the I²L npn transistor is normally biased on (low output) by a lateral pnp current-injector transistor, which is connected between the base of the npn and an external current source, switching action is accomplished by the steering of this injector current.

This is done by adjusting the base-to-emitter gate input voltage V_{BE}. A low input voltage of less than one V_{BE} (750 mV) pulls injector current out of the input through the on (low) output of the driving gate. Robbed of its base drive in this manner, an I²L transistor gate will turn off with its open-collector output rising to a high logic level.

Steering the current

This voltage level, as with any open-collector logic, is determined by the load circuit, or pull-up, utilized. In a typical I²L circuit design this is simply the clamp level at the input of the next stage—one V_{BE} (750 mV) above ground.

A high input logic level is achieved, essentially by default, when a low-impedance path of less than one V_{BE} potential is absent from the input. Deprived of a ground path of less than one V_{BE} potential, the injector current will forward bias the I²L transistor gate into the on state and produce an output low-logic level equal to one V_{sat} above ground, or typically 50 mV. It is therefore possible to achieve, by simple steering of the injector current on the npn switch, typical I²L internal logic swings of 700 mV—this from a V_{sat} of +50 mV to a V_{BE} of +750 mV.

Figure 8 shows how I²L transistor gates are interconnected to perform a basic logic function. The NAND gate logic is that of a common TTL D-type flip-flop. The schematic directly below it shows the same D-type flip-flop in I²L NAND/NOR logic at a component count of one transistor per gate. Directly below the I²L schematic is a

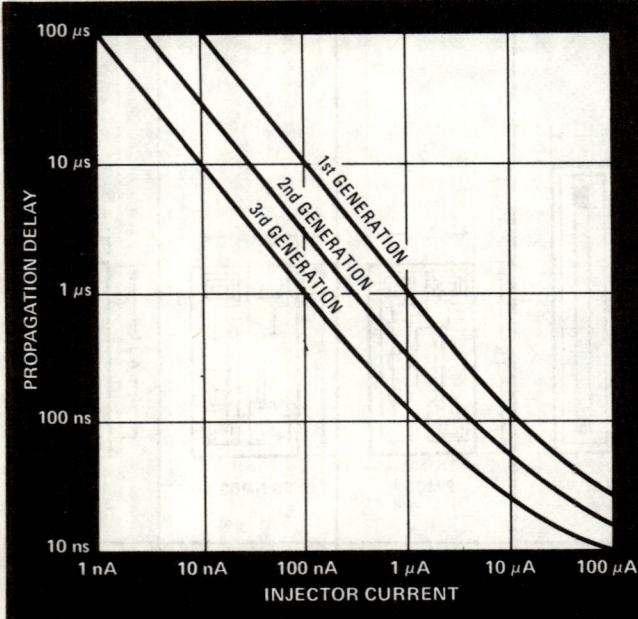

6. Only starting. Impressive as today's production I²L devices are, faster ones are coming. This year's second generation devices and next year's third generation will show steady improvements. Ten-microsecond to 20-nanosecond devices are forseeable.

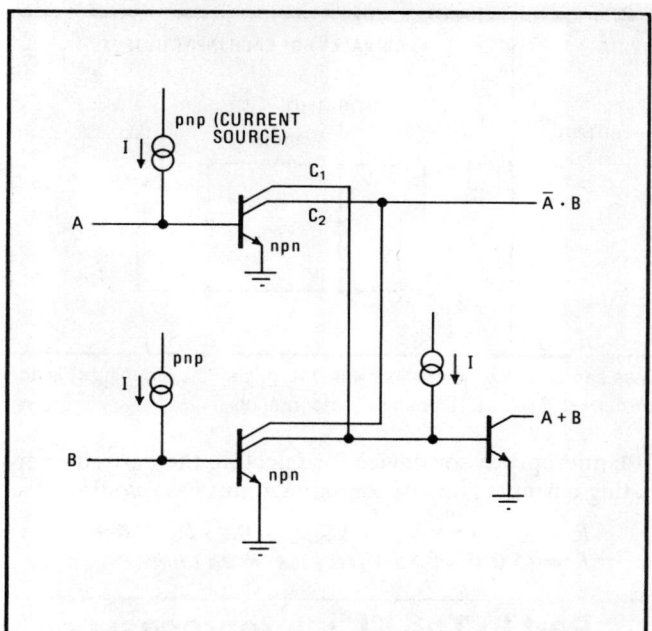

7. Sound logic. NAND functions use the multiple-collector npn switch as an inverter, where logical isolation is obtained by making the collector outputs function as isolated ANDing inputs of the next stages. NOR logic results from WIRE-ORing gate outputs.

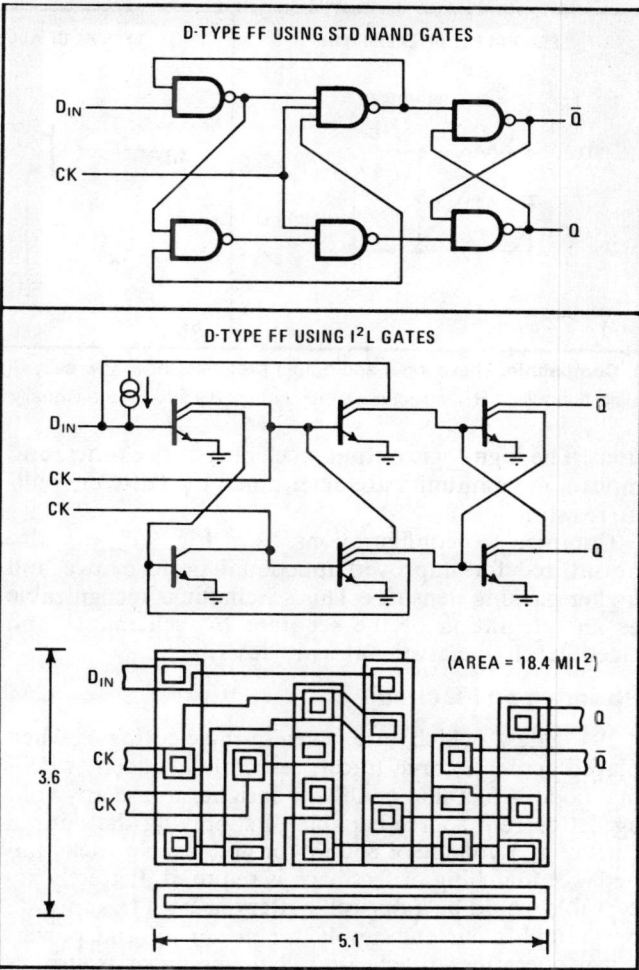

8. Easy fit. Basic to the high packing density of I²L digital circuits is its one-transistor-gate structure. Here a standard D-type flip-flop built with I²L gates takes up less than 20 square mills; it is so small it could fit under a single bonding pad.

scaled topographical drawing of the I²L D-flop. The p-injector used to power the flop is indicated along the drawing's horizontal axis. Note that an entire I²L static flip flop, which would require six 4 by 4 mil bonding pads interfaced to the outside world, would virtually fit under one of those bonding pads. It is this compact geometry that accounts for the high component density of the I²L LSI processor designs currently in production.

All told, practical I²L gates can handle a range of 6 magnitudes or more of injector current—from picoamps to microamps—at speeds ranging from hundreds of microseconds to tens of nanoseconds. They can be powered up for maximum speed, then powered down by a magnitude of 100 to 10,000 without losing functions or data (if they're memories). They do not display increased power dissipation with frequency nor produce the switching noise transients common in standard push-pull logic built with C-MOS or TTL. They require neither gold doping nor Schottky clamping, as does conventional logic in which transistors are easily saturated.

I²L logic is fully static, requiring no multiphase clocks, and temperature stability is superior, with circuits capable of military temperature range operation from −55°C to 125°C.

Designing I²L digital circuits

With the basic gate layouts of Figs. 7 and 8, a designer can use a variety of input/output circuits (Fig. 9). In the I²L microprocessor chip described in this article, input/output characteristics were selected with one objective in mind: full TTL compatibility. The input circuit, shown in Fig. 9(a), is actually an RTL configuration modified for TTL compatibility. An input threshold of nominally +1.5 volts is achieved with two 10-kilohm resistors functioning as a voltage divider, which boosts the one V_{BE} threshold of the input transistor to 1.5 v.

The input electrical characteristics, plotted in Fig. 10(a) as input current vs. input voltage, show the 10 kilohm load line and the threshold knee at +1.5 v. These high-impedance, high-threshold characteristics were chosen to reduce input loading and to increase the input noise margin over a standard TTL input, yet they retain full compatability with all 5-v logic families. The I²L inputs also utilize an input-clamping diode to limit negative excursions, or ringing, on the receiving end of a transmission line.

The output schematic and its characteristics, as shown in Figs. 9(b) and 10(b), are virtually identical to TTL or DTL open collector outputs. When turned on, an I²L open collector output will rapidly fall towards ground potential, producing a low logic level.

Standard design practice for I²L is again patterned after TTL in that I²L outputs are generally over-designed by 100%. While a typical I²L output will sink 40 mA without pulling out of saturation, the outputs of I²L logic circuits are guaranteed to sink 20 mA (10 Schottky TTL loads) at 400 mV maximum under worst-case condi-

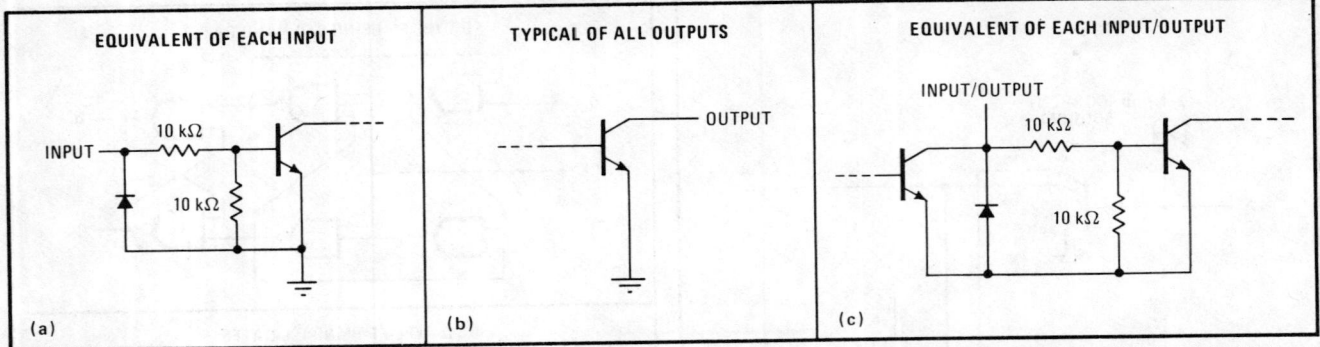

9. Compatible. These input and output sketches show how easy I²L gates can be made compatible with TTL gates. The input in (a) is actually a modified RTL structure, while outputs (b) and (c) are virtually identical with TTL or DTL open-collector outputs.

tions. The high-logic output level, output rise times, and input-noise immunity are determined by a discrete pull-up resistor.

Common I/O configurations, as in Fig. 9(c), can also be utilized for improved functional performance and higher packing densities. This schematic is recognizable as an integration of the separate I/O schematics and electrical characteristics already described.

Powering an I²L circuit

I²L gates, which are current-injected-logic when placed across a curve tracer, resemble a silicon switching diode, a fact that enables a designer to use any vohtage or current source capable of supplying the desired current at a voltage of 850 mV or greater. No tricky impedance matching or feedback is required. Perfectly acceptable would be a dry-cell battery, a 5-V TTL supply, a programable current supply for power-up and power-down operation—practically whatever power source is convenient.

If a 5-V TTL power supply were to be used, for example, a series dropping resistor would be connected between the 5-V supply and the injector pins of a typical I²L microprocessor device for selecting the desired operating current. The resistor value in this case would be:

$$R = E/I, \text{ or } R_{drop} = V_{supply} - 0.85\ V)/150\ mA$$
$$R = (5.0\ V - 0.85\ V)/0.15\ A = 28\ ohms$$

Part II: The I²L microprocessor

The first LSI digital circuit built with non-isolated I²L logic is a microprocessor chip slice designated SBP 0400, which stands for "semiconductor bipolar processor," 400 series. It is a 40-pin, 4-bit microprogramable binary processor element containing more than 1,450 gates—easily the most complex standard product bipolar logic chip built to date.

Containing all the functions required for 4-bit parallel processing (except for sequencing controls), the features of the SBP0400, as shown in the block diagram of Fig. 11, could only be duplicated by using 30 to 40 small and medium-scale TTL integrated circuits.

The chip contains:
- A 16-function symmetrical arithmetic logic unit (ALU) that has full-carry look-ahead logic.

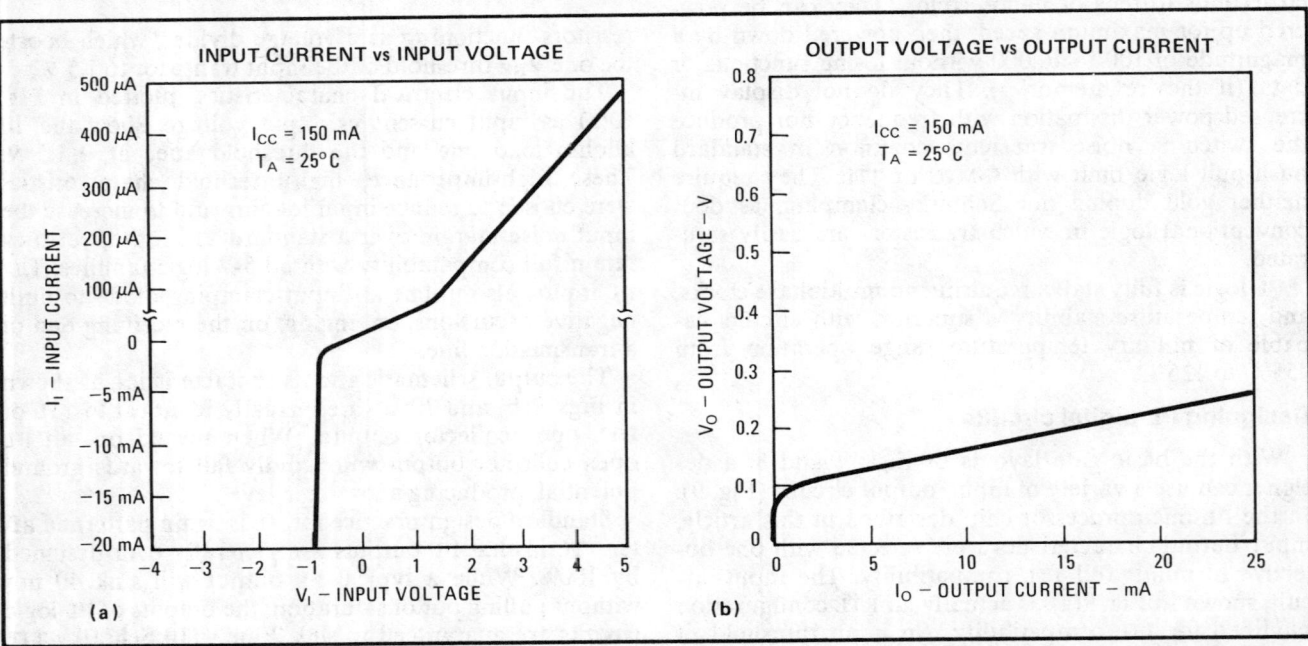

10. Plotting it. Input and output current-voltage characteristics makes designing with I²L a pleasure. The input shows a 10 kilohm load line.

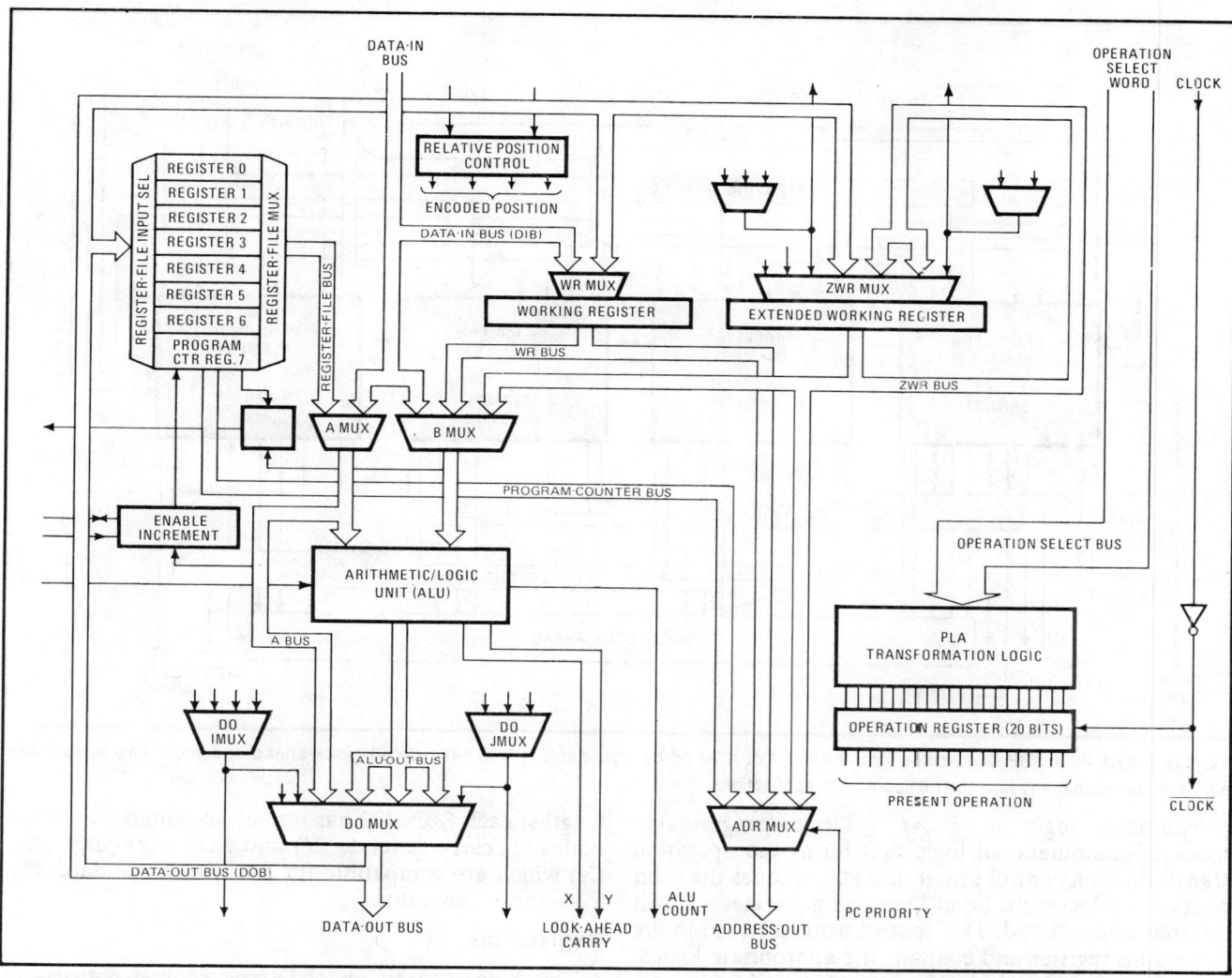

11. Organized. Among the principal blocks of the SPB0400 chip are the 16-function arithmetic logic unit (ALU), and the factory programable logic array (PLA), which provides 512 standard one-clock operations.

- An 8-word general register file that includes a program counter and incrementor.
- Two 4-bit working registers that can handle both single- and double-length operations.
- Scaled-shifting multiplexers enabling the chip to handle a wide variety of interface conditions.
- Finally—and perhaps the most innovative feature—a factory programable logic array (PLA) instead of the usual fixed-size control ROM. The 512 standard operations programed into this on-chip logic array provides a greater degree of instruction capability than is achievable by any other standard bipolar or MOS LSI processor.

This basic 4-bit I²L processor slice is directly expandable in 4 bit multiples—Fig. 12 shows the configuration for a 16-bit system. Like the single 4-bit chip, larger multichip systems provide full-carry look-ahead logic and parallel access to all control, data, and address I/O functions. It is this parallel access, together with the high bipolar speeds (typical propagation time of 110 to 530 ns at power dissipation of 128 mw), that's responsible for the device's short cycle time capability.

Thanks to the program flexibility offered by the PLA and standard micro-programing techniques, this single 4-bit slice offers a designer a repertoire of 512 one-clock operations, from which a wide range of instruction can be implemented. This compares with a fixed instruction capability of less than 80 for today's second generation n-channel microprocessors, and less than 125 basic operations today's TTL bit-slice systems. This large one-clock operation capability means that a wide range of existing designs can be emulated without loss of software compatibility or increased software investment.

Indeed, virtually any set of instructions is available. In a single one-microsecond clock cycle, for example, any one of 459 non-redundant operations can be selected, including such complicated tasks as transferring data from the processor's register to the external memory, or from memory to register, or from register to register; modifications of the operand or combinations of modifications by means of the 8 arithmetic or 8 boolean functions residing in the ALU; single or double precision arithmetic shifts, with protection of single- or double-signed binary words; single or double precision logical shifts, and so on.

Again, the key to the processor's high flexibility is the

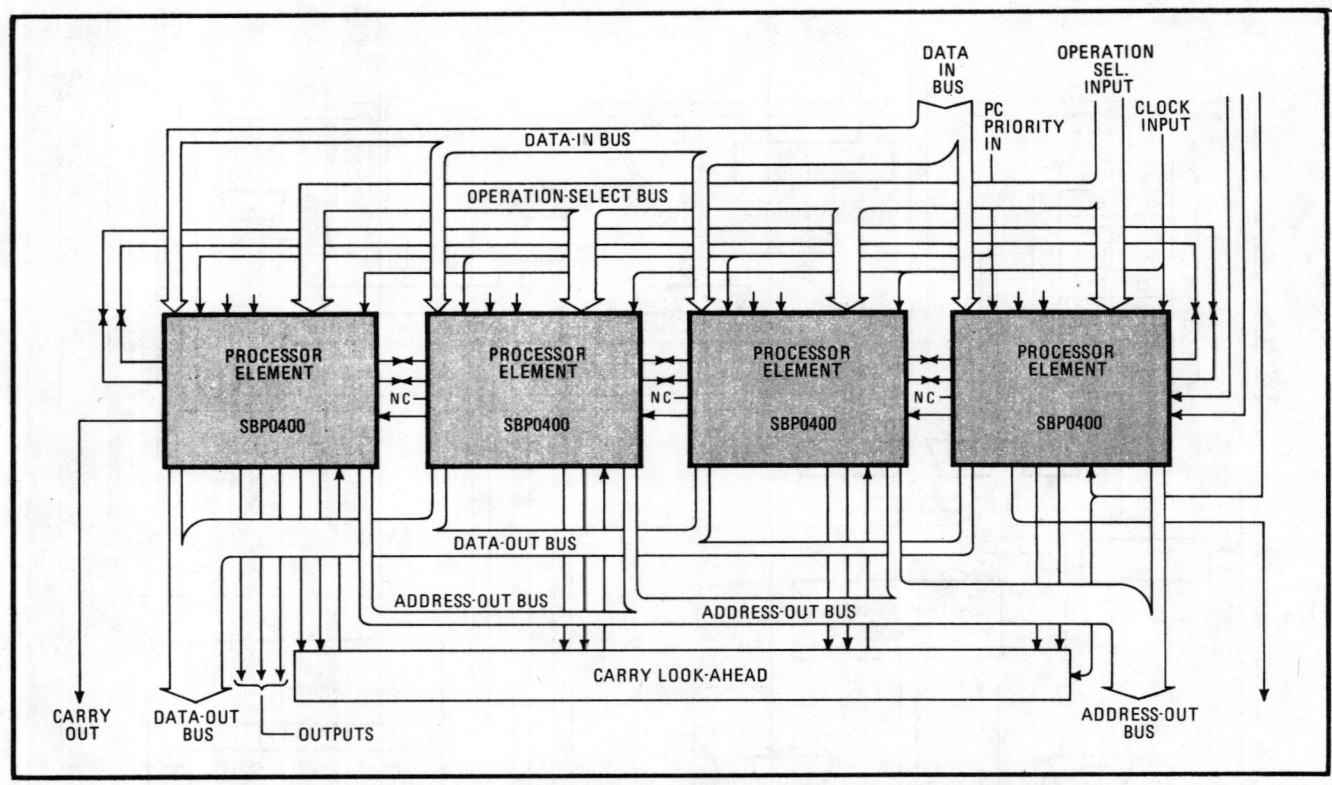

12. Expanded. Four SBP 0400 chips form the heart of a 16-bit parallel machine that has full-carry look-ahead operation. This system can efficiently emulate many low-end minicomputer applications.

programable logic array. As a factory-programable block of combinational logic that forms the operation transformation control center, the PLA decodes the 9-bit operation-select word input lines and generates a 20-bit internal control word. This control word is stored in the operations register and contains the appropriate logical operation—functional-block, bus-enable, and/or bus-select, for execution of the decoded instruction.

Using the processor

The operations register is composed of 20 D-type edge-triggered flip-flops. Upon each positive transition at the clock terminal, the operation register loads the preset PLA output. Loaded, the operations register continuously enables the various functional blocks for execution of the ongoing operation, while the PLA can be receiving the instructions for the next operation.

The 4-bit, parallel, symetrical binary arithmetic logic unit (ALU) meanwhile provides the arithmetic/boolean, operand combination/modification mechanism. The ALU, as directed by the operations register, performs one of eight arithmetic operations, or one of eight boolean operations, on either or both of two operands. The two operands are bused, one to the A input port of the ALU (Fig. 11) via the A bus, and one to the B input port of the ALU via the B bus. The A input port has access to the register-file bus and data-in bus. The B input port has access to the data-in, working-register and extend-working-register buses.

The SBP0400 has accommodations for ALU ripple carry-in and ALU ripple carry-out. To facilitate look-ahead generation across larger word sizes (over 8-bit lengths) each SBP0400 has output accommodations for both ALU carry-generate (Y) and ALU carry-propagate (X) which are compatible for use with a standard TTL look-ahead generator.

Register file

This 8-word, 4-bit set of D-type general registers is controlled by the operations register. The registers can be used as temporary storage for source data needed in existing processor routines.

An additional register file (location seven) has the added capability of performing as a program counter. Accessed in the same manner as the other files, RF7 is not only presettable but it can also be controlled externally for incrementation by one or two on the next clock transition. This capability is available at the program-counter-carry-in input and the increment-by-one-or-two input.

In addition to the integral operation (pipelining) register, implementation of overlapping instruction fetch and execute commands is further simplified as the content of the program counter is directly available at the address-out bus (AOB). Regardless of the conditions established by the present instruction, a PC priority input overrides and routes the PC data on the AOB input terminal.

For cascading purposes, the most significant output bit at intermediate and least significant package positions is available at the PCCOUT terminal. Depending on the significance of the SBP0400's relative position, these functions are under the control of the POSO and PSOI inputs. □

Schottky-TTL controller put on a chip

Four-bit microcontroller can do job of 24 TTL MSI packages and uses less power; it emulates midicomputer systems with a fraction of the DIP count

by Laurence Altman, Solid State Editor, Electronics

Large-scale integration, until recently a technology of benefit only to MOS-circuit manufacturers, has been adapted to bipolar data-processing circuitry—with significant results. Monolithic Memories, Sunnyvale, Calif., has built a bipolar microcontroller—a complete 4-bit Schottky LSI processor slice on a single chip. It can do the job of 24 TTL MSI packages and save 6 watts of power in the process. Indeed, with a gate complexity of 1,000 (the largest bipolar processor chip available), the 5701/6701 microcontroller with only 28 packages can emulate a Nova-level computer, whereas a typical Nova's CPU board requires 175 packages.

Dale Williams, marketing manager, claims that the 6701 is "ideal for upgrading or replacing existing computers because no new software is needed, and it's extremely flexible. Since the microcontroller is 4-bit expandable, machines in all classes can be emulated with a minimum number of packages—from 8-bit single-chip MOS processors, such as Intel's 8080, to the higher-performing 8-bit multichip minicomputers, right up through the 16-bit midimachines. Even the 32-bit maxis, such as the IBM-360 types, are in the 6701 range."

The 6701 microcontroller contains an impressive array of circuitry; bit shifters, a multiport 16-by-4 RAM, control registers, multiplexers, arithmetic/logic unit, and 352 bits of ROM, in addition to clocks and output-control drivers. A total of 256 instructions is possible, providing full arithmetic, logic, and shifting capabilities. There are 16 directly addressable two-port general-purpose accumulators, and a separate accumulator-extension register.

The two-address capability of the 6701 (ability to work on two accumulators simultaneously) and the powerful microinstructions permit design of hard-wired central processors having sub-microsecond cycle times or the efficient emulation of conventional machines through use of read-only memories for microprograming. The microcontroller will handle the data-flow section of

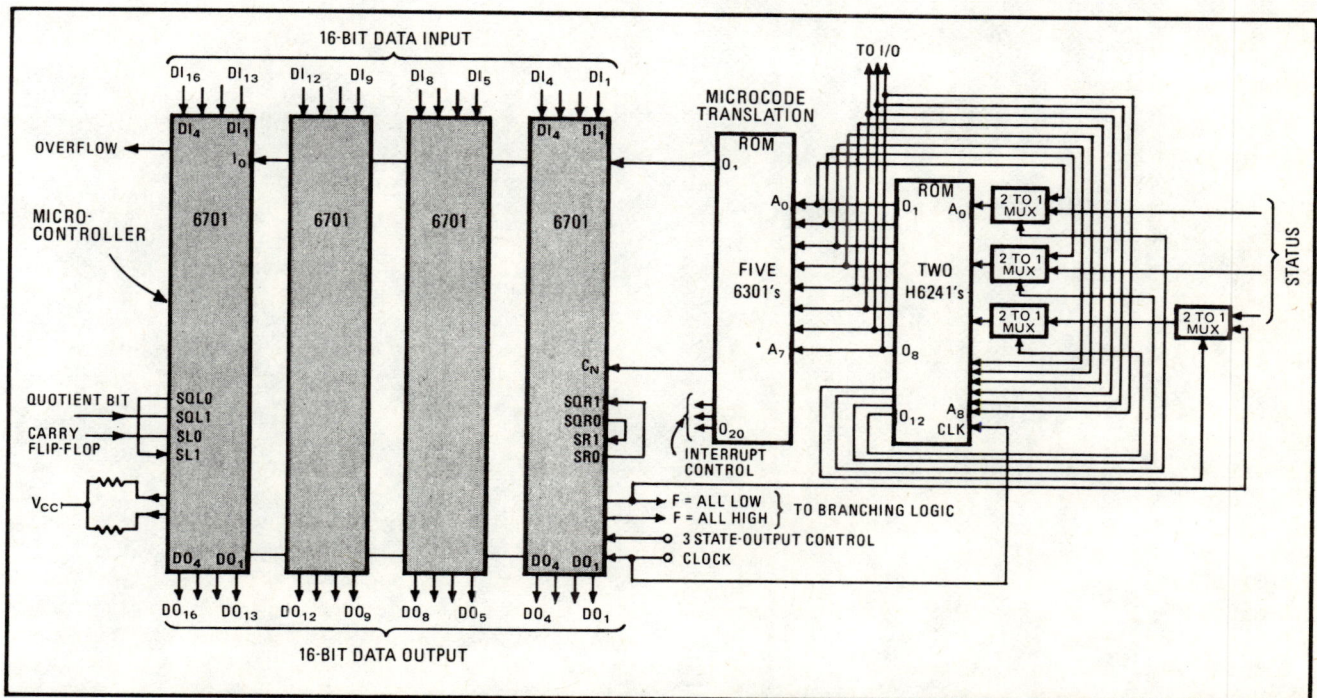

Low count. Typical special-purpose microprocessor has four 4-bit controllers, five 6301 ROMs, two H6241 ROMs, four TTL shift registers

most computers, since it is expandable to handle any word length in increments of 4 bits without significant speed degradation (look-ahead outputs are available). The 16 on-chip general-purpose accumulators give the microcontroller the type of central processor usually found only in high-performance 16-bit minicomputers and 24- or 32-bit computers.

The microcontroller can be thought of as a general-purpose 4-bit register and arithmetic/logic unit with separate A operand, B operand, and data-in and data-out ports. Additional accumulators or registers can be added by tying off-chip packages to the microcontroller's data-in pins.

When compared with its TTL MSI equivalent, the single-chip microcontroller has 350 fewer input-output pins and 19 are replaced—14 16-pin packages and five 24-pin packages. In board area, this saves about 40 square inches. To emulate the Nova-class minicomputer, for example, would require only four 6701 controllers, 14 ROMs or programable ROMs, say of the 5301/6301 type, four or five registers, three gates, and two multiplexers—a total package count of only 27 or 28.

Besides package reductions, instruction times in 6701 systems are reduced, as well—following from the 6701's speedy 150-ns cycle time. A jump, for example, is done in two microcycles that take 400 ns, compared to Nova 800's 800-ns jump time. Jump-to-subroutine takes 3 microcycles or a total of 600 ns, compared to Nova's 800 ns, Monolithic Memories says.

"Aside from emulating existing machines," asserts Williams, "the 6701 will also be useful in new applications, such as tape and disk controllers, point-of-sale terminals, process-machine control, word-processing and navigation systems, intelligent terminals, game machines, and traffic-control systems—anywhere high computer performance is required in small space using a minimal number of packages."

Part 2

Designing with Microprocessors

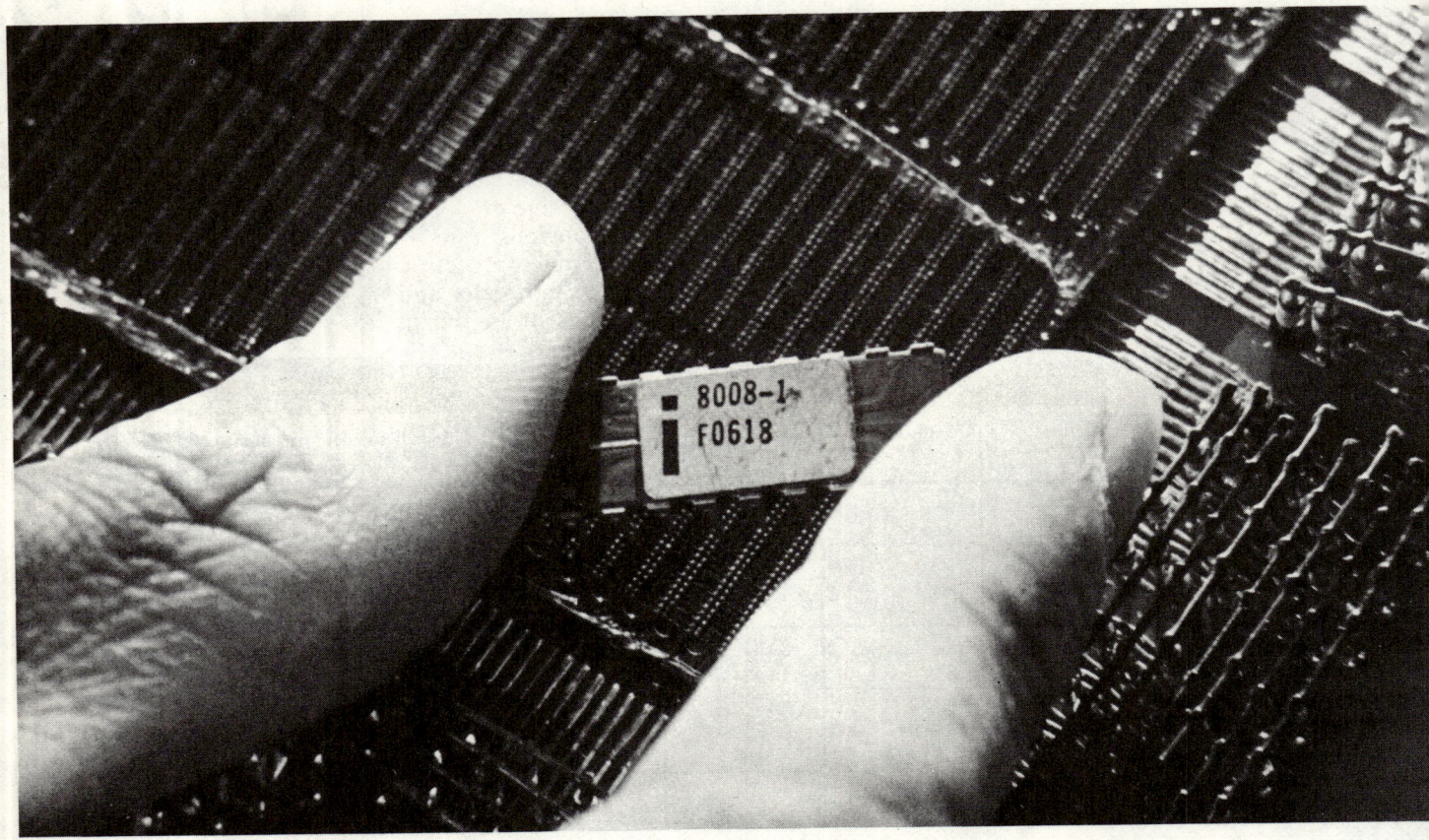

Designing with microprocessors instead of wired logic asks more of designers

When engineers accustomed to hardware logic gates tackle a job with the new microprocessors—as they're almost sure to do sooner or later—they'll need to know some of these programing techniques

by Bruce Gladstone, *Varitel Inc., Sherman Oaks, Calif.*

☐ The microprocessors recently introduced by various semiconductor companies foreshadow wide changes in the design of many electronic products and systems. These miniature computers substitute programing for logic design—an alternative that seems to surface for all but tiny specialized systems and ultrahigh-speed systems. The primary advantage of microprocessors is the short design turnaround time they make possible.

But to realize this advantage, as well as the corollary advantages of easy field alterations and inexpensive customizing, the logic or system designer will need to use new tools—some of which may be unfamiliar to him. Thus, instead of gate networks, he will use masks, comparisons, and jumps; and instead of time delays, he will use circulating loops.

Basically a microprocessor is no more—and no less—than a full-fledged processing unit essentially like the processor at the center of any computer system of any size. It has three major differences from a conventional processor: it is fabricated entirely as one integrated circuit or as a small number of such circuits; it is relatively slow, compared to most minicomputers, partly to enable its fabrication as an IC; and it sells for $300 or less. Required with the microprocessor in any working system are a read-write memory for data, another memory—possibly read/write but usually read-only—for a program, and circuits for obtaining access to limited-performance input/output gear. Generally, these peripheral circuits, each on its own IC, are used in larger quantities than the microprocessors, so that the working system fills up one or more good-sized printed-circuit boards.

When a designer uses a microprocessor instead of hard-wired logic, he determines the system functions by a program—a sequence of instructions—stored in a memory. If he uses a read-only memory, the program is immune to inadvertent alteration. Replacing the program can completely alter the function of the machine that contains the microprocessor.

Using a genuine read-only memory, of course, would run counter to the flexibility advantages of using a microprocessor, except in large-volume applications. But using a programable read-only memory, or better yet, a reprogramable read-only memory, allows an existing system to be altered quickly—in a matter of hours. As a result, a manufacturer can become much more responsive to his market.

Microprocessor characteristics

The most significant characteristics of today's microprocessors (not counting calculator sets and serial processors) are their speed, addressing modes, interrupt capabilities, and the number of internal registers. These and other characteristics are summarized in the table on this page.

The value of speed, in those applications that require it, is obvious. (Some techniques for speeding up the slower microprocessors are described later.) The more addressing modes and the more internal registers that are present in the microprocessors, the less external

TABLE 1. MICROPROCESSOR CHARACTERISTICS

		Intel MCS-4	Rockwell PPS	Intel MCS-8	Intel 8080	Signetics PIP	National GPC/P	AMI 7300
Word size (bits)		4	4	8	8	8	4-16	8
Instruction time (microseconds)		10.8 – 21.6	5 – 10	7.5–22.5 12–44 (Note 1)	2–6	<5 – <10	3.3 – 9.6	4- 32 (Note 2)
Memory size	Pgm	4,096 bytes	16,384 bytes	16,384 bytes	65,536 bytes	8,192 bytes	65,536 bytes	4,096 words (Note 4)
	Data	1280 nibbles (Note 3)	8,192 nibbles (Note 3)					65,536 bytes
No. of instructions		45	54	48	48+	64	Micro- program	Micro- program
Interrupt capability		Reset to 0 only	None	1-level vector to 8 locations	Multi- level vector to 8 locations	1-level stack to store machine state	1-level stack to store machine state (Note 5)	3-level
Address modes		Pointer Indirect Immediate Register	Pointer Immediate	Pointer Immediate Register	Pointer Immediate Register	Direct Indirect Relative Immediate Register Indexed	Direct Indirect Relative Immediate Register Indexed	Direct Indirect Relative Immediate Register Indexed
Registers		16 x 4 bits pc + 3 stack	2 x 4 bits pc + 2 stack 1 pointer	5 x 8 bits pc + 7 stack 1 pointer	5 x 8 bits pc + unlimited stack 1 pointer (Note 6)	4 x 8 bits pc + 7 stack	4 x 16 bits pc + 16 stack (Note 7)	16 x 8 bits pc + 32 x 8 stack (Note 7)
RAM & ROM		Special or standard (Note 8)	Special	Standard	Standard	Standard	Standard	Standard and special microprogram
TTL chips		Clock only	None	20–40	Clock & buffers	4–6	15–20	Clock & buffers

Notes: (1) 8008-1 instruction times are 0.6 x (8008 instruction times).
(2) Executes microinstructions from 512 x 22 microprogramed ROM at 4 μs/microinstruction.
(3) One nibble = 4 bits = ½ byte
(4) Microprogram
(5) Conditional jump MUX external to chips allows 2-level interrupt very simply.
(6) Pc stack is stored in main memory and is accessible to programer
(7) Stack is general-purpose to store pc, registers, and flags.
(8) 4008 & 4009 chips allow easy interface to standard RAM & ROM

memory capacity is likely to be required. The requirement for external memory is important because, in most systems, the memory cost dominates all other considerations. If the microprocessor can handle interrupts, it can perform more than one task at a time, and it can also do single tasks more quickly because it can overlap processing and input/output.

Many microprocessors, as indicated in the table, have a pointer-address mode. This permits a machine with a short word length to address a large memory array. And because such large arrays may require more bits in an address representation than can be contained in an instruction word, the address is kept in a special register or pair of registers preloaded by an instruction in the program. Subsequent instructions then refer to locations in the memory, which are addressed by the contents of the pointer register. However, the preloading instruction adds to the overhead in machine operation, reducing the over-all performance.

Some microprocessors also have immediate and indirect-address modes. These modes are to be distinguished from direct addressing—the simplest and most common. In any processor, an instruction word consists of an operation code (op code) and an operand code (that which is to be operated upon). When the operand code is a direct address, the processor executes the instruction on data in the location specified by that address (Fig. 1). When the operand code is an immediate address, the processor executes the instruction on the operand code itself. And when the operand code is an indirect address, the processor executes the instruction on data found at the address specified by the operand.

Indirect addressing and pointer addressing are similar, except that the address pointer is in an internal register instead of in a main-memory location. The particular mode of address is identified by the op code itself or by a flag bit associated with the op code.

Indirect addressing is a powerful tool in all software systems. It's particularly powerful in minicomputers, where the limited word length prevents direct access to more than a small part of the memory, and for the same reason, it can be equally powerful in microprocessors.

Some microprocessors are microprogramed—that is, their control sequences are stored in read-only memories in the same way as object programs, which determine each machine's function. These microprograms are functionally similar to those used in large machines and minicomputers, in which, during the last few years, they have largely replaced hard-wired control.

Available software is an important aspects of the use of microprocessors. Writing a program in machine language (directly in binary notation) is—like walking from Portland, Maine, to Portland, Ore.—not impossible, but exceedingly difficult. At the very least, an assembler or cross-assembler is necessary to convert a program written in a symbolic language into machine language. Even new assemblers are written in symbolic notation.

An assembler is executed on the same machine that is to run the object program; a cross-assembler would be executed on a different machine—most likely a minicomputer—but would produce a machine-language program that is executable on the microprocessor. Simulators, debuggers, and canned subroutines are other desirable software packages. Here, a microprogramed

1. Address modes. Three ways of addressing memory are in common use, and some microprocessors use all three. Direct mode is the simplest, immediate is handy when working with constants, and indirect often simplifies the handling of subroutines.

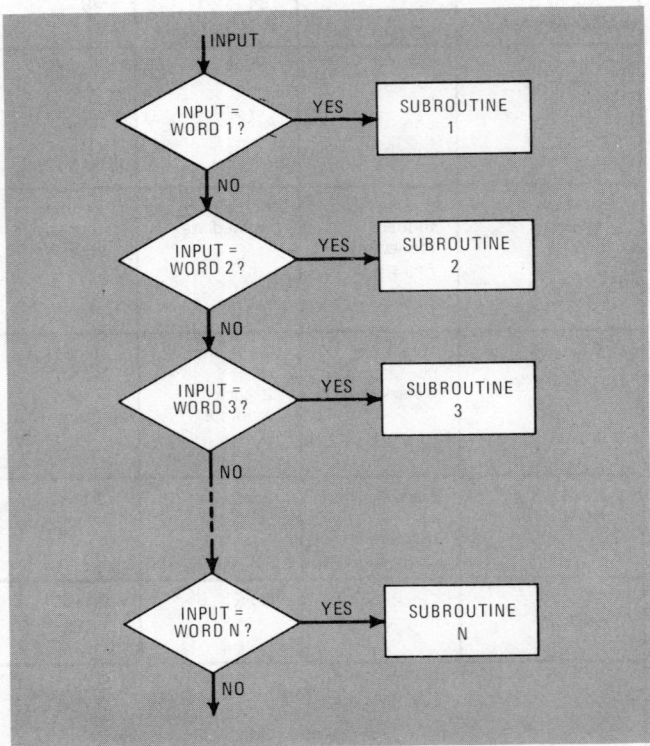

2. Sequential test. An external signal can be identified and used to trigger an internal routine by comparing it successively with several test words. A match causes a program jump out of comparing sequence to a subroutine that processes the external signal.

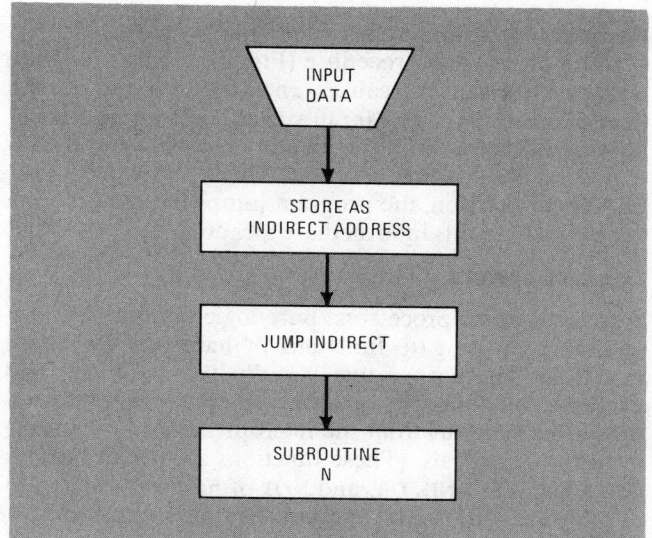

3. Indirect jump. To simplify the task of locating a subroutine, sometimes an incoming signal can itself identify the location, and the program jumps indirectly to the subroutine via the input buffer.

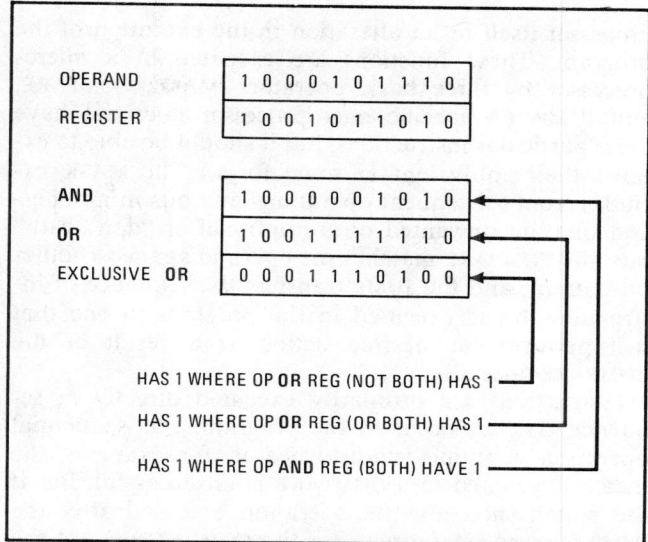

4. Logic operations. These instructions can be used to mask certain unwanted bits in a register or to generate signals that are to be sent outside the microprocessor.

microprogram has a distinct advantage—because the microprogram can be recast to make one machine emulate another, the microprocessor may be able to utilize existing software at minimal cost.

Design tools

Logic designers are accustomed to using a number of standard tools, including gate networks, time delays, counters, and discrete input/output controls. Each of these has its counterpart in a microprocessor program, but applying the programed counterparts by rote may yield an uneconomical solution to a design problem. However, careful analysis of requirements and knowledge of microprocessor programing techniques will simplify design of an optimum system.

For example, programed logic is time-shared—it works only when the program reaches a particular point in its execution. But gate networks are always available; when the correct combination of inputs appears, they generate outputs, whether the rest of the system is ready for them or not.

Gate networks consist of ANDs, ORs, and NOTs; their inputs combine in the way determined by the combination of logic blocks to produce either an output from the

---

Features of microprocessors

Two widely used microprocessors are the Intel 4-bit MCS-4 and 8-bit MCS-8 chip sets, which can be put together in various combinations to produce systems of different capabilities.[2,3] The processor chips in these two sets are, respectively, the 4004 and the 8008, for which several program routines are listed in this article. To make these routines more intelligible, brief functional descriptions of these two chips follow.

The Intel 4004 contains five functional sections: an address register and stack with an address-incrementing circuit, a set of 16 4-bit registers for indexing and general-purpose temporary storage, a 4-bit arithmetic and logic unit, an 8-bit instruction register and decoder, and peripheral circuitry.

The 16-bit registers and the instruction register are the most important sections in the present context. The index registers can be used either singly for temporary storage during computations, or in pairs to address memory and to store data fetched from the read-only memory.

The 8-bit instruction register can hold at any one time a 4-bit operation code and a 4-bit operand. Some instructions in the 4004 are of double length (16 bits instead of 8), have multiple operands, and are stored in successive read-only memory locations; they take two system cycles for execution instead of one.

The 4004 has a total of 45 instructions in its repertoire, plus a no-operation dummy instruction that uses up one instruction cycle but doesn't do anything. The 4-bit operand code in an instruction can specify, among other things, one of the 16 individual registers, or, with 3 bits, one of the eight register pairs. The upper end (most significant bits) of the register pair is the same as one of the even-numbered individual registers.

The Intel 8008 contains four functional sections: an instruction register, a local memory, an arithmetic-logic unit, and input/output buffers. The arithmetic-logic unit includes four control flip-flops—carry, zero, sign, and parity—which indicate conditions that arise during each instruction execution and are the basis for executing subsequent conditional jumps.

Part of the local memory consists of seven 8-bit registers. Of these, one, designated A, is the accumulator, which contains one of the operands and the result of every arithmetic operation. Four others, registers B, C, D, and E, may be used for any temporary storage, while the remaining two, registers H and L, contain respectively the high- and low-order bits of an indirect address in external memory. (Because external memory is limited to 16,384 words, addressed by 14 bits, register H in this application contains only 6 bits.)

processor itself or an alteration in the execution of the program. These functions are executed in a microprocessor by three basic operators—MASK, COMPARE, and JUMP. (A specific microprocessor may not have these particular instructions, but it should be able to execute their equivalent in some form.) The MASK excludes from subsequent operations any bits in an operand that are unwanted or are optional or "don't-care" bits, the COMPARE matches the operand against another bit pattern, and the JUMP transfers the sequence of instructions being executed in the program to one that will perform the desired action as a result of the COMPARE operation.

Instructions are ordinarily executed directly in sequence, as they occur in the program; this sequential operation continues undisturbed if, for example, the match attempted in a COMPARE is unsuccessful. But if the match succeeds, the operation executed after the JUMP (second operation after the COMPARE) is not the one immediately following the JUMP (Fig. 2). Here the microprocessor receives a signal from the outside world. This signal may be a pulse or level on a single wire, a series of pulses placed in order in a shift register to create a processor word, or a word received simultaneously in parallel on a group of wires.

This input, in whatever form, is compared successively with each of several previously stored words in the memory. Whenever any comparison shows that the input and a stored word are equal, the program, instead of executing the next comparison, jumps directly to a sub-routine stored elsewhere in the memory. The address of the beginning of this subroutine is the JUMP instruction's operand. Although the diagram doesn't show it, in many applications the subroutine would return to the next comparison at its completion.

In an alternative procedure (Fig. 3), the input signal, whatever its nature, causes an indirect jump to the proper subroutine. The input signal loads an address in a particular location in the memory, which is not the location of the JUMP instruction. Then, following a successful comparison, the program jumps indirectly to the subroutine via this intermediate location.

Logic operators

In some microprocessors, pure logic operators, corresponding to the gate functions of hardware logic, are available. These operators, usually the AND, OR, and exclusive-OR functions, are convenient to generate signals to be sent out from the microprocessor in response to incoming signals. (These functions are not to be confused with the AND, OR, and NOT of hardware logic.) In a program, the AND operator is the most straightforward way to perform the MASK function.

Logic operators retain 1 bits in a specified register where called for by logic 1 bits in the operand (Fig. 4)—in both the register and the operand for an AND, in either that register or the operand, or both, for an OR, and in either that register or the operand, but not both, for an exclusive-OR.

Not all microprocessors have all three of these logic operators in their instruction sets, but the designer will

TABLE 2. JUMP INDIRECT ROUTINE (INTEL 4004 CODING)		
Mnemonic	Operand	Action
FIM	1P 2	FETCH IMMEDIATE, A TWO-WORD INSTRUCTION; TRANSFERS CONTENTS OF 2ND WORD TO REGISTER PAIR SPECIFIED BY OPERAND IN FIRST WORD. (P IN AN OPERAND DESIGNATES A REGISTER PAIR.) HERE REGISTER PAIR 1 IS LOADED WITH THE NUMBER 2 -- AN ARBITRARY NUMBER THAT DEPENDS ON PREVIOUS ACTIONS IN A PROGRAM OF WHICH THIS ROUTINE IS A PART.
SRC	1P	SEND REGISTER CONTROL; ADDRESSES THE READ-ONLY OR READ-WRITE MEMORY WITH THE CONTENTS OF THE REGISTER PAIR SPECIFIED. HERE PAIR 1 IS SPECIFIED; SINCE PAIR 1 WAS PREVIOUSLY LOADED WITH THE NUMBER 2, MEMORY LOCATION 2 IS CALLED FOR.
RDR		READ DATA FROM THE SELECTED MEMORY LOCATION INTO THE ACCUMULATOR.
XCH	4	EXCHANGE THE CONTENTS OF THE ACCUMULATOR AND THE INDEX REGISTER SPECIFIED. HERE REGISTER 4 IS SPECIFIED; IT IS THE UPPER HALF OF PAIR 2. THUS WHATEVER WAS READ FROM MEMORY IS NOW IN REGISTER 4.
JIN	2P	JUMP INDIRECT TO THE ADDRESS CONTAINED IN REGISTER PAIR SPECIFIED -- HERE PAIR 2. PAIR 2 COMPRISES REGISTERS 4 AND 5; SINCE REGISTER 4 CONTAINS A NUMBER BROUGHT FROM MEMORY, AND REGISTER 5 IS EMPTY, PAIR 2 CONTAINS A MULTIPLE OF 16. THE JUMP IS TO THE BEGINNING OF A 16-WORD SUBROUTINE.

TABLE 3. LOOPING ROUTINE — MULTIPLE WORD TEST (INTEL 8008 CODING)		
Mnemonic	Operand	Action
LCI		LOAD REGISTER IMMEDIATE (2 WORDS). HERE DATA FROM THE 2ND WORD OF INSTRUCTION IS PLACED IN REGISTER C.
LLI		THE SAME; REGISTER L.
LHI		THE SAME; REGISTER H.
INP	1	READ DATA SUPPLIED BY INPUT DEVICE 1 INTO ACCUMULATOR (REGISTER A).
NDM		FORM LOGIC "AND" OF MEMORY LOCATION SPECIFIED BY CONTENTS OF REGISTERS H&L WITH ACCUMULATOR.
INL		INCREMENT REGISTER L, TO SPECIFY LOCATION OF TEST WORD.
CPM		COMPARE CONTENTS OF MEMORY LOCATION SPECIFIED BY H&L WITH THE ACCUMULATOR; IF THEY ARE EQUAL, SET THE ZERO CONDITION FLIP-FLOP.
JTZ	MATCH	CONDITIONAL JUMP, A 3-WORD INSTRUCTION; JUMP TO INSTRUCTION (SYMBOLIC ADDRESS "MATCH") SPECIFIED BY 2ND AND 3RD WORDS OF THIS INSTRUCTION IF THE ZERO FLIP-FLOP IS ON.
DCC		DECREMENT REGISTER C; IF RESULT IS ZERO, SET THE ZERO FLIP-FLOP.
JTZ	NMATCH	CONDITIONAL JUMP TO THE FIRST INSTRUCTION (SYMBOLIC ADDRESS "NMATCH") OF NEXT ROUTINE.
INL		INCREMENT REGISTER L AGAIN.
JMP	*-12	UNCONDITIONAL JUMP, A 3-WORD INSTRUCTION, TO THE ADDRESS SPECIFIED BY THE 2ND AND 3RD WORDS; * MEANS THIS INSTRUCTION AND *-12 MEANS THE INSTRUCTION 12 WORDS BACK -- THE "INP" INSTRUCTION.

TABLE 4. LOOPING ROUTINE — TIME RELAY
(INTEL 4004 CODING)

Mnemonic	Operand	Action
FIM	OP 12	FETCH IMMEDIATE (2 WORDS). LOADS 2ND WORD OF INSTRUCTION -- 12 -- INTO REGISTER PAIR SPECIFIED -- PAIR 0.
ISZ	0 *	INCREMENT AND SKIP IF ZERO (2 WORDS). INCREMENT CONTENTS OF REGISTER SPECIFIED IN OPERAND OF FIRST WORD, AND IF THE RESULT IS 0, EXECUTE THE NEXT INSTRUCTION IN SEQUENCE (SKIPPING 2ND WORD OF THIS INSTRUCTION). IF THE RESULT IS NOT 0, JUMP TO THE ADDRESS SPECIFIED IN THE 2ND WORD. HERE THAT ADDRESS IS THIS INSTRUCTION'S OWN, INDICATED BY *, SO IT KEEPS JUMPING BACK TO ITSELF UNTIL REGISTER 0 AGAIN CONTAINS 0 -- 16 REPETITIONS.
ISZ	1 *-2	INCREMENT AND SKIP IF 0 (2 WORDS). THIS HAPPENS JUST ONCE BEFORE RETURNING TO THE PREVIOUS ISZ FOR 16 MORE REPEATS, AND FOUR TIMES BEFORE EXITING PERMANENTLY -- A TOTAL OF 64 STEPS IN THE DOUBLE LOOP.
BBL	0	BRANCH BACK AND LOAD; THE OPERAND IS PLACED IN THE ACCUMULATOR. THIS RETURNS TO THE ROUTINE DELAYED BY THIS DOUBLE LOOP; THE 0 OPERAND CLEARS THE ACCUMULATOR.

TABLE 5. DISCRETE EXTERNAL CONTROLS — LAMP BANK
(INTEL 8008 CODING)

Mnemonic	Operand	Action
LAC		LOAD ACCUMULATOR WITH CONTENTS OF REGISTER C.
LLI		LOAD REGISTER IMMEDIATE; 2ND WORD OF THIS INSTRUCTION TO REGISTER L.
LHI		SAME; REGISTER H. L&H NOW CONTAIN THE ADDRESS OF THE LAMP-BANK IMAGE IN THE MEMORY.
ORM		FORM LOGIC "OR" OF MEMORY LOCATION SPECIFIED BY REGISTERS H&L WITH THE ACCUMULATOR. LOCATION CONTAINS LAMP-BANK IMAGE.
NDD		FORM LOGIC "AND" OF REGISTER D WITH THE ACCUMULATOR.
LMA		MOVE CONTENTS OF ACCUMULATOR INTO MEMORY LOCATION M (SPECIFIED BY H&L). THIS IS THE NEW IMAGE OF THE LAMP-BANK.
LAI	4	LOAD ACCUMULATOR WITH CONTENTS OF 2ND WORD OF THIS INSTRUCTION -- THE NUMBER 4.
OUT	ADD	MOVE CONTENTS OF ACCUMULATOR TO OUTPUT CHANNEL, IDENTIFYING THE DEVICE FOR A SUBSEQUENT OUTPUT OPERATION. THE DEVICE IS THE LAMP-BANK.
LAM		MOVE MEMORY LOCATION M INTO THE ACCUMULATOR. THIS BRINGS OUT THE NEW IMAGE OF THE LAMP-BANK AGAIN.
OUT	WR	MOVE CONTENTS OF ACCUMULATOR ONTO PREVIOUSLY SELECTED OUTPUT CHANNEL, THUS ALTERING THE CONDITION OF THE LAMP-BANK TO MATCH THE NEW IMAGE IN MEMORY LOCATION M.

soon find that at some cost in memory space and running time, almost any operator not explicitly included can be made up from available instructions. Because of this cost, implementing the gate functions is likely to be more economical in hardware outside the microprocessor than in the program, if their outputs are required externally. These functions pay off, however, if there is some regularity in the task they perform—for example, if one group of bits is to be compared to many test words.

In some microprocessors, this multiple comparison can be programed very compactly. For example, in the Intel 4004, the contents of any memory location can be loaded into a general-purpose register, which is specified in a JUMP INDIRECT instruction. Thus, data can modify the flow of instructions, and a multiple branch is no more than a simple procedure of looking up numbers in a table.

The routine (Table 2) requires only five instructions occupying six words. Four instructions identify the memory location—in this case an input/output device—and they bring data from that location into the accumulator and then put it into an even-numbered register—one of 16 4-bit registers in the 4004 that can also be addressed as eight 8-bit register pairs. Each even-numbered register is the upper half of a register pair, so that loading anything into an even-numbered register and leaving 0s in the lower half is equivalent to loading a multiple of 16 into the register pair. The last instruction in the routine is the JUMP INDIRECT, which refers to the register pair for the address of its destination—the beginning of a 16-byte subroutine. A maximum of 16 such subroutines can be selected.

Programed AND-OR

Another very useful technique in microprocessor programing is the use of a routine that branches back to itself in a continuous loop, together with a provision to count or otherwise limit the number of times the program executes the loop. (Without such a provision, the processor will continue executing the looped program indefinitely—chasing its tail, so to speak.)

The equivalent of an extensive hardware AND-OR network can be implemented with a looped program. Using the Intel 8008, the program (Table 3) can be written in 12 instructions occupying 21 words, only 15 of which are actually part of the loop.

First, the number of times the loop is to be executed is entered in one of the general-purpose registers; this corresponds to the number of AND gates in the hardware equivalent. Each pass through the loop brings an 8-bit word into the accumulator register, masks out any unwanted bits in that word, and compares it with a test word previously stored in the memory.

For each input word, the mask and the test word are stored in adjacent locations in the memory. Masks and tests for successive inputs are stored in successive pairs of locations. Thus, after specifying the number of passes through the loop, a pair of general-purpose registers is loaded with the address of the mask to be applied to the first input (one register can't hold a complete address). Then the program enters the loop for the first pass.

During each pass, the program fetches an input word, forms the logic AND of that word with the mask in memory, and compares the result with the test word next to the mask. If the two match, the program branches to a routine to process the input word. If the match is unsuccessful, the loop counter is decremented by 1 and tested to find out if it now contains 0. If it does, the loop has been executed the prescribed number of times, and the program branches to another task; if not, the two pointer registers that track the masks and test words are incremented, and the program goes back to fetch another input word.

Looping is also the obvious way to generate time delays. For example, to program a delay with the Intel 4004, a four-instruction seven-word routine (Table 4) can be used. Initially, the number 12 is loaded into register pair 0, which then contains 0000 1100. (In fact, the number is in the single register 1, while register 0—the upper half of pair 0—contains four 0s.) A one-instruction loop then increments register 0 over and over again, testing the contents each time until the register again contains 0000—a total of 16 steps. Another single instruction then increments register 1 once and returns to the one-instruction loop, unless the increment has placed four 0s in register 1.

Because register 1 initially contains 12, it is incremented four times—each time preceded by 16 repetitions of the incrementing of register 0; therefore, a total of 64 incrementing steps are taken by these two instructions alone. Finally, when register 1 turns up with contents 0000, the program returns to the routine that has been waiting for the completion of this time-delay loop—perhaps to permit some mechanical operation to take place. As described here, the delay is slightly more than 1.5 milliseconds, but it can be set to any amount by changing the numbers loaded into the registers and fine-tuned to a certain extent by inserting dummy instructions (no-ops) in the routine. A no-op uses up one instruction cycle—10.8 microseconds in the 4004—but doesn't do anything.

Input-output images

In designing such logic systems as digital controllers, sensing discrete conditions and generating discrete outputs are important. The conditions include switch closures, status bits, and the like. Typical outputs perform such functions as lighting lamps and energizing relays, tasks that data-processing systems rarely perform.

A microprocessor controls and monitors these signals in a unique way—it maintains an image of them in its memory. For example, one 8-bit word can sense eight status lines, treating each input signal as new data to be read and stored in one bit position of the word. And by programed bit manipulation, another word can control the lighting of eight lamps.

For instance, a program to light lamp No. 3 and extinguish lamp No. 4 in a bank of eight lamps can be written for the Intel 8008 with 10 instructions that occupy 13 words. The program (Table 5) assumes that one general-purpose register—say, register C—has previously been loaded with 0000 0100, which identifies lamp 3 (counting from the right) as the one to be turned on, while another register, D, contains 1111 0111 to point out lamp 4 as the one to be turned off; a location in memory contains an image of the bank of eight lamps, with their prior on-off status.

The contents of register C are first loaded into the accumulator, where the logic OR is formed with the image of the bank of lamps, and then the logic AND is formed with the contents of register D. The OR operation leaves a 1 in the accumulator for each lamp that should be on at the end of the routine; the AND leaves a 0 for all lamps that should be off. Because the accumulator contained only a single 1 bit before these two logic steps, only one lamp changes from 0 to 1; and since register D contains only one 0, only one lamp changes from 1 to 0.

Now the accumulator contains the updated image of the bank of lamps, which is stored back in the main memory temporarily, while the address of the actual bank is sent out through the output port. The image is then brought back into the accumulator and sent out after the address to switch the lamps.

Functions like these can be implemented with a small input/output card or subassembly containing two 8-bit registers. One of these, an input register, stores changes in external conditions that are to be sensed, and input commands transfer its contents, as required, into memory. Similarly, output commands transfer data into the other register, from which output signals can be generated as needed.

Designing systems around microprocessors

Electronic lock illustrates power of chip set to handle complex operations; adding such capabilities as I/O controllers and interrupts can expand a system

Translating logic-gate networks into program sequences, as described in the previous section of this article, is the first step toward a microprocessor-based system—but only the first step. Program sequences must then be gathered into a completed design that will perform the desired function.

An example shows how to accomplish this conversion. The logic design[1] is an electronic lock—the buzzer type often used in apartment houses, banks, and other secure areas—with a sequential combination instead of a simple button. In its standby state, the lock is closed. To open it, a button is pressed, starting the sequence. After a short time delay—a few seconds—a light begins to flash on and off at a low frequency, several seconds for each half-cycle. During each half-cycle, the button must again be pressed a prescribed number of times. If the sequence is executed correctly, a signal energizes the lock and opens it one half-cycle later, and then the circuitry returns to its standby state, reclosing the lock. A mistake in the sequence returns the circuit to standby without opening the lock.

For a half-cycle time of 4 seconds and a combination of 3-6-5—the number of times the button is pressed during each half-cycle—the state diagram appears in Fig. 5. This diagram defines the successive states the sequential circuit must occupy, and it is the starting point for either

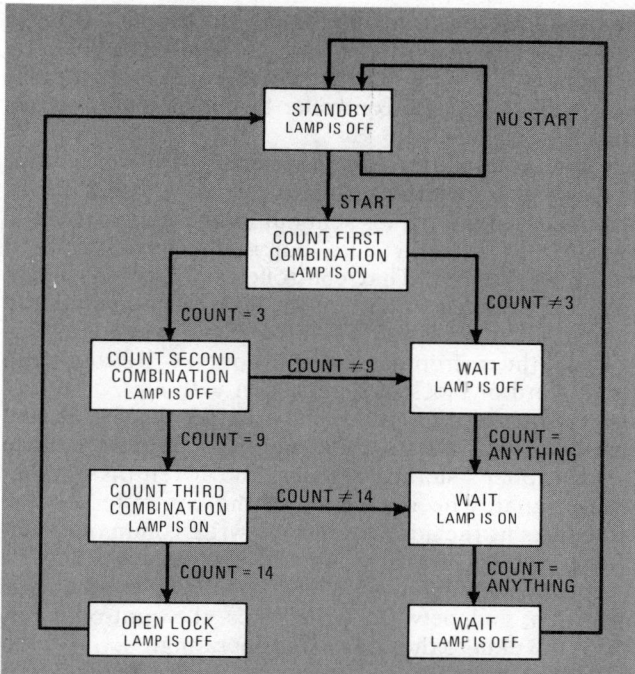

5. Electronic lock. Lock opens only when button has been pressed the correct number of times during three successive time periods. Its operation is described in this state diagram, which is the starting point for either a hardware or a programed design.

a hardware-logic design or a microprocessor program.

Because the diagram contains eight states, the sequential logic would require a minimum of three flip-flops, which together have eight combinations of on and off. The system control also would require input and output gates for these flip-flops, a four-stage binary counter, four more flip-flops, and a decoder, although all of these can be obtained as small- or medium-scale integrated circuits.

Another flip-flop or latch circuit is necessary to take the inevitable "bounce" out of the pushbutton contacts. Beyond these are a clock, which would be most easily made from an oscillator running at a kilohertz or so and another counter—more flip-flops—to divide the oscillator output down to the fractional-hertz level.

Finally, either the combination must be fixed when the lock circuit is put together, which calls for a rewiring job to change the combination, or additional complications—such as rotary switches on the protected side of the locked door—would have to be included in the design. (Driver circuits for the lamp and the electric lock are also required, but the microprocessor design will require them too.)

This list of parts that the electronic lock would require—nearly a dozen packages of small-scale and medium-scale integrated circuits—is intended to emphasize its complexity if it is designed with hardware logic. On the other hand, it is quite simple if programed for a microprocessor, which has its own counting capability.

In the Intel 8008 microprocessor, for example, the controller requires only an 85-byte program, for which a flow chart is shown in Fig. 6. The program can be stored in either an alterable or a read-only memory. In a ROM, at about 2 cents per byte, the incremental cost is $1.70.

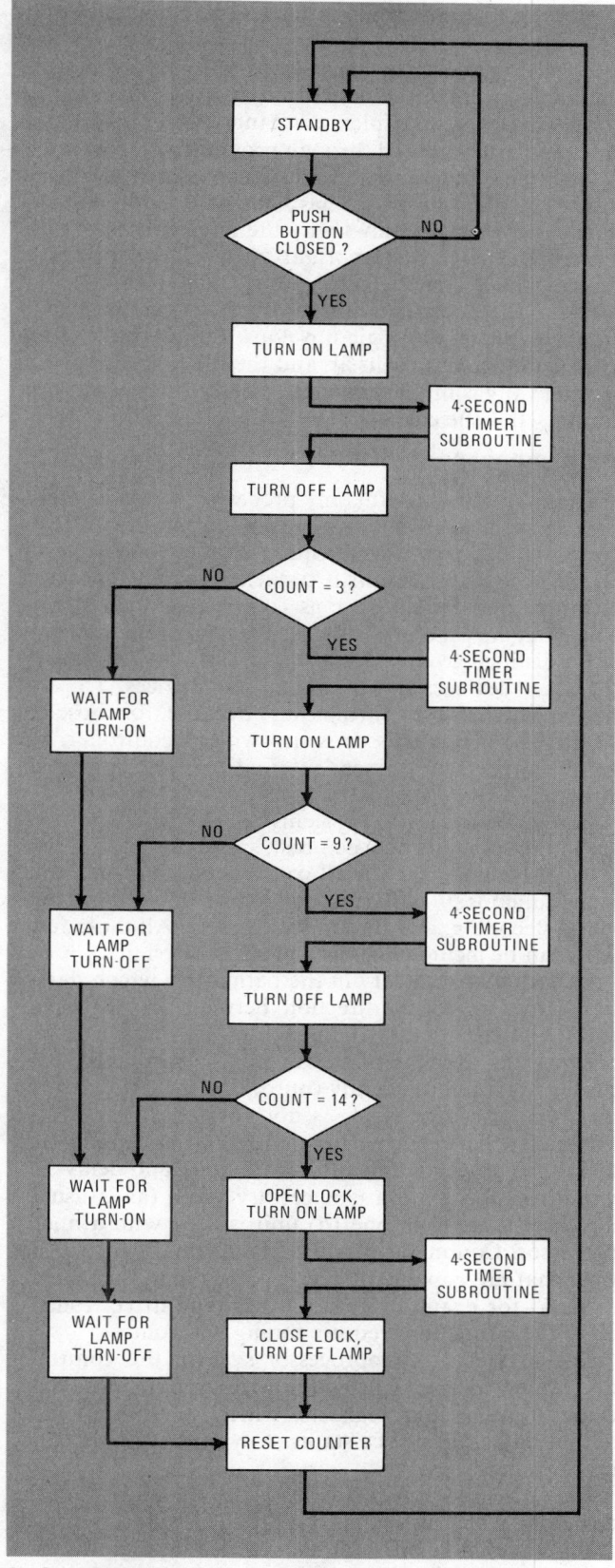

6. Counting signals. The sequence of events in the electronic lock is defined in this flow chart, which describes exactly what happens from the internal viewpoint, as opposed to the external view, of the state diagram. Blocks in the flow chart are readily translated into a program routine in any machine code or symbolic code.

Furthermore, the combination can be changed simply by reprograming. The new program could be stored in a read-only memory, to be inserted in place of the old one, or in an alterable memory that is reloaded. In the same way, more complex combinations or additional functions can be added through programing.

Thus, new functions are inexpensive, once the basic cost of the microprocessor has been paid, and the hardware logic diagram shows why the microprocessor is so powerful. The most important parts of the electronic lock are the 16-line decoder and the gate elements that compare the decoder outputs with the previous state of the three sequential-logic flip-flops. But the bulk of the logic is in the counter itself, and the microprocessor can generate any counter sequence trivially—that is, the program itself is the counter.

Input/output controllers

To do anything useful, any processor, micro or otherwise, must have one or more input/output devices connected to it so that it can acquire data to process and it can dispose of the results. I/O devices may be as simple as lamps and switches or as complex as disk storage units, but for microprocessors, they fall generally into three distinct groups: serial-bit-stream devices, single-character devices, and block-transfer devices. The first class is not discussed further here because, for those devices, the microprocessor is its own I/O controller, but for the other two classes, external control logic is required.

Many designs for I/O systems are possible, and there are many tradeoffs between cost, speed, number of lines serviced, and so on. But all controllers share four common functions: buffering, address-recognition, command-decoding, and timing and control. All these functions can be included in a rather simple design.

Buffering is necessary in the path along which data is transferred in either direction between an I/O device and the microprocessor because the two units have separate clocks and therefore are not synchronized. Synchronizing, or equivalently controlling the I/O unit from the microprocessor clock, is not advisable because the connection between the two units may be lengthy and therefore subject to difficulties with noise and delays.

Address-recognition is necessary when (as is usually the case) more than one I/O unit is used with a microprocessor. Command-decoding is necessary for I/O devices that are capable of actions other than the transfer of data—for example, rewinding a tape drive. Finally, all of these functions require timing and control.

For a typical microprocessor system, the controller diagramed in Fig. 7 provides all four functions. It includes three buffer registers, which store input data, output data, and device status. A typical write sequence involves four steps:

First, the microprocessor sends out the address of the device in which it wants to write. This address travels along a common bus that also carries data, and serves the memory, as well as the I/O system. Therefore, the address is accompanied on separate lines by an address-command and an I/O request. The address-command identifies the signals on the bus as an address, and the I/O request directs it to the controllers instead of to the memory. A synchronizing signal strobes the address into the selected controller and effectively establishes a temporary link between the separate clocks of the microprocessor and the controller at the moment the address is transferred.

Second, the addressed controller sets its address flip-flop, which generates a ready signal to the microprocessor. All the signals sent out by the microprocessor went to all the controllers, but the address identified only one of them. That controller, with ready signal, thus acknowledges receipt of the address command and indicates that it is in a condition to begin operation.

Third, the microprocessor sends out a write command and a word or block of data—again with an I/O request and a synchronizing pulse. Only the previously selected controller responds to these signals. The data goes to the controller's storage register, and it returns another ready signal. The data goes to the controller on the same lines as the address, but the write command identifies it as data instead of an address. This step may be repeated as many times as needed to complete the write operation, and between write steps, the controller forwards the data to the device it is operating.

Finally, the microprocessor sends out another address command to select a different controller. This resets the address flip-flop in the previously selected controller and takes it out of operation until it is again selected.

The first two steps of a read sequence are the same as those for write. But in the third step, the read command goes out, and the microprocessor waits for data to come back. The presence of data on the lines for the microprocessor to accept is announced by a ready signal. This cycle can be repeated as many times as needed—until a new controller is selected.

Generally, a read operation requires a delay while the mechanical device providing the data accelerates to its normal operating speed. The microprocessor can also request the controller to transfer its status information into the memory—an operation essentially identical to a read, except for the delay. The status is always immediately available in the controller, and finding it involves no mechanical processes.

Figure 7 shows the four commands—READ, WRITE, ADDRESS, and STATUS—as coming to the controller on four different lines. These could be encoded on two lines, or the four lines could be encoded with as many as 12 more commands if the I/O functions are to be expanded.

Interrupt

One such expansion might be the addition of interrupt capability to the system. In the example of the electronic combination lock, a loop at the start of the programed sequence represents the standby state. While in this loop, the microprocessor effectively runs around in circles waiting for something to happen—for someone to push the button. Similar standby loops are often incorporated in programs, but if the events they wait for are infrequent— less than once every 50 instructions or every 100 to 1,000 microseconds—the microprocessor could be doing useful work while waiting for the external event. That event must be able to cause the microprocessor to change its course of action. This capability,

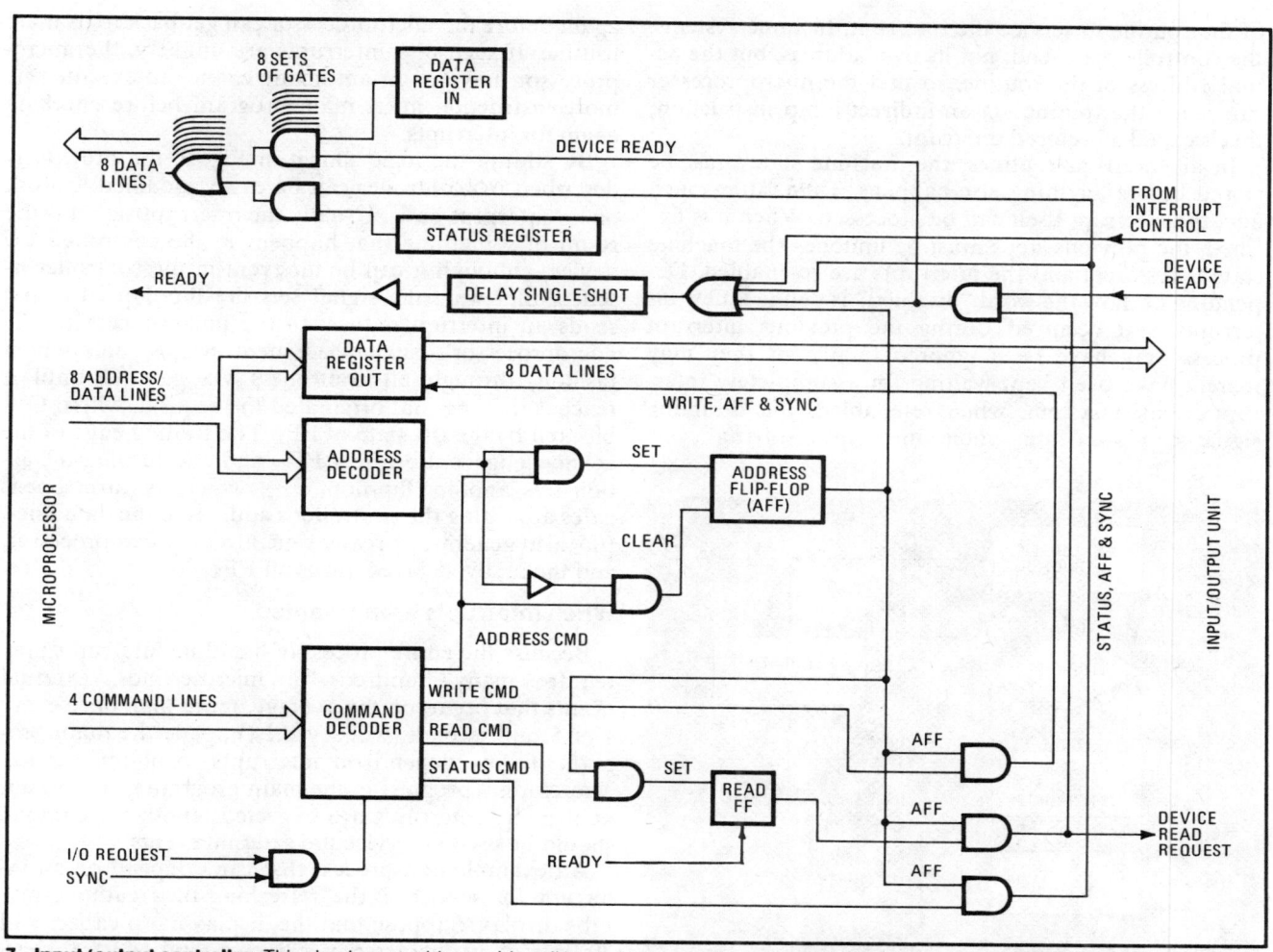

7. Input/output controller. This simple assembly provides all basic functions of any controller: buffering, address recognition, command decoding, timing, and control. These functions are required, regardless of its speed or how many lines it services.

available on some microprocessors, is called interrupt.

Interrupt is especially valuable in communications applications. Since the microprocessor often has no control over when data is to be transmitted or received, the capability to work while waiting is desirable.

Resolving an interrupt is a rather complicated procedure. First of all, once an interrupt has been recognized, the microprocessor can't afford to recognize any others until the first one is out of the way. (In large computers, interrupt priorities are sometimes installed so that a high-priority interrupt can bump a low-priority interrupt. Such complex design seems undesirable with microprocessors at present.)

Second, before the microprocessor can process an interrupt, it has to store its own state— that is, effectively to take note of where it was when it was interrupted so that it can pick up where it left off after the interrupt processing is finished. This involves transferring into a reserved part of the memory the instruction counter, which identifies the next instruction, the contents of the accumulator, and other key registers and flip-flops. The existence of only one such reserved area is the reason for recognizing only one interrupt at a time.

In general, the implementation of an interrupt system consists of replacing the wait loop in the program with an equivalent loop in hardware, which tests for the presence of an interrupt at regular intervals during machine operation. For example, the test might occur just before every instruction fetch so that the fetch is blocked if an interrupt has occurred.

An interrupt-processing routine is shown in the flow chart in Fig. 8. The degree of complication varies widely from one microprocessor to another—some have processing interrupts that are more automatic than others. For example, the National Semiconductor GPC/P has a stack memory that can completely store the machine state in only five instructions. This highly efficient technique qualifies the GPC/P for excellent real-time process control.

Daisy-chain signal

After disabling further interrupts, as described previously, the microprocessor must acknowledge the current interrupt and determine its source. For this purpose, the interrupt-acknowledge line passes through all controllers in a "daisy-chain" fashion—the acknowledge signal passes from each one to the next until the source of the interrupt stops it. By this means, I/O priority is established by proximity to the microprocessor. Arrival of the interrupt-acknowledge signal triggers the sending by the controller to the microprocessor of its address, from which the microprocessor determines the location of the routine to service the interrupt. In some systems, the controller can send, not its own address, but the actual address of the routine, so that the microprocessor can reach the routine via an indirect jump instruction; this is called a vectored interrupt.

In all interrupt routines, the machine state must be stored before anything else happens. Then, after much ado, the interrupt itself can be processed. When it is finished, the previous steps must be undone—the machine state is restored, and the interrupts are re-enabled. Depending on how the word "disabled" is defined, new interrupts that occurred during the previous interrupt process may have been ignored totally, or they may merely have been kept waiting. In a completely interrupt-oriented system, when re-enabled, the disabling signal can start the whole interrupt-resolving cycle again before the microprocessor can get back to its main routine. If such new interrupts are unlikely, the microprocessor may get an automatic chance to execute one more instruction in its main program before checking again for interrupts.

By adding the logic shown in Fig. 9, the previously described I/O controller can be easily modified to work on an interrupt basis. Usually the interrupt signal is the result of something that happens in the controlled I/O device, although it can be an event in the controller itself. Either way, the signal sets the flip-flop FF_1, and sends an interrupt request to the microprocessor. The microprocessor's acknowledgment passes, daisy-chain fashion, through all controllers via gate G until it reaches the one that originated the request, where G is blocked by the ON state of FF_1. The trailing edge of the acknowledge pulse resets FF_1, and the turning-off action sets another flip-flop, FF_2, which, in turn, opens gates admitting the controller's address to the data lines. FF_2 also generates a ready signal to the microprocessor, and the ready, delayed, turns off FF_2.

When interrupts aren't wanted

Because the entire process of handling interrupts may require many hundreds of microseconds, external events that occur, on the average, more than once every 4 or 5 milliseconds, will severely impede the main program if they depend on interrupts to obtain service. Therefore, if progress in the main program is important, or if many interrupts are expected, another technique should be used to service the external events.

An example of a process that can't depend on an interrupt for service is the refreshing of a cathode-ray-tube display. Suppose that the display has a capacity of 30 lines at 60 characters per line—a total of 1,800 characters to be refreshed 60 times per second. Refreshing requires 108,000 characters per second to be delivered to the display, or one character every 9.2 microseconds.

Many high-speed I/O processes, such as the preceding example, can tolerate relatively slow processing if the

8. Sleeve puller. A microprocessor need not stand idle while waiting for an external event—if it can keep track of what it was doing when the event finally occurs. This flow chart outlines how it can mark its place in a secondary routine while processing an interrupt.

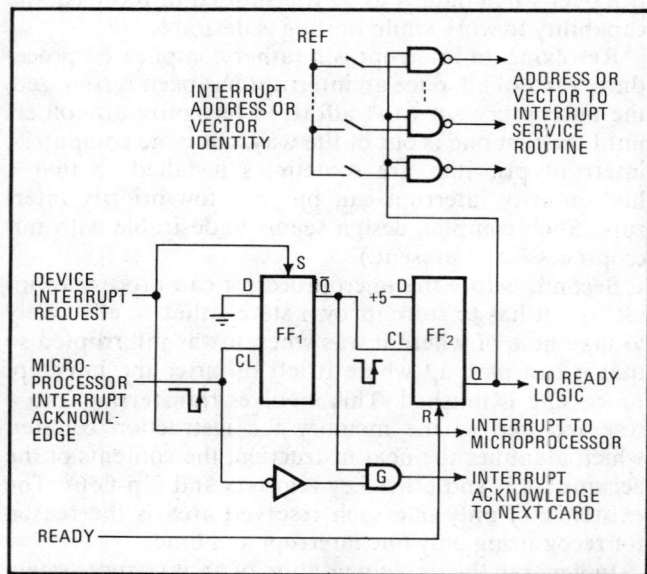

9. Additional logic. These logic blocks must be added to the simple input/output controller of Fig. 6 to enable it to handle interrupts.

data transfer to and from the unit can be fast. These processes can therefore make use of a direct memory-access channel, or DMA, the next step up in complexity and performance from a simple interrupt.

A DMA channel in a microprocessor system requires a few more controls than those in the individual I/O-device controllers, which are not affected directly by their connection through a channel to memory instead of to the processor. The microprocessor obtains access to its own memory through these channel controls in the same way that the input/output controllers do, and, since conflicts can arise, the channel's main function is to detect and resolve them. They are less likely to occur with microprocessors than with minicomputers and large computers, however, because the microprocessor usually runs slower than its memory, not faster. Conflicts in systems of any size are always resolved in favor of the input/output, because the device is usually in mechanical motion and can't afford much delay.

Once the channel is under way, the channel controller takes over the task of selecting addresses, I/O sequences, and data handling. As a result, both I/O and processing operations are expedited—the first because it is limited only by the memory cycle rate, not the instruction rate, and the second because the microprocessor need not pause in its own work to run an I/O operation.

Block input/output

Channel input/output leads quite directly to block I/O, in which large blocks of data are transferred in or out of the microprocessor by a single command sequence. Additional logic in the I/O controller is required to work, not only with addresses in the main memory and addresses of individual devices, but also with addresses within the device—such as tracks and sectors on a disk drive, files on tape, and so on.

Three major elements (Fig. 10) must be added to a basic I/O controller to permit it to handle block input/output: an I/O device-address counter, a main-memory counter, and a block counter. At the start of an operation, the device-address counter is loaded with the device's internal address—such as the sector number—the main memory counter has the address to or from which the transfer of the block begins, and the block counter contains the number of blocks to be transferred. The first READ or WRITE command sets a BUSY flip-flop. As each word is transferred, the main-memory counter is incremented, and as each block is transferred, the block counter is decremented until it passes 0, generating a borrow signal. This signal resets the BUSY flip-flop and sends an interrupt signal to the microprocessor, which is thus informed that an I/O operation has been completed.

A drum-printer controller

The preceding sections have shown how a few common logic-design problems can be solved with a microprocessor, and how controllers for use with microprocessors can be easily and quickly designed. Many of these concepts can be combined in the design of a controller for a drum printer that takes advantage of a microprocessor to control the format of the data transfer

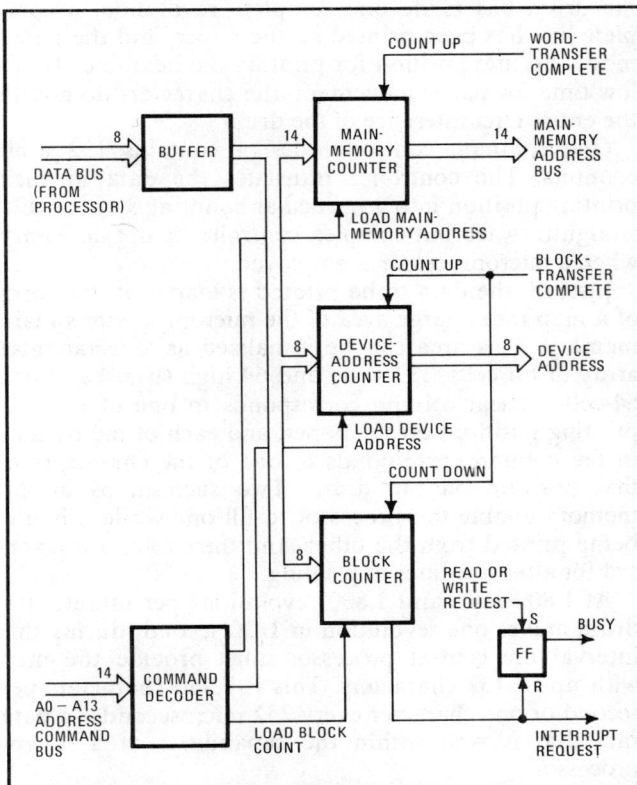

10. Block input/output. To transfer large blocks of data to or from memory, this logic is added to the basic input/output controller. It must not interfere with other microprocessor tasks, yet it must work with both internal device addresses and with memory.

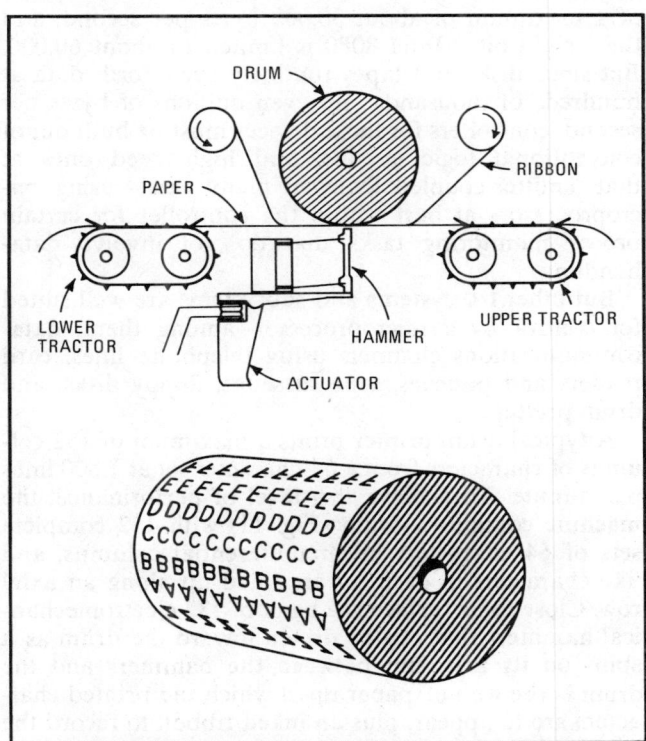

11. Drum printer. Rotating drum carries complete alphabet on its surface, repeated for each printing position across page. Separate actuator-hammer pairs for each position press the paper against the drum to pick up the imprint as the desired character passes.

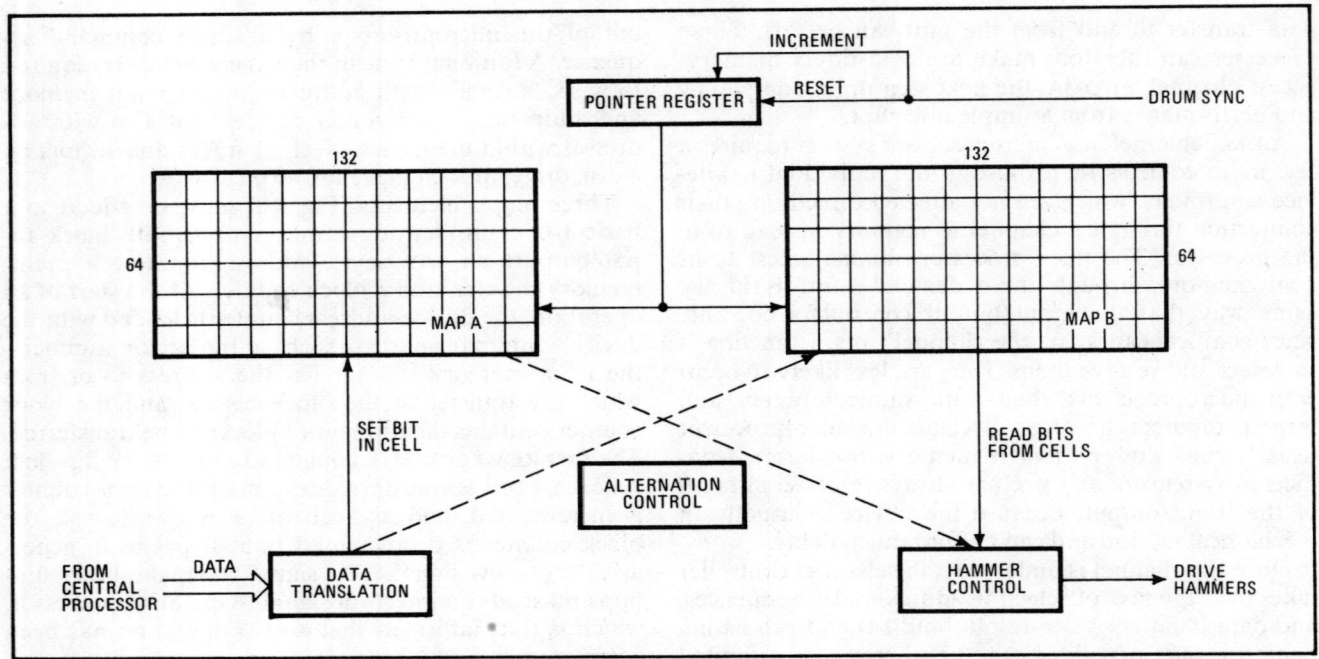

12. Printer control. Microprocessor translates data from central processor into bits in map. These, in turn, identify the hammers to be actuated to print the data in the prescribed format. Two maps are used alternately; one fills with data while the other is printing.

between a larger central processor and the printer.

Microprocessors aren't suitable as controllers in every I/O application. For example, many magnetic-tape or disk units have data transfer rates that are far beyond the capabilities of any present or contemplated microprocessor. In fact, the fastest microprocessor on the market in 1973 was National Semiconductor GPC/P, capable of a maximum of about 30,000 bytes per second, and the eight-bit Intel 8080 is limited to about 60,000. But since disks and tapes routinely spew forth data at hundreds of thousands and even millions of bytes per second, controllers for these devices must be built out of conventional logic circuits, and high-speed ones at that—emitter-coupled logic, in many cases—using microprocessors at best within the controller for certain process-monitoring tasks that do not involve data-handling.

But other I/O systems and subsystems are well suited for control by a microprocessor—among them, data-communications channels using telephone lines, card readers and punches, tape cassettes, floppy disks, and drum printers.

A typical drum printer prints a maximum of 132 columns of characters from a 64-character set at 1,800 lines per minute. To achieve this level of performance, the machine contains a drum (Fig. 11) with 132 complete sets of 64 characters in circumferential columns, and like characters in each set are lined up along an axial row. Close to its surface is a bank of 132 electromechanical hammers that can be driven toward the drum as it spins on its axis. But between the hammers and the drum is the web of paper upon which the printed characters are to appear, plus an inked ribbon to record the imprints.

As the drum turns, its position is monitored by the controller. As each of its character slugs to be printed in the 132 positions of a line approaches a point opposite the corresponding hammer, the hammer is driven forward—timed in such a way that as it reaches the limit of its travel, it prints in the desired position by pinching the paper and the ribbon between it and the drum when the desired character slug is exactly opposite it. When the drum has made one complete revolution, a complete line has been printed on the paper, and the paper moves up into position for printing the next line. To allow time for paper movement, the characters do not fill the entire circumference of the drum.

One common controller design contains 132 6-bit counters. The controller translates the data in each printing position into a particular counting step. Such a straightforward but complex controller is not necessary when a microprocessor is employed.

Instead, the data to be printed is loaded in the form of a map into a large area of the microprocessor's main memory. This area can be visualized as a rectangular array of bit cells, 132 wide and 64 high (Fig. 12). Each 64-cell vertical column corresponds to one of the 132 printing positions on the paper, and each of the 64 cells in the column corresponds to one of the characters in that position on the drum. Two such maps in the memory enable the processor to fill one while a line is being printed from the other, and their roles are reversed for alternate lines of printing.

At 1,800 lines and 1,800 revolutions per minute, the drum makes one revolution in 1/30 second; during this interval the central processor must provide the map with up to 132 characters. This is 3,960 characters per second or one character every 252 microseconds—a data rate that is well within the capabilities of a microprocessor.

The microprocessor, working as a controller, uses simple arithmetic and masking instructions to translate data received from the central processor into bits placed in the map. The character to be printed identifies the bit

> ## Cranking up the microprocessor
>
> Now that the engineer has read how to apply microprocessors to every-day design problems, assume that he orders one—from Intel, or National, or anybody. The microprocessor has an adequate quantity of read-only and read-write memory and all the necessary extraneous parts. Now, suppose that the engineer writes a program to fit his application; and assume that the program is right the first time and that it's been put into a programable ROM connected to the microprocessor system. Now, how does he start the machine?
>
> Large general-purpose computers always come with software that helps load programs into the memory and ensures that the computer starts running the program when it is turned on. This software is so cleverly designed that it seems to melt right into the scenery. The rules followed in writing the program may have been imposed, in part, by the computer hardware, but some of them were imposed by the software. However, the microprocessor doesn't have any software like this.
>
> To start any processor, some kind of number must be loaded into the program counter, which will then indicate the first instruction in the program, and the processor clock has to be started. In Intel's 4004 microprocessor, this is brutally simple—an external line, when grounded, forces the program counter to 0, and when the ground is removed, the clock starts running. If the first instruction of the program has been placed in memory location 0, grounding the reset line makes the program counter point to that first instruction, and removing the ground starts the processor.
>
> The 8008 is also simple to start, but the process is not quite so straightforward. Essentially, the machine can be made to execute an instruction that is not in the program, but which forces the program to jump to a location whose address is a multiple of 8. Any address between 0 and 56 can be used; if the first instruction of a program is in that location, the processor starts running as soon as the jump has been executed.
>
> Other microprocessors also have similar simple means of starting.

cell in the column of 64, and sets that cell to 1; all other cells in that column remain 0s. Successive characters in the line set corresponding bits in successive columns in the map.

When the map has been filled with bits corresponding to data to be printed, the map turns to the control of the spinning drum. Once per revolution, the drum generates a synchronizing signal that says the first character in the set of 64 is in a position to be printed anywhere it may be required along the line—possibly, but improbably, in all 132 positions at once. This synchronizing signal sets a pointer at row 1 in the map. If any of the 132 bits in that row is 1, the hammer corresponding to the bit position fires to print the first character in the proper column. The pointer then is incremented to row 2 as the drum continues to rotate into the next character position. This process is repeated for all 64 rows in the map and all 64 print positions on the drum.

But in reading out these map cells, the microprocessor can take, say, 8 bits at a time (assuming that it is an Intel 8008 or similar system). Thus, to print in 132 character positions, the microprocessor can take 17 memory accesses—16 of 8 bits each and one of 4 bits. (A standard line length for printers is 132 characters, but unfortunately, 132 is not divisible by 8.)

Meanwhile, the spinning drum passes one of the 64 character positions in $1/30 \times 1/64 = 1/1,920$ second, or about 521 microseconds. However, during this period, for accurately aligned smudge-free printing, all the hammers that are to be pulsed to print a given character must be pulsed within a 66-μs window. This ratio of 66 to 521 represents a rather relaxed duty cycle for the printer mechanism, allowing plenty of time for the hammers to settle back into position after firing, but during the window, the microprocessor must peel off 17 8-bit bytes from the map—less than 4 μs per byte. To handle this data rate, the microprocessor must have a DMA channel.

This printer-control algorithm can be coded for the Intel 8008 microprocessor or the new 8080 with only 72 bytes in the program. The memory maps—two—require 2,176 bytes. The 8008 isn't fast enough to run the hypothetical printer, but it can handle about 500 lines per minute, a respectable speed for some applications. The 8080, on the other hand, can handle about 5,000 lines per minute.

In an actual application, of course, a full controller would be required—with other functions, such as sequencing, vertical forms control, and various alarm functions. But the basic simplicity of a controller built around a microprocessor is apparent.

This design has several important aspects. No gate-level logic design was necessary, and no state diagrams were used. Also, only slight program changes would be necessary to control a printer with a larger or smaller character set, a different input code from the central processor, or even a more complex printer, such as a chain printer. □

REFERENCES
1. John B. Peatman, "Design of Digital Systems," pp. 211-216 and secs. 6-6, 6-7, McGraw-Hill Book Co., 1972.
2. "MCS-4 Microcomputer Set User's Manual," Intel Corp., July 1972.
3. "8008 8-bit Parallel Central Processor Unit," Intel Corp., November 1972.

BIBLIOGRAPHY
"Product Description, General Purpose Controller/Processor (GPC/P) MOS/LSI System Kit," National Semiconductor Corp., March 1972.
W. H. Davidow, "General-Purpose Microcontrollers, Part 2: Design and Applications," Computer Design, August 1972, p. 69.
Michael Davis, "Processor Interrupt Scheme Speeds Response and Minimizes Overhead," EDN, Sept. 15, 1972, p. 49.
Gerald Lapidus, "MOS/LSI Launches the Low-Cost Processor," IEEE Spectrum, November 1972, p. 33.
Yaohan Chu, "Computer Organization and Microprograming," Chapter 8, Prentice-Hall Inc., 1972.
"How to Use the CPS/1 Microcomputer System," Microsystems International Ltd., 1972.

Preparation: the key to success with microprocessors

Unwary system engineers can fall victim to time-consuming mistakes, not to mention cost, when building on new breed of semiconductors; help is available, however, for those ready to pause and pay heed

by Robert Lewandowski, *John Fluke Mfg. Co., Inc., Seattle, Wash.*

☐ A design team that takes its first crack at devising a system based on a microprocessor can be in for a trying experience. But many of the usual pitfalls can be traced to two basic oversights; they involve (1) a precipitous plunge into a project with a design group inadequately prepared for the task, and (2) failure to obtain the different kinds of help available from manufacturers, time-sharing services, and consultants.

Hardware problems, while formidable, can be solved by traditional methods. But not so for software. Microprocessor manufacturers say it is easier to turn a digital designer into a microprocessor programer rather than the other way around. While this may be true, it doesn't give a realistic picture of what can happen while a hardware designer is in the process of learning. The problems associated with becoming familiar with the microprocessor and its interfaces, and with learning programing, can at best lead to some extremely harried designers or, at worst, a poor design.

Hardware problems

Analog designers probably will not be affected, but the digital designers must become familiar first of all with the capabilities, limitations, and characteristics of the many microprocessor-system components. In addition to the central processing unit, there is a clock generator-driver, which supplies timing and synchronization to most parts of the system. There is a ROM, which contains the actual program statements executed by the CPU. There may be a memory interface device to provide address information in the correct format to allow a general-purpose memory chip to be used with a specific processor. And most systems will contain a RAM to store transient data generated by the processor during program execution.

Also, inputs and outputs will usually require interface hardware to provide timing and multiplexing so that peripheral circuitry can access the processor's data bus. In some systems, memory interface and I/O may be handled by the same hardware; other systems provide interface adapters for various types of I/O operations.

Additional hardware may also be required to interrupt processor operation for service requests, to change program flow, and to handle special modes of operation. And since the devices used within one system may span several technologies—p-MOS, n-MOS, C-MOS, and TTL—there are many different interface problems—voltage levels, propagation times, etc.—with which hardware designers must be familiar.

The software problem

Many hardware designers assume that because they have done some programing with high-level languages like Basic or Fortran, their experience will be directly applicable. Such programing is, however, a world away from the low-level languages required by most microprocessors. So while digital designers may have developed the logical way of thinking necessary to become proficient programers, the time allowed them in project schedules to get up to adequate speed in programing is frequently grossly underestimated.

If a project is on a schedule in which sufficient time cannot be given to design-team members to thoroughly learn about the device to be used, an alternative to consider is the use of a consultant.

Many consulting firms are spinoffs from microprocessor manufacturers. These people have worked on many specific applications and are familiar with both hardware characteristics and programing techniques. Some consultants will undertake the whole design—hardware and software—while others will only do the software and advise on hardware implementation. This course will allow in-house people to become experienced as they work with the consultants.

If, on the other hand, time does permit the education of staff designers, where can the education be obtained?

While there is a great deal to be said for self-made men, there are definite limits imposed when it comes to microprocessors. The information available for self-study from vendors, for example, is usually non-existent, and much of what is available is in the form of specifications not really helpful for the task at hand.

Many colleges and some community colleges now offer short courses in microprocessors and even courses on machine- or assembly-language programing. These can be useful—as can the general information available on programing minicomputers (in view of the similarity between the simple mini and a microcomputer system).

A better approach is to take advantage of seminars offered from time to time by vendors or consultants in various locations around the country. These usually last two to five days, are very concentrated, and cover the basics of hardware operation and the instruction sets used by specific devices or families of devices. The seminars usually include some "hands-on" time employing a hardware simulator, which allows students actually to write and execute simple programs. Under no circumstances, however, should it be assumed that these seminars are guarantees of expertise.

When it comes down to a matter of practice, time-shared computer services can be useful. Many such services offer proprietary programs supplied by the microprocessor vendors—programs that allow the assembly of "source" programs into "object" code suitable for execution in a microprocessor.

The source program, written in the assembly language peculiar to a particular microprocessor, consists of symbolic operation codes corresponding to the actual bit patterns that cause a given operation to occur. It also consists of symbolic labels corresponding to the actual binary addresses at which the instruction op-codes will reside during program execution. The assembly language frees the programer from keeping track of the absolute address of an instruction to which the program transfers control or to which the program branches after a logical or arithmetic test. The assembly language also keeps track of the start addresses of subroutines that may be utilized by various parts of the main program.

The object code generated by an assembler is the set of binary numbers that, when loaded in the correct sequence in the microprocessor's instruction memory, causes the processor to act in the desired manner. These bit codes are permanently "burned" or "hard-wired" into the system ROM during manufacture and provide the instructions for a microprocessor to execute.

To develop a microprocessor program, the first step generally is to establish the logical sequence of events to occur by using a flow chart or similar aid. Each operation is then converted into one or more microprocessor instructions written in an assembly language. The sequence of instructions is then keyed into a data file in the time-shared computer, and the program, or source file, is acted upon by the assembler program in the time-shared system. If there are no errors in the source program, the assembler generates an output record consisting of the object file in a suitable format for storage. This object file can be sent to a vendor who can convert the bit patterns into a usable ROM.

Since ROM manufacture is an LSI semiconductor process, the initial setup is rather costly and time-consuming. It is of critical importance, therefore, that the program be debugged and operational prior to ROM manufacture. In the case of production-LSI parts, little or nothing can be done to correct errors in the original hardware. The entire process of mask generation and fabrication of new parts has to be repeated—with time delays of two to four months for each correction.

To determine whether a program is operational or not, the time-sharing services also offer a simulation program that can execute the object program on the host computer in a manner similar to the actual microprocessor. A wide variety of information is available to the operator about the execution of his program, such as program timing, current contents of internal storage registers, addresses, and the actual instruction currently being executed. The simulator can stop operation at various places in the program and force conditions to occur within the simulated microprocessor. These features, combined with on-line editing programs that allow rapid modification or correction of source programs, make an extremely powerful system for developing microprocessor programs.

One drawback of time-shared services is their high recurring costs. In addition to the rental fee of a terminal for access, there are charges for connection time, and execution charges for use of the host computer. Also, there usually is a royalty for use of the microprocessor vendor's proprietary assembly and simulation programs. Time-sharing services also have a seemingly infinite variety of billing rates and schedules, so that comparison of costs of one service to another is virtually impossible. One can easily expect costs of $1,000 to $3,000 per month for a program development, which can easily take two to four months of peak demand time.

Prototyping systems

An alternative to the strict use of a time-sharing system (and one that provides a real-time operating-hardware situation) is the prototyping system. These are sold by various microprocessor manufacturers or independent proprietary microcomputer-systems vendors. Cost can be $3,000 to $10,000, depending on complexity and features. The prototype system can provide an operating setup that has the capability of entering and editing source programs in assembly language and executing the resultant object programs with the actual microprocessor hardware. These systems allow direct hardware interface to the instrument under development via plug-in "kluge" cards, and can contain the hardware to be used in the final system.

The main differences in comparison with the time-shared approach is the prototyping system's slower speed of execution and its lack of software or program features. Also, the editing capability is usually very limited, and in some cases nonexistent. That, together with the fact that most prototyping systems operate via a conventional ASR 33 Teletype and paper tape, make their use very awkward.

During operation of a prototyping system, the assem-

Why a microprocessor?

To name three of the chief advantages of a microprocessor-based instrument, a microprocessor can produce the following results:
- Reduction of the cost and complexity of hardware by replacing existing random-logic designs with fewer parts.
- Addition of arithmetic or computational capability unavailable with random logic.
- Achievement of a "smart" instrument that can execute a sequence of instructions under program control, and possibly to control or interact with other instruments.

The question remains: when is a given application suitable for a microprocessor? The rule of thumb today is that a microprocessor-based system is worth considering if an existing design uses 50 or more packages of medium-scale integration. But there are also other necessary preconditions, namely, that:
- There is sufficient product sales volume to approach the "knee" of the vendor's price curve.
- The application is bus-oriented, thus requiring a minimum of peripheral support hardware.
- There is a significant market advantage to be gained by features that come "free" with the addition of a microprocessor.
- There is the potential for future extension of the design techniques to other applications.

The desirability of a bus-oriented structure is based on the microprocessor's limited input/output capability. Most microprocessors transmit data on a character-serial bus (that is some multiple of 4 bits). This can, unless the system is already bus oriented, necessitate a large amount of outboard hardware to multiplex and distribute the data over wide parallel input and output structures. The extra components would seriously reduce the cost-effectiveness of the microprocessor solution.

The addition of computational ability greatly increases an instrument's usefulness, allowing it to convert measured electrical parameters—volts, ohms, etc.—into engineering units—pounds per square inch, pH, feet per second—while also performing self-calibration and fault diagnosis. It should be noted, however, that although most available microprocessors have some arithmetic capability, high speed "real-time" computation is severely limited because devices generally available have no hardware arithmetic features and must use repetitive program techniques. Speeds of execution under these conditions are well-suited for human interface, but not for high speed machine-to-machine interactions.

Front-panel controls are areas in which a microprocessor can be used to great advantage in the design of a "smart" instrument. Compare, for example, the electronic calculator to a mechanical calculator of five years ago. The mechanical calculator required that the entered data be justified with respect to the decimal location, and frequently required adjustment or re-entry of the data to accommodate the limited dynamic range of the machine.

A similar problem can be seen in a keyboard-programed frequency synthesizer that has a seven-decade display.

Entry of a number significantly smaller than full scale requires entering a number of zeros ahead of the most significant digit, making data entry rather clumsy. To implement the free-form entry with random logic requires a complex and costly design. But a microprocessor can meet the requirements easily.

One of the bonus features is the microprocessor's ability to store and recall various front-panel control settings or programs at the touch of a button. This makes it possible, for example, to store all the specific frequencies and signal levels required for production testing a narrow-band filter. A single button recalls the data previously stored, and allows the operator to examine or adjust the device under test at each critical frequency.

This technique can be extended to allow the user to enter his own programs into the microprocessor for specific applications. This requires both a complex keyboard or program entry method and a user who is familiar with programing the particular microprocessor in the instrument. Nevertheless, it can result in an extremely powerful instrument suited for a variety of applications.

A microprocessor-controlled instrument can offer sophisticated remote programing capabilities, especially when equipped with the proposed international Electrotechnical Commission general-purpose bus interface [*Electronics*, Nov. 14, 1974, p. 95]. The structure of the IEC bus is ideally suited for use with a microprocessor, allowing the instrument to take the role of listener, talker, and possibly system controller when used in the appropriate application.

At present, in instruments designed with random-logic controllers, a high price must be paid for the IEC bus option because of the large amount of additional circuitry necessary to receive or send the ASCII control characters. But the only hardware needed when interfacing a microprocessor to the bus are the bus drivers and receivers, and the random logic for both timing and recognition of addresses and universal commands. The recognition and interpretation of ASCII control characters (in the case of a listener) and the encoding of data to be transmitted by a talker are all done under program control. They may even be handled by the same methods using the same subroutines, as are used to process signals from the front panel control.

An instrument with microprocessor control can be programed to perform the controller function in a bus system, although an instrument with programing flexibility of a calculator is usually assigned this task. The control programs for a microprocessor in an application as a system controller could be very complex, requiring significant execution time, but it could represent a cost-effective solution for certain applications.

---

bly program (punched on paper tape) is read into storage in the system via some sort of monitor or control program which resides in the system's ROM. Program control is transferred to the assembler and the user's source program is read in from paper tape. The complete assembly of the source program takes two or three entries ("passes") of the entire tape, depending on the system. The object tape is generated during the final "pass" and can then be read into program storage within the system and executed by the microprocessor.

Loading the assembler, assembly, loading the object tape, and execution of the object program can easily take from an hour, for a small program, to well over eight hours for a large program. And the program stor-

Speedy look-up tables

Most microprocessors do not have built-in, hardwired arithmetic routines. They must use slower, software-controlled methods of computations. But there is a way to overcome this handicap, at least partially. Some computations can be done significantly faster with memory look-up techniques, in which tables of precomputed answers are arranged for rapid access by the processor at the time of program execution.

For example, in multiplication, the products, Z, of the single-digit BCD numbers X and Y can be stored in read-only memory, as shown in the accompanying table. The values of X and Y are first combined to form an offset address, XY, which is then added to a base address to form the actual address of the product. For example, if X = 2 and Y = 7, then XY is 27, which is added to 157 (an arbitrarily chosen base address) to form 17E (a hexadecimal number—sixteen digits, 0 through 9, plus A, B, C, D, E, and F represent decimal 0 through 15). The product, 14, is in storage location 17E.

There is much redundant information in the table (7 × 2 and 2 × 7 have separate locations), but any extra logic that would be required to remove the redundancy would probably slow down the process.

One problem with this method is that the offset addresses are handled in decimal code (actually BCD), while the actual addresses of the ROM sequentially step up in binary (actually hexadecimal). Therefore, between 09 and 10 in the offset address, there are six addresses that have no meaning in this process (0A, 0B, 0C, 0D, 0E, and 0F). These correspond to the unused storage locations shown on the table. Thus it takes 260 sequential binary addresses to handle the 100 offset addresses. Again, extra logic could be used to test values and eliminate the unused storage locations, but this would also slow down the process.

Although large amounts of memory could be required with this type of computation, semiconductor memory prices are coming down. Today one can buy ROMs containing 2,048 8-bit words for less than $30, equivalent to less than 1 cent per binary-coded-decimal digit.

XY OFFSET ADDRESS INTO TABLE (BCD)	ACTUAL ADDRESS (HEXADECIMAL)	Z TABLE ENTRY (BCD)
00	157	00
01	158	00
02	159	00
03	15A	00
04	15B	00
05	15C	00
06	15D	00
07	15E	00
08	15F	00
09	160 —*	00
10	167	00
11	168	01
12	169	02
13	16A	03
14	16B	04
15	16C	05
16	16D	06
17	16E	07
18	16F	08
19	170 —**	09
20	177	00
21	178	02
22	179	04
23	17A	06
24	17B	08
25	17C	10
26	17D	12
27	17E	14
28	17F	16
29	180 —***	18
30	187	00
31	188	03
32	189	06
⋮	⋮	⋮
97	24E	63
98	24F	72
99	250	81

Unused storage locations:
*161, 162, 163, 164, 165, 166
**171, 172, 173, 174, 175, 176
***181, 182, 183, 184, 185, 186 etc.

---

age within the system is volatile. So when the system is powered down, the stored object program is destroyed and the object tape must be re-loaded for a new execution. Data on the object tape is usually densely packed so that reading a large object program is usually less than half an hour.

Some shortcuts are available—but they cost. Some of these are: storing the assembler on PROM (programable read-only memory) within the system; the use of a high-speed paper-tape reader and punch for data input and output (five to 15 times faster than a teletypewriter); or the use of minicomputer peripherals adapted for microprocessor systems, such as cassette tape systems, floppy disk systems, CRT terminals, and line printers. These devices can reduce system operating times by factors of 50 to 150. They can also provide other benefits, such as mass data storage and low-cost/high-speed hard-copy data. But the added peripherals can easily bump system costs by more than $10,000 and require a large amount of custom interface hardware and software.

Keep in mind that assembly of the source program is not necessary each time a change or correction is made in the object program. Most prototyping systems provide for "patching" or making program corrections via direct entry of machine code into memory. For small changes, this provides a means of keeping the original program running to check for other errors. Large changes (such as relocation of large blocks of code within memory) are very difficult and can create more problems than they solve.

Another factor that can keep the assembly of large source programs from becoming a man-killing job is that the main program can be assembled in blocks with vacancies inserted for future "patches." Only an affected block need be reassembled to correct errors. When the program is completely de-bugged, the blanks can be removed and the program reassembled, creating one continuous program with no wasted space.

One frequently hears that microprocessor systems offer greater flexibility for design changes because all it takes is simple modifications to the program. This can lead the programmer into days or weeks of debugging the

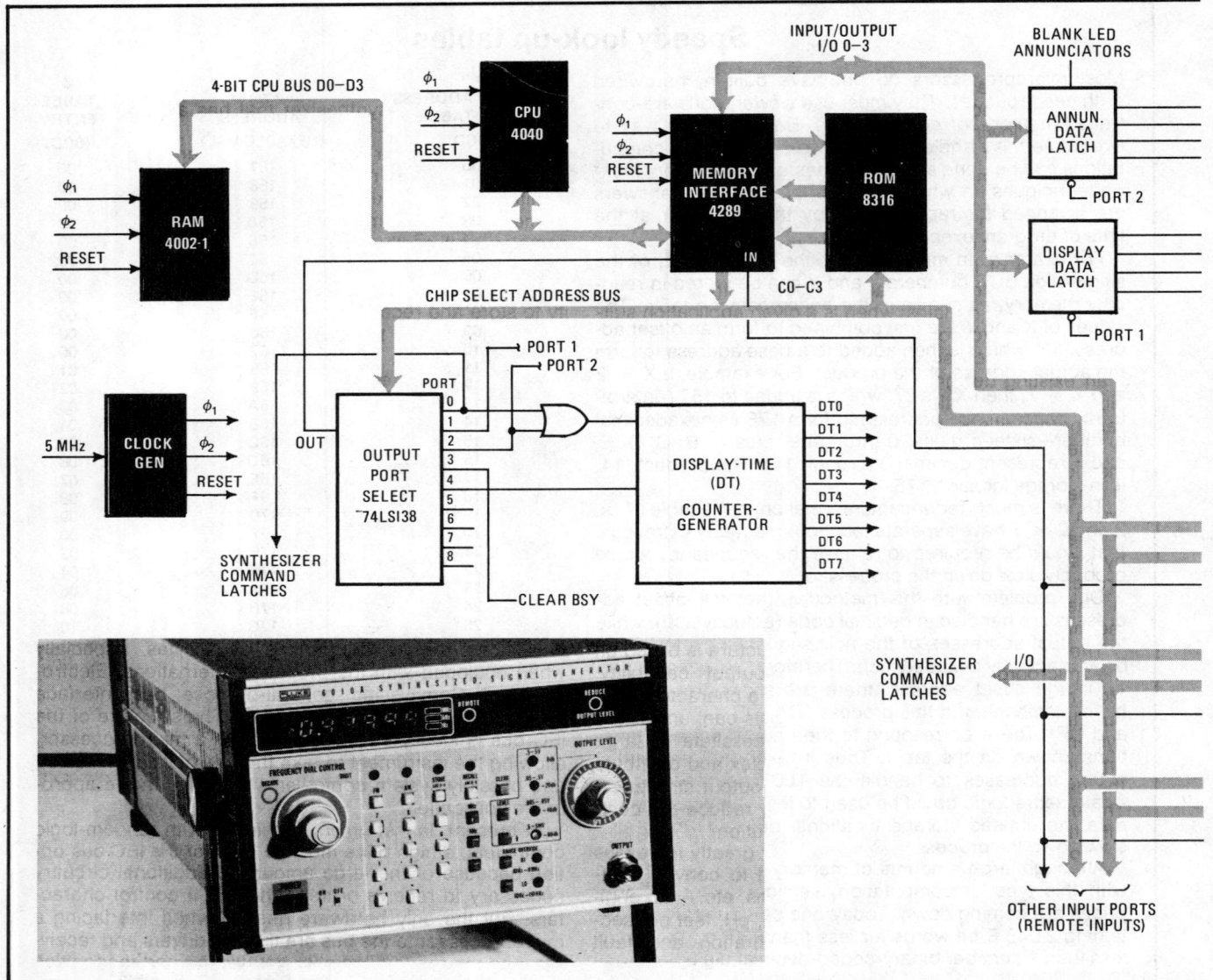

Synthesizer. In a new application, a microprocessor has been built into a 10-hertz to 11-megahertz frequency synthesizer to handle a 6-digit display, a dozen LED annunciators, and a 24-button keyboard. The chip set consists of five parts: a CPU, ROM, RAM, clock generator, and a memory interface circuit. In addition, about 30 TTL ICs are needed to handle the interfaces with other components.

"simple" program modifications. This is particularly true when the person making the changes did not write the original program. A densely packed, efficient program is like a finely "tweaked" analog circuit in which significant problems can be caused by subtle changes. A change to one part of the program can cause catastrophic occurrences in totally unrelated areas.

In-house computers

There is still another alternative, the use of an in-house computer system for program development. Microprocessor vendors have available assembly programs written in languages like Fortran, which can be used on a variety of computer systems and provide essentially the same capabilities as the time-shared services, in many cases the programs being the same. However, note that the computer required for such applications is large, costly, and may not be available.

Last of the alternative program development methods are the high level programing languages, like PL/M [*Electronics*, June 27, 1974, p. 103], available for some processors now on the market. They are similar in complexity to Basic or Fortran, where one program statement will generate many microprocessor instructions directly, as opposed to assembly languages which generate one microprocessor instruction from each program statement. These languages are relatively easy to learn. They are claimed to be within a small percentage of the efficiency of an experienced programer writing in assembly language, at least as far as the number of instructions to accomplish a particular task is concerned. However, the compilers for these languages are very large and usable only on large machines. Some time-sharing services offer them, and they may be more cost effective than assembly language methods.

Once the program development is complete and the

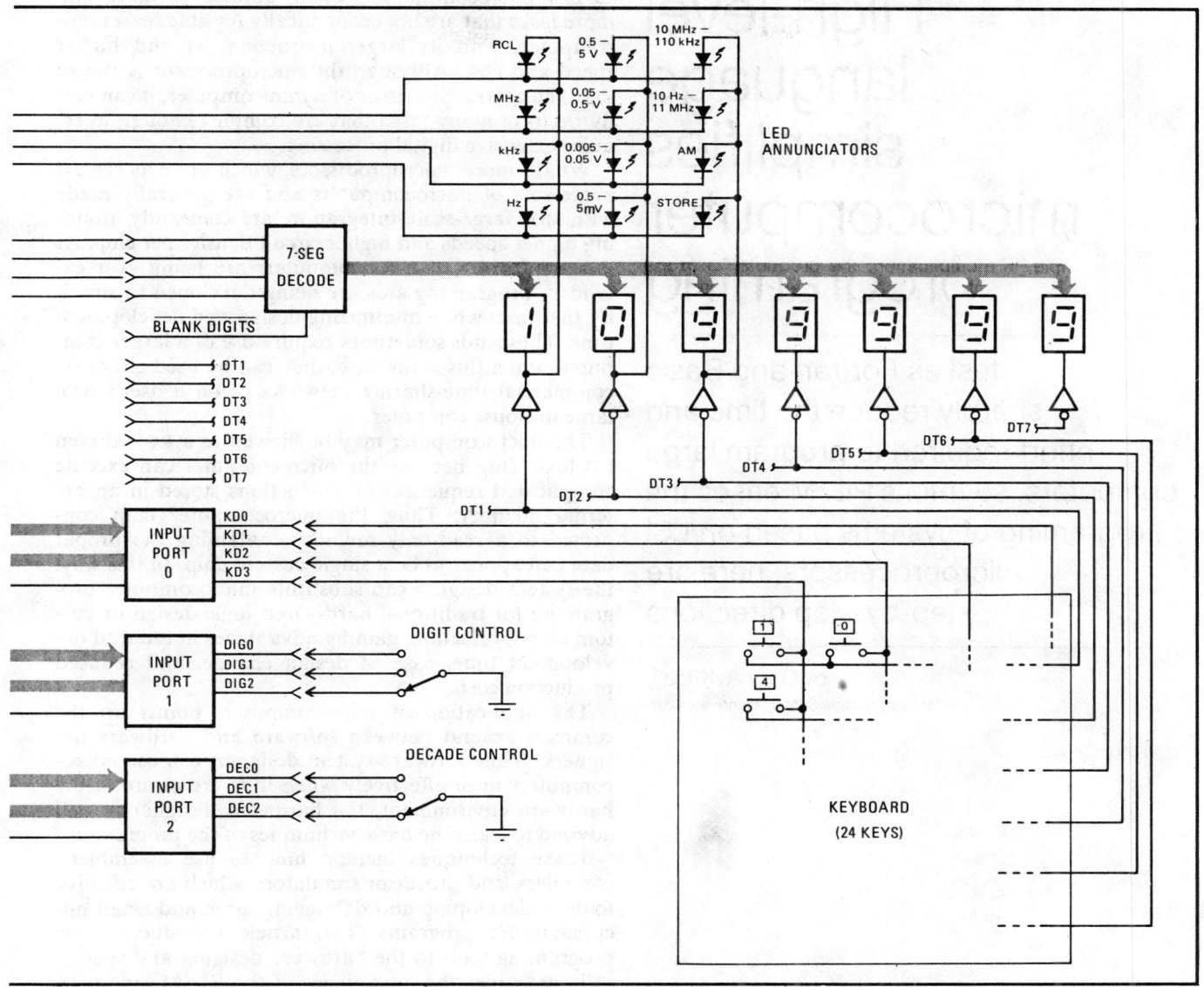

hardware design operational, the next step in the design process will be the stand-alone prototype instrument. To make this transition, a programable ROM is used to store the object program (typical PROMs have capacities of 256 eight-bit words). These devices can be programed on the prototyping system or by peripheral programing units, depending on the compatibility of the devices being used. Some PROMs can even be erased and reprogramed. Other PROMs can be programed only once, by using destructive programing methods, and once a bit is set, it cannot be erased.

An alternative method is to go directly from the prototyping system to a mask-programed ROM. However, the major disadvantage in the design cycle of this route is that they require a lead time for manufacture, which can vary from about 12 weeks for a first mask device to 8 for a last mask device. It is also possible to use PROM program storage on a production basis for a small quantity of instruments with a minimal amount of program storage in each.

The final problem area is that of production testing of the components, sub-assemblies and finished instruments. Of course, complete measurements of all parameters on microprocessor components can require extremely complex and costly test equipment. But comparable results can be attained with relatively simple functional testing, and with a minimum of additional test-equipment cost. This can be done by using a prototype instrument as a test bed and checking its performance with each new microprocessor component.

Troubleshooting and repair of functional modules or final assemblies can be best accomplished—with a minimum of aids—by direct component substitution. A word of warning, however, on preliminary inspection and handling of circuits: caution is needed so that solder bridges or other short circuits, or failed or improperly inserted parts, do not destroy expensive CPU or ROM ships at the moment of turn-on. It is relatively easy, while substituting components, to destroy several devices before a fault is located. And since most processor components are MOS, careful handling is required to prevent damage due to static electricity. □

High-level language simplifies microcomputer programing

Just as Fortran and Basic sharply reduce the time and effort required to program large computers, so Intel's PL/M eases the programing of systems based on LSI microprocessors; here are step-by-step directions

by Gary A. Kildall,
Naval Postgraduate School, Monterey, Calif.

☐ The microcomputer is being applied to more and more tasks that are not economically feasible for a minicomputer, with its larger instruction set and higher speed and cost. Although the microprocessor is slower than the central processor of a minicomputer, it can easily perform many tasks that are complex enough to require extensive digital processing.

What's more, microprocessors, which serve as central processors of microcomputers and are generally made with MOS large-scale integration, are constantly attaining higher speeds and higher circuit density per chip. As the capabilities of microcomputers are being ever extended, programing aids are being developed to simplify their use, while minimizing design and development time. These aids sometimes require use of a larger computer; when this is the case, they can be used either on commercial time-sharing networks or on a user's own large in-house computer.

The microcomputer may be viewed as a ROM-driven LSI logic chip because the microcomputer can execute complicated sequences of instructions stored in an external memory. Thus, the microcomputer chip connected to a read-only memory containing the proper data can appear to be a single custom chip. In this way, the system designer can substitute microcomputer programing for traditional hard-wired logic design or custom chip fabrication, gaining advantages in reduced development time, ease of design change, and reduced production costs.

The application of microcomputers points up the common ground between software and hardware designers. While software-system designers can use microcomputers most effectively when they are aware of the hardware environment, the hardware designer is well advised to learn the basic techniques of the programer.

These techniques include how to use assemblers, compilers, and processor simulators, which are effective tools in developing and debugging large and small microcomputer programs. This article introduces these programing tools to the hardware designer and specifically examines the advantages of the PL/M language, which make possible rapid design of systems around the MCS-8 microcomputer, made by Intel Corp.

The MCS-8 is based on the 8008 microprocessor, one of a new class of devices being offered by several manu-

1. Symbolic. This simple program for choosing the larger of two numbers takes nine lines of code in symbolic or assembly language, but typically only one line in a higher-level language, such as PL/M.

LABEL	INSTRUCTION	COMMENT
TEST	SHL B	LOAD ADDRESS OF B
	LAM	LOAD B INTO ACCUM
	SHL A	LOAD ADDRESS OF A
	CPM	COMPARE B WITH A
	JFC L1	JUMP TO L1 IF B ≤ A
	LAM	LOAD A INTO ACCUM
L1	SHL C	LOAD ADDRESS OF C
	LMA	STORE ACCUM INTO C
	END	END OF PROGRAM

facturers as a result of recent advances in semiconductor electronics. The PL/M programing aid is a good example of the service that these manufacturers can offer to simplify the use of their products.

Minimizing software costs

Like other programing tools, the PL/M approach automates the production of programs to counteract the rapidly increasing cost of software production at a time when hardware costs are decreasing. And, in addition to rapid production turnaround, the programs can be fully checked out early in the design process. What's more, the self-documentation of PL/M programs enables one programer to readily understand the work of another, which dramatically reduces program-maintenance costs and provides transportability of software between programers and to other Intel processors as they are introduced.

Additional cost reductions will also result from standardization of parts and modules, and alterability of the final program often outweighs benefits of random-logic designs or custom-chip fabrication.

The PL/M compiler, which is another program, translates the PL/M program into machine language. This compiler, which can be run on a medium- or large-scale computer, is available from several nationwide time-sharing services.

Last but not least, PL/M programs can be recompiled as improved optimizing versions of the compiler are released, as Intel has recently done. A recent revision of the PL/M compiler, for example, makes possible reduction of generated code by about 15%.

Although PL/M requires a cross-compiler—one that runs only on a larger machine—a resident compiler that uses the microcomputer itself to produce its programs is technically feasible with the advanced state of microcomputer development and today's inexpensive peripherals. Such a compiler would require several passes to reduce a PL/M source program to machine language, using the developmental system itself, and eliminating the need for large-system support.

A program for the Intel 8008 microprocessor is a sequence of instructions from its normal instruction set (see "Hardware for PL/M," p. 105) that performs a particular task. Given no programing aids, the designer must determine the machine codes that represent each of the instructions in his program and store these codes into program memory. This approach to programing quickly becomes unwieldy in all but the most trivial projects.

Nearly all manufacturers of microprocessors (and mini- and maxicomputers as well) provide symbolic assemblers—programs that ease the programing task by eliminating the need to translate instructions manually into machine-readable form. The designer can express his program in terms of mnemonics, which are abbreviations that suggest individual instructions. Then the assembler translates each mnemonic instruction into its binary representation.

Symbolic addresses

In addition, the programer can refer to memory locations by symbolic name, rather than actual numeric address; the assembler translates these, as well as the instructions. The assembler usually runs on a larger computer, although both Intel Corp. and National Semiconductor Corp. have assemblers that run directly on their microcomputer-based development systems, and symbolic programs for Rockwell microcomputers can be assembled on a machine built around that unit by Applied Computer Technology Inc. The assembler requires significantly less development and check-out time than manual translation, and there are fewer coding errors.

```
LINE        STATEMENT

 1          DECLARE MESSAGE DATA ('WALLA WALLA WASH'),
 2              (CHAR, I, J, SENDBIT) BYTE;
 3
 4          /* SEND EACH CHARACTER FROM MESSAGE VECTOR TO TELEPRINTER */
 5              DO I = 0 TO LAST(MESSAGE);
 6              CHAR = MESSAGE(I);
 7              SENDBIT = 0;
 8
 9              /* SEND EACH BIT FROM CHAR TO TELEPRINTER */
10                  DO J = 1 TO 11;
11                  OUTPUT(0) = SENDBIT;
12                  CALL TIME (91); /* WATTS 9.1 MS */
13                  SENDBIT = CHAR AND 1;
14                  /* ROTATE CHAR FOR NEXT ITERATION */
15                  CHAR = ROR (CHAR OR 1, 1);
16                  END;
17          END;
```

2. Serial sender. To print a short message on a Teletype, this routine in PL/M transmits 11 pulses at 9.1-millisecond intervals for each character in the message, stopping after the last one. The pulse train consists of one start pulse, eight data pulses, and two stop pulses.

Hardware for PL/M

The Intel MCS-8 microcomputer consists of the 8008 microprocessor plus a collection of standard read/write and read-only memories and shift registers. The 8008 is a single-chip MOS device with
- 8-bit parallel word size
- Seven 8-bit general-purpose registers
- 16,384-word address capability, in either read-only or read/write memory
- Up to 32 8-bit latched input and output ports

The MCS-8 instruction set includes register-to-register, register-to-memory, and memory-to-register transfers, along with arithmetic, logic, and comparison instructions. Conditional and unconditional transfers and subroutine calls are also provided. Input and output instructions read data from input ports and set data into output-port latches. Each of these instructions is represented in program memory by a sequence of one, two, or three 8-bit words.

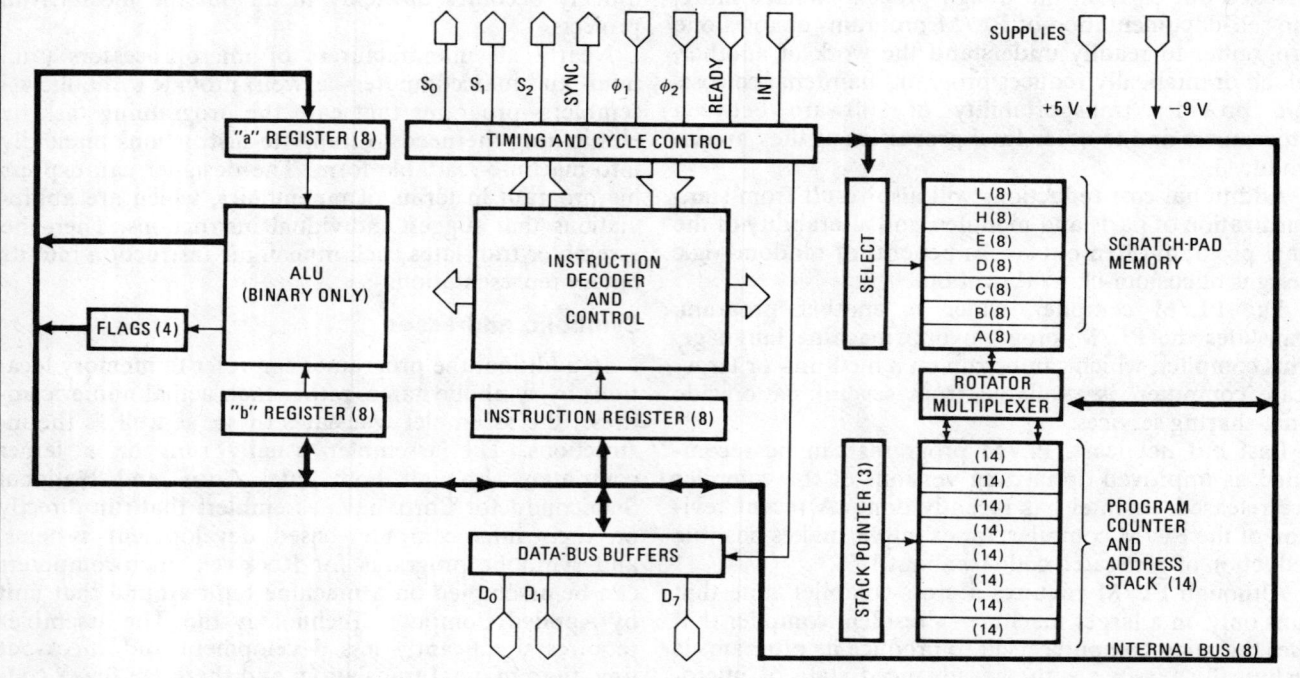

Assembly-language programing, however, is necessarily closely related to the machine architecture because instructions in symbolic code have a one-to-one correspondence with those in machine code. As a result, the programer must spend much more time keeping track of the location of data elements and proper register usage than actually conceptualizing the solution to his problem.

On large-scale computers, high-level languages have been developed to provide important facilities independently of particular machine architectures, while eliminating the trivialities of assembly languages. These facilities include program-control structures, data types, and primitive operations suitable for concise expressions of programs in particular problem environments. For example, a problem environment may be one of numerical computation, in which application-oriented programing languages like Basic and Fortran are appropriate. Or the environment may be the control of a particular class of computer and all its functions, for which system languages, which are necessarily closely related to the machine architecture, are useful.

In a system language, program statements generally correspond directly with machine-level instructions, and conversely, every machine operation is reflected in a high-level language statement. Because of this corre-

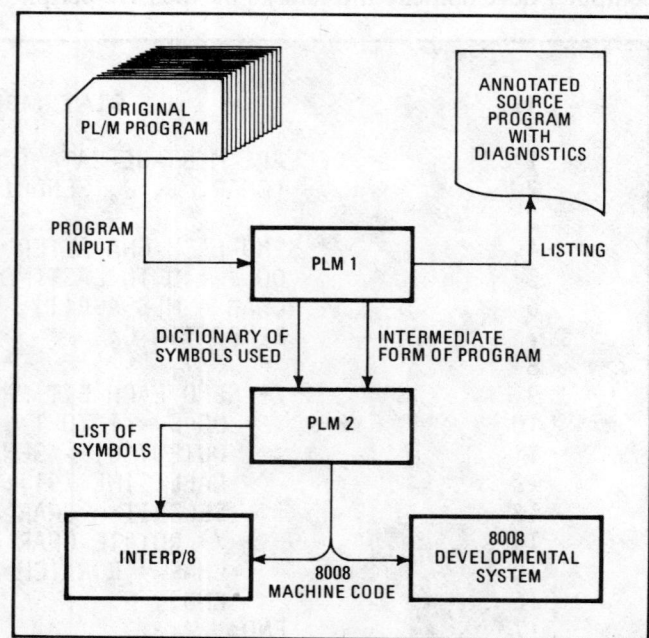

3. Compiler. Translating PL/M programs into machine language takes two passes with programs called PLM1 and PLM2, run by a larger machine. A third pass, with Interp/8, simulates the microprocessor on the big machine to check out the program.

4. SIM8-01. This Intel product checks out a program written in MCS-8 machine code or compiled into machine code from the PL/M language. Erasable ROMs store the program, and a Teletype gives input/output.

5. Intellec 8. This developmental system can check out programs written in PL/M. It also serves as a prototype for production systems based on the MCS-8.

spondence, system-language programs usually translate efficiently to the machine-language level, and the programer finds all the machine's facilities directly available to him. PL/M, an example of such a language, was designed for use with the 8008 microprocessor, and is also usable with Intel's newer 8080 microprocessor [*Electronics*, April 18, p. 95], which has more useful machine-level instructions and a considerably faster instruction cycle than its predecessor.

Nevertheless, some hardware designers, particularly those newly introduced to software systems, may prefer to work at a comfortable level, which may mean programing in absolute machine code initially and then moving to assembly language as more capability is required. Similarly, they can easily make the transition to a high-level language when programing in assembly-language becomes tedious.

In any case, the designer soon becomes familiar with various programing levels. One of these levels can then be intelligently selected as most appropriate for a given application. Each level has its own advantages. For example, a program in PL/M that compiles into about 500 bytes of memory space when using the 8008's instruction set might require perhaps as much as 30% less space if it were coded directly in assembly language. But larger programs running 1,000 bytes or more usually turn out to be more compact when written in PL/M than in assembly language because the compiler can keep track more easily of memory-reference areas, registers, and other resources. The amount of machine code generated in assembly language or PL/M varies, of course, with program complexity and style. Thus, an absolute comparison between the two is not possible.

Simple coding

The PL/M language consists of a number of basic statement types in which complicated arithmetic, logical, and character operations on 8-bit and 16-bit quantities can be expressed in a form resembling usual algebraic notation. Relational tests can be expressed in a natural way to control conditional branching throughout the PL/M program.

For example, to move the larger of two numbers in locations A and B into the location called C, either the PL/M statement,

IF A > B, THEN C=A; ELSE C=B

or the nine-instruction assembly-language program shown in Fig. 1 can be used. The statement reads, "If the value of A is greater than the value of B, then set C to equal A; otherwise set C to equal B."

Additional language structures provide iteration control to permit program segments to be "looped," or executed repeatedly a prescribed number of times. Subroutine facilities include mechanisms that are useful for modular programing and construction of subroutine libraries.

The over-all structure of the PL/M language is most easily demonstrated by a simple example. Suppose a teleprinter is connected to the least-significant bit of an output port of the Intel 8008. A PL/M program that sends a short message to the teleprinter is shown in Fig. 2; it individually times the transmission of the bits through the output port. This program can be translated into machine code loaded into the memory of the MCS-8, and then it is executed.

The program begins with a data declaration that defines a string of Ascii characters—the words "Walla Walla Wash" as shown in line 1. The 16 individual characters of this string are labeled from 0 to 15 so that they can be addressed by the program (spaces are characters, too). Four variables, or 8-bit memory locations, CHAR, I, J, and SENDBIT, are defined on line 2.

Any names

These designations are wholly arbitrary; the programer may use any names he wants, so long as he defines them before he uses them. CHAR holds each character of the message in succession for transmission, I identifies the position of the character in the message, and J controls the position of the bit in the character. The right-most bit of location SENDBIT is the next bit to be transmitted.

Since the instructions between lines 5 and 17 are executed repetitively, they are collectively called a loop. Before each repetition, the variable I is incremented until its value indicates the position of the last character in MESSAGE—in this case, 15.

First, the value of all bits in SENDBIT is set to 0 on line 7 to send a start pulse as the first bit (line 11). Then the individual bits of the selected character are sent in the inner loop between lines 10 and 16. This loop is executed 11 times, corresponding to the start pulse, 8 data bits, and 2 stop pulses, during each passage through the outer loop, beginning on line 5.

Each successive bit is sent on line 11, followed by a 9.1-millisecond time-out. This time delay is a standard feature in PL/M; the compiler implements it by inserting a wait loop in the program. The wait loop stores an appropriate number in a counter, decrements it once each processor cycle, and allows the program to continue when the counter reaches zero.

On each inner-loop iteration, the right-most bit of CHAR is selected on line 13 by the AND function, and it is stored in SENDBIT. The operation on line 15 places a 1 in the right-most position of CHAR and then rotates the result one step to the right. This step gradually fills CHAR with 1s, working from left to right in each iteration, so that two stop pulses, which are 1s, are sent properly on the 10th and 11th iterations.

The operation of the PL/M compiler and its PLM1 and PLM2 subdivisions is shown graphically in Fig. 3. PLM1 accepts a PL/M source program from a card reader, time-sharing console, or other input device. This first pass produces a listing of the source program, along with any error diagnostics, and analyzes the program structure. An intermediate file that contains a linearized version of the original program is written, and the symbols used in it are listed.

Although the linearized version does not resemble either an assembly language or PL/M, it has been reduced to a highly simplified form of the original program. PLM2 uses this intermediate file as input and generates machine code for the 8008 microcomputer.

A PL/M program can often be checked out by simulating the 8008 microcomputer's actions on a larger ma-

```
STRING COMPARISON PROGRAM
TYPE SOURCE STRING:  A  B  C  D
TYPE TEST STRING:
  A  B  C  D
*  *  *  *
TYPE SOURCE STRING:  666 666 666
TYPE TEST STRING:  6
666 666 666
*** *** ***
TYPE SOURCE STRING:  AAAAAAAABABABA
TYPE TEST STRING: AB
AAAAAAAABABABA
       *  *  *
TYPE SOURCE STRING:  XXXXXXX$
TYPE TEST STRING:  XXXX
XXXXXXX
****
TYPE SOURCE STRING:  WALLA WALLA WASH
TYPE TEST STRING:  WALLA$
WALLA WALLA WASH
*     *
```

6. Test run. Sample PL/M program produced this printout. Manually entered data is in color, and machine output is in black. Technique is valuable debugging tool.

chine. A third program, called Interp/8, is available for this purpose. The three programs PLM1, PLM2, and Interp/8 are written in ANSI standard Fortran IV, and will run on most larger computer systems.

A new version of the PL/M compiler is available for use with the extended instruction set of the 8080. Consisting of sections PLM81 and PLM82, it is accompanied by a new simulator called Interp/80. New coding is not required for the 8080. Working with old PL/M programs written for the 8008, the compiler can produce binary code requiring 10% to 20% less storage than the 8008 requires, and having the advantages of new interrupt and decimal-arithmetic capabilities.

Experience with PL/M will enable designers of future Intel microprocessors to incorporate new machine-level instructions that will make more efficient use of the PL/M language. Furthermore, if Intel so chooses, it can alter its processor architecture in future designs, as it did between the 8008 and 8080, without affecting the user of PL/M at all, except possibly to improve the performance of this application.

A number of microcomputer manufacturers are considering the use of high-level languages to augment their assembly-language products, although none have been announced yet. Several minicomputer producers, however, offer high-level applications languages, and at least one minicomputer company, Microdata Corp., provides a systems language. In fact, Microdata's MPL language [*Electronics*, Feb. 15, 1973, p. 95] closely resembles PL/M; both of them, in fact, were essentially derived from the same basic system language.

Once the PL/M program is written and checked out, the machine code is punched on paper tape (Fig. 3) and loaded into memory of a microcomputer developmental system. Again, the program is verified, and all real-time and environmental considerations are checked out. Final production systems can then be developed from this prototype. The production system, for example, may use read-only memory for the program when the developmental system's memory is read/write.

How to go on the air

Given a PL/M program and an MCS-8 microcomputer, how does a programer actually go through the compilation and execution process? As mentioned previously, the PL/M compiler is available from several nationwide time sharing services. These are the General Electric, Tymshare, National CSS, Applied Logic Corp., and United Computing Services facilities. Documentation for general programming is available from Intel Corp., and the time-sharing services provide system-dependent operating instructions.

Once the programer has a contract with the commercial service, he is assigned a work area in the host system in which he can store PL/M programs. These programs are created on line by using the time-sharing service's editor, which allows the programer to enter and alter program files. When a particular program is created, it is saved in a permanent file for subsequent compilation.

In the compilation process, PLM1 is executed first, using the saved PL/M program as input. Any diagnostic messages are printed at the time-sharing console. If no program errors are detected during the PLM1 pass, then the programer can call for PLM2. This second pass leaves code in MCS-8 machine language, which corresponds to the original program in the user's work area.

With this code, the programer may execute the Interp/8 program, which reads the machine code and simulates the actions of the MCS-8, as previously discussed. If execution errors appear during simulation, the programer can alter the original PL/M program and repeat the compilation and simulation process. When the programer is convinced the program is correct, he can punch the machine language on paper tape or other medium at his local console.

Programing at home

When a large amount of development work is to be done, the user may find it feasible to purchase the PL/M compiler and CPU simulator directly from Intel and run them on an in-house computer system. The user, at his option, can program either in batch or time-sharing mode.

The machine code produced by the compiler can be executed in several different ways. The easiest method is with a developmental system, such as the Intel SIM8-01 or Intellec 8 (Figs. 4 and 5) or equivalent prototyping hardware. These systems include hardware and software for Teletype, as well as facilities for loading and checking out programs.

The machine code is loaded into the SIM8-01 from the Teletype into erasable read-only memories. These chips are then inserted into sockets on the prototype board, and the program is executed. With the Intellec 8 developmental system, the machine code is entered from the Teletype into read/write memory, where the program can be subsequently executed and tested. Both approaches bypass the simulation stage.

After testing the program on a developmental system, a production model making use of MCS-8 and a mixture of read-only and read/write memory can be tailored closely to the final application. Although the hardware is minimized in the production system to reduce costs, the programs remain the same as in the prototype.

Developing systems

Intel Corp. has completed a number of projects using PL/M, including an assembler that runs on the Intellec 8 developmental system. This assembler's characteristics show the effectiveness of the PL/M approach to system development. For example, it has full macro capabilities, which means that a programer can define special pseudo-instructions that cause the assembler to insert sequences of instructions in the main program during the assembly process. Macros are like subroutines, except that the main program executes them as it comes to them, instead of branching out of the main stream and then returning, as it does with subroutines.

The assembler is also capable of conditional assembly, which means that it can react to such external signals as the positions of console switches at the time of assembly. Such signals indicate conditions that are not necessarily known to the programer at the time he writes the code—such as the availability of particular output equipment to which the assembler's results are to be sent.

Another useful characteristic of the assembler is evaluation of expressions at assembly time, which permits the programer to specify certain parameters algebraically instead of numerically or symbolically. Then when a program is assembled, the assembler evaluates the algebraic expressions and inserts the correct values in the machine-language program. The process requires the variables to be specified ahead of time, but it permits the programer to alter these variables by changing their specification only once, rather than every time they are used in the program. It's a great time-saver and bug-killer.

While these characteristics are not uncommon in advanced assembly languages, high-level languages that can handle them are quite rare. Yet by using PL/M, the assembler was coded in approximately 100 man-hours, and it requires 6,000 bytes of program storage—equivalent to 3,000 words on a minicomputer with a 16-bit word size. Intel estimates that the project would have taken five times as long to code and debug directly in assembly language, with little or no reduction in program-memory space. The resulting assembler is easy to maintain and alter, and, equally important, it can be recompiled for Intel's new 8080 microprocessor without alteration.

A practical example

PL/M permits many programing shortcuts, such as dividing a complex task into individual subtasks, or procedures, that are called upon when needed to simplify the job of writing the program itself. These procedures are conceptually simple and therefore easy to formulate and express in PL/M, as well as easy to check out before being incorporated in a larger program.

For example, consider a simple program for character manipulation—one that might be part of the work of a more comprehensive word-processing system. The function is relatively simple: the program asks the keyboard for two input-character strings, scans the first string for all occurrences of the second, echoes the first string, and types an asterisk under the starting position in the first string of each occurrence of the second string. A sample interaction with this program is shown in Fig. 6; all lines typed by the operator are in color.

Stated in this way, this example may seem to have little or no practical value. But it is almost identical to a program needed to fetch the strings from two different data-entry devices and do something more sophisticated than printing an asterisk when it finds a match.

This suggests a practical application—a teleprinter to check out a routine before it is embedded in a larger program. When all the bugs are out of the routine, the procedures that transfer data to and from the teleprinter can be replaced with other procedures that, for example, check sensors and turn indicators on and off. The new procedures, of course, have to be checked out in a real environment, but that's much easier when the main routine is known to be bug-free. □

PLAs enhance digital processor speed and cut component count

Programed logic arrays, which are simplified read-only memories, offer benefits of microprograming, but avoid some of its pitfalls; the advantage comes through programing addresses as well as data

by George Reyling, *National Semiconductor Corp., Santa Clara, Calif.*

☐ Engineers faced with the problem of designing digital processors and control units may use programed logic arrays, or PLAs, to get faster operation than is feasible with large-scale MOS integrated circuits, while at the same time reducing the component count below that of traditional random logic. A PLA is a read-only memory with programable addresses; when used in place of a conventional ROM, it provides the major advantages of microprograming while avoiding many of its problems.

Several vendors offer PLA products now or are expected to offer them soon. These products suggest several applications in computer design. PLAs have been used in microprogramed microprocessors and single-chip calculators made with MOS technology, where space is at a premium and the number of functions is limited. In the same way, TTL microprogramed processors may also benefit from PLAs.

And, in addition to their potential use as control memories, one of the most straightforward applications of PLAs is in address transformation in conventional control memories. They may also be used with registers directly in peripheral-device controllers to implement the flow charts of state diagrams. This reduces design time and permits fewer errors.

Other applications include code converters, implementing decision tables, and, where only one task is required for any given set of input conditions, a single PLA may be used as a condition-driven lookup table or code converter, giving the address of the program to be executed directly.

The anatomy of the PLA

Like a conventional read-only memory, a PLA is a matrix of crosspoints; a mask superimposed on the matrix during its manufacture establishes connections at some crosspoints and leaves other crosspoints open. Each connection is usually a transistor or a diode, so that energy can flow in only one direction through the connection, eliminating spurious "sneak paths" through the array.

The matrix of a PLA is divided into two parts (Fig. 1). In the first part, input signals (and their complements, usually internally generated) are selectively connected to product-term lines in such a way that certain combinations of inputs produce a logically true signal on one or more of the product-term lines. These lines are inputs to the second part of the matrix, where other selective connections transfer the true state from each product-term line to one or more output lines.

In fact, the only difference between the PLA and the ROM is that, in the ROM, *all* combinations of inputs cause an output to appear—whereas in a PLA some combinations may have no effect, and some groups of combinations may be indistinguishable, as described later.

Effectively, the second part of the matrix is pro-

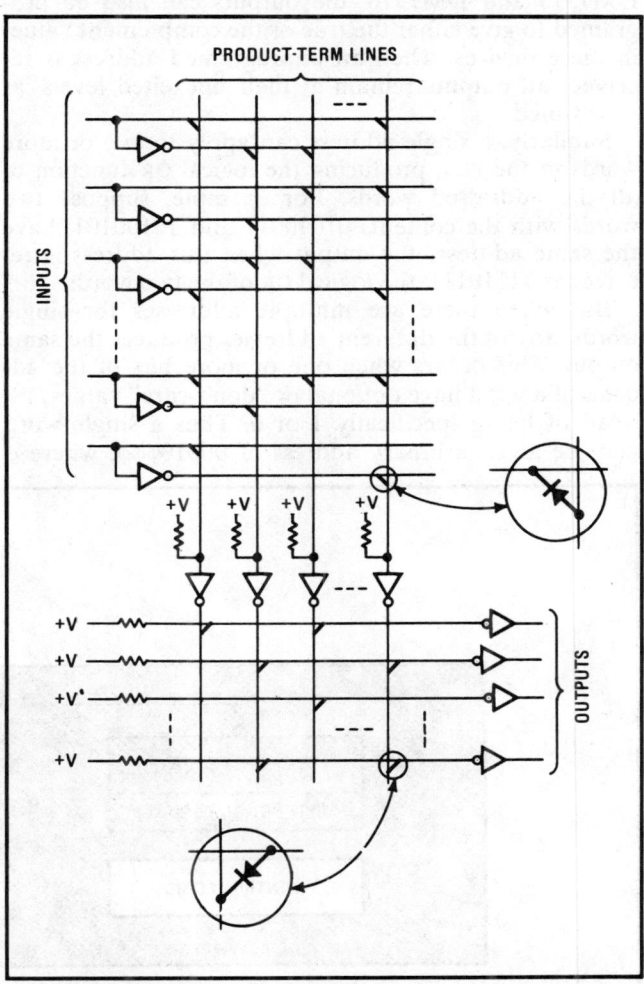

1. Programed logic array. Like a ROM, a PLA is a matrix, but addresses are programed, as well as data. Using optional bits in an address permits two or more addresses to point to one word.

> **Don't be confused**
>
> Programable logic arrays now offer many advantages in microprograming digital processors and control units. But storing a microprogram in a PLA is not the same as using a PLA as a collection of programable AND and OR gates to construct a random-logic controller. The latter is a valid alternative to the use of read-only memories as truth tables, and it may be a quicker way to complete a design. The use of both ROMs and PLAs in random-logic design is already well documented.

gramed at the time of manufacture with the PLA's data, while the first part contains its programed addresses, also specified during manufacture. Because the addresses are programed, the PLA can cope with certain special address conditions more easily than a ROM can. These special cases include unprogramed addresses, single addresses for multiple words, and multiple addresses for single words.

An unprogramed address input doesn't read any word of the PLA, so that all bits of the output, in general, remain at 0. (In some PLAs, such as National's parts DM7575 and DM7576, the outputs can also be programed to give either the true or the complement value; in these devices, when an unprogramed address is received, all outputs remain at their unexcited levels, as programed.)

Similarly, a single address can apply to two or more words in the PLA, producing the logical OR function of all the addressed words. For example, suppose two words with the contents 01010011 and 10100101, have the same address; the output when this address is received is 11110111, the logical OR of the two words.

But when there are multiple addresses for single words, any of the different addresses produces the same output. This occurs when one or more bits of the address of a word have optional or "don't-care" values; instead of being specifically 1 or 0. Thus a single word may be given a binary address of $00010\phi\phi\phi$, where ϕ represents an optional value; this word appears at the PLA output when any address in the decimal range 16 through 23 inclusive (binary 00010000 through 00010111) is sent to the PLA input.

Optional values are supplied to the address of a word in the PLA simply by leaving both the true and complement input lines unconnected to the product-term lines in the address part of the PLA matrix. The ϕ symbol is used because it resembles a 1 superimposed on a 0.

This use of optional address bits is the basis of the PLA's advantage over the ROM, which requires exhaustive decoding to achieve the same results. For the three special cases mentioned, the ROM must respond to every address. It must produce an all-0s word for a meaningless address, corresponding to the PLA's unprogramed address; a word specifically programed with the logical OR of two or more other words, corresponding to the single address for multiple words; and separate identical words for nearly identical addresses, which can't contain optional bits.

Furthermore, the PLA can implement several simple functions by using only part of the structure for each function; or complex functions can be implemented by connecting several PLAs in series or parallel.

Microprogramed processors

Most microprogrammed computers and processors have two levels of programing: the microinstruction level and the external instruction level. External instructions are stored in the main memory (Fig. 2), and microinstructions, which direct the basic functions of the processor, are stored in the control memory.

Microprograms may be "horizontal," that is, have instructions with many bits that individually control all parts of a processor in a single cycle at relatively high speed; or they may be "vertical," with fewer bits encoded in groups to specify different kinds of processor controls, requiring several cycles per instruction. Vertical microprograms run more slowly, but they are easier to write and to modify.

Control memories are often implemented with read-only memories; but in some instances, a read-only

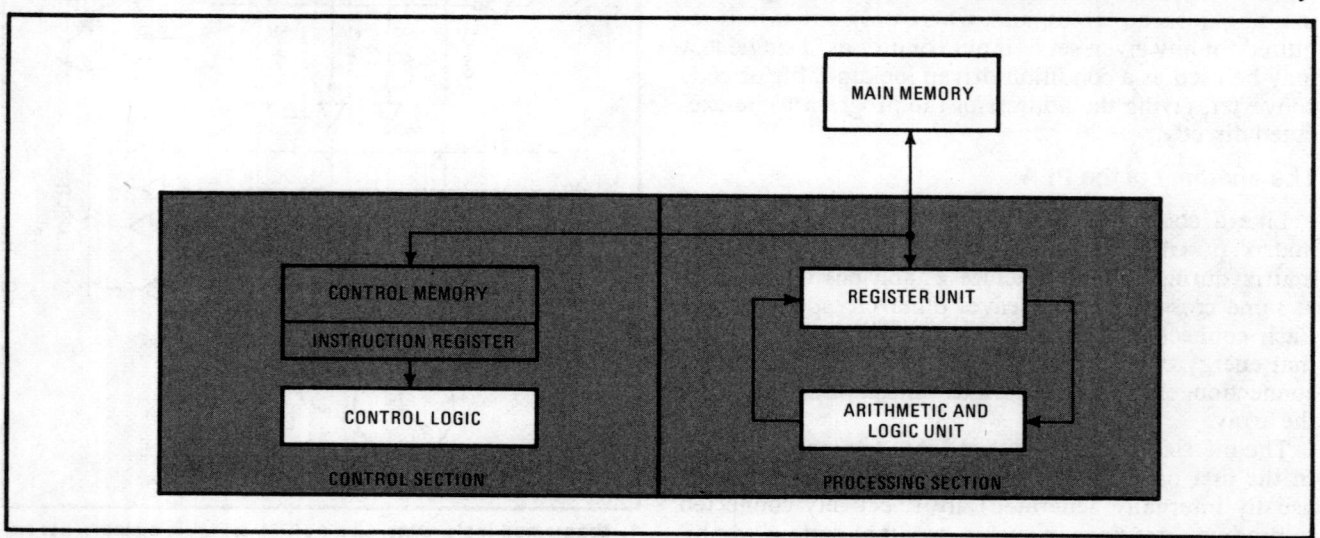

2. Microinstruction control. Basically, the operation code of an instruction in the user's program (external) is interpreted as an address specifying, in the microprogram (internal), the beginning of the routine that executes the external instruction.

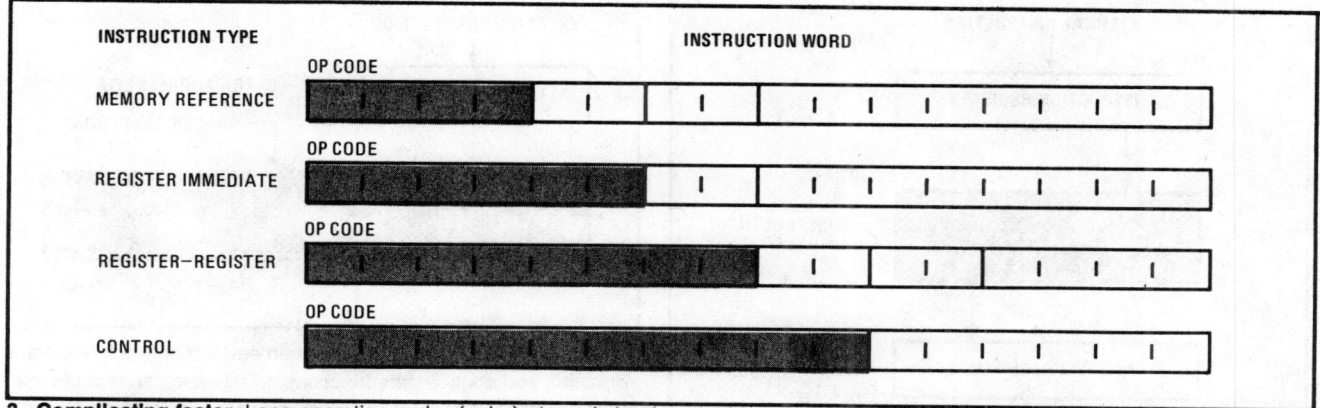

3. Complicating factor. Long operation codes (color) at user's level may address nonexistent control-store locations. Short ones may not address all of a store. Other instruction-word parts (black) specify such locations as main-memory address and internal register.

memory requires more complex control logic that can be simplified with a PLA. The need for address transformation in control memories is also shown by a consideration of how the microprogram is brought into the operation of the processor.

Problems with variable formats

The microprogram is a collection of microroutines, each one a series of microinstructions corresponding to a particular external instruction. For example, the microroutine for a REGISTER ADD instruction would obtain data from two appropriate registers, route them through the adder, and store the result in a designated register.

The address of the microroutine in the control memory is, most simply, the operation code of the external instruction. The code is interpreted as an address after the entire instruction is fetched from main memory and placed in the instruction register by a separate microroutine. As such, it points only to the first word of the microroutine; successive words, if any, are taken in the proper order as the microroutine is executed, under direction either of external logic or of certain bits fed back from the control memory output.

But this simple approach presents a considerable problem when the operation code for various instructions in a particular processor are of different lengths. Some of them may have more bits than are necessary to address the control store—which implies that some operation codes, interpreted as binary addresses, may point to nonexistent control locations.

Choice, not coercion

For example, consider the instruction format for a hypothetical but typical computer using 16-bit instructions (Fig. 3). The operation code varies from 4 to 10 bits in length. The control store may contain only a few hundred words, but the 10-bit operation code can address a maximum of 1,024 locations. Thus it should not specify the address of the microroutine directly because the address would sometimes exceed the storage capacity. Furthermore, even if the control store contains more than 1,024 words, the microprogramer should have the choice of starting addresses for his microroutines, rather than having them specified directly by the operation code, so that he can avoid awkward problems that can arise, for example, from almost identical operation codes.

Suppose the ADD and SUBTRACT codes are almost identical. This is not unreasonable because both call for two operands to be put through the adder, and they differ only in that one of the operands in SUBTRACT is complemented (all 1s replaced by 0s and vice versa) before adding. Both operations, therefore, would be controlled by almost identical microroutines, and their operation codes might differ in only one bit. If that bit is in or near the least-significant-bit position of the code (the right end), the two microroutines would begin in consecutive or nearby locations in the control store, and they may therefore overlap. On the other hand, if the bit that distinguishes ADD from SUBTRACT is in or near the most-significant-bit position of the operation (the left end) the two microroutines would begin in locations far removed from one another in the control store, and may overlap wholly unrelated microroutines.

Thus, an arbitrary operation code should be transformed into a convenient control store address (Fig. 4). Past designs have performed this function with logic

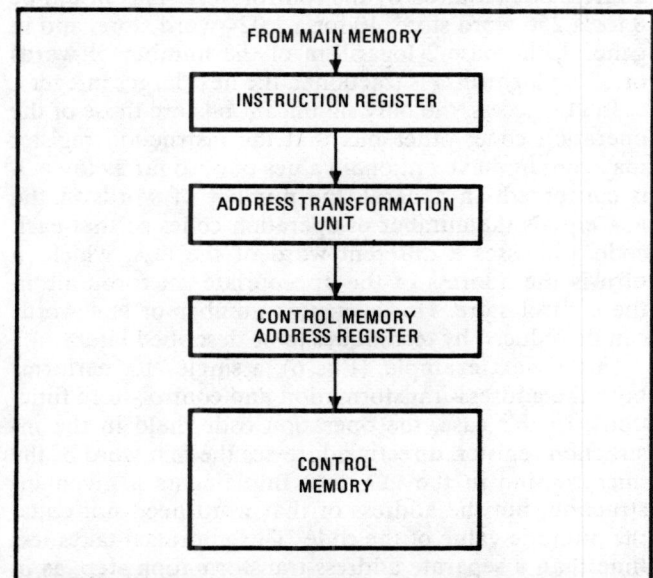

4. Address transformation. Having operation code generate a control store address overcomes difficulties of addressing the store directly and permits efficient microprogram organization.

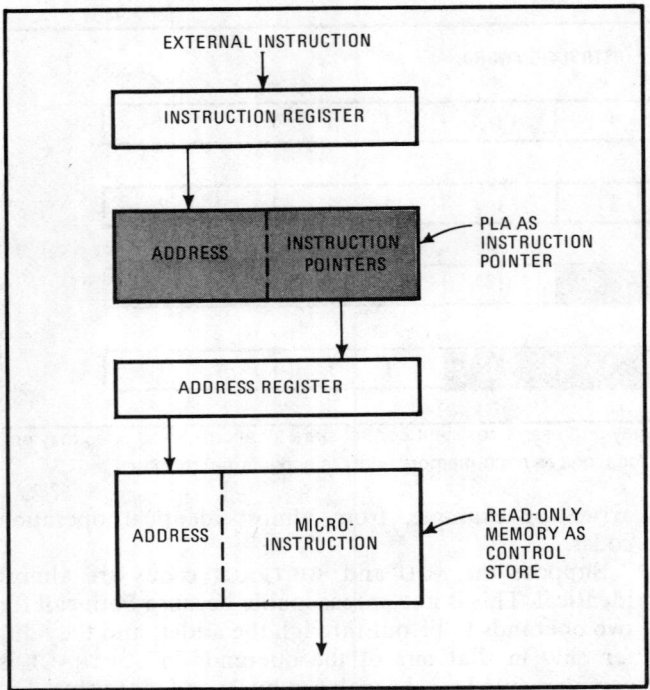

5. PLA plus ROM. Simplest address-transformation technique uses PLA in path between instruction register and conventional ROM. Longest operation code defines number of PLA inputs.

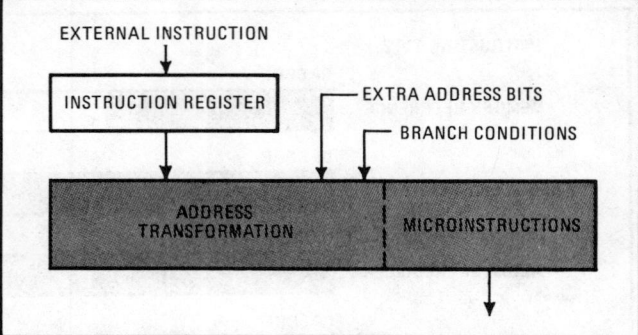

6. PLA instead of ROM. One PLA can perform both address-transformation and control-store functions quickly and can react to interrupts directly. But, since it has many inputs, it is quite large.

gates and multiplexers, but the choice of operation codes and starting addresses has been limited by the need to minimize the logic complexity.

Alternatively, the address transformation may be implemented with a PLA in any of three ways, shown by the following examples:

The first case (Fig. 5) combines a PLA for address transformation with a conventional read-only memory for a microprogram. The number of PLA-address inputs equals the number of bits in the longest operation code, while the number of PLA outputs equals the number of address bits required by the control store. This would be 8 for a 256-word store, 10 for a 1,024-word store, and in general, the base-2 logarithm of the number of words or, if the logarithm is fractional, the next larger integer.

In PLA access, the only significant bits are those of the operation code; other bits that the instruction register may contain have optional values of ϕ, so far as the PLA is concerned. In general, the number of words in the PLA equals the number of operation codes so that each code addresses a different word of the PLA, which in turn is the address of the appropriate microroutine in the control store. However, this number of PLA words can be reduced by techniques to be described later.

In the next example, (Fig. 6), a single PLA performs both the address-transformation and control-store functions. In this case, the operation code, held in the instruction register, directly addresses the first word of the microroutine in the PLA that implements a given instruction, but the address of that word need not equal the numeric value of the code. This approach takes less time than a separate address-transformation step, as in the previous example.

A significant advantage of this PLA application is that it can eliminate explicit testing for microinstruction branching by using the conditions that might be tested as address inputs to the PLA instead. With this technique, the arrival of an interrupt triggers the appropriate microroutine immediately so that the interrupt is processed quickly. On the other hand, every input, including the extra condition inputs, must be made available to the address-programing lines in both true and complement form, requiring an inverter on the PLA chip for each of them. This requirement for inverters means that the PLA must be very large in physical area—even for a relatively small number of words.

The third example uses separate PLAs for address-transformation and control-store functions (Fig. 7). When used in minicomputers, this approach often has the smallest number of bits of any of the three examples—for two reasons. First, the main PLA as a control store is smaller than the read-only memory of the first example and has fewer inputs than the combined PLAs of the second example. Second, the address-transforming PLA contains only one word for each different external instruction format, in contrast to one for each different external instruction, and this PLA is therefore likely to contain less than a dozen words.

The outputs of the address-transforming PLA drive an array of AND gates through which the operation code passes to the input of the main PLA. Because of these gates, all bits that are not part of the operation code in that particular format appear as 0 to the main PLA. Since the second PLA input must accept the operation code with the longest format, the unused bit positions in shorter formats, assumed to be the least-significant bits, are available for incrementing from word to word in a microroutine, or for bringing in such special lines as interrupts or feedback lines from the PLA output. These lines must be properly multiplexed to prevent their interference with long-format operation codes.

Extensions to micrograming

PLAs can be applied not only to conventional single-level microprograming, as demonstrated by the preceding examples, but also to modifications of the microprograming concept. One modification is to divide the PLA into several parallel parts for functionally separate portions of the processor—such as control of the arithmetic/logic unit, register control, interrupt control, and input/output control. This "horizontal" approach has fewer bits and simpler interconnections in certain appli-

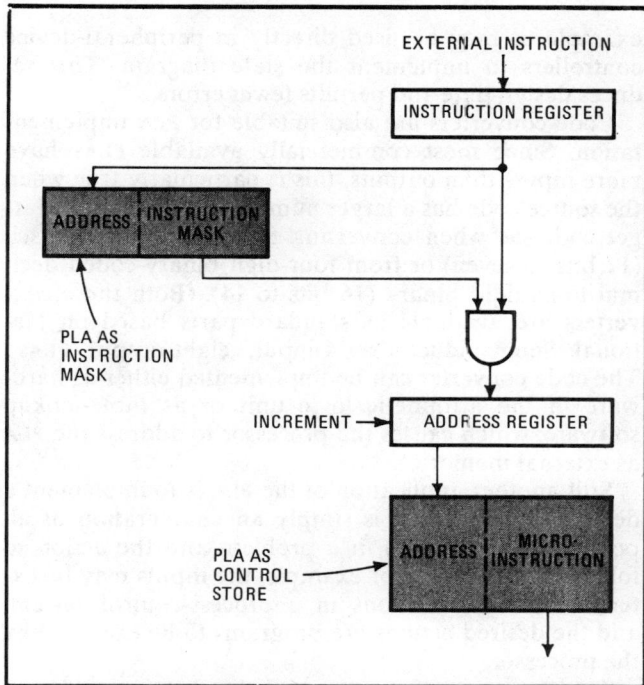

7. Two PLAs. Division of labor between two PLAs reduces total number of bits in control logic and simplifies interrupt-processing and ordinary word-to-word microroutine-incrementing.

cations, but is more difficult to program than the traditional microprogram structure.

Another modification is to use two or more levels of control store. This "vertical" approach may be used in combination with parallel partitioning. Thus, a microinstruction may cause the execution of a sequence of control instructions at an even lower level. "Vertical" and "horizontal" partitioning affect system speed somewhat analogously to the speed trade-offs of vertical and horizontal microprograming.

Partitioning in TTL designs is somewhat limited by the PLA configurations available, but may become more commonplace as new products are announced.

Minimization

Using "don't-care" bits in the PLA address reduces the number of words required. Logic designers are familiar with standard minimization techniques for multiple-output combinational networks, which can be applied as well to the PLA, considered as an array of AND and OR gates. These techniques can also be applied by computer programs—probably the most valuable general-purpose way to reduce a PLA, except that minimizing a network with 14 inputs and eight outputs sometimes requires a lot of computer time.

Minimizing PLAs for microprogram storage can often be done manually or with simplified computer assistance. The most significant reduction in microprograms can be made by combining identical microinstructions at different addresses into a single term. This requires the addresses to differ by 2, 4, 8, 16, and so on—that is, in one bit position, which is programed as ϕ.

A substantial further reduction can sometimes be made at the assembly-language level, looking for microinstructions that perform the same function but have different bit patterns. These can be detected much more easily at the assembly-language level than at the bit level. For example, ADD R2, R1, R1, which means "add the contents of register 2 to the contents of register 1 and store the result in register 1," is functionally the same as ADD R1, R2, R1, but it has a slightly different bit pattern. Computerized text-manipulation systems are very useful for finding these assembly-language equivalences.

Another simple trick combines two or more microinstructions into one by the use of optional bit values. For example, a microprogram might contain two instructions, "OR, 0, R2, R3," and "OR, R1, 0, R3." Both

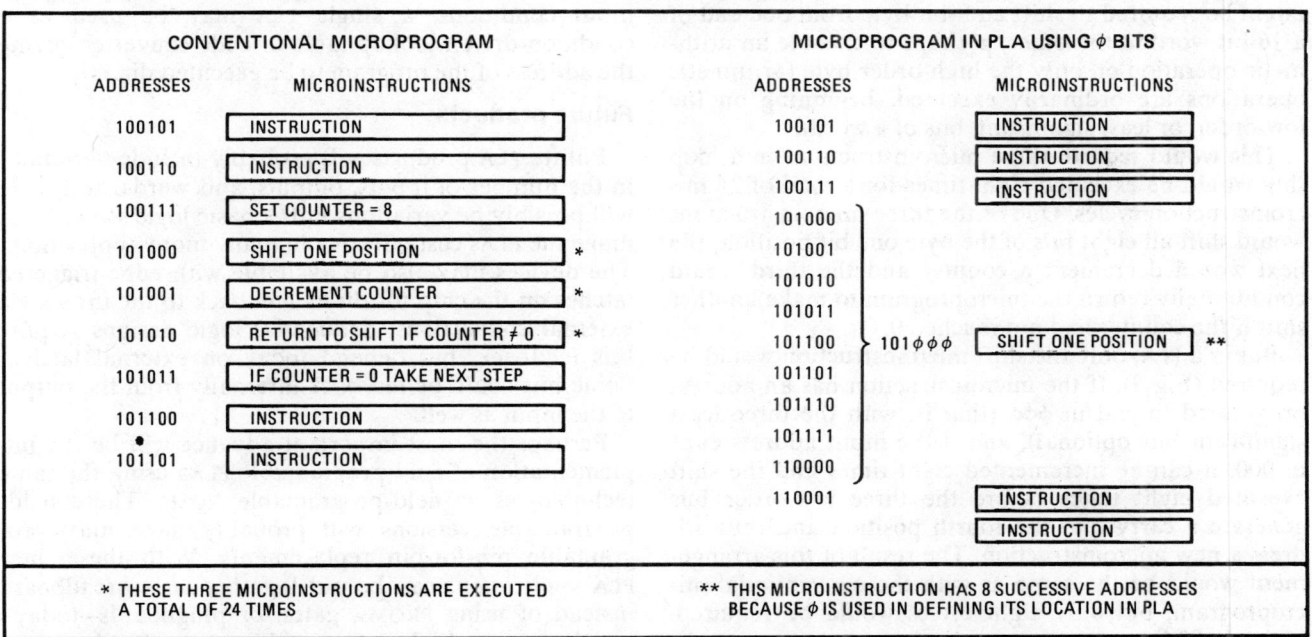

8. Simplifying a microroutine. With optional bits in the address of a word in a PLA, several different input addresses can point to that word, and thus cause the microinstruction to be repeatedly executed. Here, address ending in $\phi\phi\phi$ can repeat one step eight times.

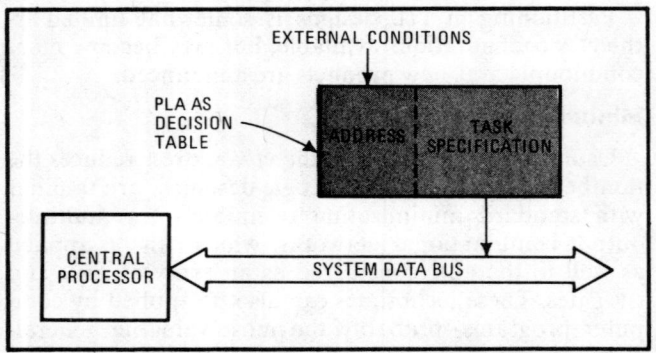

9. PLA as decision table. When it's convenient to specify the response to all contingencies by looking them up in a table listing, the table can easily be made of a PLA. It's used as if it were a peripheral device connected to a computer's data bus.

instructions effectively call for a 1 to be inserted in a register called R3 in each position where either or both of two other registers contain a 1. However, both instructions, by the designation 0, fail to specify one of the source registers, so that the other source works with what is assumed to contain only 0s. As a result, both instructions effectively move the contents of one other register into R3.

Meanwhile, a third microinstruction might legitimately perform the OR function on the contents of registers R1 and R2. But if the two data-move microinstructions have addresses differing in only one bit, then replacing that bit with an optional value calls for the full OR microinstruction without using up an extra word to hold it.

One word for three

Still another use of optional values permits some program loops to be replaced with single short routines that are executed repetitively by the judicious use of addressing. For example, a conventional microprogram might be required to shift an 8-bit byte from one end of a 16-bit word to the other, perhaps to execute an arithmetic operation on only the high-order byte (arithmetic operations are ordinarily executed, beginning on the low-order, or least significant, bits of a word).

This would require three microinstructions in a loop that would be executed eight times for a total of 24 microinstruction cycles. One of the three microinstructions would shift all eight bits of the byte one bit position; the next would decrement a counter and the third would conditionally return the microprogram to make another shift if the counter had not reached 0.

But in a PLA, only the shift microinstruction would be required (Fig 8). If the microinstruction has an address programed to end in φφφ (that is, with the three least significant bits optional), and if the input address ends in 000, it can be incremented eight times and the shift executed eight times before the three low-order bits generate a carry into the fourth position and thus address a new microinstruction. The result of this arrangement would be the same as with the conventional microprogram, but only eight cycles would be required, instead of 24.

The PLA may be used for numerous functions in a processor system other than microprogram control. For example, it may be used directly in peripheral-device controllers to implement the state diagram. This reduces design time and permits fewer errors.

Code converters are also suitable for PLA implementation. Since most commercially available PLAs have more inputs than outputs, this is particularly true when the source code has a larger number of bits than the target code—as when converting from Hollerith to Ascii (12 bits to seven) or from four-digit binary-coded decimal to straight binary (16 bits to 14). (Both these converters are available as standard parts based on National Semiconductor's 14-input, eight-output PLAs.) The code converter can be implemented either as hardware in the arithmetic/logic unit or as table-lookup software, which causes the processor to address the PLA as external memory.

Still another application of the PLA is to implement a decision table, which is simply an enumeration of all possible contingencies in a problem and the action to follow in each case. For example, the inputs may be external binary conditions in a process-control system, and the desired actions are programs to be executed by the processor.

The structures of the PLA and the decision table are exactly analogous—the condition entries drive the address inputs, and the data-output bits represent the desired actions. The PLA is connected as a peripheral device to the system's data bus (Fig. 9). When the processor reads the PLA, it executes the tasks specified by true bits. Decision tables are often implemented in software, but considerable time and program storage can be saved by using PLAs because decoding the tasks specified by a PLA's output-bit pattern is much easier than the full software approach. Furthermore, even this task of scanning the bits and sequentially generating the addresses of the routines to be executed can be implemented with a PLA to give even higher speed.

Where only one task is required for any given set of input conditions, a single PLA may be used as a condition-driven lookup table or code converter, giving the address of the program to be executed directly.

Future products

Future PLA products will probably include variations in the number of inputs, outputs, and words, and there will possibly be variations in the basic logic structure to make the PLAs cost-effective in many more applications. The devices may also be available with edge-triggered latches on the chip for direct feedback to the inputs via external connections. Sequential logic designs require this feedback, but depend today on external latches. Some bits could be fed back internally from the output to the input as well.

Perhaps the most important advance will be the implementation of field-programable PLAs using the same technologies as field-programable ROMs. These field-programable versions will probably have mask-programable pin-for-pin replacements. With these, new PLA applications can be put together on a breadboard instead of using PROMs, gates, or plugboards—today's usual practice. Field-programable PLAs will also allow their use in low-volume applications, where the cost of mask-programing is not justified. □

Designing microprocessors with standard-logic devices, Part 1

Application-oriented processors that utilize standard-logic families like ECL or Schottky TTL are an economical alternative to random-logic designs and perform better than MOS microprocessors

by Robert Jaeger, *Signetics Corp., Sunnyvale, Calif.**

☐ MOS microprocessors are growing in popularity mainly because digital systems designed around them require relatively few integrated circuits. They do have drawbacks, however. They are slower and less flexible than random-logic TTL systems, and they are not widely second-sourced.

But there is a third design route available to meet certain system requirements: the small, applications-oriented processor built with standard high-speed logic devices, either ECL 10K or Schottky. These "standard-logic processors" perform about as well as random-logic TTL designs and use logic families available from four or five major sources. Although they require more ICs than metal-oxide-semiconductor microprocessors, they can replace random-logic TTL designs that need five to 10 times as many devices. By designing his own processor, an engineer can minimize system costs by including only as much capability as he needs, and can provide special features that would be unavailable in an off-the-shelf MOS device.

Part 1 of this two-part article will outline the requirements for the three basic processor elements—the register/arithmetic/logic unit, the control memory, and the input/output circuitry. Part 2 will discuss how proper selection of the microinstruction format can minimize control-memory size; it will also cover memory branching and outline some designs for standard-logic processors.

Processors

A processor, whether in a large computer or in a hand-held programable calculator, differs from random-logic designs in two important respects. First, the processor performs a sequence of logic or arithmetic operations. By contrast, in a typical random-logic design, several operations, such as data manipulation or system input and output control, can take place concurrently. One of the requirements in a random-logic design, in fact, is to ensure that these concurrent operations do not interfere with each other. Second, a processor can modify its sequence of operations on the basis of the results of previous operations.

It is worth repeating that a processor is not a computer—although it can be designed to function as the central processing unit (CPU) in a computer system. In this application, the processor interfaces with the main memory and controls data transfer into and out of the system. A CPU, then, is a processor with special features and capabilities.

Functions of ICs

Each IC function in a system can be classified as either arithmetic/logic, control, or interfacing. In an average system containing 100 to 300 devices, about 35% are used in arithmetic/logic functions, 40% for control, and 25% for interfacing. Depending on the particular product and design approach, this breakdown will vary somewhat—but seldom more than 10% in a system with more than 100 ICs. A processor design can incorporate all the arithmetic/logic and control functions in one small subsystem. In addition, the use of bussing techniques can reduce the number of internal interfacing functions needed. Because of this, whether a processor requires one, two or 20 devices matters far less than the question of whether a processor can be used instead of random logic while still maintaining the necessary system performance level.

A system with 100 to 300 ICs will use various types of devices to implement the arithmetic/logic, control and interfacing functions. Table I shows a breakdown of these devices into five classifications and the percentage of each used in a typical system. These numbers are representative of many different designs and types of products.

A basic processor, shown in Fig. 1, has three sections. The register/arithmetic/logic unit, or RALU, performs all the logical and arithmetic functions on system data and replaces the buffer registers, counters and shift registers used in a random-logic design. The RALU is controlled by the control memory, which provides it with instructions specifying different operations. The

*Now with MSI Data Corp., Santa Ana, Calif.

TABLE 1: DEVICE USAGE IN TYPICAL RANDOM-LOGIC DESIGNS	
30%	Counters, shift registers, latches
10%	Decoders and multiplexers
35%	Gates and flip-flops
15%	Interface
10%	Miscellaneous

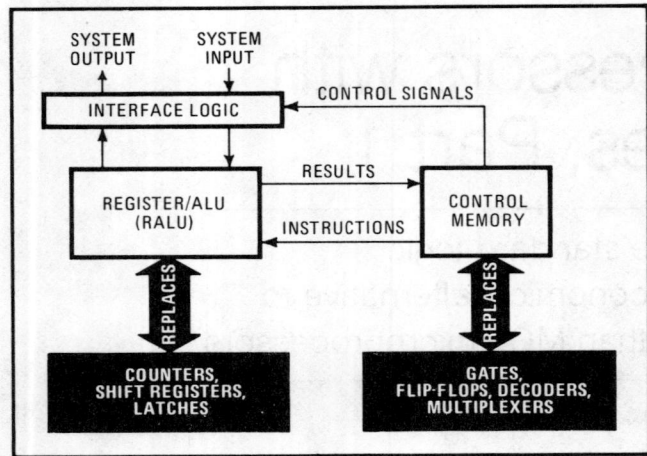

1. Basic processor. Replacing large numbers of registers, counters gates, flip-flops, decoders and multiplexers, are three basic components comprising a processor: the register/arithmetic/logic unit (RALU), the control memory, and the associated interface logic.

control memory replaces gates, flip-flops, decoders, and multiplexers used in random-logic designs. The control memory also steers data into or out of the RALU through the interfacing logic.

Figure 2a shows a RALU design that uses only four devices to perform the same function as 16 individual registers, counters or shift registers. Although this and the other examples shown here use ECL 10K devices, the concepts and techniques apply equally well to any standard-logic family. ECL 10K does, however, have several advantages in this type of application. It is the fastest standard-logic family and obtains a higher level of performance from a system of a given size. The open emitter outputs minimize the need for multiplexers by allowing wire "ORing" of outputs. The ability to terminate critical path signal lines with their characteristic impedances eliminates ringing and overshoot and permits system speed to approach that of the logic devices more closely. Finally, ECL 10K is designed to operate at high speeds without an increase in operating power, in contrast with Schottky TTL, where power dissipation increases rapidly above 20 megahertz.

memory also receives "feedback" signals from the RALU, indicating the results of a current or previous RALU operation, and is capable of modifying its sequence of instructions on the basis of these signals. The

The combination of a small random-access memory, arithmetic/logic unit (ALU), shift register, and latch shown in Fig. 2a provides an extremely versatile basic

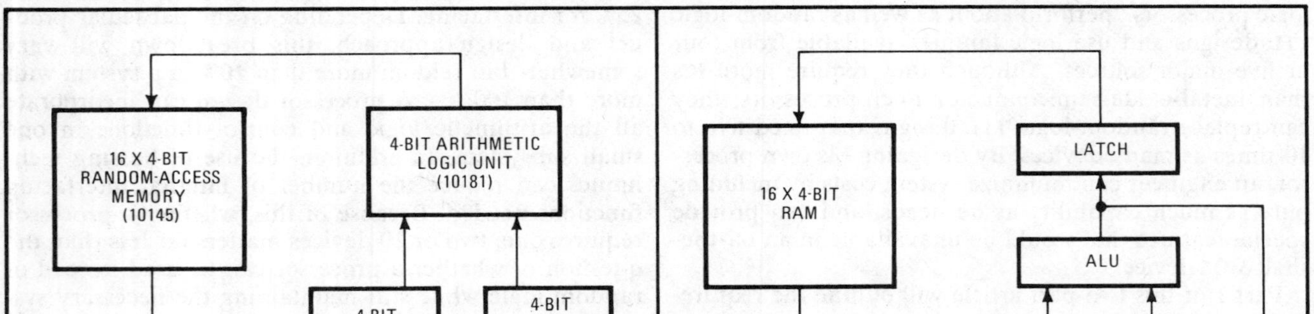

2. Variations on a theme. Four versions of the basic RALU configuration, are implemented with 10K emitter-coupled-logic devices, although other standard logic families could be used. A four-device configuration like (a) can replace 16 individual registers and counters.

Processors vs random logic: a cost comparison

Are high-speed, standard-logic processors only a way of providing higher-performance microcomputers? Or are they also cost-competitive with random-logic TTL designs? In the table shown, the total costs for random-logic TTL designs using 100, 200, and 300 devices are compared with the total costs for three different sizes of processor using TTL read-only memories, programable ROMs, and ECL 10K logic devices. The IC costs were calculated from prices for comparable device quantities.

This shows that, as a substitute for random-logic TTL designs with more than 165 ICs, even a complex 8-bit ECL processor is less expensive. Processor designs using Schottky TTL will be about 30% cheaper than the ECL versions, bringing the crossover point still lower.

The table also shows that the total cost of a random-logic design is highly insensitive to reductions in the price of the ICs. A 10% drop in IC prices results in only a 2.5% drop in total system cost and can easily be wiped out by a small increase in overhead costs. The processor designs, by contrast, use expensive devices which make up almost all of the total system costs. Not only are these devices dropping in price at rates twice that of TTL, but any IC price reductions translate almost entirely into over-all cost reductions.

It is not strictly true that smaller systems have the same overhead cost per IC as larger systems since this figure tends to get larger as IC count decreases. However, even if the figure should double to $2.40 per device, the effect on the total system cost for the processor is to add only $20 to $40, and the effect on its crossover point with a random-logic system is negligible.

Other benefits of processors, which can contribute to cost reductions throughout the life of a product, include shorter design times, common logic for different product models, fewer part types, higher reliability, ease of field modification, special features for custom requirements, and longer product life without redesigns.

COST COMPARISON	IC cost*	Overhead cost**	Total cost
Random-logic TTL			
100 ICs	$ 40	$120	$160
200 ICs	80	240	320
300 ICs	120	360	480
Simple 4-bit ECL processor			
13 ICs, plus 8,192-bit memory	$125	$ 20	$145
Simple 8-bit ECL processor			
18 ICs, plus 8,192-bit memory	$160	$ 26	$186
Complex 8-bit ECL processor			
25 ICs, plus 16,384-bit memory	$225	$ 40	$265

*Assumes average selling price of 7400 TTL logic at $0.40.
**Average is $1.20 per IC, and includes cost of connectors, wiring, pc boards and board checkout, cabinets, fans, IC test and assembly, and power supply.

---

building block for a system. Any of the memory locations may be treated as a 4-bit counter and incremented or decremented by passing the word from the memory through the ALU and back into the memory. Transferring a word through the shifter is enough to perform a shift-left or shift-right operation. A word may also be moved from one location in the memory to another. (Actually, the 16-by-4-bit memory replaces more than 16 individual counters or registers, since the on-chip address decoding replaces a 4-to-16 decoder and the multiplexed outputs replace four 16-to-1 multiplexers.)

It might be expected that accessing a word from the RAM, passing it through the latch and ALU, and writing it back into the RAM would take longer than simply incrementing a counter. However, the whole operation takes a maximum of only 45 nanoseconds, allowing the memory to be accessed and a word incremented or decremented at a 22-MHz rate. This is comparable to the maximum counting frequency of a 74163 TTL counter, which is specified at 25 MHz. While the basic four-device RALU can replace 16 individual registers and counters, merely adding another RAM in parallel and "ORing" the outputs provides a five-device RALU that replaces 32 individual devices.

In addition to incrementing, decrementing, and shifting, the RALU may be used to perform many other operations on words stored in the memory. If one RAM word is loaded into the latch and another into the shifter, the ALU can perform a total of 16 logic and 16 arithmetic functions on the words taken from the memory. The ALU's performance of these functions eliminates the need for specialized MSI devices in the design.

Figure 2 also shows some possible variations in the basic RALU, each of which has features which may be valuable in a particular application. Of particular interest is the design that uses RAMs containing their own output latches. This eliminates the need for a separate latch in the RALU.

Shift linking and carry linking

In those cases where data formats are wider than 4 bits, the basic RALU may be expanded to accommodate them in either of two ways. The simpler and more straightforward is to widen the data path by adding more of each device to form an 8-, 12-, or 16-bit design. Each additional 4 bits of data path requires four additional devices. The other alternative is to include a provision in the 4-bit RALU for multiple word operations;

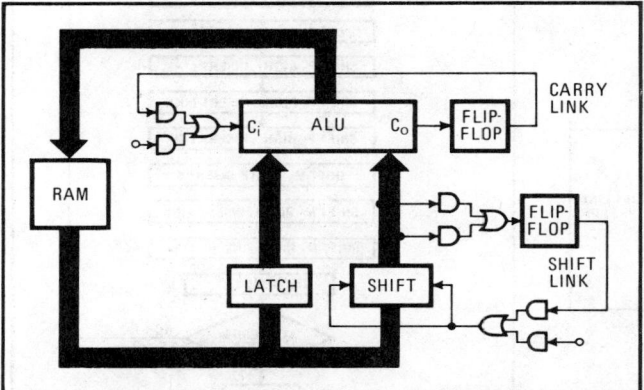

3. Togetherness. Adding "shift linking" and "carry linking" features to the basic RALU enables it to handle words of any width by operating on their segments in sequence, but at lower operating speed.

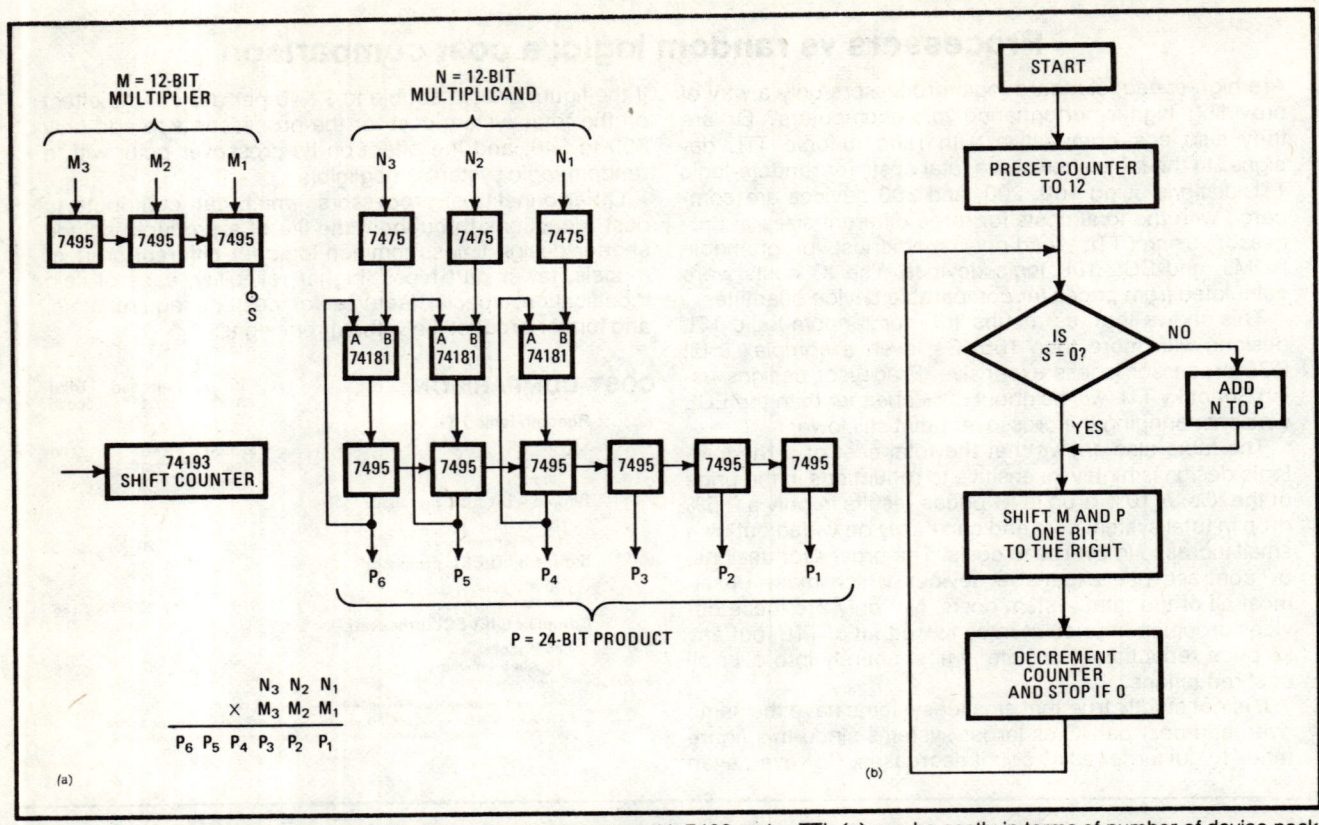

4. Complex way. Building a multiplier using a random logic design with 7400 series TTL (a) can be costly in terms of number of device packages. Flowchart for the 12-by-12-bit multiplier, in which sequence is performed at each bit position, is shown in (b).

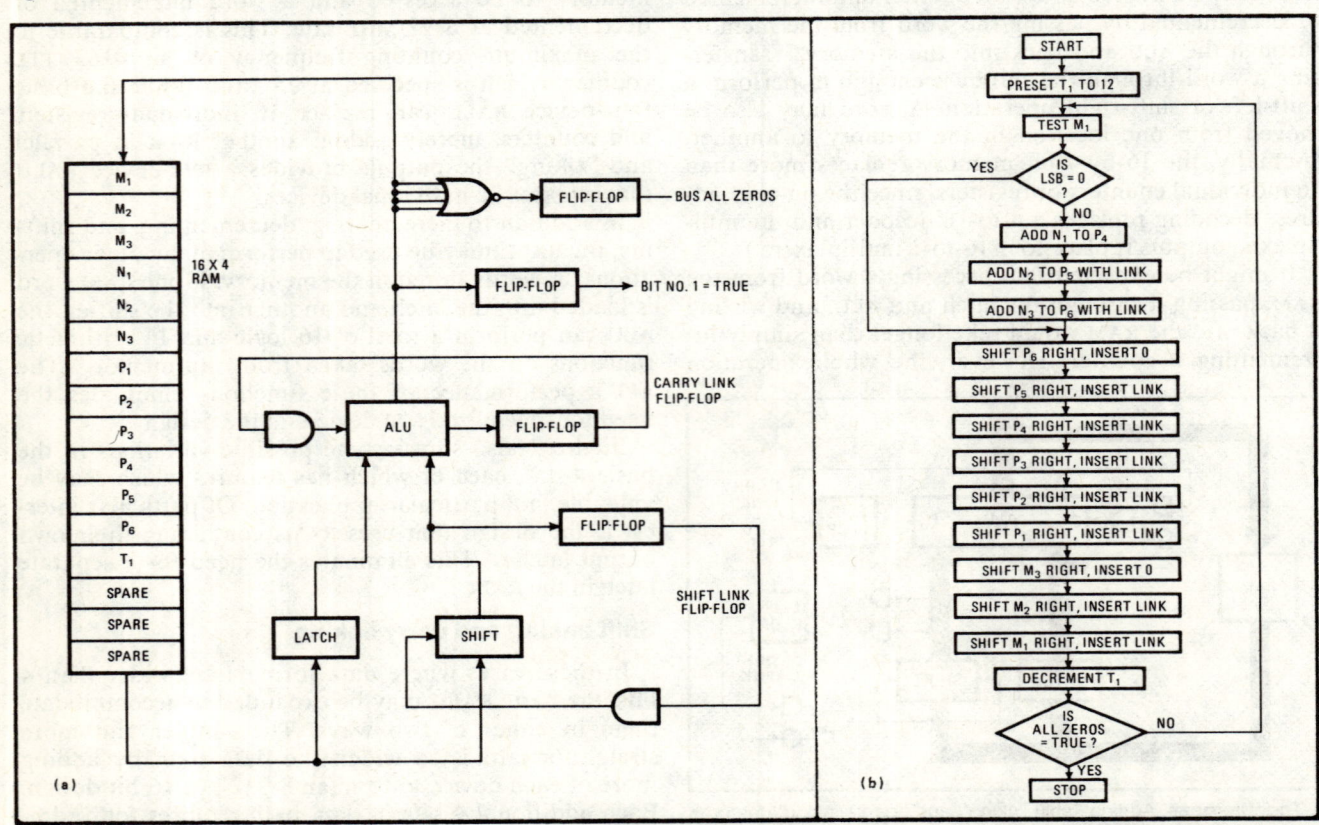

5. Simple way. Multiplier, equivalent to that of Fig. 4 and implemented with a 4-bit RALU design, operates at a reduced speed—but halves the part count. For larger numbers, the reduction is even greater. Sequence of operation is shown in (b).

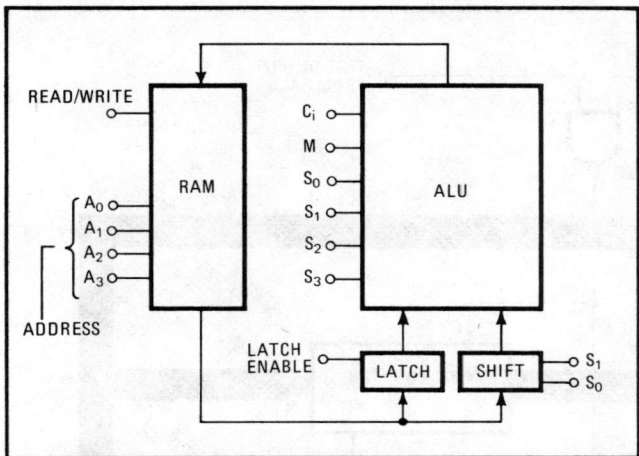

6. Control. Any size of RALU requires a minimum number of 14 control inputs, as shown in this diagram.

that is, to enable it to operate 4 bits at a time on data more than 4 bits wide.

Figure 3 shows a 4-bit RALU with two link flip-flops added. One stores the bit output from a shift operation, and the other stores the carry output from an arithmetic operation, so that the results from one operation can be linked to the next. With this technique, a 12-bit word, stored in three 4-bit memory locations, can be incremented or decremented. Although the operation takes three times as long as the same function performed with a 12-bit RALU, it requires far less logic. Linking can be used in a sequence of operations to operate on a number of any size up to the entire bit capacity of the memory.

More complexity

Using a sequence of simple operations, a RALU can perform more complex logical or arithmetic functions. Figure 4a shows the design of a 12-by-12-bit multiplier implemented with a random-logic design. The flowchart describing the operation is shown in Fig. 4b. If the least significant bit (LSB) of the multiplier is a logical 1, the 12-bit multiplicand is added to the most significant 12 bits of the partial product, and the multiplier and partial product are shifted right one bit. If the LSB is 0, no addition takes place, but the multiplier and partial product are still shifted one position to the right. This operation is performed at each bit position in the multiplier.

Figure 5a shows a 4-bit RALU with carry linking and shift linking that can perform the same function. It also tests the least significant bit of the ALU output and tests for an all 0s condition.

Figure 5b lists the sequence of operations required to perform the multiply operation. In this example, a RALU using seven devices can perform the same function as a specialized random-logic design that requires 16 devices. The RALU, of course, operates much more slowly but, where high speed is not important, this permits halving of the parts count. For multiplying numbers longer than 12 bits, the reduction becomes even larger. In addition, because the RALU memory locations are not committed to specific system functions, the same location could be used for other purposes, such as converting the binary product to BCD digits.

It was stated earlier that about 40% of the devices in a typical digital system are needed for the control and timing functions. Control memories, in the form of high-speed read-only memories and programable ROMs, can provide the same functions with many fewer devices, and, because the RALU provides the system data functions, this greatly simplifies the control-logic requirements.

Control memories

The purpose of the control memory in a processor design is manifold: to supply the RALU with signals that select a source and destination for data, and control the functions of the ALU and shifter; to control the input or output of data between the RALU and interfacing logic; and to send a sequence of signals to the RALU that will determine which system function the RALU is to perform. Basically, then, the control memory provides the RALU with individual control signals, and sequences the RALU operations to enable it to perform a system-level function like a multiply operation.

Figure 6 shows the 14 control inputs to the basic 4-bit RALU. These inputs specify a memory address, memory read or write operation, ALU function, and shift operation. Significantly, the number of RALU control inputs is independent of the RALU data width—that is, an 8-, 12-, or 16-bit RALU would each require the same 14 control inputs. However, as features are added, such as linking, bus testing and extra latches and shifter inputs, the number of control inputs increases.

Figure 7 shows a simple control memory consisting of a ROM/PROM array and two 4-bit counters that provide an 8-bit array address. The width of the array is determined by the number of control signals that must be supplied to the RALU and the number of bits used in presetting the array counters. Each word in the array constitutes a microinstruction—that is, it specifies a RALU operation and provides an 8-bit number which can be used to change the array address. The 8-bit counter can address an array that is up to 256 words deep. Incrementing the array counter provides a sequence of these microinstructions to the RALU. This sequence defines the series of RALU operations that results in a system-level function.

In this example the 10136 ECL binary counter is used to address the array. With the counter function select input, S_2, at a logic 1 level, the counter will increment, and at a logic 0 level it will preset. The logic state of this signal will determine whether the counter increments to select the next microinstruction or presets to select a microinstruction in another part of the array.

Input/output

Regardless of how fast the control memory can be accessed or the RALU can operate on data, the performance of the processor will be seriously impaired if the input/output facilities require cumbersome and time-consuming program steps. Consequently, interfacing a processor with other system elements easily and economically becomes a prime design consideration.

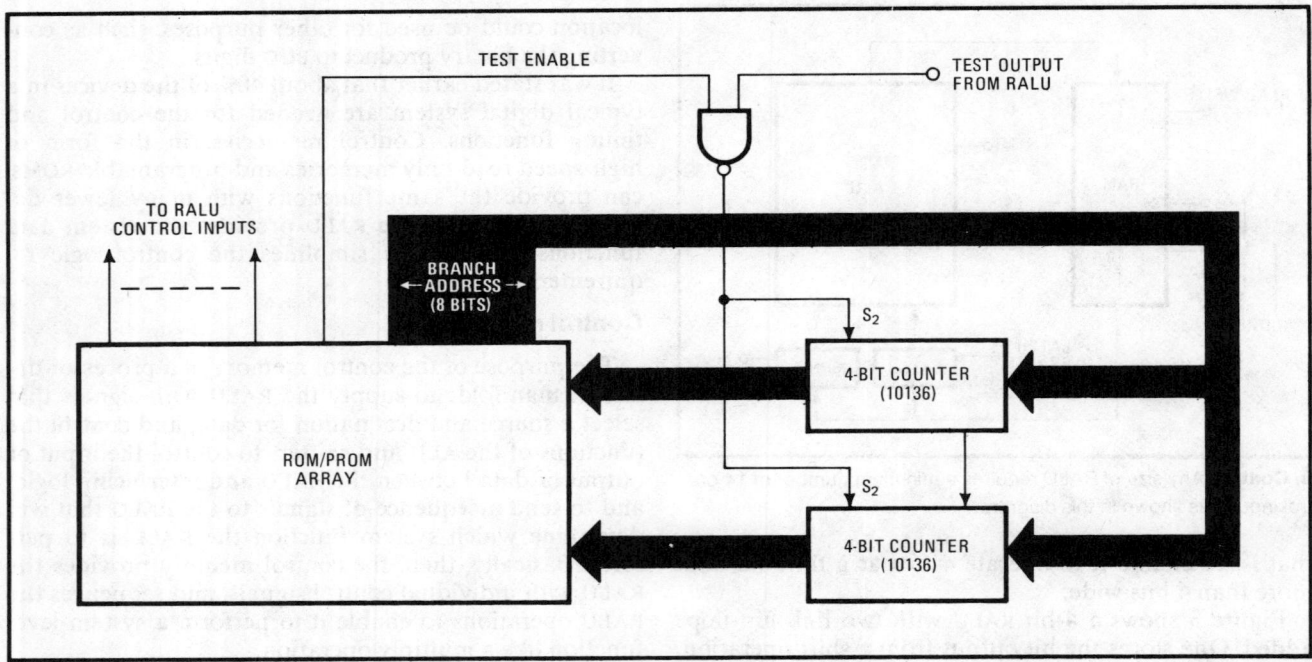

7. Control memory. Width of the ROM/PROM array in this control memory depends on the number of control inputs to the RALU and the number of bits used for presetting the two 4-bit counters which address the array to select appropriate microinstructions.

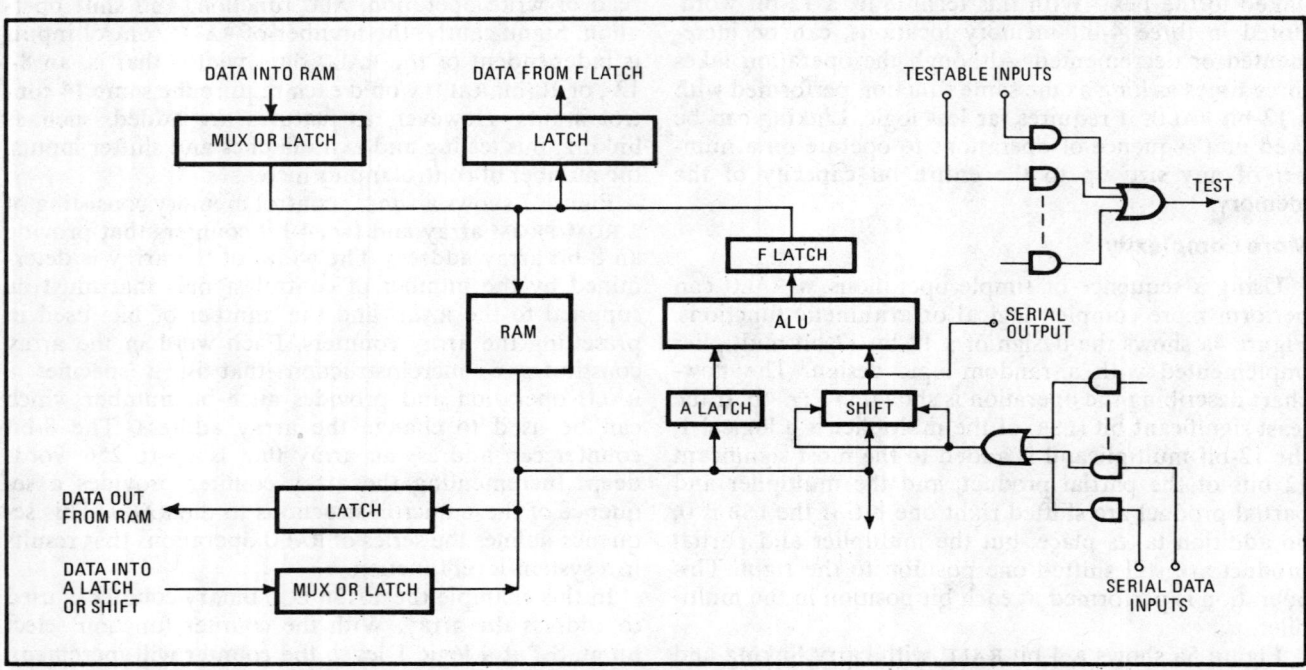

8. Flexibility. One great advantage to standard-logic processors is the ability to place interfaces at almost any point. Here such interfaces are provided at RAM and shifter inputs and outputs. Also, it's fairly simple to provide additional testing or control functions at other points.

One of the most useful features of a processor design utilizing standard-logic devices is its unique ability to provide an interface at any point in the processor logic. Figure 8 shows a processor with interfaces at the RAM input and output and at the shifter input and output. Inputs can be tested directly with "test and branch" instructions which sense the state of one or more input lines. Similarly, by decoding a set of bits in an instruction, a single pulse or set of pulses may be sent from the processor to set or clear flip-flops or to perform some other external control functions.

I/O instructions, then, can be simply extensions of other processor instructions. As an example, instead of transferring a word from the RAM to shifter or "A" latch, the word may be transferred directly to an external register or bus. The ability to interface different system elements to different points in the processor can reduce to an absolute minimum the external interfacing logic required in the system. □

Designing microprocessors with standard-logic devices, Part 2

In comparison with TTL random-logic systems, many fewer devices are needed to build high-speed standard-logic processors; but even fewer are necessary when the particular application requires less than optimum performance

by Robert Jaeger, *Signetics Corp., Sunnyvale, Calif.* *

☐ Processors built with standard high-speed logic take a middle course between MOS microprocessors and random-logic TTL designs—they're faster and more flexible than MOS chips and use many fewer ICs than the random-logic systems. For different applications, they can be optimized in several different ways, as Part 2 of this two-part article describes. (Part 1, which appeared on pages 93-98, discussed their basic elements: a register/arithmetic/logic unit or RALU, a control memory, and input/output circuitry.)

Generally, the number of devices needed to build a standard-logic processor can be reduced whenever the acceptable level of performance is less than the highest attainable. When speed is not crucial, for instance, the microinstruction format can be modified to reduce the number of read-only memories or programable ROMs required by the control memory. Different types of memory branching can also be used sometimes to reduce memory size and/or program length. The flexibility of the approach will be illustrated by two standard-logic processor designs.

The role of the microinstruction

A single microinstruction from the control memory may cause the RALU to perform one operation (called monophase) or more than one (polyphase), and the designer should choose carefully which best suits his system. Figure 1 shows four different kinds of RALU operations, which require one, two, or three phases.

The advantage of polyphase RALU operations is that complex microinstructions, such as "read-modify-write," are executed by the RALU in the shortest possible time. Once the microinstruction has been accessed, the RALU needs no further reference to the control memory. Execution time is limited only by the propagation delays of the RALU logic elements.

* Now with MSI Data Corp., Santa Ana, Calif.

1. Monophase or polyphase. RALU operations typically require one or more steps to complete after a single microinstruction is received. More complex microinstructions can be executed faster with polyphase operation, but this often dictates additional decoding logic and more control inputs than with monophase.

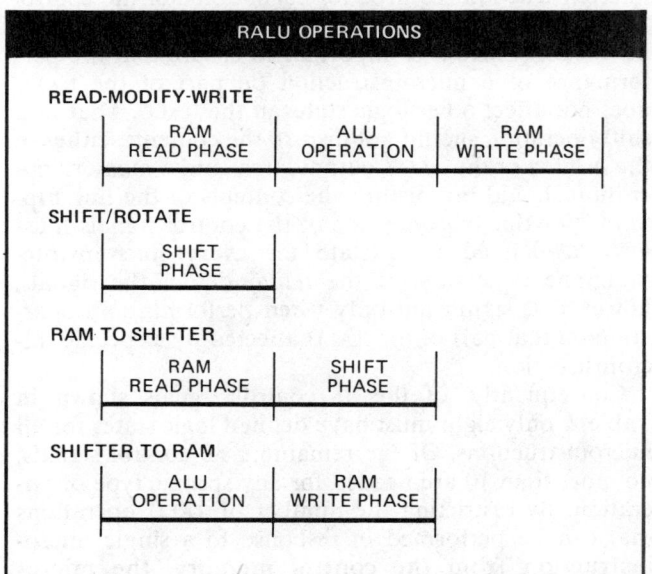

TABLE 1: POLYPHASE VERSUS MONOPHASE CONTROL INPUTS

	Number of RALU control inputs used
Polyphase microinstructions	
Increment RAM word	17
Branch if K is equal to contents of shifter	17
Rotate shifter and branch if LSB = 0	18
Rotate shifter and load result into RAM	21
Monophase microinstructions	
Transfer RAM word to A latch	7
Transfer RAM word to shifter	7
ALU operation (A, B to F latch)	10
Shifter operation	6
Test and branch	7
Load 4-bit K input to A latch	6

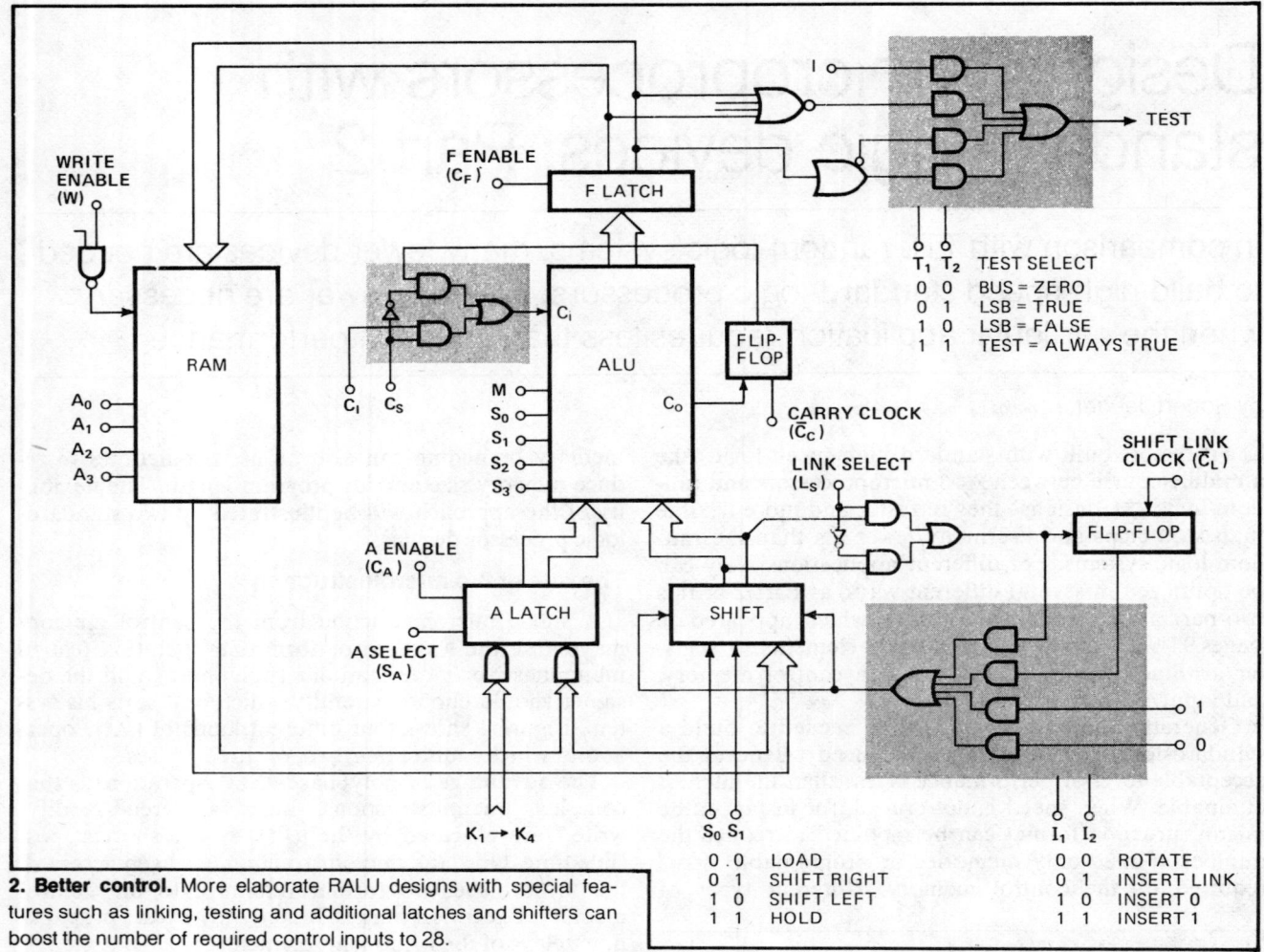

2. Better control. More elaborate RALU designs with special features such as linking, testing and additional latches and shifters can boost the number of required control inputs to 28.

Another advantage is that a sequence of RALU operations can be specified by a single microinstruction. This provides a kind of instruction encoding, which reduces the number of instructions needed in the control memory to perform a given system function.

There are several disadvantages, however, which argue against the use of polyphase operations, unless the system needs the speed. First, if a fixed-phase sequence is used for each microinstruction, the simpler ones will take as long to execute as the more complex ones. If a variable-phase technique is employed, additional decoding logic is required to select the phases to be used in executing each microinstruction. Second, a wide microinstruction is required from the control memory to provide control signals to all the RALU control inputs. This precludes the possibility of encoding the microinstruction to reduce its width, and also increases the required size of the control memory.

Table 1 shows some possible monophase and polyphase microinstructions, together with the number of RALU control inputs that must be specified in order to execute them. The RALU in Fig. 2 has 28 control inputs and a highly flexible 38-bit microinstruction format. However, most microinstructions, particularly if they specify a monophase RALU operation, would not require all 38 bits for every operation, and restricting microinstruction capabilities can yield significant savings in the size of the control memory, and therefore its total cost.

Table 2 shows five types of operations that can be performed on the RALU and the number of bits in the microinstruction required for each. Some of the control signals must have a defined logic state for every microinstruction, since it is important to ensure that the performance of a microinstruction on part of the RALU does not affect other logic states in the RALU. That is, a shift operation should not disturb the contents, either of the A latch or the ALU's output latch, and a memory operation should not disturb the contents of the link flip-flops. For this reason, some of the control signals must have a defined logic state for every microinstruction. The logic state of the remainder of the signals, however, is significant only when performing an operation on that part of the RALU affected by a specific microinstruction.

Consequently, of the 38 control signals shown in Table 2, only eight must have defined logic states for all microinstructions. Of the remaining 30 control signals, no more than 10 are needed for any specific type of operation. By restricting the number of RALU operations that can be performed in response to a single microinstruction from the control memory, the micro-

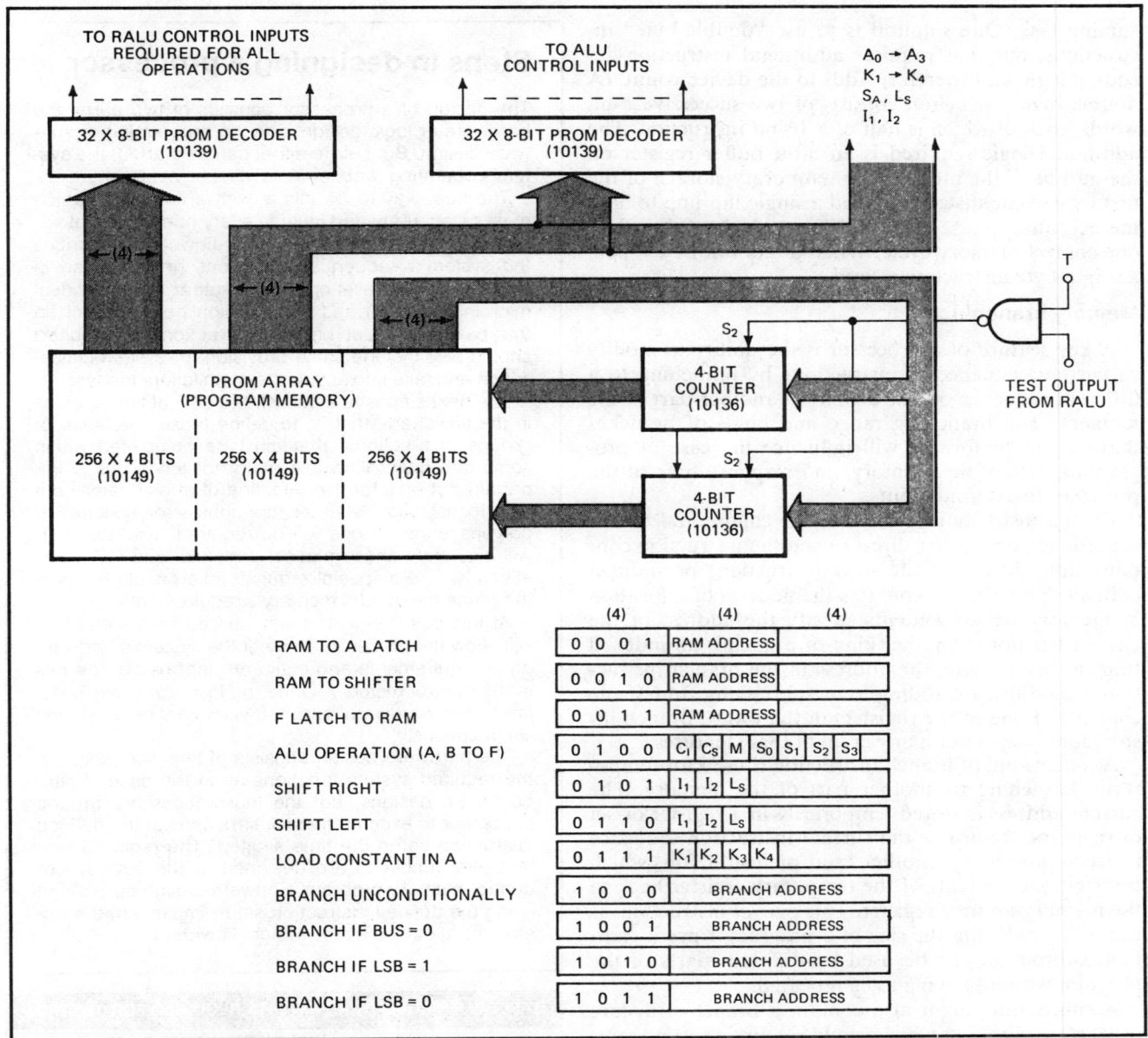

3. Encoding. Microinstructions can be arranged in such a way as to minimize size of program memory. This control memory, which was built with ECL 10K components, uses microinstructions with 12-bit word lengths, examples of which are shown at right.

instructions need never be wider than 18 bits—and the number of ROMs or PROMs needed to store those microinstructions can be reduced.

Further reductions in the width of the microinstructions can be achieved by encoding the bits they contain. Basically, the control memory provides the RALU with control signals that specify an operation, and with a sequence of microinstructions that tell the RALU to perform a more complex, system-level function.

Encoded microinstructions

These two functions can be separated, with one part of the control memory providing the microinstruction-decoding function, and the other part providing the sequencing function. The bit positions in the "sequence" or "program" memory, then, do not have to bear any direct relationship to a specific RALU control input, since this function is left to the instruction decoder. The microinstructions to be used in the processor can be designed to minimize the size of the program memory and provide the most efficient utilization of the memory bits.

Figure 3 shows a control memory that has a 12-bit microinstruction. The 10139 is a 32-by-8-bit ECL PROM, used for decoding the microinstructions, and the 10149, organized 256 by 4 bits, is used as the program memory. A list of possible microinstructions that might be used with this design is also shown.

It's possible to encode a microinstruction in only 8 bits, but it is then extremely difficult to define instructions that reference memory (branching) or those that contain data or constants. Such instruction sets are possible, though, and one is being used in one of the newer MOS microprocessors. Writing useful programs with these instructions, however, is a tedious and time-con-

101

suming task. One solution is to use "double-byte" instructions, but that requires additional instruction-decoding logic and therefore adds to the device count. (A double-byte instruction consists of two successive 8-bit words, each of which is half of a 16-bit instruction. The additional logic required is an 8-bit buffer register on the output of the memory for temporary storage of the first byte of the instruction, and a single flip-flop to hold the execution phase of the processor during more than one control-memory cycle. When 8 bits will be enough, a single-byte instruction is used.)

Memory branching

A key feature of a processor is the ability to modify its current sequence of instructions by branching to a different sequence of instructions in another part of the memory. The branching range and kinds of branches that can be performed will influence the ease of programing, size of the memory, and response time of the processor to external inputs.

Branch instructions can be either conditional or unconditional, and either direct (when the instruction contains the address of the next instruction) or indirect (when the instruction contains the address of a location in memory whose contents specify the address of the next instruction). Another kind of branch is an indexed branch. In this case, the address in the branch instruction is modified by adding to or subtracting from it the contents of one of the registers in the RALU. Branch instructions may contain any or all of these features.

Another kind of branch instruction is used for temporarily branching to another part of the memory. The current address is stored temporarily in a register or set of registers. Return to the current-instruction sequence is accomplished by another kind of instruction, which transfers the contents of the temporary register back to the memory-address register. This pair of instructions is useful for reducing the size of a program, since a common subroutine can be used by different parts of the program without having to be repeated.

A subroutine might also contain a branch-and-store instruction within it, which would require a second temporary storage register for saving the second return address. This set of temporary registers constitutes a return-address stack, which may be implemented either by using registers in the RALU or by storing the address in an external memory.

The usefulness of a return-address stack depends heavily on the particular processor application. A stack reduces memory size the most when the program repeatedly uses the same subroutines. But it also increases the program's execution time, since the branching instructions have to be added to the program to reduce the memory requirements.

Central-processing units

The central-processing unit in a computer system is a special application. The function of the CPU is to provide an interface to the main memory, which, by implication, is larger and slower than the processor's control memory. The processor receives instructions from the main memory and transfers data to and from it. The

Steps in designing a processor

The design of a processor consists of two parts: the hardware or logic design, and the programing or software design. But before either can be started, the system's operating requirements must be established.

The best way to do this is with a flowchart, which must be accurate and include every operation that will be required of the system. This flowchart describes the system's sequential operations (in this case in terms of system-level operations rather than individual microinstructions) and the decision points (which in this case represent branch instructions). The chart should also include some provision for system initialization and take into account system failure modes.

The next step is to establish the critical timing paths in the flowchart—that is, to define those functions, or groups of functions, that must be completed within some maximum allowable period of time. This is important not only for the selection of a logic family but also to establish whether monophase or specialized polyphase instructions will be required. The flowchart will also show those places, particularly in I/O operations, where a specialized instruction could be used to reduce the control memory's requirements.

At this point an instruction set can be defined that will allow the processor to meet the system's performance requirements and make efficient use of the bits in the control memory. Once the instruction set is defined, the hardware and software can be designed simultaneously.

The hardware design consists of implementing, not the required system functions as in the case of random-logic designs, but the logic necessary for the processor to execute those instructions in the defined instruction set in the time allotted. The required system-level functions are designed in the software or control-memory program. Software design consists of using the defined instruction set to implement the operations specified by the system flowchart.

TABLE 2: MICROINSTRUCTION BITS REQUIRED FOR CONTROL

	RALU control inputs	Number of bits used per microinstruction					
		All	RAM	ALU	Test and branch	Shift	$K_1 \to K_4$ to A latch
RAM	W	1					
	A_0, A_1, A_2, A_3		4				
A latch	C_A	1					
	S_A			1			1
Shift	S_0, S_1	2					
	I_1, I_2					2	
	L_S					1	
	C_L	1					
ALU	$C_I, C_S, M, S_0, S_1, S_2, S_3$			7			
	C_0	1					
	C_F	1					
	T_1, T_2				2		
	Branch address				8		
	K_1, K_2, K_3, K_4						4
	Test enable	1					
	Total	8	5	7	10	3	5

number of instructions can be quite large—usually more than 100—and they specify operations to be performed on data in the registers, as well as data transfers between the memory and peripheral devices. In this situation, the main memory can be treated as another external interface.

The processor sets up the main-memory address either by incrementing a number used as the program counter or by specifying the address of a main-memory location for a data transfer. The main-memory address may be formed by adding or subtracting the contents of a register from memory data (indexed addressing), by using memory data as address pointers (indirect addressing), or by using memory data directly as the next memory address (immediate addressing). It is the function of the processor to interpret the instructions from the main memory and to perform the sequence of operations on the RALU and interfaces specified by it. As the first step in the processing of a main-memory instruction, the processor may sense the state of an input line

4. Little leaguer. This 4-bit emitter-coupled-logic processor requires only 13 devices over and above a read-only-memory/programable ROM array. Multiple-byte instruction capability can be added with more logic.

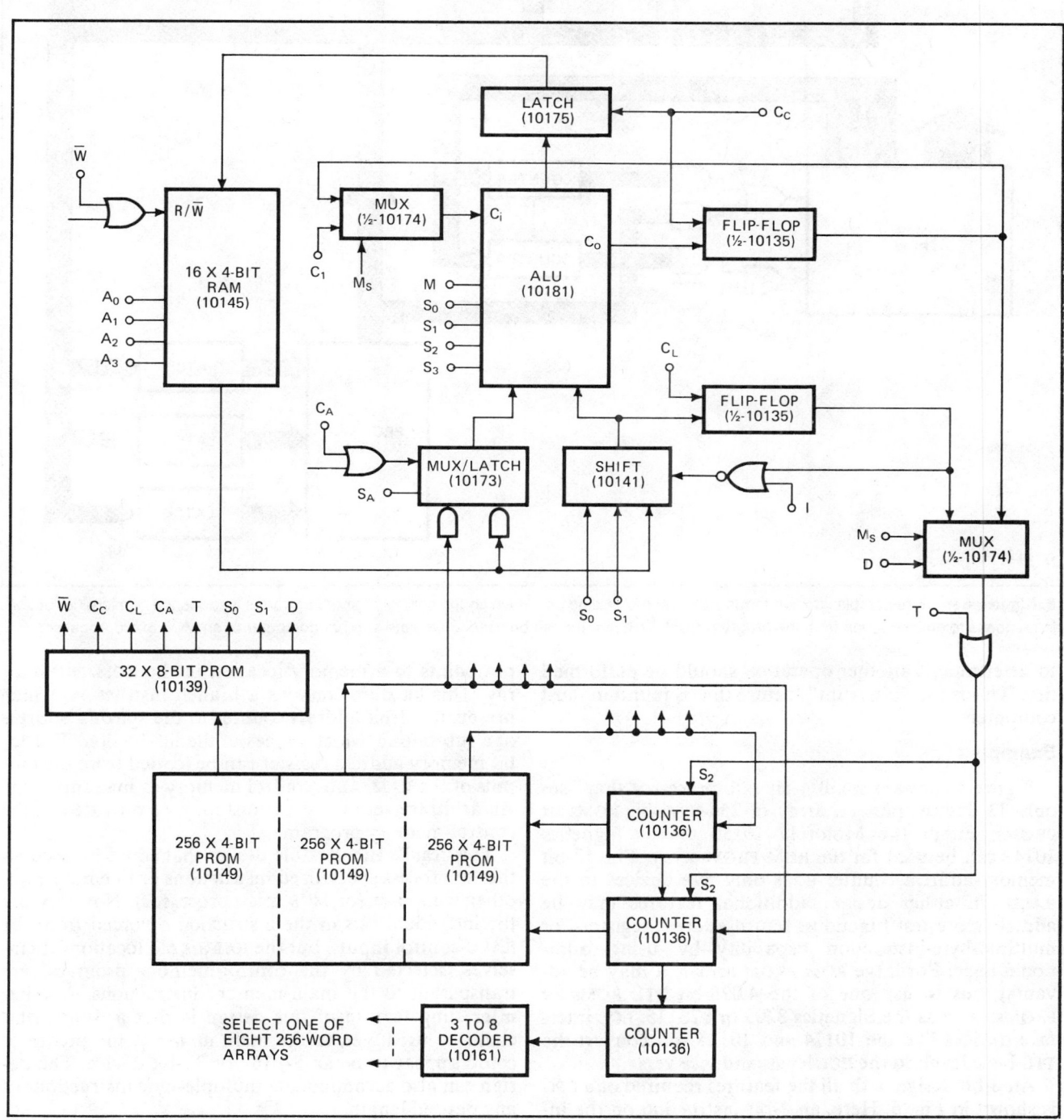

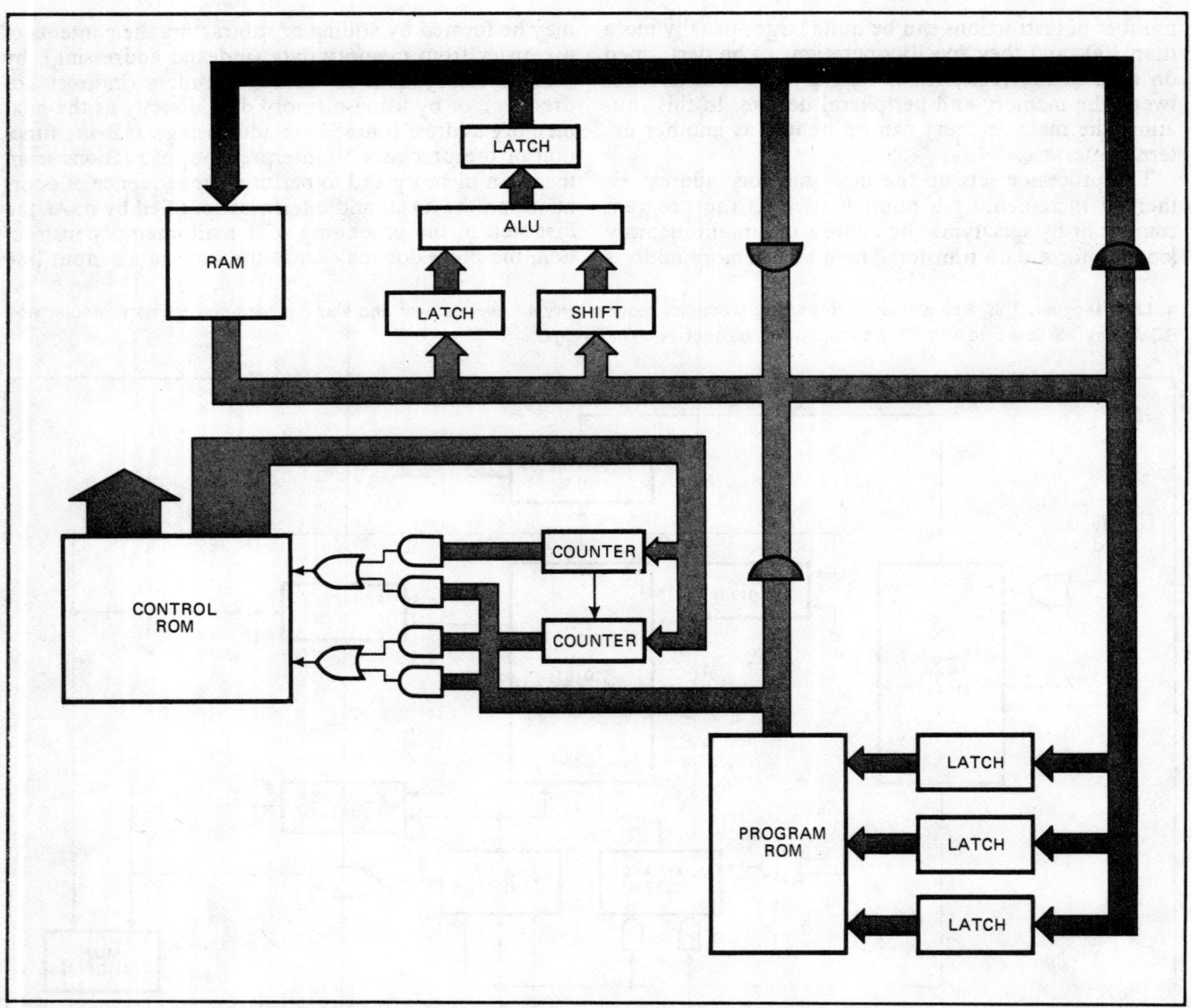

5. Big leaguer. More complex design forms a central processing unit in which the control memory performs a sequence of microinstructions in response to an instruction from the program ROM. This feature can be used to emulate another computer or an MOS microprocessor.

to determine if another operation should be performed first. This is the "interrupt" feature that is found in most computers.

Examples

Figure 4 shows a small 4-bit ECL processor that uses only 13 devices plus an array of 256-by-4-bit ROMs or PROMs. Either the Motorola 10150 or the Signetics 10149 can be used for the ROM/PROM array. The 12-bit memory-address counter adds only five devices to the RALU. In either design, additional features may be added—more test functions, return-address registers, or multiple-byte-instruction capability—by using additional logic. For large ROM/PROM arrays, it may be advantageous to use one of the 4,096-bit TTL ROMs or PROMs, such as the Signetics 8205 or 82S115. ECL interface devices like the 10124 and 10125 will convert the TTL-logic levels to the ECL levels and vice versa.

An 8-bit design with all the features required of a CPU is shown in Fig. 5. Here, an 8-bit instruction on the input points to a memory location in the ROM/PROM array. This location contains a branch instruction, which presets the 8-bit address counter to the starting address of a subroutine, which processes the instruction. The 16-bit memory address register can be loaded from the outputs of the RAM, ALU, control memory or main memory. An arbitrary set of instructions may be provided in the control-memory program.

This results in a flexible design that could be used either to process specialized instructions or to emulate another computer (or MOS microprocessor). Not only are the individual bits in the instruction divorced from the RALU control inputs, but the RALU RAM locations themselves, selected by the control-memory program, are transparent to the main-memory instructions. Another interesting feature of this design is that a 4-bit RALU could be used, yet, to the main memory, the processor could appear to be an 8-, 16-, or 32-bit device. The design can also accommodate multiple-byte instructions of any desired length. □

ROMs in microprocessors can test themselves

by John B. Peatman,* David G. Dack, and David A. Warren,
Hewlett-Packard Ltd., South Queensferry, Scotland
*Now at Georgia Institute of Technology, Atlanta, Ga.

Read-only memories that contain the programs and constants needed in a microprocessor-based system can be given self-test capability by reserving one word of the ROM for a bit-for-bit parity check on all the other words. The approach can detect any of several possible ROM malfunctions.

As illustrated in the diagram, the check word can be, but need not be, the last word in the memory. Each of its bits is selected to force an odd number of 1s (odd parity) in the corresponding column of the ROM. Even parity won't work.

To check the contents of the ROM, the microprocessor reads out every word in the ROM and performs a cumulative parity check—an exclusive-OR operation on each bit. At the end, the result should be a 1 in every bit position of the accumulating register.

If the specific microprocessor's instruction set doesn't include an exclusive-OR instruction, it can execute the equivalent operation in a subroutine.

This self-test always detects single errors, whole-word errors, data output lines stuck at 1 or 0, and address input lines stuck at 1 or 0. It sometimes detects address lines short-circuited to each other, output lines short-circuited to each other, and multiple random errors. Each of these has its own effect on the test.

Single errors occur at random as a result of flaws in the chip, or occasionally when a bit in a programable ROM reverts to its unprogramed state—unlikely in recent versions of programable ROMs. Any single error changes the parity of its column from odd to even.

Multiple errors in a single word change the parity of every column involved. They occur only rarely.

If a data output line is stuck at 1 or 0, there may be a short circuit to ground or to a power line from wiring connected to that output, or the output driver circuit may be dead. Since most ROMs have a total capacity equal to a power of 2, the number of words is even, and the stuck output line looks like an even number of 1s or an even number of 0s—thus creating an even parity. (This is one reason why even parity in the check word won't work.)

If an address input line is stuck at 1 or 0, it may similarly indicate a short circuit somewhere in or near the ROM, or a dead bit position in the address input buffer. This fault renders exactly half of the words inaccessible; an attempt to read all the words in the memory will read the other half twice, necessarily generating even less of the true contents of the addressed word. Which pair is presented again depends on the circuit family and the logic state definition. With a random distribution of 1s and 0s, half the words will present an incorrect bit in one column or the other.

For multiple random errors in the ROM, even parity. (Even if a user perversely loads a whole ROM with two identical groups of words, contents of the one location reserved for a check word must necessarily be different from its image in the other half of the memory.) Likewise, if two address lines are stuck, a sweep of the ROM reads one quarter of the words four times, again giving even parity.

Of the kinds of fault detected with uncertainty, short circuits in address and data lines can occur either on the chip or in associated wiring. A short circuit between two address lines causes the lines always to have the same logic state. They correctly address one quarter of the words in the ROM when they both should be 0, and another quarter when they both should be 1; but when they are supposed to be different, for access to the remaining half of the ROM, they address one of the same-state quarters instead. Which quarter is addressed depends on the circuit family and the definition of the 1 and 0 states; in some cases a short-circuited 0 pulls a 1 down, while in others a 1 pulls a 0 up. This may or may not cause a parity error; if the inaccessible words themselves have even parity in all columns, the remaining words generate odd parity and thus don't upset the check-word parity. Assuming the distribution of 1s and 0s in the ROM to be random—an assumption that's not necessarily justified—the probability of an error in any one column is 0.5, and the probability of an error somewhere in n columns is $1 - (0.5)^n$. If $n = 8$, this probability is 0.996, which is close to certainty.

If two output lines are short-circuited, those two lines always present the same bit pair, either 00 or 11, regard-results if any column has an odd number of errors.

The self-test is intended to be performed on individual ROM chips, each with its own check word, even if the system contains multiple chips. This pins down the location of detected errors to particular chips, which a single check word over a whole system can't do. □

ROM ADDRESS			ROM CONTENTS				
0	0	0	1	0	1	0	
0	0	1	0	1	1	0	
0	1	0	0	1	0	1	
0	1	1	1	1	1	0	
1	0	0	0	1	1	0	
1	0	1	1	0	1	1	
1	1	0	0	0	0	0	
1	1	1	0	1	0	1	← CHECK WORD
			1	1	1	1	← PARITY

Self test. Reserving one location in a read-only memory for a check word enables a variety of faults in the ROM to be detected.

Counter keeps track of microprocessor interrupts

by Douglas M. Risch
Woodward Governor Co., Fort Collins, Colo.

A counter for keeping track of the number of times a microprocessor executes its interrupt-enable and interrupt-disable instructions permits the use of nested interrupts. With nesting, a routine that interrupts another program can itself be interrupted by a subroutine, which may be subject to still another interrupt, and so on to almost any desired depth. By this means, the power of the microprocessor to implement complex logic designs can be greatly extended.

A single microprocessor can often be assigned several related tasks, which it executes in rotation, either with a fixed amount of time devoted to each task, or to interrupt on a demand basis. A program yields when the interrupting program requires service.

However some programs may contain segments that must not be interrupted. For instance, if a routine that fetches information from a multiplexed analog interface (Fig. 1) is interrupted after the input channel is selected, but before that channel's signal moves to the analog-to-digital converter, erroneous information could be transmitted. Or, when a multiple precision operation is under way (Fig. 2), an interrupt after the first word is loaded into the register, but before the second, may generate an incorrect output for a period much longer than normal in this period.

These examples show why the newer microprocessors include interrupt-enable and interrupt-disable instructions with their interrupt capabilities. Simpler microprocessors can implement these instructions with hardware (Fig. 3). But a simple enable/disable capability would be insufficient when a program that would disable the interrupt called a subroutine that would also disable the interrupt. The subroutine, when finished, would enable the interrupt before the program could tolerate enablement.

The solution is to remember how may interrupt-disable instructions were given and to prevent interrupts until each disable instruction has been matched with an enable instruction. A hardware implementation (Fig. 4) is just a modification of the simple enable/disable logic, including an up/down counter to remember the number of disable signals. A corollary software solution is also possible; it merely implements the up/down counter in a memory location instead of in a separate register.

Interrupt-disable commands can be nested as deeply as $2^n - 2$ for the hardware implementation, using an n-stage counter, or $2^n - 1$ for the software implementation, where n is the number of bits in a word. □

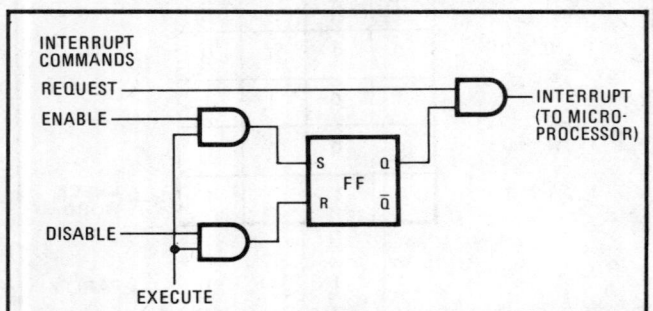

1. Multiple precision. When desired precision requires more than one word, all bits must be loaded before an interrupt can be tolerated. This prevents an incorrect level from appearing at the output.

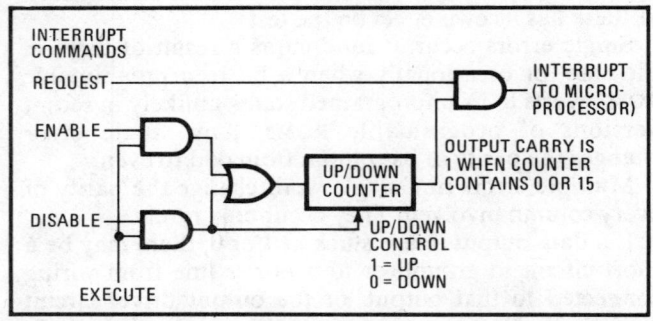

3. Counter for nesting. Successive disable and enable instructions step the counter respectively up and down. Only when enables have canceled previous disables can interrupts pass.

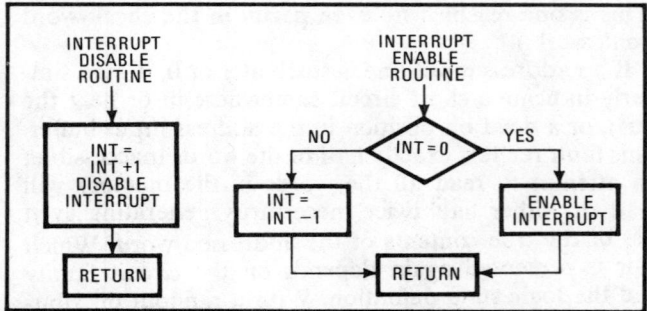

2. Interrupt gate. An enable instruction, stored in the flip-flop at execution time, permits subsequent interrupts to pass. A disable resets the flip-flop and blocks following interrupts.

4. Software counter. These routines count the enables and disables as does the counter in Fig. 3, but the count is stored in a memory location called INT, rather than in a separate register.

part 3
applications

Single-chip microprocessors open up a new world of applications

Having freed system designers from the constraints of hard-wired logic, microprocessors are achieving new highs in performance and radically reducing the cost of computer control

by Laurence Altman, *Solid State Editor, Electronics*

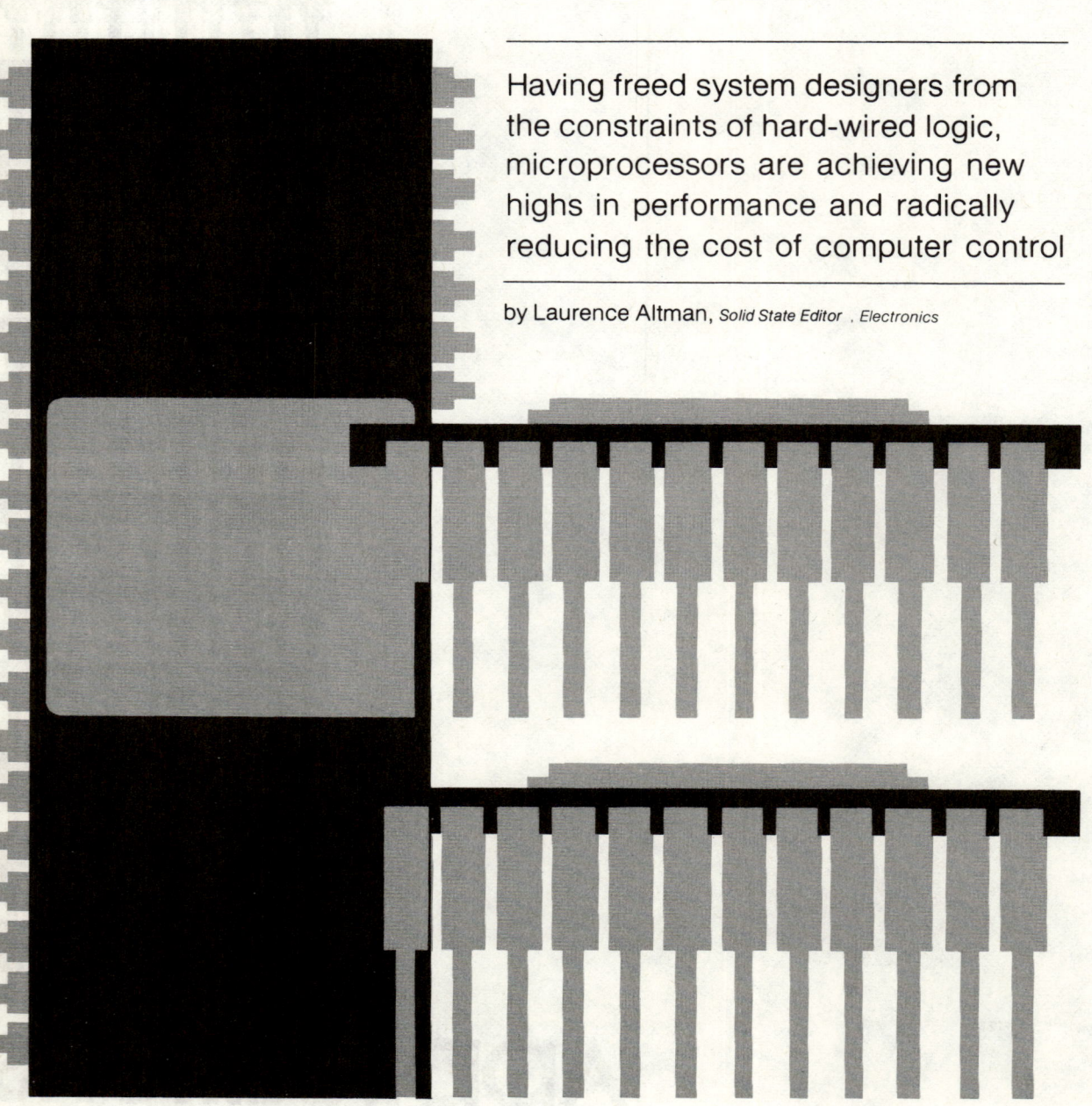

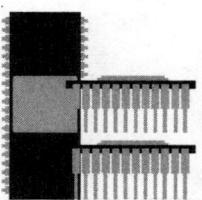

☐ The first single-chip high-performance microprocessors are rolling off the production lines, splendid confirmation of the power of large-scale integration. These second-generation microprocessors, together with a handful of matched memory and logic circuits, provide equipment designers with the full power of computer hierarchy at unprecedentedly low cost—about the price of a dozen medium-scale TTL integrated circuits.

Inexpensive computer control—that is the miracle of the new microprocessor. All the other advantages inherent in its innovative organization are secondary, even the versatility that results from the ability to simulate logic with software and to reprogram corrections and system changes quickly with no changes in hardware.

The implications of such cheap, distributed one-quarter-horse computer power are only beginning to be understood. A Teletype computer terminal capable of transmitting 300 bits of data per second can now be implemented with 12 LSI packages costing less than $300. Traffic-light controllers can be built with 12 microprocessor family packages, where an equivalent TTL design requires 200. A simple gas-pump meter needs one microprocessor and only nine other packages, an electronic scale needs eight chips. A digital instrument panel displaying five functions can be built from a five-chip microprocessor family, plus display circuits. A microprocessor control system already is operating in experimental automobiles, monitoring dozens of operational parameters at a potential component cost of less than $200. No other electronic method could perform these functions at a practical cost.

Indeed, the microprocessor is really the first truly general-purpose LSI logic device—calculator chips are decidedly special-purpose. That's because the microprocessor, replacing hard-wired logic, offers the twin advantages of LSI circuitry and programability.

Software-implemented logic, few packages, low power-supply and cooling requirements, and few pc cards and connectors simplify system re-evaluation, redesign, and testing. They also reduce assembly costs and inventory requirements.

Using software programs to affect the behavior of the processor instead of hardware interconnections may be an unfamiliar technique to many circuit designers, but pays off by boosting system performance. A typical software program consists of a series of orders or commands to the processor stored in a companion read-only memory. Since ROMs are easy to program—and programable ROMs easy to reprogram—the microprocessor's behavior can be much more conveniently adapted to a changed application than if extensive, time-consuming changes in hardware were necessary. New designs, too, can be turned around faster because a standard microprocessor architecture can be used along with a different ROM program for each new application.

Designing systems with microprocessors is still largely

1. The big attraction. Built using standard TTL hardware, this microprogramable processor circuit requires 451 packages on five circuit boards. Using advanced MSI logic and read-only-memory programing, it requires 114 packages on one board. Yet the same circuit, when built with today's n-channel LSI techniques, can be packed into one 40-pin microprocessor package—Motorola's new M6800 system.

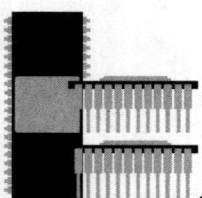

uncharted, but some rules of thumb are beginning to emerge. Since a complete microprocessor system requires from five to 50 ICs—including clocks, control logic and memory, and peripheral buffering—microprocessors should only be considered for a sequential digital design requiring more than 50 hard-wired logic ICs. Such a design will have more than a trivial number of steps to its logic flowchart and will also have some logic or arithmetic data-processing requirements. At the same time, the speed cannot be too fast, say, not more than 5 to 10 microseconds per instruction.

These system requirements, clearly less stringent than those handled by today's minicomputers, would cost $2,000 to $20,000 to build with hard-wired logic. But with microprocessors costing a 10th of that, their range is almost inexhaustible: point-of-sale terminals, electronic cash registers, inventory-control systems, credit-card verification systems, process, numeric, and machine control, automatic test systems, digital instruments, traffic controllers, communications systems, peripheral controllers, navigational systems, game machines. This is the domain of the microprocessor.

How to choose a microprocessor

Selecting a central processing unit (CPU), the major component in a microcomputer design, is a matter of deciding the best way to process the data. For example, data word length may be fixed by the processor design or it may be variable if the design allows multiple processor chips in parallel. A variable data word length is to be preferred when the needs of a variety of applications must be satisfied. For instance, a 16-bit CPU chip could be programed into 4-bit words for BCD display control, calculators, or cash registers, 8-bit words for CRT terminals or data concentrators, 12-bit words for handling the output of a-d converters, 16-bit words for general-purpose processing, or even 24- to 32-bit words for high-accuracy or high-throughput applications.

Instruction power is the next feature to watch out for in a CPU chip. Because the power of individual instructions and methods of counting may vary widely, the number of instructions in the set executed by a microprocessor is a poor index of its usefulness. The only realistic method of comparing instruction sets is to experiment with programs typically required for the intended applications and to compare the execution times and number of bits of storage they use.

Often overlooked in choosing a microprocessor is its interface structure—that part of the CPU which connects the arithmetic and logic unit and the control memory with the input/output peripheral circuitry. Clearly, this structure should adapt easily to a variety of system parameters without imposing a high overhead in hardware or software. The application may demand anything from a simple low-cost bus (either parallel or serial) having separate input, output, and address lines and heavily dependent for its control on the processor, to a sophisticated, high-speed, bidirectional bus with addresses and data multiplexed over the same lines. For maximum flexibility, look for provisions for input/output control, which allow convenient interfacing with peripheral components of varying response time. On the other hand, fixed I/O timing may provide higher I/O speed. In any case, the microprocessor I/O circuitry should directly interface with the 5-volt bipolar logic required to drive I/O lines; if not, buffers will be necessary, adding expense and needing more in the way of power requirements and board space.

Since the memory is often a major portion of the system cost, its selection is nearly as crucial as the CPU's. Read/write memories (random-access memories or RAMs) are best used for variable data storage and for program storage during program development. Programs for prototype or preproduction systems are often stored in a programable ROM, while a ROM is used during high-volume production.

What's available

The rush with which microprocessor devices are appearing—and will continue to appear throughout the year, according to semiconductor manufacturers—is a tribute to the intensity of the demand for them. They fall into three classes.

The pioneering 4-bit microprocessor systems were

What a microprocessor is . . .

. . . but first, what it isn't. A microprocessor is not a computer but only part of one. To make a computer out of a microprocessor requires the addition of memory for its control program, plus input and output circuits to operate peripheral equipment. Also, the word is not short for microprogramable central processing unit. For, though some microprocessors are controlled by a microprogram, most are not.

What a microprocessor is, then, is the control and processing portion of a small computer or microcomputer. Moreover, it has come to mean the kind of processor that can be built with LSI MOS circuitry, usually on one chip. Like all computer processors, microprocessors can handle both arithmetic and logic data in a bit-parallel fashion under control of a program. But they are distinguished both from a minicomputer processor by their use of LSI with its lower power and costs, and from other LSI devices (except calculator chips) by their programable behavior.

In short, if a minicomputer is a 1-horsepower unit, the microprocessor plus supporting circuitry is a ¼-hp unit. But as LSI technology improves, it will become more powerful. Already single-chip bipolar and C-MOS-on-sapphire processors are being developed that have almost the capability of the minicomputer.

built largely with p-channel MOS calculator technology, examples being Intel Corp.'s MCS-4, Rockwell International Corp.'s PPS-4 system, and Microsystem International Ltd.'s MC-1. Next came the 8- and 16-bit p-channel processor sets that are extensions of the early 4-bit units. These devices, while intended for applications up to the minicomputer level, generally require either multichip CPUs or considerable peripheral circuitry. Intel's MCS-8 and National Semiconductor Corp.'s IMP-16 are the most popular examples of each kind. Into the third and newest class, considered by many to be the second generation of microprocessors, fall the new n-channel 8-bit systems like Motorola's MC6800 and Intel's 8080 chips, which, together with matched memory and input/output circuit interfaces, form a completely self-contained large-capacity microcomputer family of chips.

Introduced late in 1972, the 4-bit microprocessor units were the first to provide the microprogramable parallel processing required in many keyboard and slow-throughput terminal and process-control applications. Indeed, using as few as two devices, like Intel's 4004 CPU chip plus a 1,024-bit ROM, a 4-bit microprogramed dedicated computer could cost less than $50.

Intel's basic MCS-4 system, however, was designed for general applications. Its single-chip CPU performs all control and processing functions and interfaces directly with ROMs, which store microprograms and data tables, and RAMs, which store data and pseudo-instructions. This system communicates with input/output devices, found here on each ROM and RAM chip. In addition, a 10-bit parallel shift register is provided to expand the system's I/O capability. Thus just four chips are needed for complete microcomputer capability.

Even this relatively simple 18-pin 4-bit package provides up to 45 instructions, cycling in 10.8 microseconds with standard two-phase clock operation. The system can drive up to 4,096 8-bit ROM words (16 chips), 1,280 4-bit RAM characters (16 chips), 128 I/O lines (without a shift register), and unlimited I/O capability with shift registers. And, adding even more to the MCS-4's flexibility and further accelerating the design cycle, the CPU and RAMs may be interfaced with conventional electrically programable and erasable ROMs, allowing fast program development and quick prototype realization.

Equally versatile is Rockwell's 4-bit PPS system, which comes complete with five compatible support circuits: a 256-by-4-bit RAM, a 1,024-by-8-bit ROM, a RAM-ROM combination chip containing a 704-by-8-bit ROM and 76-by-4-bit RAM, an I/O buffer, and a multiphase clock generator (Fig. 2).

The CPU in this system can directly address up to

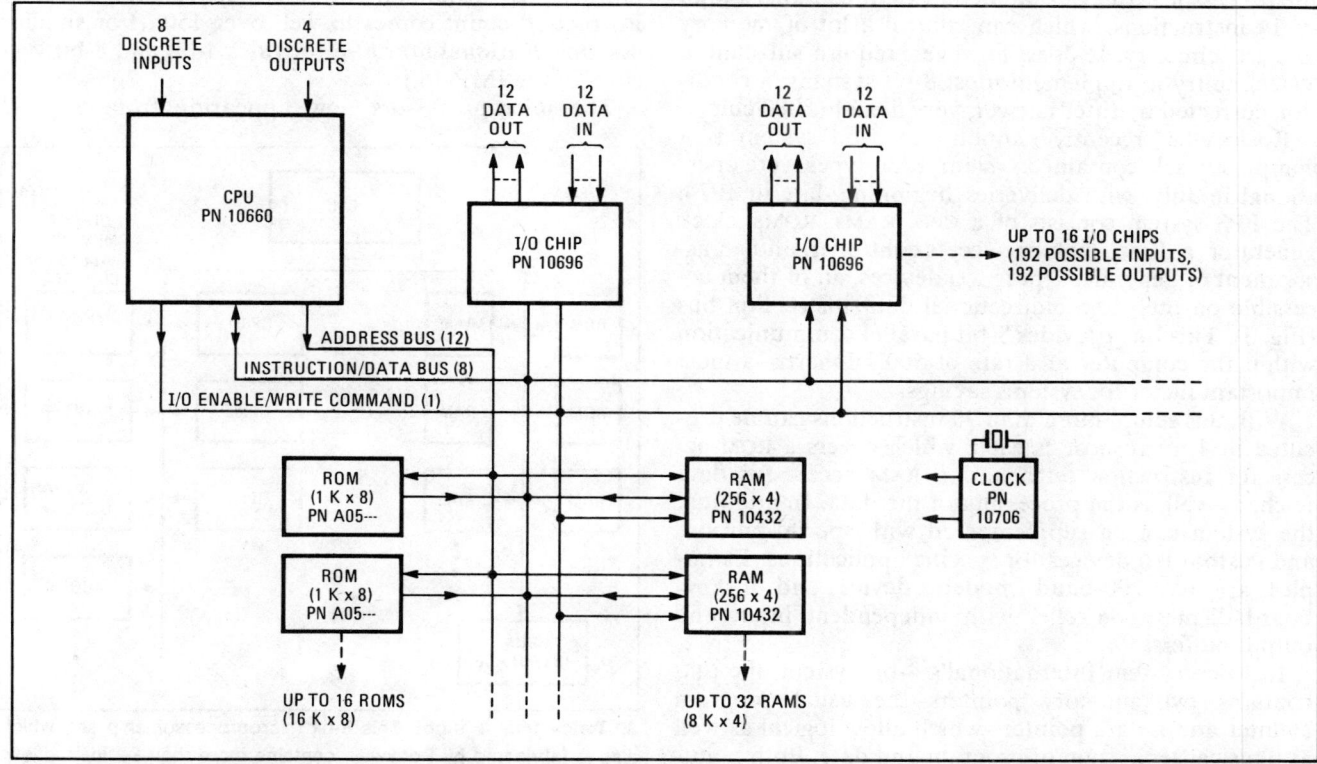

2. Four bits' worth. In Rockwell's self-contained 4-bit PPS system, versatility is a major design asset. Five compatible elements—CPU, RAM, ROM, a RAM-ROM combination chip, and an input/output buffer—provide up to 4,096 8-bit ROM words and 4,096 4-bit RAM words.

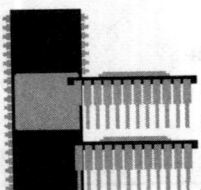

4,096 8-bit ROM words and as many 4-bit RAM data words over its 12-bit parallel address bus. This large number of data words gives this family the capability of a 4-bit minicomputer. The basic instruction set contains 50 instructions, and instruction fetch and execution time is a speedy 5 microseconds.

Apart from power and clock-signal requirements, 21 multiplexed lines interconnect the CPU with ROM, RAM, and I/O circuits. These lines, as shown in Fig. 2, are functionally grouped into 12 parallel address lines, eight parallel data lines, and one write command and I/O enable line. The address lines originate at the CPU and are time-multiplexed within it to provide direct addressing capability for up to 4,096 locations on both ROM and RAM. In addition, the ROM has two chip-select inputs and the RAM has one chip-select input, which may be directly controlled by discrete outputs from the CPU or I/O circuits to expand on memory without the need for auxiliary circuitry.

The move to eight bits

For greater capacity, both Intel and Rockwell are extending their 4-bit p-channel systems to 8-bit capability. The Intel MCS-8 is an 8-bit fixed instruction set and consists of a single MOS chip in an 18-pin DIP. Also on the chip is an 8-bit data/address I/O bus that interfaces the processor with external memories. It contains a total of 14 instructions, which can control a lot of memory and I/O circuitry. It does, however, require substantial TTL circuitry to implement most 8-bit systems, a condition corrected by Intel's newer, very flexible 8080 chip.

Rockwell's recently announced 8-bit system is a completely self-contained system. Prototypes were operational in July, with deliveries beginning late in 1974. The PPS system consists of a CPU, RAMs, ROMs, clock generator, a direct-memory-access controller, and an assortment of general-purpose I/O devices, all of them accessible on the same bidirectional data/instruction bus (Fig. 3). This bus provides 8-bit parallel communication within the computer at a rate of 500 kilohertz—a most important factor for systems savings.

With this setup, more than 90 instructions can be executed in 4 microseconds each, which covers a ROM access for instruction fetch and a RAM access for data fetch, as well as the processing of the data. In addition, the system can be supplemented with special-purpose and custom I/O devices for specific applications. Examples are a 1,200-baud modem device and a keyboard/display controller with independent input and output buffers.

In Microsystem International's 4-bit system, the CPU contains two memory pointers—the usual program counter and a data pointer—which allow logical as well as physical separation of program and data. Both pointers are 12 bits long and can directly address 4,096 memory locations. Each memory location contains 4 bits of data. Up to 34 kilobytes may be addressed over field switching in the typical MC-1 microcomputer.

Even more powerful is National Semiconductor's multi-chip CPCP CPU, shown in Fig. 4, from which National's IMP-16 systems can be built. It can provide computing power that ranges from simple 4-bit keyboard address capability right up through full 16-bit minicomputer capability. In IMP-16 systems, processing is done by four 4-bit arithmetic logic units controlled by microprogramable ROMs. With this arrangement, data exchange happens over a 16-bit-wide data bus, while I/O and control operations take place over a set of 16 general-purpose addressable registers (called FLAGs).

Consisting of a five chips, this CPU is contained on a board along with 256 words of random-access and 512 words of read-only on-card memory. Also available on the card are external interface circuits such as an address bus, data input and output buses, additional control FLAGs, system timing lines, and an interrupt input.

In essence, the IMP-16, which is expandable to 32 bits, is composed of four 4-bit ALU slices, each with control registers, ALU logic, and I/O data lines. The control ROM contains all control logic and microinstruction storage necessary to control the ALU chips. A total of 43 instructions is available though, if one considers the multiplicity of branch conditions, I/O FLAGs, and general-purpose accumulators in the system, the effective instruction count comes to well over 150. (For smaller systems, National now also provides 4-bit and 8-bit versions of the IMP-16.)

The microprocessors now appearing from a good

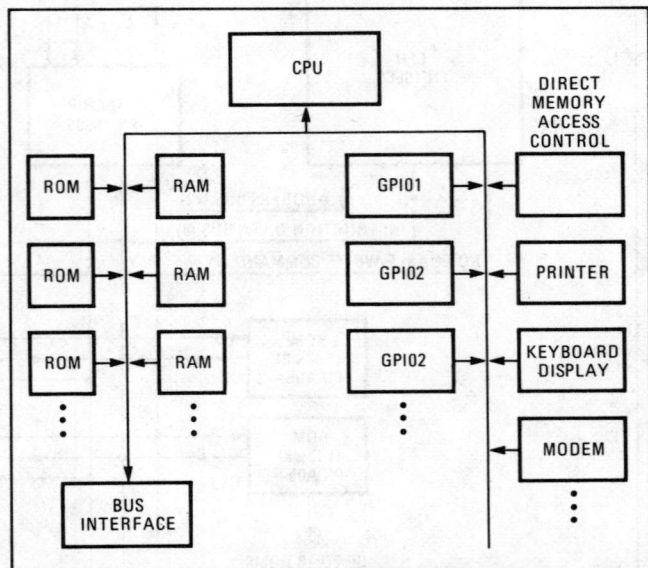

3. Twice four is eight. This 8-bit microprocessor chip set, which also is fabricated by Rockwell, contains more than 90 instructions with 4-microsecond execution times. All of the components shown work directly off the CPU.

many semiconductor manufacturers take full advantage of the knowledge gained in the past two years and incorporate those features that have proven most effective for the greatest variety of applications. What is obviously wanted is a single-chip 8-bit CPU device, offering 70 instructions or more, at speeds above 1 megahertz, with an extremely flexible input and output structure, and requiring only a few support memory and logic circuits to do most 8-bit jobs. Above all, these support circuits must be easy to use—that is, work directly with the CPU without requiring additional buffers and power supplies. Moreover, the CPU must be able to work directly with standard memory products. This adds up to a need for a self-contained 8-bit microcomputer set of chips—one CPU, and maybe five or six matched memory and logic hang-on packages.

The new generation

To build them, most manufacturers have settled on n-channel technology because it can pack many memory and logic structures onto one CPU chip, provides high capacity, and operates at high speed from 5-v (TTL) power supplies. Since the new n-channel memories would be directly compatible with such CPU chip, ease of use falls out automatically.

Besides the 8-bit n-channel microprocessors that have already arrived from Intel and Motorola, standard n-MOS products are also evident from Texas Instruments, American Microsystems, Signetics, National, Fairchild, General Instruments, and Western Digital. Rockwell and MOS Technology Inc. are staying with p-channel, and RCA has already announced a C-MOS microprocessor prototype.

The Signetics device, called PIP for programable integrated processor, is a single-chip 8-bit unit in a 40-pin DIP. The customary address logic, control memory and ALU are organized around a bidirectional 8-bit data bus, and there are also 15 address lines for handling external memory and I/O circuitry. In the PIP device, the address logic handles all instructions. It also includes a return address stack that lets eight subroutine levels be stacked.

As for RCA's C-MOS microprocessor, the two-chip 8-bit design has all the advantages that C-MOS circuits offer. (A single-chip version is under way.) It can operate off power supplies providing anywhere from 5 to 15 v, it

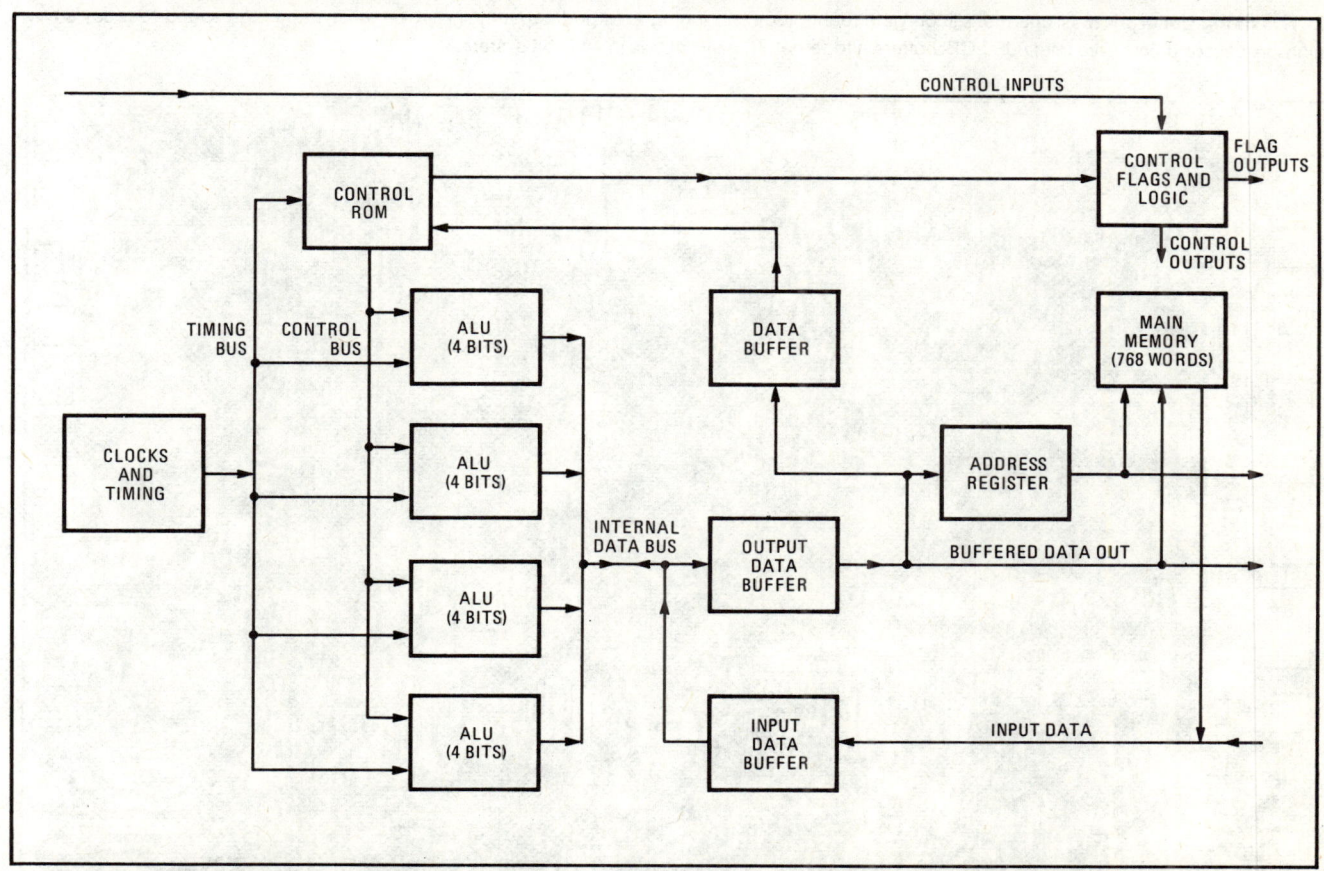

4. Sixteen-bit systems. The block diagram of National Semiconductor's IMP-16 microprocessor system shows that the system is made up of four 4-bit ALU slices with control registers, ALU logic, and I/O data lines. Altogether 43 instructions are available.

has high noise immunity, and it dissipates power at the microwatt level. Needing so little power and being easy to use, the chip set will be particularly useful for low-cost high-volume applications, and the C-MOS process could make it especially attractive for use in cars.

The microprocessor will come in a 40-pin package and can be used with any mixture of RAM, ROM, and peripheral I/O circuits. It is capable of addressing up to 65,536 8-bit bytes, so that quite large and flexible processing systems could be implemented, even though it has only 25 instructions. What's more, when operating from a typical supply of 10-12 V, the machine cycle time is a respectable 3 microseconds. And using a standard 1-microsecond RAM, the chip set has a maximum 6-µs fetch-execute time for any instruction.

Another manufacturer favoring C-MOS for microprocessors is Intersil, which is developing a 12-bit single-chip CPU to work with its C-MOS and n-channel memories. Intersil chose a 12-bit structure so that designers could use software programs that already exist for PDP-8A systems—and in fact, when combined with appropriate memory and I/O hang-ons, the 12-bit unit can perform all the MSI functions of the PDP-8A minicomputer but needs only a fraction of the packages.

The implications of all this activity are tremendous. Indeed, many observers feel that the MOS microprocessor families now just emerging will have a bigger impact on the electronics industries than any other semiconductor device has had so far. Quite soon, too, improved LSI structures should result in single-chip microcomputers combining the CPU, I/O, and memory in one LSI device. Moreover, the same sort of excitement is being generated around the bipolar LSI processor work that's now a priority in many semiconductor laboratories; for that technology, too, points to full-instruction minicomputer capability on a few LSI chips, but at even faster speed. □

BIBLIOGRAPHY
George Reyling Jr. and Alan J. Weissberger, "Microprocessor components and systems," (unpublished, but available from the authors, National Semiconductor Corp., 2900 Semiconductor Drive, Santa Clara, Calif. 95051).

5. The rising generation. N-channel silicon-gate technology is bringing enlarged capacity, great versatility, and high speed to today's new microprocessor chips. This Intel 8080 CPU offers altogether 78 instructions in an 8-bit system.

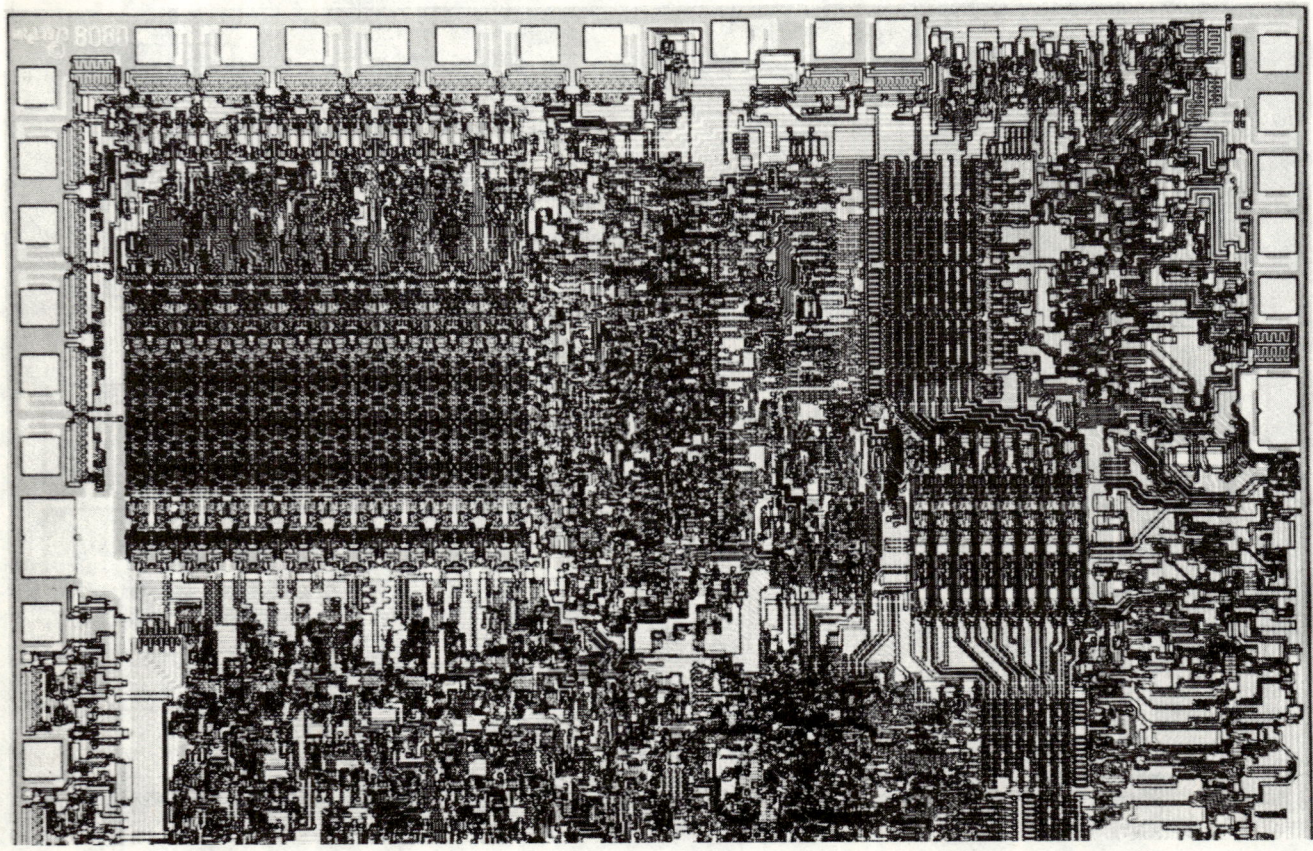

Diverse industry users clamber aboard the microprocessor bandwagon

LSI processors are not only expanding
capabilities of traditional products
—from instruments to consumer wares—
they're also creating completely new markets

☐ Industrial-equipment designers like them because they can be tailored economically to bring computer capability to jobs where minicomputers represent overkill.

Communications-gear designers are enthusiastic because their flexibility can solve problems presented by the ever-changing multiplex and modem specifications.

Instrument designers are looking forward to making them the basis of families of "smart" instruments that can evaluate data and react accordingly, without boosting instrument costs significantly. And even computer manufacturers are eyeing them as perfect companions to their TTL-based central-processor modules.

It's no wonder, then, that microprocessors are engaging the attention of equipment designers of all persuasions and manufacturers from a wide variety of industries. As a result, the growth of microprocessors is projected to leap from last year's $10 million to $800 million in the next five years. More dramatic yet will be the increase in the value of new end equipment built around LSI processors, expected to exceed a staggering $10 to $15 billion a year by the end of the same period.

What has caused the sudden microprocessor boom? Simply stated, LSI technology has reached the level of sophistication where it can provide the logic and memory performance needed to perform a growing number of computer functions at low cost. Programable LSI circuits—the calculator was the first—combine the flexibility of custom design with the cost advantages of readily available standard products. The user can change his design or add features to it merely by changing a program in a read-only memory. No mask changes are needed. And he is saving money by replacing many dozens of logic packages with a few LSI chips.

Impressive as today's microprocessors are, they are only the most visible aspect of what is clearly becoming an LSI-processor revolution that will completely change computer and computer-control design. Today's LSI processors are at the capability level of the small and not-so-small computer. But more powerful LSI-processor and computer-component chips that are now starting to appear far exceed the requirements of today's microcomputer applications.

Built with bipolar and improved MOS techniques, these faster and more complex components go to the heart of minicomputer-based systems, nourishing more and more equipment-design applications. These are the LSI programable chips computer manufacturers themselves have been waiting for. At last, the full benefits of LSI programable technology can be applied to the large computer, ushering in a new era of high-performance computer control at lower cost.

These articles bring together the experiences of the first microprocessor users—the promises and problems of designing with this powerful technique. The entire range of electronic-equipment designs has been researched—industrial, communications, consumer, commercial, instrumentation, and computer technology. Included are details on such varied systems as process and numerical controllers, word processors, data loggers, communications controllers, intelligent terminals, point-of-sale systems, games, toys, advanced calculators, self-calibrating instruments, automobile controls, and all the rest.

Also included is a section that contains tips on software and design aids. Finally, Bill Davidow, manager of microcomputer systems for Intel Corp., adds up the design advantages of microprocessor-based systems to show their impact where it counts most—on the bottom line.   —Laurence Altman, Senior Editor

Industrial Automatic control proliferates

by Alfred I. Rosenblatt, Associate Editor

"The microprocessor is going to set the industrial-equipment marketplace on its ear. The technology will never be the same again." That opinion was expressed by a market planner at a semiconductor house developing a microprocessor-chip set for one of the manufacturers of process-control instrumentation. The prediction is borne out by developments in the industrial marketplace. What's more, prospects for dramatic improvements are as bright for piece-parts manufacturing as for process control.

Although less than three years old, microprocessors are already finding their way into a host of new industrial equipment—factory-automation systems, machine-tool control, data-acquisition systems for such jobs as monitoring apportionment of meat for hamburgers, electronic scales, control of conveyor lines, numerical control, robot manipulation of piece parts, data-sensing, and component-insertion. They are also being used for environmental monitoring and phototypesetting.

These microprocessor-based systems offer the flexibility to adapt manufacturing systems to changing demands and upgrade them as production expands. All that is necessary is for chips containing new instructions to be inserted when peripherals are changed, equipment is added, or the system itself is modified. Changes and modifications are much more difficult when conventional hard-wired circuitry must be replaced.

What's more, manufacturers are happy about decreases in manufacturing costs that result when a relatively few microprocessor chips replace tens of discrete SSI and MSI circuits. Not only are fewer components required, but the microprocessor obviates the necessity to fabricate many more components manually into hard-wired logic arrays and insert these boards into the control systems. However, where speed is critical, hard-wired designs may do better for some time to come.

As the capabilities of microprocessors are expanded, they are taking over many of the tasks—at a pleasant reduction of costs—previously performed by minicomputers, but for which a considerable amount of the power of minicomputers is wasted. Replacing the purchased minicomputers may also increase the amount of value added for a manufacturer in his final product with a consequent increase in profits.

Taking over the factory

The availability of powerful low-cost microprocessors is also hastening the transition to the efficient distribution of computer power through employment of hierarchical computer systems in factories. The microprocessors and microcomputers perform dedicated tasks under the control of minicomputers, and the entire complex is tied in to large central computer systems.

What's more, the microprocessor is making it possible for manufacturers of process-control equipment and systems virtually to go into computer-manufacturing. Bruce H. Baldridge, director of corporate marketing and product planning at Foxboro Corp., Foxboro, Mass., points out that microprocessors are going to seriously influence the make-or-buy decision so that "a company like Foxboro could buy a micro chip, put it on a board, and it would be putting us in the computer-manufacturing business without the expense of getting deeply involved in the technology."

The importance of the microprocessor to industry is summed up by Edwin Lee, president of Pro-Log Corp., a Monterey, Calif., systems-design firm that also offers a line of microprocessor modules, "Within 12 to 18 months, anyone who hasn't incorporated a microprocessor in his design will either be serving a very special application or he's going to be very uncompetitive, as far as hardware is concerned."

Another consultant calls this "an explosive situation—anything that's cheap and reasonably powerful changes things. Anyone doing anything with hard-wired electronics who doesn't look at and consider microprocessors is making a big mistake."

A recently completed study on factory automation by Quantum Science Corp., a New York-based industrial-research company, estimates that by 1984, industry will

APPLICATION OF MICROCOMPUTERS TO FACTORY AUTOMATION					
	Machine tool control (units/year)	Robots (units/year)	Product testing (units/year)	Facilities monitoring (units/year)	Total cost
1974	300	10	300	150	760 @ $1,000 each avg.
1979	3,400	2,850	500	300	7,050 @ $400 each avg.
1984	7,800	14,000	1,000	600	23,400 @ $300 each avg.
Estimates courtesy of Quantum Science Corp.					

be buying 27,300 microcomputers a year at an average price of $300 each. Accumulated over the years, these numbers will have an incredible effect on the factory's operation, increasing the efficiency and cost-effectiveness of production. The average unit price today is $1,000 according to the Quantum Science study.

Perhaps most unusual is Quantum's prediction that programable manipulators, or robots, will mushroom with the aid of microcomputers from 10 units installed in 1974 to 14,000 a year by 1984. About half that many—7,800 a year—are expected to be used for machine-tool control, a mammoth increase from the present base of 300 a year. And about 3,900 new microprocessors a year are predicted to handle communications between the various tools and computers in another 10 years, whereas now only 50 units a year are now being sold for that purpose. Product-testing is expected to account for 1,000 units per year by 1984—more than a three fold increase—and facilities-monitoring will rise to 600 a year—a four fold increase.

Perhaps the earliest to recognize the potential of the new microprocessors were manufacturers of industrial-control equipment. For example, Comstar Corp., Minneapolis, first started using microprocessors two and a half years ago, and now it has more than 700 microcomputers installed. Applications include assembly-machine control, automatic weighing and batching systems, materials-handling systems, remote monitoring and control, data entry, and automobile-traffic control.

One particularly strong market for the microprocessors is in materials-handling. For Beatrice Foods' new frozen-food warehouse in Chicago, for example, Comstar has installed six microprocessor systems. Each controls 50 motors in a network of more than 300 conveyors that transport boxes from the freezer to trucks. On the way, they go through sorters, convergers, divergers, and conveyor-belt changes, but the controller keeps track of every box for its entire trip.

"In earlier warehouses, Beatrice used electromechanical-relay control, with limit switches for actuation," says Tom Walstrom, regional sales manager for Comstar. "Something like our system could have been designed and built with relays, but it might never have worked. It would have been too complex to be practical and much too large to maintain."

Numerical controllers gain

For several reasons, microprocessors also have an excellent potential for being built into stand-alone numerical controllers for machine tools, which are now fabricated with hard-wired logic. Microprocessors can sharply reduce the component count in the controllers while offering easy modifications of programs and functions, which are now possible only with much more expensive systems built around minicomputers.

Although the major N/C suppliers like Allen-Bradley Co., Bendix Corp., and Cincinnati Milacron Co. aren't saying much about their interest in microprocessors, smaller companies and even newcomers to the field, with little or no product base and inventory to worry about, may jump in. General Electric Co., the largest N/C supplier, only last month announced that it had begun using a microprocessor in one of its numerical controllers.

One newcomer is Cambridge Thermionic Corp., Cambridge, Mass., a manufacturer of IC sockets and terminals. But rather than compete head-on with the giants, Cambion's recently introduced PMC-1 microcomputer numerical control is aimed at applications that may have been too expensive for N/C until now, says Lyndon Wilkes of the N/C marketing group. The PMC-1, which operates point to point, rather than on a continuous path, is aimed at simple positioning for such applications as insertion, wire-wrapping, and machines for drilling printed-circuit boards. In its open-loop configuration, it can position a tool to within .001 inch.

Price of the unit is less than $4,000, including the controller, which is built around the Intel 4-bit MCS-4 microprocessor set, plus a two-axis motor drive and a stepping power supply. The price is about $1,000 less than the lowest-priced hard-wired controller available, asserts Wilkes.

Manipulating the controls

As indicated in the block diagram, the control and arithmetic units in the Intel 4004 chip allow the CPU to acquire and manipulate control logic and data from the memory sections of the microcomputer and generate the outputs called for in the parts-making program.

Control programs containing the logic which, in con-

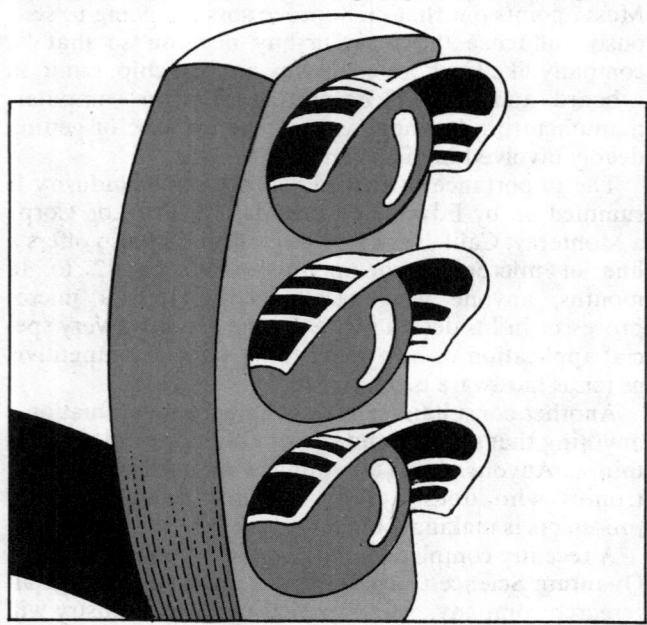

ventional N/Cs is hard-wired, is stored in read-only memory. The ROM controls interfacing for a maximum of 32 inputs and outputs. In addition, the ROM section contains the microprograms and data tables that the central processor must execute to control the tool. The unit can accommodate a maximum of six ROMs, each containing 256 by 8 bits, or programable ROMs, if field programability is desired.

A random-access memory—there can be a maximum of four devices, each containing 256 by 8 bits—serves as a scratchpad for the central processor. The RAM temporarily stores and releases data and instructions needed on a priority basis by the CPU as it executes the control programs stored in ROM. The parts-making programs themselves are written by the user, just as for a hard-wired controller. Then they're entered into the controller via punched-paper tape. For production runs, however, these programs could also be stored in a programable ROM.

Likewise, the ROM output interface controls the dispatch of signals to the X- and Y-axis motor drivers and the display readouts. RAM storage controls output to the tools and tape-reader motor. An automatic reset clears the CPU and RAM, resetting the system back to microprogram step one. A two-phase clock circuit provides the timing signals needed by the CPU.

Other components of the system include a ROM input-control interface that monitors inputs from control-panel switches, a paper-tape reader, tool feedback, and an X-Y jog-select mode.

All active components in the control section are contained on a single plug-in printed-circuit board—a decided advantage for maintenance and trouble-shooting, points out applications engineer Howard Atwood. Moreover, because the control has fewer parts, Atwood says the company can deliver a unit in one month or even two weeks, as opposed to the three to six months it would take to put a hard-wired control together.

Bending metal

A microprocessor-based system also controls a metal-stretching and bending press designed by Varitel Inc., Beverly Hills, Calif. About as large as a good-sized room, these giant machines have generally not been amenable to control by off-the-shelf numerical controllers, as have other machine tools, because of the great differences in their design caused by the spread in the size and type of parts they are called upon to fabricate. Hard-wired logic systems are generally used, and each press requires a custom-designed controller.

Although custom designing is still a problem, Varitel president Bruce Gladstone estimates that use of microprocessors can cut design time to a third or even a quarter of the time required to program a hard-wired system. To program the National Semiconductor IMP-16 card used by Varitel, the operator first bends the metal by manual controls. Two angular and two linear multiplexed analog-to-digital converters transmit to a tape cassette the amount of stretch and other factors involved in making the bend. The operator can edit the information as he goes.

When the information on the cassette proves to be accurate, it is transferred to the IMP-16's on-board erasable RAM. The RAM's capacity of 256 by 16 bits is adequate to provide 12-bit accuracy, achieved through two digital-to-analog converters that drive linear servos. As an added benefit, Varitel provides a small panel that plugs into one of the IMP-16 slots for servicing and troubleshooting. The panel contains its own memory.

The new microprocessors could also affect the design of programable controllers, which are themselves solid-state replacements for hard-wired banks of electromechanical relay logic. The present solid-state designs are also hard-wired and hence would be excellent candidates to be replaced by microprocessors.

But because of the many inputs derived from the assembly-line machines being controlled, present CPU speeds are generally too slow, says senior systems engineer Ronald D. Malcolm at Modicon Corp., Andover, Mass. Hard-wired designs will offer as fast or faster processing speeds for some time to come, but the microprocessors could allow more features to be added at lower cost, says Malcolm.

In addition, the microprocessors shorten design time "a great deal," he adds, as well as reduce the physical size, power-supply requirements, and cost. However, for use in its larger controllers, Modicon is considering a 16-bit bipolar monolithic microprocessor with a 150-nanosecond microinstruction time that is being sampled by Monolithic Memories.

And Modicon, a pioneer in programable controllers, has already applied microprocessor technology to peripheral products. For example, Intel's MCS-4 set is designed into the P-500 impact printer introduced last winter, as well as the manually operated programing panel for its smallest controller, thereby speeding up the panel's response time.

Controlling traffic

One of the greatest potential applications of microprocessors is to control street traffic. Indeed, Multisonics Corp. of San Ramon, Calif., with 10 years of experience in this application, predicts that intersection-control systems constitute the wave of the future for microprocessors.

Tom Seabury, chief engineer, points out that controllers can be designed for each intersection's needs.

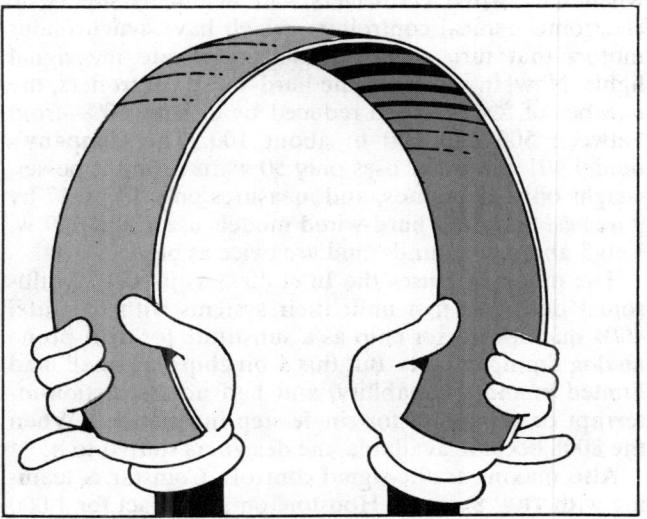

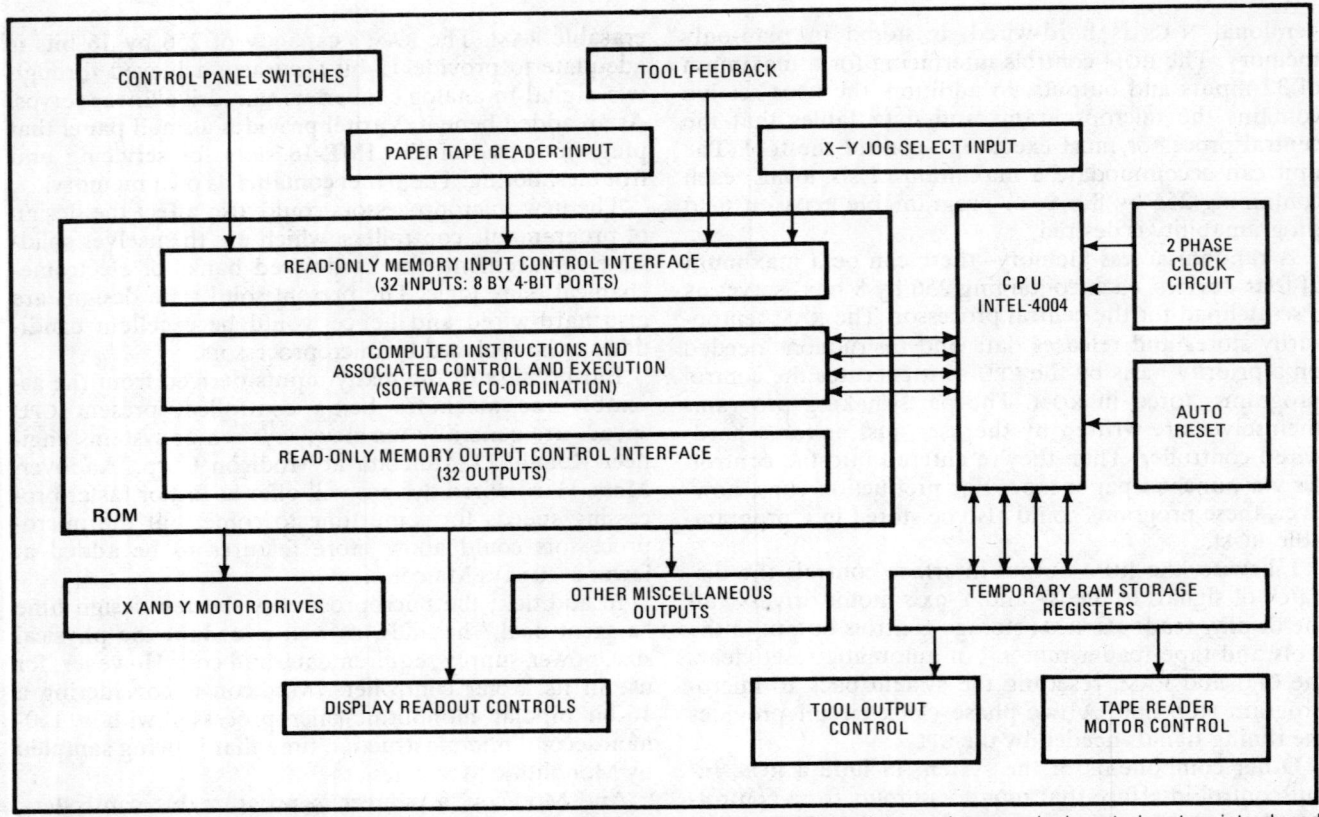

1. Numerical control. An Intel 4004 microprocessor chip is at the center of the PMC-1 point-to-point numerical-control system introduced by Cambridge Thermionic Corp., Cambridge, Md. Programs can be changed simply by plugging in new read-only-memory chips.

"Some traffic schemes, for example, require that all vehicles stop while pedestrians cross in a 'scramble' fashion," he says. "The conventional random-logic controllers need wiring changes to allow this, while with the microprocessor, all we have to do is plug in a different ROM package."

Seabury says the microprocessor is ideal for the stand-alone intelligent intersection controller. Minicomputers, the other alternative to hard-wiring, provide power that is wasted in such a dedicated application, and they are unable to withstand the severe environmental conditions without major design modifications.

The switch to microprocessors is coming at a time when hard-wired controllers had begun to supersede electromechanical controllers, which have synchronous motors that turn switch drums to operate the signal lights. Now, in replacing the hard-wired controllers, the number of ICs has been reduced by at least 60%—from between 500 and 600 to about 100. The company's model 901 controller uses only 50 watts of input power, weighs only 41 pounds, and measures only 17 by 17 by 9 inches. Standard hard-wired models use about 200 w, weigh about 80 pounds, and are twice as big.

The model 901 uses the Intel 8008 as its CPU. Multisonics designers first built their systems with the Intel 4004 microprocessor chip as a substitute for drift-prone analog timing circuits. But this 4-bit chip was small, had limited memory capability, and had no instruction-interrupt or capability for single-step instructions. When the 8008 became available, the designers shifted to it.

Also making traffic-signal controls, Comstar is teaming with TRW Systems, Houston, on a contract for 1,000 microcomputers for the city of Baltimore.

Microprocessors are also providing information to help humans improve the quality of the earth's environment. In one application, microprocessors are being installed in remote data-gathering stations that are keeping tabs on such conditions as water and air quality at sites proposed for nuclear-power plants.

Watching the environment

By preprocessing data and determining right at the remote site whether or not it falls within certain preset limits, "we can economize greatly on data-transmission costs because we send back only important data," explains Melvin Couchman, director of marketing and planning for NUS Corp., Rockville, Md. Ordinarily, as many as a half dozen remote stations are tied to a central data-gathering station via telephone lines. In addition to screening out unnecessary and redundant data, the microprocessor-based systems can also run calibration and diagnostic tests of the remote instrumentation to determine whether or not it's functioning properly, a task that might otherwise have to be handled from the central site.

The new systems, built around Computer Automation's LSI-2 unit, also cost less than if they'd been built with hard-wired logic, Couchman points out. But even more important is the capability of programing the microprocessor to tailor the operation of each remote station to specific requirements. "We just change the programable ROM in the field with a new program, or we put in a read/write memory and use the same basic physical hardware," says Couchman. "It would be much more complicated to change hard-wired logic."

Other types of data-acquisition systems are also feeling the effect of microprocessors. Quindar Electronics Corp., Springfield, N.J., has expanded the capabilities of its system, which is designed to monitor the operation of utilities, partially process the data, and send necessary information to the central computer [*Electronics*, 5/30/74 p. 34]. Process Computer Systems Corp., Ann Arbor, Mich., has designed a system that monitors torque applied to fasteners on an auto assembly line [*Electronics*, 6/13/74 p. 42].

Another company, Doric Scientific Corp., San Diego, Calif., has introduced a new data-monitoring system that not only sharply expands the number of monitored points—to as many as 1,000, an order of magnitude increase over the capacity of an earlier hard-wired unit—but also increases the kinds of parameters that can be monitored. Doric's new microprocessor-based Digitrend 220 monitors and records dc voltages and currents, as well as thermocouple outputs, in such diverse areas as the textile, petrochemical and pulp and paper industries.

The system handles as many as six different types of functional ranges at a time— double the capacity of Doric's hard-wired Digitrend 210. Moreover, with room for plug-in interfaces, it can send this data out to as many as four separate peripheral recording or transmission devices, such as magnetic-tape recorders or teletypewriters. In contrast, the Digitrend 210 handles but a single peripheral.

Doric relies on an Intel 8008, with as many as three PROMs, four ROMs, and two RAMs in a bus-organized structure. The memories contain input instructions for handling data, coefficients for linearizing the nonlinear thermocouple inputs, for scaling, for reading out measurements directly in both the fahrenheit and celsius scales, for limiting alarms, and scratchpad memory for aiding in linearization and formatting.

The new unit was designed to do more than its hard-wired predecessor, but comparable configurations would cost 25% more, admits chief engineer Freeman Rose. However, it performs all its functions in just about the same space as its predecessor.

Moreover, the microprocessor approach is "quite a bit" cheaper than if Doric had gone to a minicomputer, Rose continues. At any rate, Doric did not want to "boggle the mind of the customer" with a mini and the software that would be needed. With the microprocessor, changes are made by simply plugging in a new memory, rather than substituting a hard-wired logic board. Doric is looking at such new n-channel microprocessors as the 8080 to expand the capability of its system still further by offering such operations as trend analysis and averaging.

Typesetting makes headlines

For typesetting, a typical microprocessor-based system would consist of a module containing all the processing and memory functions. One module, built by Varityper division, Addressograph Multigraph Corp., East Hanover, N.J., contains the Intel 8008, which offers the large instruction capability required by phototypesetting equipment, plus the required programable ROM,

ROM, and RAM, an input bus, and printer and teletypewriter interfaces.

Not only is Varityper able to add processing capabilities to its top-of-the-line phototypesetter that sells for some $15,500, but processing can be included in lower-end products as well. In the past year, the company has introduced a phototypesetting controller called the Amtrol, built around the Intel 8008. The results couldn't have made management happier. Varityper engineers have built a family of 16 standard plug-in modules that they can just about pull off the shelf and apply to new products as they're needed.

This summer, for example, the company will introduce a composition machine that will sell for less than $10,000, yet have decision-making capability. This could never have been accomplished at such a low price with the special-purpose minicomputer that Varityper had been buying since 1969. The old mini was "markedly" more expensive than even the full Amtrol controller, and the modular family enables Varityper to tailor the processing power to each application.

Other advantages abound. The new processor is far more compact and reliable, and its plug-in design makes it easy to troubleshoot and service in the field. Moreover, customers seem to prefer the microprocessor design to hard-wired logic, says Joseph A. Verderber, of the office of product management, because it's easier to upgrade the system by adding features through a plug-in read-only memory.

Microprocessors have already begun to have a tremendous impact on many industries that have repetitive processes to be controlled. In the future, their application is likely to be limited solely by the imagination of the design engineer. Although cheap now, microprocessor prices will come down still further. Within a decade, an entire microcomputer with 4 kilobits of memory could cost less than $150, predicts a market consultant at Quantum Science Corp. That price earmarks the device for an ubiquity similar to that enjoyed by today's hand-held calculator.

Communications
Data-handling gains flexibility

by Stephen E. Scrupski, Communications & Microwave Editor

A strong tide is running in favor of replacing analog communications with digital methods. Microprocessors are accelerating this trend, bringing on a new wave of "intelligent" digital communications equipment. Multiplexers, code converters, error checkers, input/output controllers—all are natural applications for microprocessors. However, their full impact is yet to be felt; most communications-equipment suppliers are still in the feasibility-model and prototyping stages, while the speed limitations of present-day microprocessors are still inhibiting their wider usage.

As in other industries, communications designers like the flexibility and the low costs offered by microcomputers. Custom routines for individual tasks can be quickly changed simply by changing the contents of the programable read-only memories that hold the programs. This is particularly useful in digital communications, where many different codes and message protocols are in use and where the processing chores do not require the capabilities nor justify the cost of minicomputers.

Microcomputer hardware and software can be designed in parallel. While the printed-circuit boards are being laid out to accommodate the almost standard parts of the microprocessor complement, software design can proceed independently, and the two designs can be merged late in the product's development cycle, allowing for system optimization in a minimum of design time. What's more, when a microcomputer breaks down in a communications system, recovery time should be substantially less than in any other kind of system. Service technicians can carry standard circuit modules that are compatible with any of their company's equipment, requiring only new programing to take the place of a failed unit.

Micro teams with mini

An example of how a microprocessor and a minicomputer can be teamed up is in the message-switching units (Fig. 1) being developed by Action Communication Systems Inc., Dallas, Texas, in which microprocessors serve as front ends for Data General Corp. Nova minicomputers. The switchers are used in networks of private terminals, such as those employed by police departments to access records in a state capital or the National Crime Information Center in Washington, D.C. The company has installed several such systems. In the Texas network, for example, more than 500 terminals are located in police headquarters throughout the state.

These switchers, now in the prototype stage, will speed up the switching action and allow higher data rates. They will do this by relieving the minicomputers of certain standard operations—the "dirty work" that must be performed on all messages, such as converting them to the proper code for processing by the Nova and scanning the incoming character strings to identify different control sequences.

"What we're trying to do is eliminate any character-by-character handling by the Nova and allow it to handle only blocks of data," says Action design engineer Michael Fannin. By allowing the minicomputer to do the more complex tasks while the microprocessor handles the menial chores, he predicts that this configuration will raise the processing speed by about an order of magnitude, from the 1,000 or 2,000 characters per second to 10,000 or 20,000 characters per second.

Action is using National Semiconductor's IMP-16C processor for this application "because of its powerful instruction set," says Fannin. "Although it has a slower cycle time than some of its competition," he adds, "it does more with its instructions."

In the system (Fig. 1), circuit controllers interface with the communications circuits and perform serial assembly and disassembly of the characters at data rates as high as 19,200 bits per second. The microprocessors interface with the controllers and perform four functions:
- Convert character codes.
- Scan messages for key characters.

- Edit message headers and text.
- Check character calculations.

One microprocessor can handle the 19,200-b/s rate. It also interfaces with the 64,000-character semiconductor random-access memory, which buffers message blocks between the microprocessor and the central minicomputer.

In such applications, the microprocessor serves primarily as a piece of hardware, since the custom features still reside in the minicomputer's program. In effect, Action is using the microprocessor as a low-cost way to achieve large-scale integration. Many communications designers consider that this is the primary benefit of the microprocessor.

Arliss Whiteside, senior department consultant (essentially a senior scientist) in information processing at the Bendix Research Laboratories in Southfield, Mich., says, "A microprocessor is just another component—and a few too many people consider it something magic. I think they're oversold."

Whiteside goes on to explain that the microprocessor, in his view, is simply a way to cash in on the benefits of large-scale integration—lower costs through fewer packages—without entering a multi-thousand-dollar program to develop custom LSI. "I call it standard LSI," he adds, "LSI that is standardized, flexible, and built by the manufacturer in the quantities that are necessary to justify the design costs for an LSI chip."

Handling the full load

Such a viewpoint is supported in applications where the microprocessor assists a minicomputer. But in others, microprocessors shoulder the full load of data processing. Collins Radio Corp. in Dallas, for example plans to use microprocessors in an intelligent repeater for a private microwave data-transmission system now being built.

In the system, several data links surround a central-hub repeater terminal that switches one link to another upon request. The data signal carries address information that is decoded by the microprocessor, which then routes the message through the hub repeater to the proper receiving terminal. Although this is still an experimental project, according to Collins, the experiments have nothing to do with the microprocessors—the unknown factors are in the radio communications.

In this instance, the microcomputer's small size helps it beat out a minicomputer for the application—the repeaters have to be man-transportable and battery-powered. To further reduce the power drain, Collins engineers are replacing the TTL circuits recommended by the microcomputer manufacturer with complementary-MOS circuits. To conserve battery power, Collins is also using C-MOS chips for the random-access memory and programable read-only memory. However, the use of C-MOS instead of TTL slows down the system from the microprocessor's basic 1.4-microsecond cycle time to about 4 µs.

Considering tradeoffs

The reduced speed affects the architecture of the system, since extra memory is required to compensate for it. As the message is received in the processor at the hub repeater, it is stored in a buffer memory, and the microprocessor goes right to work processing the information. By the time the message is completely received, the microprocessor has extracted the processing and routing information, and the message is ready to be retransmitted to its destination.

The reduced speed also prevents Collins engineers from using the microprocessor for what should be a natural function—error-checking. The expected maximum data speed of 500 kilobits per second is just too fast for today's microprocessors. Error-checking therefore is done by hard-wired logic. However, if the transmission speed were lower—say, in the range of 50 kilobits per second—the microprocessors could be used to perform error-checking, says Collins design engineer Dale Walls.

Or, if the microprocessor could be operated at its design cycle speed of 1.4 µs, Walls says it would be "aw-

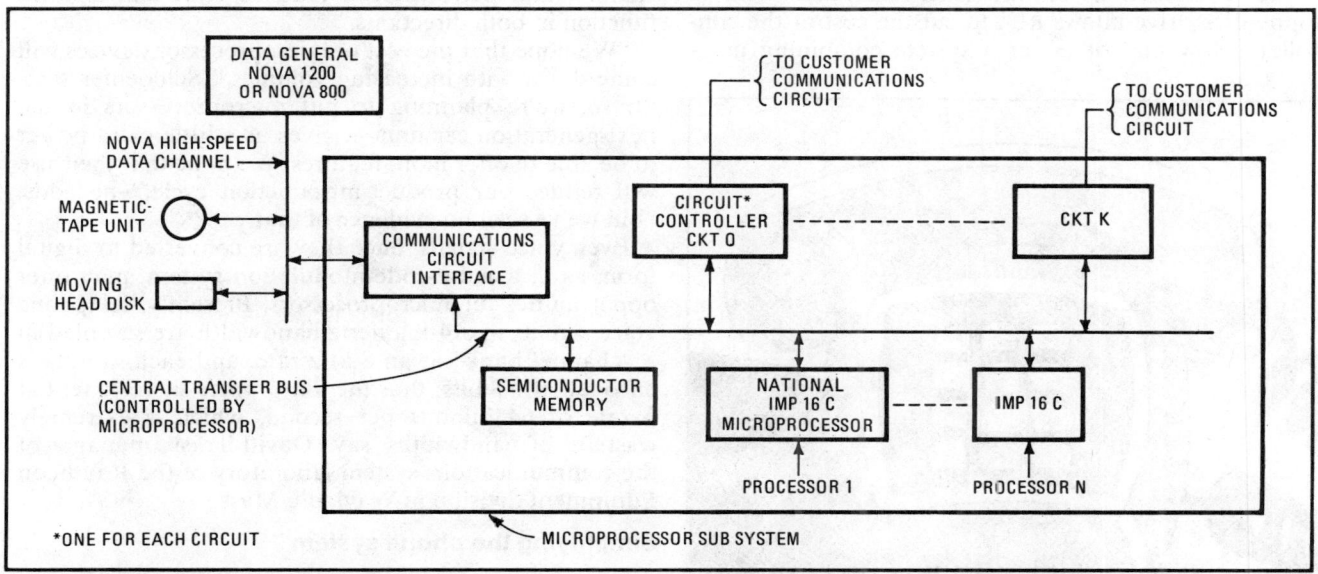

1. Nova helper. In message-switching units built by Action Communication, a National Semiconductor IMP-16 microprocessor handles character-by-character decoding so that Nova minicomputer can concentrate on handling full blocks of data, increasing system speed.

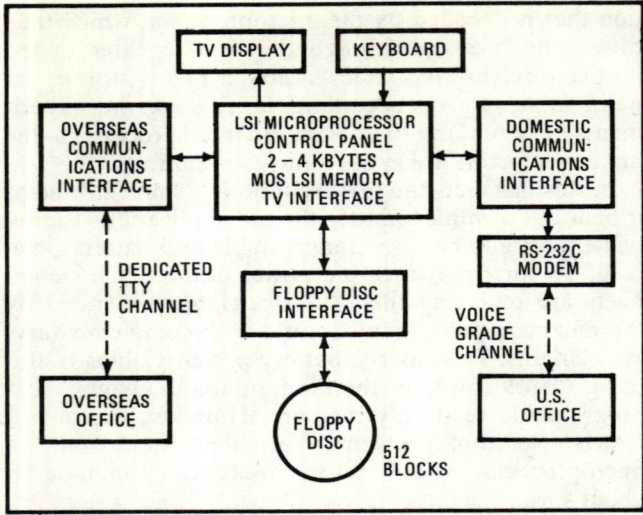

2. Interpreter. A microprocessor handles conversions of codes and speeds to allow a domestic data processor to communicate with an overseas network via the RCA Global Communications system. Easily changed software helps customize system.

fully close to being applicable for error-checking." The limiting speed of today's microprocessors however, will soon be overcome by a new generation of faster devices built with bipolar or sapphire-based MOS technologies, while 4-bit processor slices capable of instruction times of 10 to 50 ns are expected to be available by the end of the year.

Interfacing between nations

A microprocessor is the sole computing component in a programable controller built to handle international leased-data channels. Developed jointly by RCA Laboratories, Princeton N.J., and RCA Global Communications Inc., New York, the controller connects RCA's Cosmac, a two-chip C-MOS microprocessor and associated semiconductor RAMs, to a floppy-disk drive for mass storage of messages.

The combination of the microcomputer with a floppy-disk drive allows RCA to cut the cost of the controller below that of either a system combining magnetic tape with a minicomputer or hard-wired logic. The single basic design, easily customized by software, meets a variety of different customer needs, while at the same time offering improved maintainability.

The microprocessor's job is to provide all the conversions necessary to interface a domestic communications network with an overseas network (Fig. 2). Signals, codes, speeds, character formats—all must be often reconciled to allow the two networks to communicate with one another. And, since each private user who leases a channel from RCA has his own unique combination of such parameters, use of hard-wired logic would require long development times and an abundance of specialized equipment that would have to be maintained.

Minicomputers, although they offer programability, are simply too expensive to be considered for this application, according to RCA, since they have too much computing power for the few lines that must be controlled. Another tangential problem, RCA claims, is that often the customer has only partial knowledge of his own needs, and the microprocessor programability offers RCA engineers an easy means to add needed features at later stages.

Helping the police

In another police-oriented application, Motorola's Communications division, Schaumburg, Ill., is using a microprocessor in a computerized mobile terminal system, first installed for the Atlantic City, N.J., police in 1973. Each squad car carries a light-weight terminal with a full keyboard and plasma alphanumeric display. Using the terminal, a policeman can access files at his local station, at the state headquarters, or even at the National Crime Information Center.

An 8-bit microprocessor is built into the base-station unit, says Jerry Schloemer, manager for command and control products at Motorola. The microprocessor acts as a communications interface to the computer at the next higher echelon, controlling the coding on the radio channel and performing a reduced store-and-forward function in both directions.

"We hope that the cost of microprocessor devices will come down with increasing volumes," Schloemer says. "If so, we're planning to put microprocessors in the next-generation car unit—it gives us a little extra power to be able to offer more features. We hope that their use will reduce our product-introduction cycle," he adds, "but we've seen no evidence of that yet."

Even voice signals, once they are converted to digital form, as in a pulse-code-modulation system, may offer opportunities for microprocessors. Presently, telephone voice signals in a 4-kilohertz bandwidth are sampled in a "channel bank" at an 8-kHz rate, and each sample is encoded into 8 bits; thus the 4-kHz voice signal is sent at a rate of 64 kilobits per second, which is extremely wasteful of bandwidths, says David Trask, manager of the communications system laboratory of the Raytheon Equipment division in Wayland, Mass.

Simplifying the phone system

He points out that telephone engineers have given much thought to ways to reduce the bit rate necessary

Calling all cars. Microprocessor in Atlantic City, N. J., police station controls message-coding for keyboard terminals used in squad cars.

for each voice signal and thus to expand the capabilities of the transmission system. For example, many algorithms have been proposed for a processor that would note an instantaneous value of the voice signal and predict the value during the next sampling period. Then, when the next sample actually appears, the processor would transmit only the difference between the actual and predicted values.

If the algorithm is effective, it would only require a few bits, rather than the full 8 bits presently used. An identically programed microprocessor at the receiving end would then reconstruct the full voice signal. In fact, he envisions a telephone set that has the sampling and microprocessor circuitry built right into the back so that digital signals are sent to the telephone central office directly from the set itself.

Microprocessors are being designed into a somewhat similar system at Harris Electronic Systems, Melbourne, Fla. Harris is building encryption devices for secure digital-communications systems and, says Ray Glenn, associate principal engineer at Harris, the microprocessor makes a good pseudo-random noise generator. One microprocessor can be programed to encode a digital signal, and an identical microprocessor at the receiving end can decode the signal.

If fabricated with medium-scale integration, such a system might require up to about 75 packages, but a microprocessor would cut the count to only 10 to 15 packages, Glenn estimates. He points out that microprocessors are being used at Harris to control the output-power levels of radio-frequency transmitters throughout the day. Temperature changes, Glenn says, cause the power level to drift, but a simple 4-bit microprocessor can store a control algorithm that enables the microprocessor, when presented with digital information on the output level, to bring the level back to the desired point.

It is clear that microprocessors are taking over many of the routine applications in communications equipment. And regardless of whether the designer views a microprocessor as merely another component—a way to get standard LSI— or as a radical new component that offers small-scale programing, nearly all analog, as well as digital, communications gear will benefit from its impact.

Consumer/commercial Microprocessors go public

by Gerald M. Walker, Consumer Editor

Manufacturers of commercial and consumer products have for some time taken the lead in applying advanced semiconductor technology. Their adoption of microprocessors is no exception. In a sense, microprocessors are accelerating the timetable for equipment and systems already deemed feasible in both the commercial and consumer markets.

In addition, development of totally new products not yet identified will sweep these markets in the same way that the personal electronic calculators came from nowhere into international prominence. Thus, microprocessors are having it both ways—enhancing present-day equipment while promising completely new products for offices, stores, households, and entertainment centers.

Included in commmercial equipment containing microprocessors now on the market are terminals for point-of-sale and supermarket checkout, scales, terminals for investment houses and the finance industry, automated back tellers, processors for business-inventory control, equipment for supermarket in-store packaging, and portable data terminals.

Among the products using microprocessors in the comsumer and related markets or on the drawing board for the near future are sophisticated games, gambling equipment, cable-television transmission hardware, do-it-yourself instrument kits, and photographic-film developers. Further down the pike are automobile on-board processors that perform such tasks as controlling combustion timing (Fig. 1), exhaust emission, transmission operation, and anti-skid and diagnostic systems.

It's in the household that the explosive new product—the home computer—is expected to emerge. The most obvious door into the home is the television set, which can make good use of a data-communications processor. By then, microprocessors will have to be quite different from today's products, not only in bit capacity, but also in basic environmental configuration and price.

In the entertainment world, the microprocessor offers the simulation of games at a level of sophistication until now reserved for military and space projects. In its civilian format, simulation makes games realistic by the capability to cram programing, memory, feedback, and real-time processing onto a single chip. Certainly Disney's "Land" and "World" are proving the wide attraction of family fantasy via simulation. The subject of a movie spoof about a year ago, an adult fantasyland designed around simulation techniques is now more than science fiction.

In general, the advantages of microprocessors to commercial/consumer-equipment designers boil down to the tradeoffs between hard-wired and programable logic. For instance, point-of-sale cash registers built with hard-wired packages have performed both as stand-alone units and minicomputer-controlled terminals. By changing to microprocessors, POS-equipment manufacturers gain the important advantage of adapting their basic equipment through programing to the needs of individual stores.

On the other hand, the problem most frequently mentioned by manufacturers of commercial/consumer equipment using microprocessors is the difficulty of refining the very software that they also say is the microprocessor's major advantage over hard-wired circuits. Equipment makers feel that microprocessor suppliers are not equal to the task of providing software support, forcing users to become immersed in programing.

Some of the commercial-consumer products using microprocessors are hardly a generation removed from electromechanical design. Yet the totally different requirements of the technology have made the switchover from hard-wired logic to microprocessors as traumatic for designers as the original change from an electromechanical to an electronic approach.

As C.W. Kessler, vice president of corporate engineering and advanced development for NCR Corp., Dayton, Ohio, points out, engineers familiar with Boolean equations and logic families, which were adequate for the design of hard-wired equipment, must now add complex instruction sets to their repertoires for microprocessors. They must be prepared to live with the sequential operation of microprocessors, which is slower than the parallel operation of chips using standard logic like TTL.

In addition, Kessler suggests, "There is a horde of new problems in choosing the right microprocessor, and these have become corporate-level decisions. After all, you're tied to one supplier, once work is completed on hardware and software. There's a lot hanging on the source selection, since you don't have a second source."

POS-terminal producers took different routes to arrive at use of microprocessors. For example, National Semiconductor's Systems division began applying them as a direct result of its ties to development by the semiconductor operation. Because of the close relationship, programs presented little problem. However, the main challenge was to teach test personnel to debug semiconductor chips the way programers debug a computer. This conversion required training because microprocessor faults are much more difficult to isolate and correct than failures on a standard LSI chip.

At American Regitel Corp., San Carlos, Calif., application of a microprocessor made it possible to design a terminal combining stand-alone "intelligence" and peripheral-communications capability. Such mechanical attributes as communications routines are specified in read-only memory, while the logical attributes at the human and exterior interfaces are specified by instructions residing in random-access memory. The former are concerned with fixed procedures, while the latter must be variable to permit application of a wide range of sequences, tax tables, and keyboard checks.

Most of the jobs assigned to the controller are performed at the speed of the terminal operator, and the program responsible for driving the printer has a throughput of only 30 to 100 characters per second. Because the arithmetic is not a major difficulty, and transactions are done at human speeds (communications functions require logic throughput of 200 to 300 characters per second), a general-purpose microprocessor that could fetch in 3 to 10 microseconds was adequate, putting the task well within the capacity of 4-bit processors.

NCR presently employs Intel MCS-4 microprocessors in two products—a bank-teller terminal and a point-of-sale terminal—and will soon introduce four others that use microprocessors. Their functions are quite different.

Inside the NCR 279 financial terminal, for instance, microprocessors control the keyboard, printer, and credit-card reader, do the teller's arithmetic, transfer data, and act as computer-interrupt. In the NCR 255 supermarket register, the microprocessor is essentially a back-up element to provide the terminal stand-alone capability, should the remote computer-controller fail. The microprocessor makes it possible to do away with dual minicomputers to control terminals unless the customer wants the redundancy.

Another teller terminal using microprocessors has been built by Financial Data Science Inc., Orlando, Fla., and about 100 are presently in the field. The model 108 contains three MCS-4s—one for printer control, one to provide stand-alone processing in the event of communications failure to the central computer, and one to control the keyboard and perform calculations.

> **Microprocessor knowhow**
>
> Not only are microprocessors changing the design of equipment, they are also changing the demands on the designers who use them. A list of the skills and tools needed for the new generation of microprocessor applications engineers, recently drawn up by Herman Schmid of General Electric, is awesome.
>
> He states that engineers must thoroughly comprehend the organization, operation, and performance of the processor's CPU; control of input/output; the organization and operation of RAMs, ROMs, and programable ROMs, plus such interface circuits as analog-to-digital and digital-to-analog converters; operation of peripheral equipment; the operation of multilevel priority-interrupt systems; the operation of control-panel circuits; and the operation of such various logic families as TTL, p-MOS, n-MOS, and C-MOS.
>
> But that's not all. For designing firmware, this same engineer must also have extensive knowledge of programing. This designer needs to be an expert in software for machine-level, micro-level, and assembler-language programing. Finally, the microprocessor engineer must be familiar with such interface operations as the performance of converters and signal-conditioning.

The first and third applications could have beeen performed by hard-wired logic, but stand-alone processing backup would have required a minicomputer. By applying the microprocessor to the keyboard, total package count was reduced 30%, and total cost was lowered to slightly less than what hard-wired logic would have been. In addition to the 108, which is meant for savings-and-loan institutions, the model 151 is also available for full-service automated bank tellers. It uses one microprocessor, essentially as a calculator.

Automating inventory

The manufacturer that probably has the most units containing microprocessors in the field is MSI Data Corp., Costa Mesa, Calif. This firm has delivered about 10,000 portable data terminals for use in taking and recording inventory or other data at remote locations.

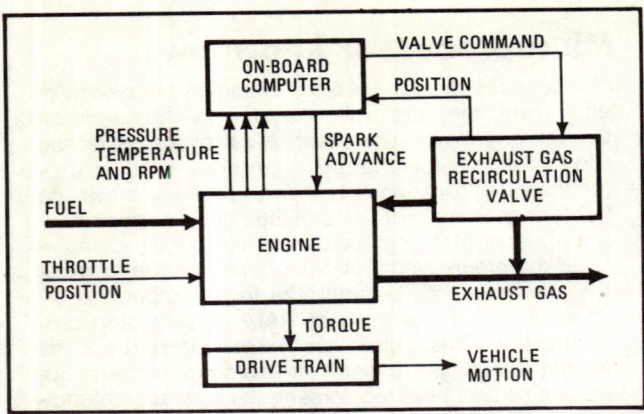

1. Economy car. One microprocessor will be used in an automobile for spark-ignition timing and exhaust-gas recirculation-valve control.

Each terminal contains one MCS-4 microprocessor.

The MSI battery-powered model 1100, which has semiconductor memory, and the model 2100, which has a magnetic-tape cassette, look like plump hand-held calculators, except that the keyboards have special symbols, and just below the LED displays are function switches for transferring data to telephone modems. Data such as supermarket inventory or warehouse stockroom supplies is entered through the keyboard and recorded either on a tape cassette or in solid-state memory, depending on which of the two models is used.

Afterwards, this data is communicated by telephone to a MSI receiver at some control location. Depending on the model used, 7,000 to 20,000 characters of information can be transmitted in less than three minutes, eliminating several data-handling steps required in manual or even punch-card procedures.

MSI originally designed these terminals with TTL to control the displays, computations, and interface circuits. Later models were converted to complementary-MOS chips to reduce battery-power dissipation. But the need for flexibility to meet a variety of uses for remote terminals made microprocessors attractive replacements for the control logic. At the same time, delays in delivery of standard chips made the change to microprocessors even more attractive.

Larry Hendricks, manager of the Electronic Engineering department for MSI, points out that previous experience in designing a minicomputer controller for data terminals was valuable in learning how to design with microprocessors. In fact, MSI now uses a minicomputer that it designed and built to serve as a communications controller to write the microprograms.

Hendricks complains that microprocessors are still difficult for many designers to learn to use because there's no easy applications track; hardware-oriented engineers stumble on the software, while software-oriented programmers get confused by LSI technology.

He also cites three other current problems. First, he would like microprocessor manufacturers to stick with one device long enough to establish an industry standard such as the 1103 chip. Second, Hendricks is uncomfortable with single-source purchasing, particularly since MSI is now buying microprocessors in relatively large quantities to support production of about 1,000 portable data terminals a day. The third problem is the need for a more sophisticated system that nonprogramers can use for microprograming.

While microprocessors are essentially used for what Hendricks calls "bit-banging," that is, simple and slow processing chores, he believes that there's a danger of trying to apply them for too many functions. "It may seem possible to substitute a microprocessor for every minicomputer," he says, "but you have to watch out that you're not sending a boy to do a man's job."

Singer patterns its own

Although most microprocessor users, especially commercial manufacturers, have been concerned with dependence on sole-source purchasing, Singer Corp., New York, has alleviated this situation by designing its own microprocessor at the firm's research laboratory in Fairfield, N.J. At least three semiconductor houses are qualified to use Singer's masks to produce the chip. In fact, one of the design constraints was to be conservative enough to keep producibility within the capability of at least two suppliers—not an easy task.

The result is the Advanced Byte-Oriented (ABO) microcomputer, an 8-bit, n-channel MOS processor measuring 191 by 202 mils. The 40-pin unit is designed for a variety of Singer products, including point-of-sale terminals built by the Business Machines division in San Leandro, Calif. It's microprogramed internally from a 6,000-bit ROM, rather than from separate chips.

One reason Singer designed its own microcomputer was to follow the course of its electronic end products into what the firm calls "distributed computing," that is, loading each piece of equipment with as much processing capability as possible. Thus, in a Singer POS terminal, the ABO is heavy on processing capability and light on arithmetic-calculation functions.

Microcomputers from semiconductor suppliers need both capabilities, whereas a custom design could downgrade the less important attribute. Of a total of 256 instruction codes, 50 are basic, and the instruction time is typically 10 microseconds. According to Singer, prototypes of its microprocessor are now being manufactured by two sources.

The Business Machines division presently has a terminal with a single microprocessor also of Singer de-

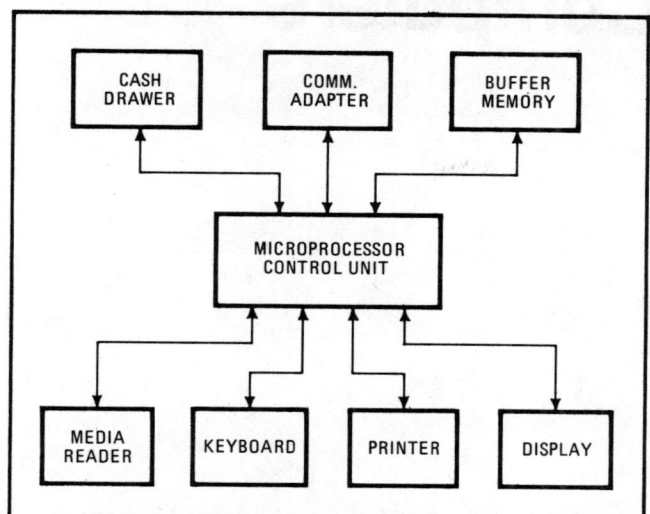

2. POS microprocessor. In a stand-alone point-of-sale terminal, the control unit carries out microinstructions stored in a ROM.

sign. However, unlike the ABO, this unit has five 12-kilobit ROMs outboarded to instruct the microprocessor. The function of the microprocessor-control unit (Fig. 2) is to direct the flow of data between the I/O devices and the buffer memory and to perform arithmetic chores. All data transfers within the microprocessor and between it and the I/O devices are accomplished by means of a source-destination bus, consisting of a 5-bit source address, a 5-bit destination address, and a 6-bit data bus. Because each register inside the microprocessor and in the I/O devices is addressable, it can act as either the source or the destination in a data transfer. However, intercommunications are minimized, and interface requirements for the I/O devices are simple because the terminal is bus-oriented.

Steering for Detroit

An example of what an automobile-microprocessor system might look like is a Ford Motor Co. advanced development. Figure 1 shows the bare bones of a digital control system, designed to maximize fuel economy. It is being road-tested, but it won't be ready for a standard car for some time. This system uses two microprocessors and other custom-LSI devices to control timing of spark ignition and position the exhaust-gas-recirculation (EGR) valve by using several engine inputs.

Ford engineers decided to use a microprocessor because attempting to compensate an analog programable spark-timing controller over the worst-case of auto temperatures turned out to be more expensive than a digital control system. The microcomputer made it easier to program changes in engine design than to use hard-wired logic. Ford uses a 12-bit microprocessor with the program and associated coefficients, which describe the engine-control algorithm stored in a ROM.

The present engine-control software is contained in about 1,500 12-bit words. The system also includes an 8-bit analog-to-digital converter with an eight-channel multiplexer under CPU control to measure the outputs of engine and EGR-valve transducers. The key reason for using a microprocessor for this application is to be able to design the same hardware for all engine and transmission variations in several different models, changing only the software to match each car.

Actually the idea for computer-like management of timing, combustion control, emission control and transmission control has been considered by the advanced engineering departments of the auto Big Three for some time. There is also a possibility for microprocessors to handle such safety functions such as antiskid braking and on-board diagnostic systems.

The game's the thing

A unique, but significant, application of microprocessors to games is exemplified by a bowling game Bally Manufacturing Corp., Chicago, has been marketing since last October. Sold to distributors for $1,600, about 85 of the electronic game, Bally Alley, are now installed. Each contains one Intel 4004 CPU, four programable ROMs, a RAM, and one 1,024-bit ROM, in addition to some 250 discrete power transistors and silicon-controlled rectifiers.

The electronics package in Bally Alley is vital to give players the right "feel," not only in the scoring, but in the fall of the "pins," the roll of the "ball," and posting the odds normally associated with making various shots. None of this could have been done in the size and cost required of an arcade game without the microprocessor.

The microprocessor monitors the placement of the ball when it is sent down the lane by a player (one to four can play at any one time), keeps tabs on the pins, and metes out free games and credits. In controlling the scoring, the microcomputer tracks pin patterns. A player can decide at what place along the bottom of the lane to let go of the simulated ball, and the microprocessor calculates from program instructions how many balls have been used before recording the score on an incandescent-lamp display. Bally is now looking at microprocessors in 8-bit configurations for other games, as well as gambling equipment it builds.

Computers

Peripherals now, mainframes later

by Wallace B. Riley, Computers Editor

Although much of the shouting about microprocessors has been about consumer and industrial applications, these programable large-scale integrated circuits are also impinging on the way computer manufacturers themselves are designing data-processing systems.

For manufacturers of large mainframes, the impact is mainly in peripheral and control equipment because today's microprocessors are generally too slow and limited to perform large-scale processing. For minicomputer manufacturers, however, the low-cost versatile LSI processor goes to the very heart of their designs and promises to open up a whole range of higher-performance capabilities at lower costs.

A major advantage of microprocessors is the smoother design iterations that can be wholly or partially achieved by reprograming a microprocessor instead of rewiring a major part of a prototype design. These design iterations are necessary in almost any development cycle because the original specifications have to be modified as development proceeds. The goal is a design that meets the original specifications to some degree while being both manufacturable and marketable. In conventional designs, iterations often take the form of building and rebuilding a succession of prototypes—an expensive and time-consuming process.

The main use of microprocessors with the large mainframes has been in peripheral equipment and controllers. Their application inside the computers themselves has been like only a distant rumble of thunder because until now they have been too slow. However, a new generation of chips now on the drawing board promises to overcome that shortcoming.

Microprocessors have thus far proved of value primarily in low-cost, low-speed equipment, such as cathode-ray-tube terminals and magnetic-tape cassette drives. Their main benefits have been to facilitate customization and addition of power at a lower cost than previous designs and to increase the processing capabilities of remote terminals.

Makers of punched-card machines, floppy-disk-storage units, and devices of similar complexity say they may use microprocessors in their next design cycles. However, they have thus far found the LSI chips too slow or too limited in some other functions. These companies are expressing great interest in such microprocessors as Intel's new 8080 [*Electronics*, 4/18/74, p. 95], mainly because of its expanded instruction set and the order-of-magnitude increase in speed.

Microprocessors cut costs and reduce system complexity while simplifying customization of otherwise standard designs. For example, Beehive Medical Electronics Inc. of Salt Lake City, Utah, can adapt its Superbee terminal easily to a variety of applications because it uses the Intel 8008-1 chip. And, although the microprocessor replaces only some of the circuitry of the company's earlier model, it adds new functions and adapts easily to each customer's application.

A trend changes

Significantly, the burgeoning interest in microprocessors reverses one important trend that has been shaping up during the past few years—the execution in hardware of many functions traditionally left to the software. This tradition was established in the early days of computers, when gates cost $100 apiece and programmers were paid clerical wages. These rates made the minimization of hardware imperative and the proliferation of software initially unimportant.

But since then, costs of hardware and software have moved inexorably in opposite directions. Today, some functions that would have cost astronomical amounts for 1954 hardware can be implemented now for little more than pocket money, while software has grown to almost unmanageable proportions in the form of operating systems, time-sharing, and so on—all in the name of efficient use of hardware.

The low cost of hardware has made microprocessors possible—simple enough not to require software of the complexity remotely resembling an operating system and cheap enough for inefficient use without adding significantly to the cost. As a result, some new functions can be implemented in software that considerably simplifies design and alteration—without the headaches associated with large software systems.

Peripherals and controllers benefit

In the peripheral devices themselves, microprocessors take a substantial load from a controller or central processor. For example, Digi-log Systems Inc., Horsham, Pa., uses microprocessors to control a display's refresh memory, its communications interface, its editing functions (inserting and deleting words, phrases, and paragraphs, and rearranging them as directed from the keyboard), as well as other display characteristics.

A variety of optional capabilities is available with the basic models. Customers select the capabilities they want, and modules programed to perform the desired tasks under software control are shipped with the system. In most other terminals, these functions are performed by hard-wired logic, which can be added or removed from a system only with difficulty.

However, some designers who have tried the Intel 8008 for these functions have criticized it as not being fast enough and not having a large enough instruction set to do an adequate job. Again, the 8080 chip is viewed as a substantial improvement, although it's still too new for users to have accumulated much experience with it.

The Beehive and Digi-log terminals illustrate one of two trends in the computer-terminal market—their microprocessor-based units offer greater power and a higher level of customization, yet at lower cost. The other trend is to the "dumb" terminal under control of the central computer, which provides a simple way to "look into" a computer to see what's going on. "There'll always be a market for a dumb terminal," says Richard Kaufman, director of marketing at Applied Digital Data Systems Inc., Hauppauge, N.Y. Because of these two extreme requirements, the intermediate terminal that has only a small amount of logic capability will disappear. But the best way for designers to keep up with the trend toward smarter and smarter terminals is to use microprocessors to provide the "smartness."

Building controllers

Builders of mechanical peripheral equipment that contains minimal electronic circuitry have no need for microprocessors. However, builders of controllers for this equipment, as well as the manufacturers that build both the mechanical devices and their electronic controls, are more enthusiastic about microprocessors for

---

Microprocessor aids the mini

Perhaps partly because of a certain degree of overselling by microprocessor manufacturers and partly because of misunderstandings of what a microprocessor is and what it can do, there has been some speculation that the advent of microprocessors means the end of the smaller minicomputers. This is most emphatically not true. On the contrary, by enhancing the capability of the minicomputer, the microprocessor opens a whole new range of applications for the minicomputer that it couldn't touch economically before.

In many of the new applications, the capabilities of microprocessors and minicomputers have been combined to increase the effectiveness of the entire system at only a small increase in cost. For example, David Methvin, president of Computer Automation Inc., describes attempts to drive a series of remote terminals from a single minicomputer. "It didn't work very well," says Methvin, "because the minicomputer's speed and short word length are generally adequate to drive no more than two or three terminals."

But by designing into each terminal a microprocessor to handle some local processing and relieve the control minicomputer of the drudgery, it can easily do the higher-level work for the entire network. "In this way," concludes Methvin, "the advent of the microprocessor creates a new market, not only for itself, but also for the minicomputer, which previously had to yield to something bigger and costlier."

Microdata Corp., Irvine, Calif., a leading producer of microprogramed minicomputers, has not yet begun using the single-chip p-channel-MOS microprocessors in any of its computers. However, Richard Vahlstrom, technical director, foresees a possible utilization of the devices in peripheral equipment whenever they become cost-effective. Meanwhile, Microdata has introduced its Micro-One, a one-board bipolar processor that is both software- and firmware-compatible with the company's older 800 and 1600 series minicomputers and with their peripherals [*Electronics*, 5/30/74, p. 142].

Digital Equipment Corp. and General Automation Inc. have already recognized this trend, as shown by their recent product announcements. General Automation now has two minicomputers based on silicon-on-sapphire microprocessors, while DEC's microprocessor module, an extension of its long-standing line of logic modules, is based on Intel's 8008 microprocessor—one of some 53 circuits on the card. The PDP-8/A is the company's latest version of the line with which it more or less invented the minicomputer market back in 1965. The original PDP-8 was a discrete-component computer in a big box 34 inches high and almost two feet square. But now the complete set of 79 PDP-8 instructions can be executed by an assembly of components on a single printed-circuit board measuring 15¾ by 8½ inches, not including the memory.

The PDP-8/A makes extensive use of LSI, but none of the circuits is a microprocessor. Future versions of this and other DEC computers may include circuits that would be called microprocessors today. William Hogan, marketing manager for logic products in DEC's components group, describes the microprocessor module as the first of a series of products that will use any appropriate semiconductor chips with the right combination of cost and performance.

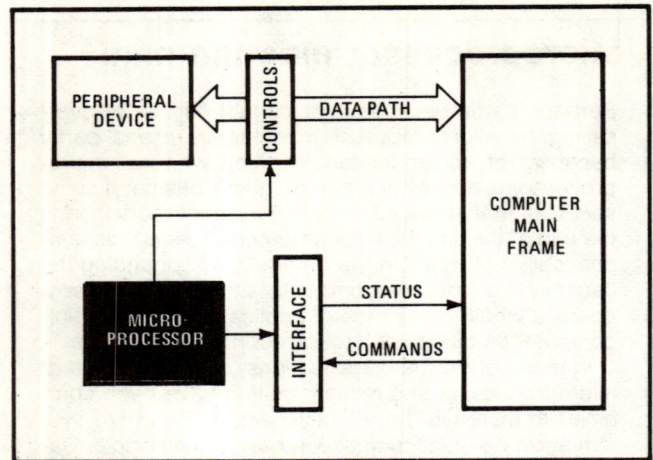

1. Interface and control. Today's microprocessors are applied in computer systems primarily where they do not affect data flow, but that limitation will only last until their performance improves.

use in the interface and control sections of their machines (see Fig. 1). The interface section responds to signals from the central processor and generates status signals to it. The control section sets up the device controller for a particular task. But neither of these functions is concerned with the actual passage of data through the controller, which may involve such steps as serial-to-parallel conversion, assembly of words from bytes, and error detection and correction.

Although the enthusiasm of controller designers, like that of terminal designers, is tempered by the performance level of presently available microprocessors, they look forward to a new generation of microprocessors now on the drawing board. The higher performance of the new microprocessors will enable them to graduate to full use in the data path as well.

New single-chip processors made with silicon-on-sapphire and bipolar technologies are expected to promote such a graduation by reducing the typical execution time to the range of 50 to 500 nanoseconds (from today's 2 to 20 microseconds) and increasing the number of instructions toward 200 (from today's 40 to 75).

Specifically, Intel is reported to be working on a bipolar microprocessor that can execute instructions in as little as 500 nanoseconds. In MOS, Rockwell's Microelectronics Group, one of the earliest to exploit sapphire technology, is developing more powerful processor chips. They already supply devices to General Automation for their LSI microcomputer line. Also, Inselek Corp., Princeton, N.J., has proposed a C-MOS-on-sapphire microprocessor that could handle a data rate of 3 megabits per second with its cycle time of 300 ns. Inselek says the device will be available early in 1975.

For its paper-tape emulator, Remex, a unit of Ex-Cell-O Corp., Santa Ana, Calif., chose the Intel MCS-4, a chip set that includes the 4004 4-bit microprocessor. The emulator is a magnetic-tape cassette drive that works with a minicomputer like a paper-tape reader.

Currently, the programs for the emulator are stored in programable read-only memories—the kind that can be erased under ultraviolet light. Program bugs turned up by the first few customers can be easily corrected. Later, when change activity has died down somewhat, Remex plans to switch, perhaps first to fused-link ROMs, which can be updated but not erased, and eventually to masked ROMs that can't be changed in the field at all, except by physically exchanging one part for another.

Stamp out logic monsters

Decision Data Corp., also of Horsham, Pa., indicates great interest in microprocessors—particularly in data recorders. In these peripherals, a few microprocessors replace a multitude of interconnected integrated circuits. The company manufactures a line of punched-card machines—both the old standard 80-column type and the newer, smaller 96-column equipment for IBM's System/3 and similar computers. The line includes a data recorder, which is a sort of combination keypunch, card reader, card punch, and printer, with various other outputs available and usable either on line with a computer or as a stand-alone device.

"Data recorders are monsters in logic," says Thomas Richardson, vice president for engineering, referring to the multitudinous functions that the machines perform. Present designs, he says, use 700 to 800 small-scale integrated-circuit packages, plus as many as 400 signal lines to interconnected equipment—clearly a prime territory for an invasion by microprocessors. Richardson indicates that the company will begin to move in this direction before the end of 1974, initially with its own design implemented with medium-scale ICs and later graduating to bona fide LSI microprocessors.

Despite the advances already made, development of faster, more powerful microprocessors is continuing. Although today's microprocessors have word lengths of 4 to 8 bits and instruction-cycle times of 2 to 20 microseconds, at least one 12-bit unit has already been developed in Japan [*Electronics*, 3/21/74, p. 111]. And semiconductor manufacturers in the U.S. are working feverishly to increase speeds.

What's more, LSI processors being made with bipolar and SOS technologies are yielding processor chips that blur the distinctions between the capabilities of the microprocessor and the small minicomputer. Indeed, the LSI miniprocessor is already on the design bench.

Instruments

Systems are getting 'smarter'

by Michael J. Riezenman, Industrial Editor

Anyone who has ever twiddled the controls of a pulse generator, wasted a couple of hours trying to recall how to use a scope's delayed-sweep feature, or laboriously calculated the standard deviation of a set of measurements knows that it takes detailed knowledge and refined techniques to use a complex modern instrument properly and efficiently. But soon, microprocessors will bring about a new generation of "intelligent" instruments that will automatically relieve the operator of routine procedures. And most of these "smarter" instruments will be cheaper than the ones they replace.

Instruments can be made less costly because, in many cases, the software techniques used with microprocessors will be cheaper than the hard-wired logic and mechanical switches they replace. Probably multi-instrument systems can benefit even more because microcomputers should replace minicomputers or programable calculators in small systems and do much of the repetitious work so that much cheaper minicomputers or calculators can be designed into larger systems.

Many cost-related benefits can be expected from a whole new class of small computer-controlled instrument systems that would be too expensive if built with minicomputers or even programable calculators. And for large systems that need minicomputers as controllers, microprocessors may be able to make significant reductions in the costs of the computers by using them as preprocessors in the instruments that are controlled by, and are feeding data to, the minicomputers.

These reductions should be significant. The intelligent application of, say, $400 worth of microcomputer components in each of five or six instruments may make it possible to replace a Digital Equipment Corp. PDP-11/45 minicomputer that costs about $16,000 to $18,000 in an appropriate configuration, with a PDP-11/40 at a cost of about $12,000.

The straight bench instrument that can probably realize the greatest cost reduction by use of a microprocessor is the frequency synthesizer. A high-resolution synthesizer uses a large number of expensive electromechanical switches and a great deal of complex logic circuitry simply to tell the frequency-generating circuitry what to do. Replacing these switches with simpler, cheaper ones or with a keyboard and replacing the logic circuitry with a microprocessor will, in most cases, justify the cost of the microprocessor, even if it brings no other benefits.

Of course, microprocessors will provide a whole host of such other benefits as data-formatting for the instrument's input/output interface. Moreover, the microprocessor will enhance accuracy and reliability through the use of special routines for self-diagnosis and the elimination of systematic errors.

Automating testers

Already several manufacturers have introduced microprocessor-controlled instruments. Among them are the in-circuit IC testers built by Testline Inc., Titusville, Fla.; the model 76A automatic capacitance bridge made by Boonton Electrics Corp., Parsippany, N.J.; the Qualifier 901 IC tester made by Fairchild Systems Technology, Palo Alto, Calif.; the Digitrend 220 recorder made by Doric Scientific Corp., San Diego, Calif.; and the interfacing circuitry used by Tektronix Inc., Beaverton, Ore., to marry the digital processing oscilloscope with the company's model 31 programable calculator.

Most of these pioneering applications use the microprocessor more as a manipulator of bit patterns than as a number-cruncher. The microprocessors are used more to set up tests, perform interfacing chores, and control other subsystems than to process the data that the instruments have acquired.

The IC testers are perhaps the best examples of this emphasis, since, strictly speaking, these instruments acquire no numerical data at all. They use the microprocessors for the quick and easy setup of complex input-bit patterns and comparison of actual and expected output-bit patterns without resorting to either expensive minicomputers or so-called performance

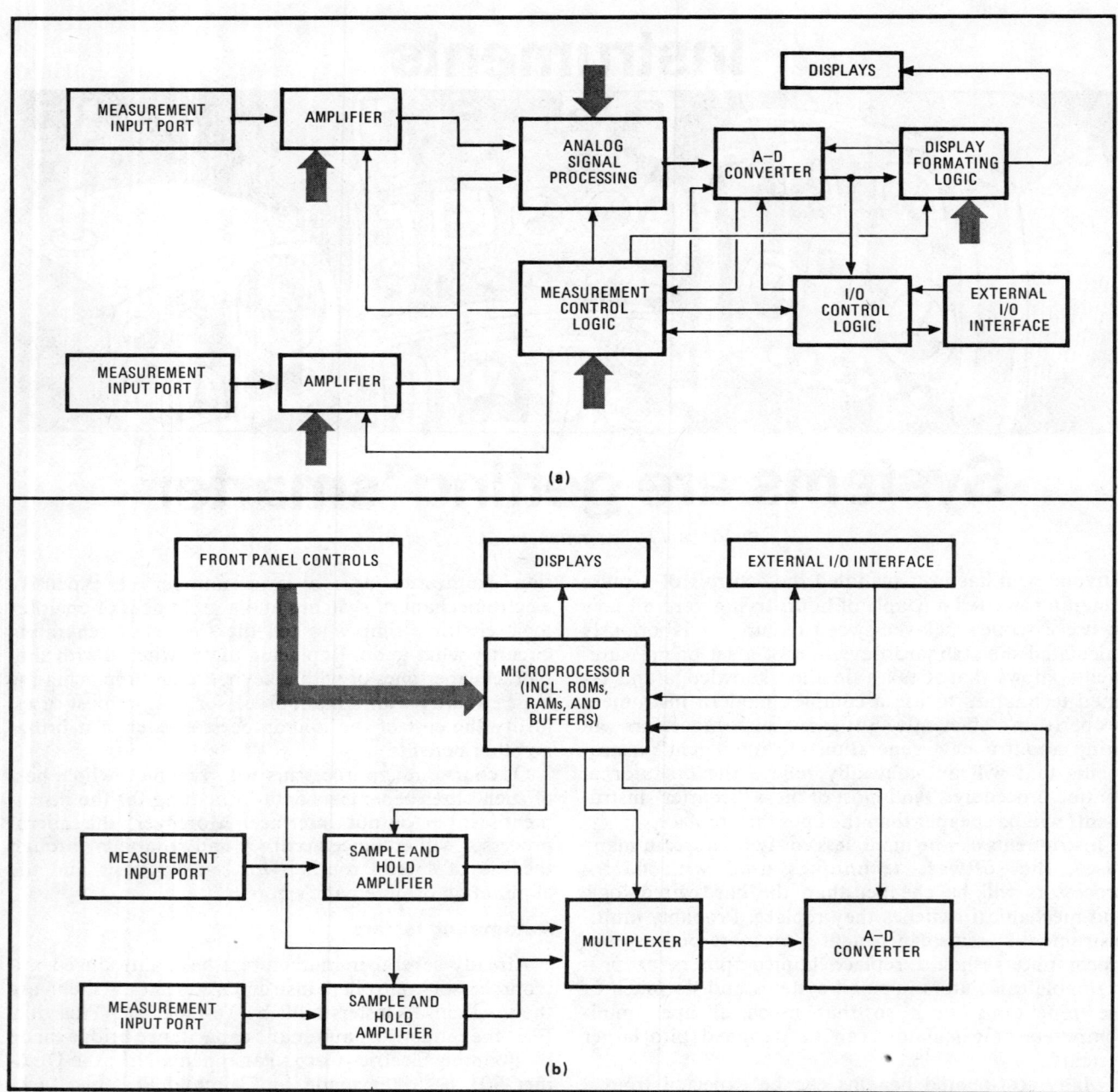

1. Generalized instrument. Typical digital-readout instrument is really an analog machine with a lot of digital control and display circuitry tacked onto it (a). In particular, signal processing is performed by conventional analog means. With microprocessor, a-d converter is moved up front so that most processing can be done digitally (b). In both diagrams, signal paths are shown in color, and control lines are in black.

boards. One of the additional benefits of the Qualifier 901 is a thorough self-test routine. Under control of the microprocessor, the machine checks itself out every time a program is loaded into it.

While they use the microprocessors largely for control, the Boonton capacitance bridge and the Doric recorder also exploit the processor's ability to do a bit of numerical calculation, as well. The capacitance bridge directly measures only capacitance and conductance. It then processes these numbers to find such quantities as equivalent series resistance, equivalent parallel resistance, Q, dissipation factor, and percentage of deviation from a preset reference.

The Doric Digitrend 220 recorder is programed with a set of linearizing equations for various thermocouples. Instead of using different linearizing networks for each of the six common thermocouples (types J, K, T, E, S, and R), the instrument does it all with software. (See p. 87 for more details on this instrument.)

A generalized microprocessor-controlled instrument and its conventional digital counterpart are shown in Fig. 1. The exact nature of the instrument is not specified, but it may either be a two-channel voltmeter or a wattmeter.

The main point is that the conventional version of the generalized instrument (Fig. 1a) does all of its processing, which may include such difficult operations as multiplication and linearization before the output is digitized. Also, the conventional instrument needs lots of logic circuitry to control the making of the measurement, to format the digital display, and to handle the I/O interface with any other equipment to which it may be connected in a system.

The microprocessor-controlled instrument, on the other hand, (Fig. 1b) converts the data into digital form as close to the front end as possible and does all of its signal processing digitally. Its potential for cost reduction comes from the capability of a single microprocessor to do the signal processing and also handle all of the interfacing and formatting chores that would require literally hundreds of TTL packages.

Getting 'smart'

The most dramatic impact of microprocessors on instrumentation will be in the creation of new "smart" instruments for a host of new applications. A smart instrument is one that performs a significant amount of internal arithmetic processing. From a number of inputs (either signals or switch positions), it calculates an output to display and/or performs additional processing.

Indeed, smart instruments, like people, may be expected to come with a wide range of intelligence. At the low end of the spectrum may be a digital voltmeter for communications applications that can be programed to make, say, 1,000 measurements and then display their mean and standard deviation. For this, the microprocessor, together with associated control memory and I/O circuitry, would perform all the logic-management functions.

Assuming that very fast measurement times aren't needed, such a system could be built of one of today's 8-bit n-channel microprocessors, together with, say, eight 1-kilobit random-access memories to supply 8,000 bits of main memory and the associated read-only memory for control, plus I/Os. The entire system could be implemented with fewer than 20 LSI packages—only a tenth of the more than 200 standard TTL circuits that would be needed.

A somewhat smarter instrument might modify its own behavior as a result of its calculations. An example of such an instrument already exists—it is Hewlett-Packard Co.'s model 3805A distance meter. This surveyor's tool measures distances by measuring the time required for an infrared beam to travel from the instrument to a reflector and back.

Since atmospheric perturbations can affect the readings, the meter is programed to make 3,000 measurements and to calculate their mean and standard deviation. Then, if the standard deviation is within a specified limit, the mean is displayed as an accurate reading. If the standard deviation is out of spec, the meter makes as many additional measurements as are necessary to get it within spec. If, after it has made 32,000 measurements, the instrument still fails to get a sufficiently good standard deviation, it displays the mean in flashing numerals to tell the operator that the measurement conditions are less than ideal.

The next level of instrument made possible by microprocessors could, by today's standards, be called geniuses. These instruments will probably be most noteworthy for their high degree of human engineering.

Their value may best be appreciated by considering the hairy problems that one may encounter when using a complex pulse generator or oscilloscope. Highly skilled engineers, not to mention technicians and service personnel, can easily waste several hours refamiliarizing themselves with instruments that they haven't used for several months. Even an instrument that one has used every day can present problems if someone else borrows and returns it with some small, seldom-used, control out of its usual position.

Building 'geniuses'

Microprocessors can and will be used to generate a "genius" class of instruments, but how it will be done is uncertain. One can imagine an oscilloscope that has had most of the knobs and switches replaced by a keyboard through which one punches in such parameters as the sweep speeds, vertical sensitivities, and triggering modes needed for any particular application.

Seldom-changed controls might be automatically set to preprogramed states from which they could be changed, via the keyboard, if desired. The status of the machine could be presented on the cathode-ray tube by a character-generator similar to the one already available on Tektronix' 7000 series scopes. In addition to simply presenting the machine's status, the CRT readout could also warn of incompatible instructions or of valid, but unusual, measurement conditions.

In a sense, oscilloscopes and other measurement tools aren't difficult to deal with because they present the user with displays, which, if abnormal, warn that corrective action is needed. The myriad possibilities for error in setting up signal generators, synthesizers, and other signal sources, on the other hand, can drive an engineer to a psychiatrist. Few users of pulse-generators can claim that they have never set the pulse width to a duration longer than the period defined by the selected repetition rate. And on some complex two-channel pulsers

Who invented the microprocessor?

Intel Corp. certainly deserves the credit for exploiting the microprocessor concept and was the first to market microprocessors, although much credit must also go to the many companies and individuals who contributed in some way to the development of large-scale integration.

Remember Viatron? In 1968, the Burlington, Mass., firm startled the world by announcing its intention to build a data-handling system that would rent for $40 a month in its basic configuration. [*Electronics*, Oct. 14, 1968, p. 193]. Heart of the Viatron unit was an 8-bit microprocessor run by a primitive program in a read-only memory. But the company encountered serious financial and management problems, and it went bankrupt after about two years.

Meanwhile, General Electric Co. found itself designing integrated logic circuits for some of its terminals, duplicating much of the work from project to project, but not generating enough volume on any one of them to justify the use of custom-designed LSI—until somebody thought of a customized *programable* LSI circuit. GE then developed an eight-chip basic logic unit, or BLU, that could be used without change with different programs in many different terminal designs—essentially what is done today with microprocessors.

---

that have separate controls for such settings as amplitude, offset, delay, pulse width, and trigger mode, the fact that these highly interactive controls have been set wrong is not always obvious.

The microprocessor can unravel that complexity. If all of the instrument's operating information is fed in through a small keyboard-controlled processor, the instrument could simply refuse to accept an input that is incompatible with earlier instructions. Alternatively, electronic stops could be programed into the machines, and a small light-emitting-diode display could be positioned above a vernier pulse-width control. As the control is rotated to increase the pulse width, the display would reflect its position, so long as the pulse width did not conflict with any other control settings.

If such a conflict arises, the machine might be programed to ignore the control setting and to set only the maximum pulse width that could be accommodated. The LED display would keep the operator informed of what is happening by always showing the actual pulse width being generated, regardless of the front-panel control setting.

Although each of the ways in which a microprocessor might be used in an instrument has been discussed as a separate idea, it should be clear that, at least until their prices are reduced considerably, the devices will be used primarily in applications where they can perform several functions.

Most industry sources agree that an instrument would have to sell for at least $2,000 to $3,000 to justify the inclusion of a microprocessor. There is no upper limit to the size of instrumentation systems in which microprocessors could be included, since even systems large, complex, and costly enough to justify the use of a minicomputer may benefit from the inclusion of microprocessors as preprocessors.

Peak picker

Such an application might be in an analytical chemistry laboratory, where a single, fairly small minicomputer could control, say, two or three mass spectrometers and a dozen gas chromatographs if each of them were equipped with a microprocessor programed to act as a peak-picker. The outputs of these analytical instruments, if drawn by a chart recorder, are typically a series of peaks separated by nulls. Unfortunately, closely spaced peaks tend to blend into each other, which makes it difficult to decide exactly where the peaks are.

An experienced human operator can locate the peaks by eye, but it takes a fairly complex computer program to do the job. If the computer is to do all the peak-picking, it would have to be an extremely fast machine with a lot of memory. Adding the microprocessors brings the task well within the capabilities of a minicomputer of modest size.

Improvements are imminent

Thus far, only a handful of commercially available instruments contain microprocessors. But this state of affairs in no way indicates a lack of interest in them by the major instrument houses. Quite the contrary.

Although details are not yet available, it is clear that microprocessors are responsible for previously unavailable or unaffordable capabilities that will be offered in several new meters, counters, signal sources, and oscilloscopes before this year is out. The designers of these instruments speak of "totally new approaches to the making of measurements" but, understandably, they refuse to elaborate on what that means right now. However, the next six months promise plenty of excitement for the makers and users of electronic instrumentation.

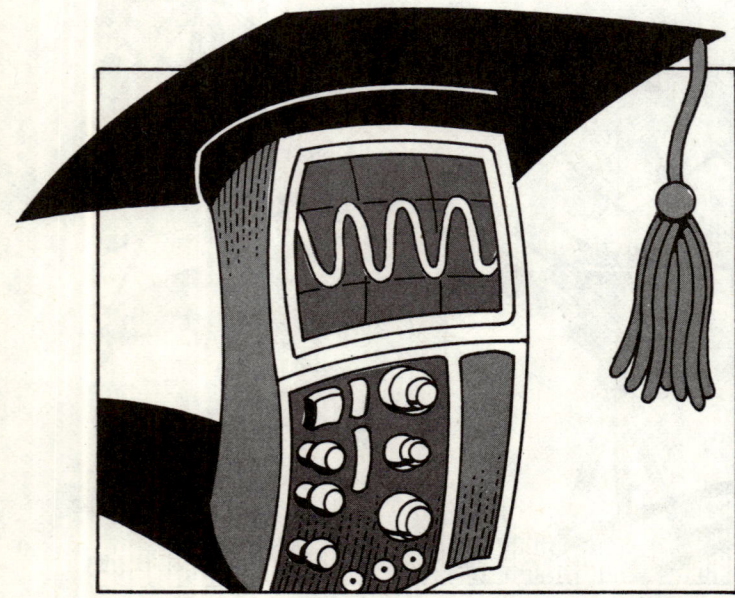

Design

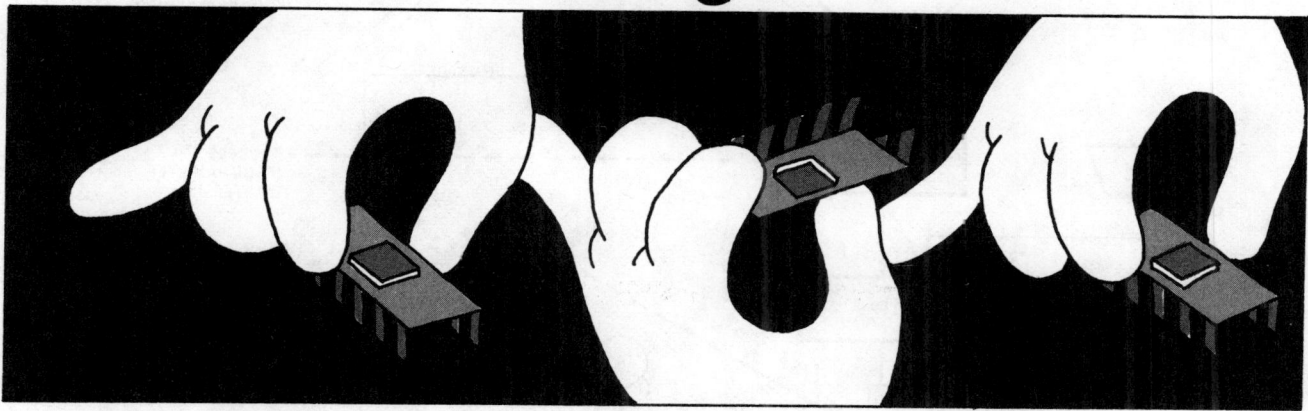

Blending hardware and software

by Wallace B. Riley, Computers Editor

It's a whole new world, but it's really not all that different from what the engineer is accustomed to. Supposedly, EEs experienced in the conventional approach to design—flip-flops and gates—might expect to encounter difficulty expressing their design ideas in term of software. But, although the end result of a software development effort looks different on paper from the traditional logic diagram, it is basically identical.

An engineer's usual approach begins with a set of functional specifications, which he translates into a block diagram and then reduces to the level of individual gates. The completed design is assembled on a breadboard, built into a prototype, and then, with a series of tests and redesigns, reduced to a form that can be manufactured in volume and sold at a profit. Meanwhile, it may be undergoing simulation on a computer as part of the design refinement.

Likewise, software design begins with functional specifications, but it is translated into a sequence of instructions, rather than into an array of gates. The paper design usually involves a flow chart, which shows events graphically in the proper order, together with conditions that can cause the order of events to change. The first step can be a high-level flow chart, which closely resembles the block diagram. This is broken down into a form in which each block in the flow chart represents a single instruction in the program. Standardized shapes of blocks in the flow diagram have evolved (Fig. 1) so that one person can more easily follow the logic of another person's work. [For an example of applying a flow chart to either the hardware or software implementation of a specific design, see *Electronics*, Oct. 11, 1973, p.97.]

For some individuals, software is a problem until they get the hang of it. At some companies, teaching engineers how to program and programers the limits of hardware has turned out to be a great enlightenment on both sides. But the highly motivated people who undertook the project knew that understanding microprocessor software would be essential sooner or later, and they have managed to overcome any obstacles to understanding. Still other companies have assigned the task to younger engineers who had no previous strong commitment to either hardware or software designs, and who, therefore, made the transition easily.

In the last analysis, any intelligent person who can lay out a procedure accurately one step at a time can learn to write a program for a microprocessor.

Support is essential

Some users and potential users of microprocessors express concern about the level of software support from the manufacturer. Since microprocessors come from semiconductor houses, those users fear the vendors don't have the capacity to offer the assistance that is expected from the IBMs or the DECs.

The concern is largely unfounded because the need for software support, compared to the requirements of large computers, is small indeed. But to the extent that microprocessor users have had no previous exposure to computers, they may need to be led through thickets of unfamiliar concepts to get their applications working.

Support for a large general-purpose computer is significantly different from support for a minicomputer, and it differs even more from the kind of support that a microprocessor user will need. And since a general-purpose computer is likely to cost its user hundreds of dollars an hour, he doesn't want to shut it down even momentarily if he can avoid it—not even to load new programs into it. To protect him from unnecessary expense, manufacturers offer operating systems, which are software packages designed to keep the machine running under all but the most catastrophic conditions, as well as various aids that simplify the task of writing programs for the large computer.

But a minicomputer is likely to be operated in a dedicated application so that a single program runs over and over indefinitely. Furthermore, it's sufficiently inexpensive that its occasional stopping between jobs or when an error occurs is only an inconvenience, not a major expense. Minimakers also offer support, in the

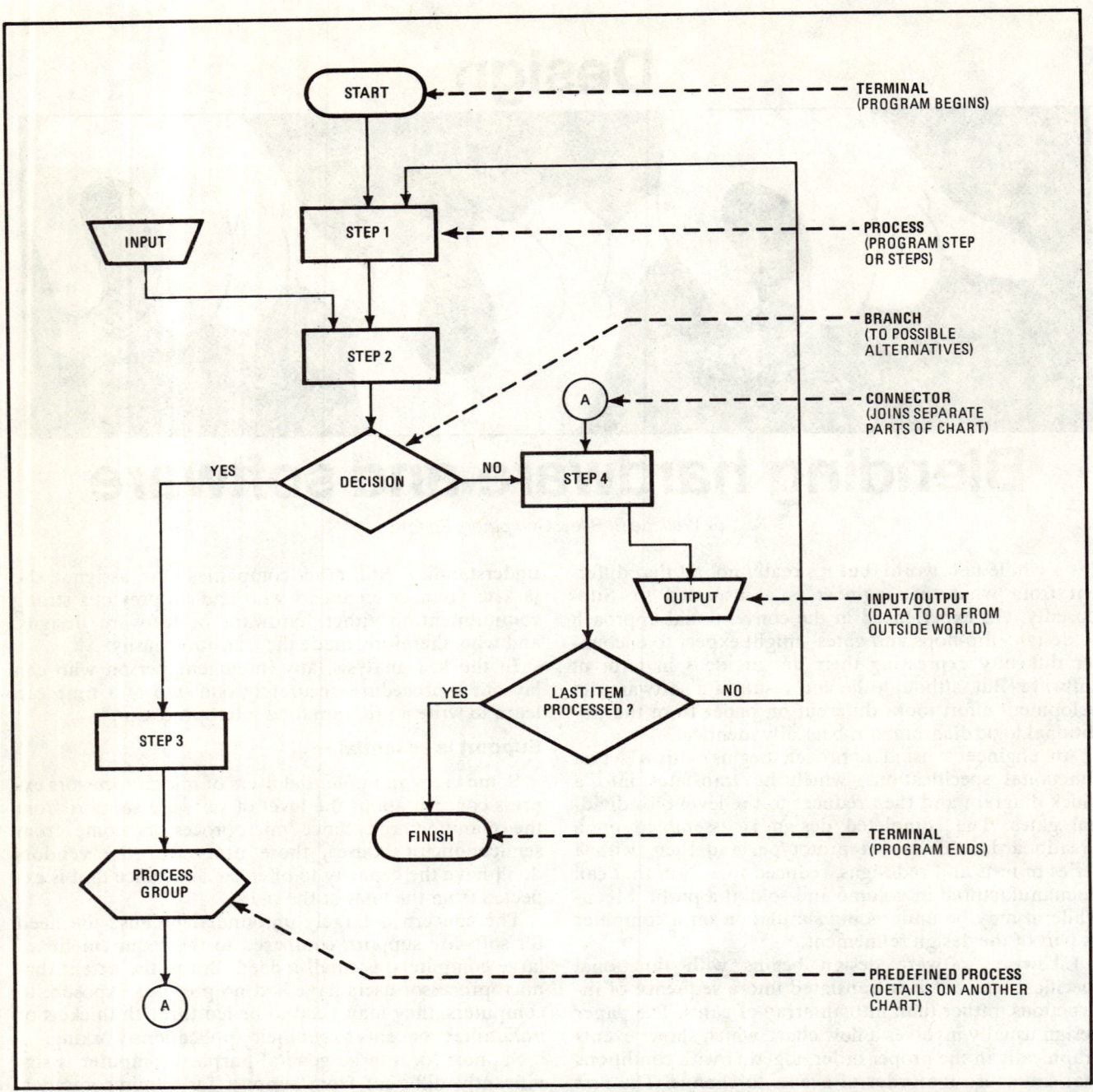

1. Flow-diagram conventions. These are among standard shapes that simplify communications via flow charts. Also often used are specific input/output functions, such as a torn sheet of paper for a printout, a tape reel for magnetic tape, or a cylinder for a disk or drum.

form of some kinds of programing aids and perhaps a relatively low-level time-sharing system. Of course, there's maintenance of the hardware, but this is far short of the support that is expected from the manufacturer of a general-purpose computer.

None of this kind of support applies in any way to microprocessors, except possibly in the form of higher-level programing languages like PL/M [*Electronics*, 6/27/74 p. 103]. Like the average passenger automobile, a microprocessor remains economically feasible, even though it may be "parked" 90% of the time. Its program is likely to be wholly in a read-only memory, making it even more dedicated than a dedicated mini. It doesn't even need hardware maintenance, because it can't be patched the way a board or chassis can.

For users wholly unacquainted with the art and science of computer application, extensive support from the vendor will be necessary. By and large, this support is available now—in the form of users' manuals, programing manuals, application notes, and similar documentation—and it shows no signs of abating. But in all probability, using microprocessors won't be a wholly new experience for most people. Many engineers have already used minicomputers in some form or have enlisted the aid of various computer-aided-design programs. And, as indicated previously, most of those who have already tried microprocessors haven't found the software a serious problem.

138

Processors and product costs

How microprocessors boost profits

by William Davidow, Intel Corp., Santa Clara, Calif.

When the first single-chip microprocessors were introduced two years ago, few designers or project managers could foresee how massively these devices would influence creation of new products and services. To most, the microprocessor was merely another interesting LSI device to be evaluated and built with some memory and interface chips into prototype equipment.

But as designers became familiar with the early microprocessors and equipment began to benefit from them, respect grew for their capability and versatility. Rapidly there arose an awareness throughout the electronics industries that the microprocessor was indeed a significant extension of computer technology. Suddenly, the concept of distributed computer power became a reality, applicable to a host of new equipment.

There are compelling and fundamental reasons for the dramatic success of today's microprocessors:
- Manufacturing costs of products can be significantly reduced by designing around microprocessors.
- Development costs and time are reduced.
- Products can be rushed to the market faster, which enables a company to seize advantages in sales and market share.
- Product capabilities are enhanced, and manufacturers can economically add features that boost profits.
- Product reliability is increased, leading to a corresponding reduction in both the cost of service and warranties.

Microprocessors enable designers to replace hardware with software. Using programed logic, they can

TABLE 1: NUMBER OF ICs REPLACED BY A READ-ONLY MEMORY		
ROM size (bits)	Gates replaced	ICs replaced
2,048	128 – 256	13 – 25
4,096	256 – 512	25 – 50
8,192	512 – 1,024	50 – 100
16,384	1,024 – 2,048	100 – 200

TABLE 2: SYSTEM MANUFACTURING COSTS PER IC	
IC	$ .50
Incoming inspection	.05
Pc card	.50
Fabrication	.05
Board test and rework	.10
Connector	.05
Discretes	.05
Wiring	.10
Power	.10
Cabinetry, fans, etc.	.10
Total	$ 1.60

now substitute a handful of ICs for a large number of conventional random-logic networks. In such a system, the information about logical sequences and the output responses provided from input signals are stored in a few memory chips instead of in relatively expensive interconnect patterns on printed-circuit cards.

Use of microprocessors saves money and time at every stage of the product's life cycle. These savings are passed on to the customer in products with greater capabilities and higher reliability than has ever before been attainable. Microprocessors are not only improving the performance of established products, they are bringing about completely new products. They are beginning to permeate every walk of life.

Memory replaces random logic

If microprocessors were fast enough with their programable techniques, they could replace all hard-wired logic. But as the speed of new generations of microprocessors is increased, they will move into more and more designs now implemented with conventional ICs. And although each new application has its unique structure, it's possible to estimate the package reduction that accrues when hard-wired random logic is replaced by programable techniques.

Again, the microprocessor replaces logic by storing program sequences in memory, rather than implementing these sequences with gates and flip-flops. While it is impossible to prove quantitatively, designers use a rough rule that they can replace one gate by using 8 to 16 bits of memory. Therefore, if the average hard-wired logic circuit contains on the order of 10 gates, Table 1 indicates that a single 4,096-bit read-only-memory can replace 50 MSI packages. Each new 16,384-bit ROM save as many as 200 IC packages in every design. No wonder system designers are being so quickly convinced of the capability of microprocessors to reduce IC complexity.

Reducing manufacturing costs

Clearly, reduced IC complexity translates directly into reduced product costs. Table 2, which presents a detailed analysis of the sources of these surprisingly high costs, shows that the average sale price of an integrated circuit today is approximately 50 cents. Incoming inspection and testing cost an average of 5 cents more.

Many companies are now buying aged and tested circuits for their applications to increase system reliability, and this adds about 15 cents to unit costs. A simple printed-circuit card may cost as little as 25 cents for each IC position, but the average cost in most applications for high-quality cards is closer to 50 cents. (In some systems, costs of sophisticated multilayer cards can go as high as $1 per location, and if wire-wrap assemblies are used, the cost per IC position can reach the $2 mark.)

Next, board test and rework add another dime to system cost, while the cost of a connector, divided by the number of ICs per printed-circuit card, frequently exceeds 5 cents. Then the system requires such components as resistors, capacitors, and power-bus bars, which add another 5 cents per IC.

Systems frequently average one wire or more per IC position, and the wires—even those installed by automatic equipment—frequently cost more than 10 cents each. Finally, the cost of power supplies and mechanical packaging add another 20 cents. Altogether, the minimum system cost approaches $2 per IC.

Table 3 shows the potential system saving in manufacturing costs that can be achieved by using a microprocessor. The savings are derived by assuming that the typical manufacturer can save $1.50 to $3 by displacing a single IC, after which the cost of implementing an equivalent system with a microprocessor is taken into account. In moderate volumes, a system such as the MCS-4, made up of 16,384 bits of ROM, a processor, and a minimal amount of RAM, can be purchased for less than $100. This system has the potential of displacing $150 to $600 of manufacturing cost in a system.

Reducing development time

Use of microprocessors simplifies nearly every phase of product development. Because of the extensive design aids and support supplied with microprocessors, it

TABLE 3: SAVINGS IN USING PROGRAMED LOGIC		
ROM size (bits)	IC replaced	Savings
2,048	13 – 25	$19.50 – $78
4,096	25 – 50	$37.50 – $150
8,192	50 – 100	$75.00 – $300
16,384	100 – 200	$150.00 – $600

TABLE 4: HOW MICROPROCESSORS REDUCE DEVELOPMENT TIME AND COST		
	Conventional system	Programed logic
Product definition		Simplified because of ease of incorporating features
System and logic design	Done with logic diagrams	Can be programed with design aids (compilers, assemblers, editors)
Debug	Done with conventional lab instrumentation	Software and hardware aids reduce time
Pc card layout		Fewer cards to lay out
Documentation		Less hardware to document
Cooling and packaging		Reduced system size and power consumption eases job
Power distribution		Less power to distribute
Engineering changes	Done with yellow wire	Change program in PROM

is relatively easy to develop applications programs that tailor the devices to the systems and then implement these systems in very short turn-around times. Indeed, a principal reason for the increasing popularity of microprocessors is the speed with which products can be developed, designed, and rushed to the market. Discussions with system designers indicate development cycles have frequently been shortened by as much as six to 12 months to only a few weeks.

Table 4 tabulates a number of the steps in a system-development cycle and the effects of the microprocessor on the design-cycle time—designing becomes easier, faster and less costly. Surprisingly, product definition is frequently speeded up as soon as the decision is made to use a microprocessor because the incremental cost for adding features to the system is usually small and can be easily estimated.

For example, adding such features as automatic tax-computation to an electronic cash register may require only the addition of a single ROM, which has a minimal effect on total system cost, power dissipation, and packaging requirements. But adding the same function by means of IC logic might require two or three fairly large pc cards filled with SSI and MSI logic packages.

Building around microprocessors also reduces the time needed for system design. When the engineer decides to use a microprocessor, he designs by programing—potentially a more organized and faster way to design than by using logic diagrams. What's more, the ready availability of extensive software aids, such as simulators, assemblers, editors, compilers, and monitors, reduces the cost of program development. These aids also reduce the time needed for system debugging. Pc-card layout time is reduced simply because fewer cards need to be laid out.

Getting to market fast

When product-design cycles can be shortened, obviously new products can be rushed to the market faster. This permits companies to either beat out the competition or effectively respond to competitive moves. Figure 1 shows what typically happens in a competitive program when one company beats another to the market. Assuming that both companies have about the same marketing capability, the company that introduces the product first usually can gain a greater share of the market (Fig. 1a) and reach a mature sales volume more quickly.

Figure 1(b) shows the price erosion characteristic of most products during their life cycles. This erosion means that the company introducing the product first will not only sell more but will sell at a higher price. In

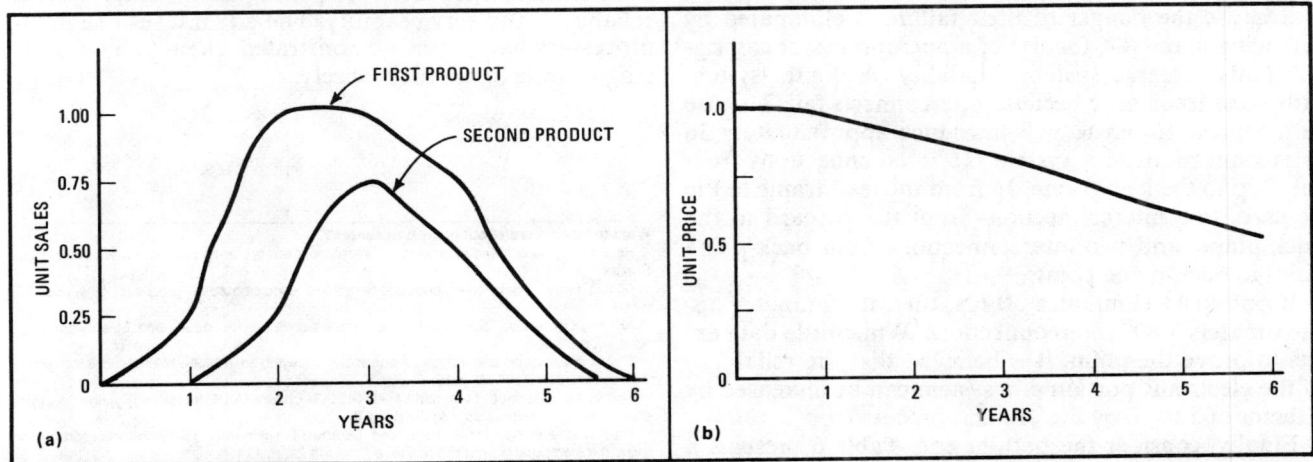

1. Market jump. Microprocessor design helps get equipment to the market fast, resulting in a greater share of market than second entry (a) as product matures. What's more, first product shows a slower rate of price erosion (b).

TABLE 5: PROJECTED INCOME FROM FIRST AND SECOND PRODUCT

FIRST PRODUCT

Year	Price	Unit sales	Income
1	$1.00	.25	$ .25
2	.90	1.00	.90
3	.80	1.00	.80
4	.70	.75	.52
5	.60	.25	.16
		Total	$2.63

SECOND PRODUCT

Year	Price	Unit sales	Income
1	$1.00	0	$ .00
2	.90	.25	.23
3	.80	.75	.60
4	.70	.50	.35
5	.60	.10	.06
		Total	$1.24

TABLE 6: HOW MICROCOMPUTERS AFFECT CORPORATE PROFITS

	Without microcomputers	With microcomputers
Sales	100%	100%
Cost of goods sold	−55	−45
Gross margin	45%	55%
Development		
Engineering	8 %	6%
Documentation	1.5	1
Warranty	1.5	1
Marketing	20	20
G & A	3	3
Engineering and marketing costs	34%	31%
Before-tax profit	11%	24%

this hypothetical example, the first product to the market generates about twice the total income that the second product does (Table 5). As a result, the advantage gained by application of a microprocessor to achieve early product introduction can have a much greater impact than merely reducing manufacturing costs.

Again, since product features can be added to equipment built around microprocessors simply by adding more program storage, many manufacturers are taking advantage of this characteristic to increase the value of their products. For instance, makers of point-of-sale-equipment are adding automatic tax-computation to cash registers by merely increasing the ROM size. Instrument makers are adding automatic calibration to their instruments. Makers of vehicular-traffic-light controllers are adding automatic sensing of traffic loads to their basic equipment and adjusting the duration of the signals. From a profitability point of view, these optional features, many of which are requested by the customer, are frequently sold at 10 to 20 times the cost of adding them. Some companies have been able to earn sizable profits from marginal products and services through the application of microcomputers.

Because the danger of their failure is eliminated by replacing many ICs, the use of a microprocessor can significantly increase system reliability. A digital system fails most frequently because interconnects fail. The use of a typical 16-pin IC will introduce approximately 36 interconnections in a system (16 interconnections from the chip to the lead frame, 16 from the lead frame to the pc card, two interconnections from the pc card to the back plane, and two interconnections from back-plane point to back-plane point).

If one ROM eliminates 50 ICs, then it eliminates approximately 1,800 interconnections. While little data exists to prove the point, it is believed that the reliability of the electronic portion of a system can be increased by a factor of 5 to 10 by use of microprocessors.

Finally, consider the bottom line. Table 6 presents a comparison based on information from users of the profit-and-loss statements of a hypothetical product line before and after the use of microprocessors. The product using the microcomputer has a smaller final cost because the manufacturing costs of systems containing microcomputers are generally lower than those built with conventional ICs, and the enhanced capability of many microprocessor-system products enables manufacturers to charge more for their equipment.

In addition, the shortening of development cycles and the elimination of much documentation can save a company another 2.5%. Warranty and service costs, such as those associated with stocking spare parts and training service engineers, can also be greatly reduced. The net effects of all these savings can frequently increase product-line profits by 10% to 20%.

The challenge is here. The design and cost advantages of putting computation and decision-making into equipment are clear messages to product-planning managers for all kinds of manufacturers, many of whom have been outside of the orbit of the electronics industries. These technical managers are finding that the use of microprocessors can affect such basic ingredients of corporate success and failure as manufacturing costs, market share, development costs, time, system reliability, and serviceability. The advantages of microprocessors have been demonstrated already. The challenge now is to use them wisely. □

Want to learn more about microprocessors?
Here are some additional articles on microprocessors that have been published in *Electronics*:
  Kildall, Gary, "High-level language simplifies microcomputer programing," June 27, p.103.
  Altman, Laurence, "Single-chip microprocessors open up new world of applications," April 18, p.81.
  Shima, Masatoshi, and Faggin, Federico, "In switch to n-MOS, microprocessor gets a 2-μs cycle time," April 18, p.95.
  Young, Link, Bennett, Tom, and Lavell, Jeff, "N-channel MOS technology yields new generation of microprocessors," April 18, p.88.
  Tarui, Tadaaki, Namimoto, Keiji, and Takahashi, Yukiharu, "Twelve-bit microprocessor nears minicomputer's performance level," March 21, p. 111.
  Electronics staff, "The minicomputer comes on," Oct. 25, 1973, p.98.
  Gladstone, Bruce, "Designing with microprocessors instead of wired logic asks more of designers," Oct. 11, 1973, p.91.

part 4
Microprocessor round-up

Electronics/February 21, 1974

New microprocessor design cuts gates

While nearly all commercially available microprocessors hover at the 2,000-gate mark, a unit that can perform as well with less than half the number of gates may seem unlikely. But a new design, called Hummingbird, which uses part of a computer's main memory as a register file, makes possible a 12-bit parallel microprocessor with only 700 logic gates and a 16-bit unit with only 900 gates, according to Wynne Calvert, who heads his own computer company in Boulder, Colo.

Like most microprocessor designs, Calvert's calls for an external memory—the processor itself comprises only an arithmetic unit, a few working registers, and the necessary control logic. But most other microprocessors also contain a number of internal general-purpose registers that store operands and intermediate results between accesses to the main memory.

Because Calvert's design uses main memory as a register file, the speed of his system suffers—"by a factor of about two." But for many applications, Calvert says, high speed is not necessary.

Tradeoffs. Calvert describes his design as being completely parallel. "The Intel 8008 requires two cycles just to specify the address of data in memory, before it can actually work on that data," he says. "In my design, that's not necessary." Calvert does admit to a tradeoff: this highly parallel operation requires the microprocessor to be mounted in a 44-pin package. The multiplexing of pin functions would permit the use of a smaller package, but the multiplexing would reduce parallelism and require additional external circuits to demultiplex the pins.

Calvert has built engineering models of the two microprocessors with conventional TTL gates, and he has assembled the software to make them work. He is now negotiating with one semiconductor manufacturer to produce the design commercially as a single large-scale integrated circuit.

The process would probably be some form of MOS, like most other microprocessors. Calvert points out that the gate count is in the vicinity of the upper limit achieved to date with C-MOS, in which p- and n-channel circuits are paired at the expense of circuit density. "If we can implement this design in C-MOS," he says, "our speed will be increased and the power dissipation decreased. We could achieve a 2-μs command cycle." □

Electronics/May 16, 1974

Microprocessor runs recorder

"Smart" terminals are already finding wide use in business data-processing applications. Now it looks as if the availability of microprocessor chips heralds the era of "smart" instruments and instrument accessory systems.

One of the first may well be a smart digital data-acquisition system developed by Doric Scientific. The multipoint Digitrend 220 recorder uses an Intel 8008 microprocessor control, plus semiconductor memory, and can scan and record 20 to 1,000 points at speeds to 20 points per second.

The points can be programed for up to six functions per system. Standard ranges and functions are four linear dc voltages with resolution to 1 microvolt and automatic ranging at high speed, six thermocouple inputs (J, K, T, E, S, and R) with built-in cold-junction compensation and digital linearization for direct temperature display in C° or F°, and two ranges of current transmitter inputs to handle process signals of 4–20 milliamperes and 10–50 mA.

Special functions, ranges, and scaling for standard or nonstandard transducers are available at an additional cost. Point skipping is included at no cost when point programing is ordered.

Group programing is available instead of point programing for a single function by groups of 10 points. This feature is extremely convenient for large systems where the first couple of hundred points can be point-by-point programed and the other hundreds can be group programed.

Time of day is displayed and recorded in hours, minutes, and seconds, also included is a power-failure indication. Precision self-test is a built-in feature.

Among the nine interface circuit cards that are available as options to couple to pheripheral equipment are: external alarm relays, computer access with parallel BDC output, serial output for 7-track or 9-track incremental magnetic tape recorder, serial output for paper-tape punch, serial output for Teletype, and output drive for modem.

A fixed data panel is available for entering data to be recorded prior to each scan. This feature is also available with an auto-calendar circuit, which automatically advances the date every 24 hours. Optional selective alarm provides up to 32 independent alarm points.

The use of plug-in read-only memories and programable ROMs in the Digitrend 220 permits selection of desired features and allows future expansion at a minimum additional cost. The base price is approximately $3,000 with 60 day delivery.

Electronics/May 16, 1974

Tester checks microprocessors

The whole question of how to thoroughly test semiconductor-memory components hasn't been laid to rest yet, and already there's a component that promises an even bigger testing challenge—the microprocessor. It appears to require a completely different test approach from other semiconductor devices—

one more akin to checking out a large computer than to testing logic or memory devices.

Macrodata Co. has developed a new test system, the MD-104M, to test microprocessors and related parts adequately. The tester is priced at $30,000 to $40,000, rather than the $150,000 to $200,000 now typically required for such a system.

The only adequate way to check a microprocessor, contends William C. W. Mow, Macrodata president, is to find out if the instruction set, which may have 75 or more instructions, works. Testing the part for its logic patterns as it's clocked won't ensure that the part is good, he says.

Microprocessors, like semiconductor memories, are pattern-sensitive; the sequence in which the instructions are programed can affect operation of the part and uncover subtle problems. Another problem is that so few microprocessor chips are in use that people can only guess at the most prevalent failure modes, says marketing vice president Joseph Rivlin.

Computer. The MD-104M includes a 10-megahertz special-purpose computer with 64 data bits (the MD-104 uses 16 bits for memory testing) plus parametric capability and interfaces to test microprocessors. An interface board is now offered with the system for the Intel 8080, and boards will be forthcoming for other parts that are or will be on the market.

Programing will be the key to testing the microprocessor, and, although the best techniques are not yet clear, Macrodata says the system is flexible enough to accommodate the programs that are ultimately proven optimum. The tester's computer, which can perform such exercises as loops and branches, address 65,000 addresses directly, and it can be expanded to several million. In this way, the MD-104M can, in effect, simulate the operation of the computer in a real environment.

Modular. The parametric capability of the system is provided in modular form, with the test operation able to choose up to the five or six parameters that are deemed most critical. Typical examples for a device manufacturer would be probe continuity, leakage, a unique dynamic test for drain current while the device is being clocked, and breakdown. The device user might choose thresholds and input and output leakage. These tests, on plug-in cards, would also provide the capability for classification into categories.

Timing tests are also possible, but Rivlin suspects they won't be considered vital for microprocessors. The system also tests memories and other parts. Testing time, however, may be very important. Mow says it may run about ½ minute because of the enormous number of steps required. The MD-104M is designed to support two test heads, and four of the MD-104M's can be controlled by a single MD-1041 controller, so that eight positions can be run simultaneously.

Electronics/May 30, 1974

Micro CPU smartens dumb remotes

A remote data-acquisition and monitoring system developed for utilities illustrates how the new breed of microprocessors-on-a-chip will be increasing the intelligence of dumb terminals. And in the process, it shows how to ease the work load on both computer and personnel at complex central master stations.

With initial units to be shipped in July, Quindar Electronics Corp., Springfield, N.J., now has developed its smart remote terminal to handle basic data reduction, thereby taking the load off the central monitoring computer to which it is tied. Moreover, the terminal can also perform programed control functions that, until now, had to be relayed in proper sequence from the central master station. Thus, the remote terminal can on its own be involved in such things as the sequential starting and stopping of power generators.

"It's a big change for us," declares Stanley Green, Quindar's manager of research and development. A long-time supplier of remote data-monitoring gear for utilities and pipelines, Quindar had relied on multiplexed digital signals containing the monitored data to be sent back over telephone lines to a master station. Years earlier, Quindar had switched to the digital control from discrete tone generators.

Bogged. "We originally went to the digital system because, as systems became more complex, the number of tone channels got very large," explains Green. "But even with a fairly large computer, the system could become data-logged because the dumb remotes had to send everything back to the master station." The result was that even the master station became bogged down when responding to the needs of many remote stations.

With a micro-processor—National Semiconductor's IMP-16 central-processing unit—designed into the remote stations, plus "special buffering for the power utility environment," the remote station only sends back the data it has to. This could include such things as the monitored points that fall out of present limits or indicate changes in the system's status.

Green points out that buffering for the microprocessor is extremely important and that it would be prohibitively expensive to buffer an off-the-shelf minicomputer to withstand the sharp transients found on power lines. All essential programing of limits is done in a 4,096-bit read-only memory. Transitory information for calculations, such as readings from analog transducers, are stored in 1,024-bit random-access-memory chips.

Over-all view. The system itself consists of plug-in printed-circuit boards, containing such items as the four-chip central processor plus the buffering ROMs and RAMs, analog-to-digital conversion, multiplexer, and a transceiver/modem card, which transmits the digital signals over voice-grade telephone lines.

Coding of the signals is done in software, rather than in hardware, Green says. Quindar uses a 16-bit word in its system to "tag" events with time from an absolute time source. This couldn't be done by the older, hard-wired remote stations, he says. Now, if a disturbance occurs in a power grid, for example, the events can be tagged with a time base so that a history of the event can be reconstructed to millisecond accuracy.

Typical instruction times must be executed within 8 to 10 microseconds, says Green, which can be easily done by the National part. As for programing the microprocessor, Green reports this has been remarkably simple so far. ☐

Electronics/June 13, 1974

Microprocessors add new twist to torque-monitoring

Since Federal auto-safety regulations now extend to the amount of torque applied to tighten fasteners during assembly, a Flint, Mich., company has put together a microprocessor-based system for monitoring torque at remote assembly-line locations. And the system is already earmarked for several General Motors plants.

Process Computer Systems Inc. designed its Torque Certification System to monitor, control, and provide hard-copy documentation for the 30 to 50 critical fasteners installed in a vehicle. Although each remote unit can stand alone, high-speed data links can connect as many as 256 remote microprocessor terminals to a host minicomputer to obtain factory-wide information.

Each microprocessor terminal, in turn, can handle up to 25 torquing tools so that a single 16-bit minicomputer—a Hewlett-Packard 2100—and 256 small satellite processors can accommodate some 6,400 tools. Moreover, the builders of the system say it has uses, not only in the defect-conscious auto industry, but in other industries faced with excessive field repair, replacement of fasteners, or new Federal quality and safety standards. In the auto industry, for example, assembly plants must employ additional personnel to check and often to retorque critical fasteners.

Each satellite terminal, sealed in an environment-proof enclosure, is built up of standard modules, also developed by Process Computer, in what is called a Plant box. The company's CM4400 microprocessor module uses the 8-bit Intel 8080 chip and includes six 8-bit registers, 8-bit accumulator, 8-bit parallel arithmetic unit and 16-bit stack pointer. Four different memory modules may be used in any combination for up to 64 kilobytes of read-only and random-access memory for storing data, data tables, and application software.

Also included in the Plant box is a teletypewriter that prints torque readings and out-of-tolerance messages, along with summary reports for all tooling connected to the stations. The date and time of day can be included, as well. At the option of the user, an alarm light or buzzer may be substituted for an out-of-tolerance printout. A general-purpose interface at the host minicomputer matches each Plant box to the computer via the high-speed serial communications lines.

Stripped threads seen. The data itself comes from dc strain gages on each torquing tool. These gages send over a shielded cable low-level dc analog voltages that indicate the actual torque characteristic of each fastening operation. Equivalent torque voltages are stored in memory, and the processor is able to calculate actual torque applied to a fastener. The system also includes a special tool-controller module that provides excitation for the transducer, as well as transducer-signal amplification, peak-torque detection, an automatic tool shut-off signal when maximum torque is reached, and 10 bit analog-to-digital conversion for output to the microprocessor card.

In addition, a timer determines how long it takes the transducer signal to get from the threshold where torque is first applied to peak. This enables a fault such as crossed threads on a fastener to be detected immediately—the fastener would be torqued to a final value in only 50 milliseconds, when it should have taken 100 to 300 ms. Moreover, stripped threads might show up when a relatively long time is taken for torque to build up—say 400 ms.

Communications between the host minicomputer and each Plant box are serial at 40,000 to 160,000 bits per second, using the company's high-speed serial input/output controller modules. A standard interface module—PCS series 2000—is used as well.

Originally, Process Computer had thought of using Hewlett-Packard minicomputers at each of the remote stations, says chief engineer Richard Barnish. However, the microprocessors offer several distinct advantages, he points out. The systems cost less and also allow the company to boost the value that it adds to the product. What's more, the microprocessor cards are better able than the minis to withstand the severe factory environment. ☐

Electronics/June 27, 1974

Microprocessor controls tester

Because they are much lower in cost and complexity than minicomputers, microprocessors are spurring the development of reasonably priced automatic test systems. One of the latest is a system, the model 400, developed by Data/Ware Development Corp. for in-factory tests. The company has delivered one to Sony Corp. of America for testing color-TV tubes, and the system, which is completely automatic, has many other uses, particularly in checkout of devices.

The test is organized in a familiar manner for automated checkout. An Intel MCS-4 microprocessor chip set controls the input/output buffer, which, in turn, programs and controls power supplies, measuring instruments and a relay matrix. To the MCS-4 are added both read-only and random-access memory. Both fixed and programable sources can be used; the filament voltage for the tubes can be fixed, for example.

This system provides for programing the points at which forcing voltages are applied to the unit under test, the voltage values, the measurement points, and the measurement-current scale. Proper selection of these parameters adopts the model 400 to almost any device to be tested, says Data/Ware vice president Dale V. Schmidt.

In checking color-TV tubes, each gets more than 20 different tests, results are compared to preselected limits, and go/no-go indication is provided. Results for the test are printed, along with the serial number of the tube tested.

The model 400 can contain multiple power supplies, providing maximum outputs of 1,000 volts and power of 100 watts. Measurements are made by a programable digital ammeter that is accurate to within 0.1% and has ranges of 1 microampere to 2 amperes, full scale. The relay matrix uses 32 double-pole, double-throw, telephone-type relays.

Go/no-go signals, LED digital readouts, audible alarm, and a 10-column printer are among the outputs. Programs are stored in ROMs, each containing 4,096 words, which can be changed as desired.

Price and availability of the system depend on the specific capabilities required.

Electronics/September 19, 1974

Microprocessors invade control gear, but builders wary

While the inherent conservatism of the machine-tool industry could be expected to hamper the penetration of microprocessors in its equipment, a few producers are building them into everything from loaders for programable controllers to highly sophisticated computer numerical-control (CNC) systems. For the most part, however, exhibitors at this month's International Machine Tool Show in Chicago were still wary.

"Every time we reach out for a microprocessor—boom, there's a more capable one on the horizon," says one manufacturer. Equally distressing is the lack of alternate sources for available versions, and the devices' relatively slow speeds mean that users build additional hard-wired logic to handle such critical tasks as circular interpolation for contouring purposes.

Nevertheless, major numerical-control manufacturers—General Electric, Allen-Bradley, and Bendix—agree that there's a place for on-board computers in machine tool control and suggest that microprocessors can eventually grab much of the market.

Cost-effective. The largest producer of numerical-control equipment for machining and metalworking showed for the first time a new microprocessor-based system. General Electric's Mark Century 1050 control system is built around the National Semiconductor Corp. 16-bit chip set, and boasts capabilities— such as the control of up to six axes of motion—usually found only on more expensive minicomputer-based systems. Additionally, it incorporates some features that just haven't been available—diagnostics for both the machine and the control, for example, points out James P. Conley, manager of domestic sales at GE's Numerical Control operation, Waynesboro, Va.

"We went the microprocessor route because it was the most cost-effective," he says. "It also enabled us to do something that everyone has talked about for years—to make a modular control. Each axis requires only one printed-circuit board." The biggest advantage of microprocessors in machine-tool control, adds sales engineer Charles Freed, is higher reliability than either hard-wired logic or minicomputers. That is because a large

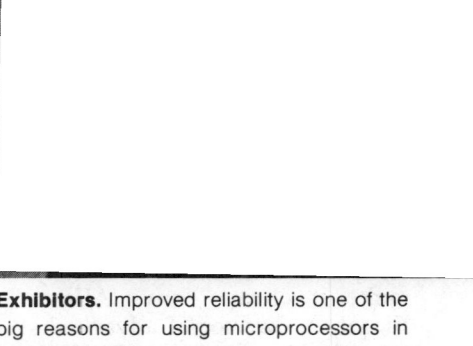

Exhibitors. Improved reliability is one of the big reasons for using microprocessors in their new NC controller, according to Charles Freed (top) and James P. Conley of GE's Numerical Control operation.

number of ICs are replaced by a small number of LSI packages.

Yet the GE system makes major use of hard-wired logic to get around the slow-speed microprocessor for specialized calculations such as conversion between metric and English units, cutter compensation to adapt to different cutting tools, and circular interpolation to generate the necessary axis moves to cut an arc.

New mini too. Bendix Industrial Controls division, Detroit, also introduced its new CNC system—a system that it had earlier said would include a microprocessor. Instead, the DynaPath System 5 is based on the Data General Corp. Nova II minicomputer. "As we proceeded down the microprocessor path, we found ourselves building so much hardware that we felt we couldn't afford to sell such a hybrid system," notes Timothy B. Faricy, manager of NC product marketing. "Theoretically, it should work, but in order to compromise for the slow speed of the microprocessor, so much of the system is hard-wired that it's unwieldly."

Bendix started with a bus concept—latching more and more microprocessors on a bus to accommodate growing complexity until a mini could be latched on and the microprocessors—which Faricy points out are not yet cost-effective—eliminated.

Both the General Electric and Bendix systems are designed for the same users, and feature essentially the same capabilities. Neither manufacturer will discuss pricing, except to say that its approach is substantially cheaper than the other's.

On the other end of the scale, General Automation Inc. introduced an open-loop, continuous-path stepping-motor controller built around its LSI-12 microcomputer with a silicon-on-sapphire microprocessor. "We used the microprocessor to get some advantages of computer control, but basically to make it cheap," says Allan G. Fiegehen, director of advanced systems for the Anaheim, Calif., firm. "A $5,000 controller with any features at all is unheard of in this industry." The GA system is called the Adapt-A-Path L-100.

Microprocessors are also showing up in loaders for programable controllers. Modicon Inc., Andover, Mass., will begin next month to ship its Model 284, a controller that will replace from 15 to 100 relays. It's using an Intel MCS-4 in the programing panel to alter from one to four 256-bit programable read-only memories on site.

And Westinghouse Electric Corp.'s Control Products division has decided to supplement the Datapoint CRT terminals it's now using to load its PC 400 programable controller with a Westinghouse-built version of the controller that includes an Intel 8008 microprocessor. □

Electronics/November 14, 1974

Microchips meet buyer resistance

Microprocessors were a hard sell at the recent Instrument Society of America conference and exhibit in New York, but few were buying.

Manufacturers of measurement and control equipment at the annual event substantially agreed that microprocessors will wind up in their equipment—particularly in data-acquisition systems and programable controllers. However, most of them aren't quite ready to buy the new chip sets.

Applications engineering takes time, the potential customers insist, and they want to evaluate competitive products, including those that have been announced but are not yet available for delivery. Several readily admit to window-shopping—they are interested, and they're looking, but they won't buy until the price drops.

At the same time, some systems manufacturers are disturbed about the prospect that microprocessors will be marketed much like certain products in the computer industry, which are announced well in advance of their actual availability. This practice could even slow the adoption of microprocessors in their hardware, they contend.

Monday look. Microprocessors, says Robert O. Wilson, president of FX Systems Corp., Saugerties, N.Y., are "something we look at every Monday morning. We're keeping up with all the developments and looking forward to using them, but they're still not economical for our products."

Wilson says he can replace all but four of the 13 function cards in his Series 1 programable data-acquisition system, but will hold off for about a year, when he expects the price to fall significantly. He'll hold off even longer on using microprocessors in programable controllers, he adds, because "they don't have the horsepower yet."

Allen-Bradley Co., Cleveland, uses a microprocessor in one of its programable controllers to decode binary information for generating graphics, but not for control functions. "We evaluated a number of microprocessors before we went with one," says an Allen-Bradley systems engineer, "but as for controls, we'll probably stick with core memory for a while just because it's reliable and low-cost. We'll get there, but we're not going to dive in [to microprocessors], I'll tell you that."

The systems division of Struthers-Dunn Inc., Bettendorf, Iowa, uses microprocessors only when building a large number of systems in different configurations. "We program for each job," says Robert H. Rech, general manager. "But in all jobs, we've had the customer pay for the programing," which he describes as difficult and time-consuming.

Another firm, Modicon Inc., which bills itself as "the programable controller company," recently introduced a system using microprocessors to handle 23 data-transfer functions. "I'm getting more speed, and that means I can add more functions," says Fred U. Henderson Jr., regional manager. "It may even give us a cost-reduction in terms of what we can do in control functions. But we really won't know until we get into it."

Mark Levi, director of National Semiconductor Corp.'s Microprocessor group, says his company has designated measurement and control as one of the three prime markets for its microprocessors, along with communications and terminals. "We're telling the end user that he should be talking with his vendor about the flexibility that microprocessors can provide."

But Levi admits that equipment makers' investment in existing products is something National and other chip suppliers will have to contend with, at least for a while. "In the late 1970s, we'll see dedicated microprocessor systems," concludes Levi. "It makes the 'smart' instrument a reality." □

Microcomputer on four chips needs no external circuits

Most of today's MOS microcomputers are designed around single central processing chips containing all control and processing functions. The chip is connected via buses to standard general-purpose memory and input/output circuits.

But West Germany's Olympia Werke AG in Wilhelmshaven is developing a concept that could increase flexibility and decrease the number of circuits needed for performing many control and processing applications. Borrowed from calculator design, the new concept treats the microcomputer as a special function and partitions it into four large-scale-integrated circuit chips. Unlike most of today's microcomputers, these LSI chips operate only with each other.

Moreover, the chips are self-contained and do not require additional standard memory and I/O interface circuits for implementing most microcomputer applications. For simple controller functions, for example, as few as two chips would suffice, while for complex 8-bit process-control systems the full set, together with external standard random-access-memory components, would be needed.

Desk top. The first units of what Olympia calls its CP 3-F chip set are slated for a desktop computer with printer—basically a calculator with memory—to be marketed next year. And Olympia, a $270 million subsidiary of AEG-Telefunken, the German electronics giant, undoubtedly intends to use the chip set in other products as well. In addition, a Telefunken spokesman asserts that some 25 European equipment makers are interested in the chips for their own products. He declined, however, to identify any of them.

Circuits will be supplied by three European semiconductor manufacturers beginning early next year, with equipment from Olympia coming to market a few months later. The circuit manufacturers are AEG-Telefunken in Heilbronn, West Germany, and General Instrument Europe and SGS-Ates, both based in Italy. Significantly, all circuits are interchangeable even though different MOS technologies are being used by the three to implement the designs. AEG-Telefunken is using a double ion-implanted metal-gate process, SGS-Ates a silicon-gate process, and General Instrument Europe an aluminum-gate-nitride process.

Setup. The four-chip system consists of an 8-bit parallel CPU containing a 48-byte RAM and 8-bit I/O channel, a microprogramable read-only memory, a data RAM and a combination microprogramable ROM and data RAM chip. These chips have been designed so that a functional system can be built without the use of external logic or control registers. The minimum configuration consists of the 8-bit CPU chip with a 48-instruction set having a minimum cycle time of 5 microseconds, plus the microprogramable ROM chip.

These two chips contain all the logic, binary, and decimal operations, as well as other processing functions necessary for simple controller systems. The set of 48 instructions is sufficient to handle instructions for most controllers and many processors—for example, logic, binary and decimal operations, shifting, constant multiplications, and subprograms. The microprogramable ROM is organized in a convenient 1,024-by-8-bit format. Four registers serve as address counters and recirculating memories, and two I/O channels handle the bus requirements for all the 8-bit-instructions.

If more computing power is required, a user can select the data RAM and ROM/RAM chip. The data unit consists of a 128-by-8-bit RAM, address register, and an 8-bit I/O channel that is designed to interface directly with the CPU chip. The program and data memory are contained on a 768-by-8-bit ROM and an 18-by-8-bit RAM that have been designed to interface directly with the other members of the family.

The microprocessor set can be used for even more complex systems, since it is possible to expand the memory capacity to 16,000 8-bit words without additional I/O circuits. Along with the system, Olympia will supply a Fortran cross-assembler, a simulation program, and necessary test equipment. All circuits are supplied in a 40-pin dual in-line packages that operate from −5-volt and −17-V power supplies. □

Millions predicted for microprocessors

Despite great interest shown this year in microcomputer chip sets, only about 100,000 will have been shipped by the year's end, according to Norman F. Zimbel, a member of the consulting firm of Arthur D. Little Inc., Cambridge, Mass.

But Zimbel, speaking last week at the Arthur D. Little-sponsored First National Microprocessor Conference in Boston, estimated this number will grow to anywhere between 2 million and 3.5 million units per year in about five years, with a total market value of between $280 million and $475 million.

Lincoln Young, marketing manager for microcomputers at Motorola Semiconductor Products division, Phoenix, Ariz., is even more optimistic. In five years he estimates there will be more than 16-million microcomputers in use, breaking down to 4.8 million in computers, 8.4 million in industry, 2 million in consumer products, and 1 million in Federal systems.

Young says that in 1974 the market price of an OEM product using a microprocessor now averages $1,000, and this will drop to $500 in 1976.

About 80% to 90% of microprocessors will be sold as chip sets rather than individual devices, he believes, and in the future he looks for larger, more cost effective packages of standard building blocks.

Coming. About 80% of the cost of a microprocessor is for memory and input/output circuitry, and David F. Millet, also of ADL, looks for some changes. In the near future he sees non-volatile semiconductor memory eliminating the need for backup power supplies. And he also anticipates that there will be larger, easier to use memories matched to their central processing units. But he notes, "It is in I/O devices that the microprocessor industry is truly in its infancy." The additional transistor-transistor logic needed to interface to the microprocessor chips eliminates many of the benefits of large scale integration (see page 33). The external circuitry adds considerably to the cost of the system.

He sees the development of more "idealized" I/O devices—ones that will accept and enter data with timing and levels matched to the requirements of the CPU. An extra but important advantage of this is that it could relieve the CPU for more important functions and increase throughput. This could allow designs which might have used two or three microprocessor chips to get by with only one. □

Electronics/December 26, 1974

Microcomputers emphasize input-output

In some control and communications applications for microcomputers, data processing capacity is not nearly as important as input/output efficiency. Scientific Micro Systems, a subsidiary of Corning Glass Works, is taking aim at a number of such applications with a family of four systems called MicroControllers.

Applications include control of machine tools, intelligent instruments, and peripherals and communications tasks such as data acquisition, switching, and concentration.

Each of the four microcomputers, with modifications dependent on specific applications, contains the following: a microprocessor with an instruction time of 300 nanoseconds; up to 4,096 words of ROM/PROM program storage; up to 256 bytes of RAM working storage; and—most importantly—from 32 to 224 individually addressed I/O connection points. Prices range from about $385 in 100 quantities for the basic System 10 MicroController to $1,580 for the top-of-the-line fully implemented System 40. Each package contains three hermetic ceramic modules: the processor (containing the program storage, a program counter, an arithmetic logic unit, and 12 registers having a repertoire of eight instructions), the interface vector (a program-addressable, buffered connection between the controlled elements of a user's system and the MicroController), and the working storage module.

"What all this means," says James Geers, marketing vice president, "is that control, status, and data lines of user devices are immediately accessible by the MicroController program. There's no speed penalty for talking with the outside world because the input data is treated with the same speed the internal registers are operating at—300 nanoseconds."

I/O data may be addressed in various field sizes, from a single bit up to 8 bits. This feature means, Geers says, "that only those control and status points of immediate interest may be directly accessed without masking."

Scientific Micro Systems has also checked out the architecture in a MSI prototype, which will be made available as a MicroController simulator for program modification and control during MicroController system debugging. Using a symbolic programing language, the system can be programed, says Geers, with an assembler-level instruction set, reducing concept-to-manufacturing time as much as 50%.

Electronics/March 20, 1975

TRW Systems sets gate-density record for bipolar logic

Emitter-follower logic, although 10 years old, has been fashioned by TRW Systems Group into one of the industry's most powerful computer-circuit technologies. So the big payoffs from bipolar LS may not all go to glamorous new processes like integrated injection logic.

Under the direction of the manager of the Microelectronics Center, Barry Dunbridge, one-chip processors containing more than 17,000 EFL devices (over 5,000 gates) have been built at the Redondo Beach, Calif., company. Such device density is over 10 times that of today's most complex transistor-transistor-logic LSI processor chips.

The improved EFL process was developed for in-house custom programs under Air Force contracts, but can easily be transferred to commercial semiconductor production. TRW already has agreements with semiconductor manufacturers, who are enthusiastic about the high yields on large chips offered by the relatively simple three-diffusion (3D) process (see "Motorola readying LSI emitter-follower logic . . ." p. 30). For example, the on-wafer yield for a die measuring 300 by 300 mils is 30%.

Such high yields signal TRW's near-attainment of a major semiconductor-development goal—a low-defect bipolar process capable of packing 10,000 gates on a chip [*Electronics*, March 6, p. 57]. This so-called 10K bipolar LSI excites computer and semiconductor manufacturers alike, many of whom are counting on it for the step-function improvement in price and performance that will explode demand for medium and large computers even further.

Hardware. Using only 11 chips, Dunbridge's group has built a high-performance 16-bit microprogramable parallel computer for an Air Force signal-processing system. A companion circuit for the system's front end is a signal-processing arithmetic unit that contains 14,000 bipolar devices on a single, high-yield 302-by-360-mil chip [*Electronics*, March 6, p. 32]; it dissipates only 5.1 watts at clock-cycle speeds of 120 nanoseconds. Better yet is another TRW processing chip, the MPY-1, which, with over 17,000 devices, must hold the bipolar density record.

According to Jim Buie, one of the key designers on the EFL project (and also the inventor of TTL in

1961), the 16-bit computer has now reached the final debugging stage. The machine is composed of eight 4-bit-slice microprocessor chips that make up both the central programable address unit and the operand arithmetic unit (see p. 29). The three remaining chips are a 16-bit parallel multiplier [*Electronics*, Jan. 23, 1975], a control chip for microprograming, and a single jumbo input/output chip.

More coming. Buie points to even more impressive developments with a triple-diffused LSI process that has been extended into the higher-performing current-mode-logic configuration. "With CML," says Buie, "we can boost the frequency range of our 3D transistors to approximately 30% of the actual transistor cutoff." This permits the devices to operate two to three times faster than before. And since CML and EFL can be made directly compatible, a designer can use them side by side on a chip to optimize the performance of different segments of the circuit.

For example, CML is faster but more limited for combinational logic functions than EFL, so that in an EFL-CML D-type flip-flop, the internal registers could be built with CML, the gates with EFL. The resulting flip-flop runs with a propagation delay of only 25 ns (for a typical load of 80 picofarads) while dissipating only 32 milliwatts.

Paralleling these circuit advances is the development of advanced 3D LSI designs that could improve still more dramatically the speed-power product of today's 3D techniques and lead to still higher levels of bipolar complexity. It all boils down to gates that occupy a quarter of the space of TRW's already tiny EFL structures.

In addition, these gates may be built with transistors operating at cutoffs as high as 500 MHz, almost five times faster than in present EFL circuits. As a result, a typical 300-by-300-mil processor chip dissipating only about 5 W could accommodate an incredible 50,000 devices—probably enough for a full 16-bit miniprocessor. □

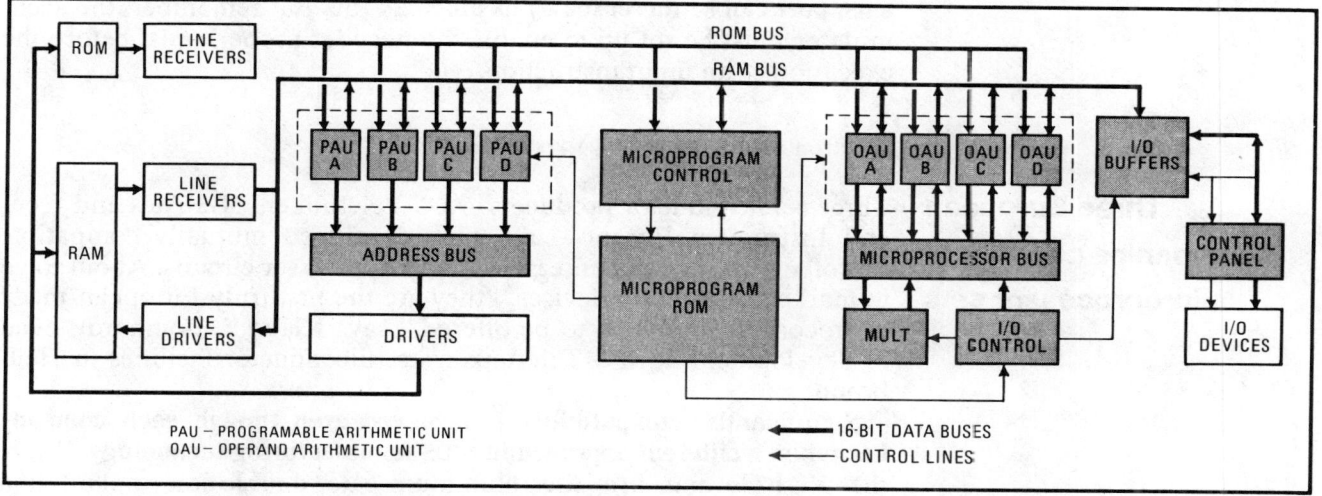

Speeder. Sixteen-bit computer built with TRW's high-yield emitter-follower logic has a typical instruction cycle time of 120 ns. Under TRW license, Motorola Semiconductor plans to start producing the parts and may announce a new MC5800 chip family by September.

Electronics/May 2, 1974

IC-fault tester makes use of microprocessor

Microprocessors are finding their way into instruments for testing integrated circuits via a small Titusville, Fla., company called Testline Instruments. What the firm has done in its AFIT (automatic fault-isolation tester) is to use **a brute-force in-circuit test, controlled by a microprocessor, to pinpoint both IC and board failures.** This is a departure from the usual technique of resorting to ever more powerful computerized diagnostic schemes in which elaborate procedures are applied to a board's input/output connector.

The simplicity of Testline's system saves time and money, claims president Roger Boatman. Use of a microprocessor instead of a minicomputer means that Testline **can sell its AFIT for $8,800, compared with around $25,000** for computer-controlled machines, he says. And even though a clip must be moved from IC to IC, says Boatman, the Testline method is faster because each test is performed so quickly, and faults are isolated down to specific ICs.

Electronics/June 13, 1974

Microprocessor designs demand tighter logic

Besides cost-saving benefits, microprocessor-based designs have another, less obvious, advantage over equivalent systems built with hardwire logic. Because they need software control, microprocessor designs require the whole system to be analyzed before any portion of the design can be attacked. **The old hardwire cut-and-try piecemeal logic design tricks won't work any more. This forces a designer into more rigorous, iterative methods, with their attendant flowcharts and optimization techniques,** which in the end results in a tighter logic design. The only problem: **you must learn to implement software.**

Electronics/August 22, 1974

How to give the 8008 a thousand input ports

The number of input ports for the popular 8008 microprocessor is **normally limited to six**—but you can make it accept many more than that, says Perry Lyne, a project engineer of Vidar Autodata Inc., Mountain View, Calif. You just take advantage of the fact that the 8008's accumulator can be latched into the lower memory address during the execution of an input instruction. Then, **by decoding this address along with the port select, the number of actual inputs channeled through each port can be increased by as much as 256.** But remember, the accumulator must be set up to enable the decoder properly just before the execution of an input instruction.

Electronics/September 19, 1974

Three European companies coordinate microprocessor sets

Three semiconductor producers—AEG-Telefunken, SGS-Ates and General Instrument Europe—have each developed mutually compatible sets of MOS large-scale-integration microprocessor circuits. About to go to market as standard devices, "they are the first truly European-made microcomputer circuits to be offered," says Klaus E. Bomhardt, head of development at AEG-Telefunken's semiconductor facilities in Heilbronn.

Significantly, **compatibility is achieved even though each company has taken a different approach in MOS manufacturing technology.** While the West German firm uses aluminum-gate, double ion-implantation techniques, Italy's SGS-Ates employs silicon-gate MOS, and GI Europe, also headquartered in Italy, uses aluminum-gate nitride methods. All circuits are eight-bit p-channel versions, and the technologies involved in making them reflect the respective companies' strengths in MOS manufacture. The p-channel route was chosen because of the economy this technique offers.

The circuits are now in the pre-production stage and **first applications will be in a microprocessor system built by Olympia Werke AG, an AEG-Telefunken subsidiary.** The system, CP3-F, is a table-top calculator-printer that will come off Olympia's production lines in Braunschweig next year. Talks with other potential circuit users are already being held.

Such project-oriented cooperation in MOS LSI circuitry, says Richard Epple, development coordinator at Heilbronn, is an answer to the demand by most European circuit users for a second or third source. "But it is also an answer to the challenge posed by the American dominance in MOS technology—a dominance underlined by the fact that more than 40 companies in the U.S. are active in the MOS field."

Electronics/October 3, 1974

How to design with microprocessors

To be published this month is a new book that's packed full of hard-to-get information on **how to put together a cost-effective design with microprocessors.** For example, it tells the system designer how to slash 20% to 50% off the chip count of a board using the Intel 8008. Title of the 300-page book is "Micromputer Design." Although it's based largely on the 8008 and Intel's newer 8080 microprocessor, it does describe other types now available and **generalizes the design techniques so that they are applicable to any 8-bit unit.** Offered by Martin Research Ltd., 1825 S. Halsted St., Chicago, Ill. 60608, it will sell for $100.

Electronics/November 28, 1974

Now there's a kit for bipolar LSI systems

We've seen several MOS microcomputer design kits recently, but Intel's kit for developing Schottky bipolar LSI systems is the first of its kind to come to our attention. **For $720, Intel says, you get enough computing elements to build a high-performance 16-bit CPU or controller** and enough other devices, device documentation, and design aids to design other systems. The company also promises to **send kit buyers updated documentation and selected new members of the family during 1975.**

INDEX

American Microsystems Inc., AMI 7300, 61
Collins Radio Corp., 123
Data/Ware Development Corp., test system, 146
Emitter-coupled logic, designing with ECL or Schottky TTL, 93-104
Emitter-follower logic, improved, 150-151
Fairchild Semiconductor Corp., 29
   F8 (a family of 4 n-channel chips), 29-34
   isoplanar MOS process, 29
General Electric, 136; control system, 147
Intel Corp., 2, 16, 136
   processors, 2-6
   3000, Intel's bipolar LSI family, 43
   3001 MCU (microprogram control unit), 42
   3002 CPE (central processing element), 42, 44, 45
   3003, 43, 44
   4001 ROM, 2, 3, 6
   4002 RWM, 2, 3
   4003 SR, 2, 3, 6
   4004 CPU, 2-5, 63-67, 73
   8008 CPU, 4, 63-67, 73
   MCS-4, 2-6, 10, 61
   MCS-8, 10, 11, 61, 82
   8080, 11-12, 16-21, 61, 73
   PL/M language, 80-86
   SIM8-01, 83, 86
   Intellec 8, 83, 86
Intersil, and C-MOS, 114
Macrodata, MD-104M test system, 145
Microdata Corp., MPL language, 85; Micro-One processor, 131
Microprocessors, definition of, 110
Microsystem International Ltd., MC-1, 111-112
Monolithic Memories, 57
   6701 microcontroller, 57-58
   Nova, 57-58
Motorola Semiconductor Products Inc., 9
   M6800, 9-16
   p-MOS, 9, 11, 37
   n-MOS, 9, 11, 113
   MC6800, 11, 16, 111
   MC6850, 11
   C-MOS, 114

National Semiconductor Corp., 2, 22
   MAPS, 4
   IMP-16, 10, 24, 112-113, 119
   Processing and control element (PACE) CPU, 27
   CRC (card-reader controller), 28
   GPC/P, 61, 69
Olympia Werke AG, partitioned chip set, 149
Process Computer Systems Inc., torque monitor, 146
Prototyping hardware, Intellec 8 and SIM8-01, 83, 86
Programed logic arrays pp. 87-92; and TTL, 91
Quindar Electronics Inc., smart data terminal, 145
Random logic, 95
RCA, 113
Rockwell International, 7
   PPS-8, 7, 111
   PPS-4, 13, 111
Scientific Micro Systems, input/output efficiency, 150
Signetics, PIP microprocessor, 61, 113
Texas Instruments, 49-56
   integrated-injection logic (I_2L), 49-56
   complementary metal-oxide semiconductor (C-MOS), and I^2L, 50,52
   p-MOS, and I^2L, 50
   MOS, and I^2L, 50
   n-MOS, and I^2L, 52
   silicon-on-sapphire, and I_2L, 52
   S8P0400, 54-56
Tokyo Shibaura Electric Co., 35
   Toshiba TLCS-12, 35-40
   silicon-gate transistors, 37
   bipolar, Schottky, 41; integrated-injection logic (I^2L), 49-56
   Schottky, 41; and I^2L, 52; microcontroller, 57-58
TRW Systems Group, improved EFL, 150-151
TTL, and I^2L, 49-56; partitioning with PLA, 91; Schottky, designing with ECL or, 93-104
Viatron, 136
Wynne Calvert, Hummingbird design, 144